Marx family

Adamson, Joe
    Groucho, Harpo, Chico - and sometimes Zeppo;
a history of the Marx Brothers and a satire on
the rest of the world.   Simon and Schuster,
c1973.
    464 p.   illus.

GROUCHO, HARPC

A History of the Marx Brothers
and a Satire on the Rest of the World

NEW YORK

CHICO

and sometimes ZEPPO

by JOE ADAMSON

SIMON AND SCHUSTER

SBN 671–21458–6
Library of Congress Catalog Card Number: 72–87944
Designed by Edith Fowler
Manufactured in the United States of America

1   2   3   4   5   6   7   8   9   10

Portions of this book have appeared in various periodicals under the following titles:
"The Seventeen Preliminary Scripts of A Day at the Races," Cinema Journal, Spring, 1969.
"Joe Adamson on Monkey Business," Film Comment, Fall, 1971.
"Duck Soup the Rest of Your Life," Take One, December 8, 1971.
The editors of these publications have kindly consented to allow this material to be reprinted in the form for which it was originally intended. In the case of contradictions, all material is to be considered in its final form only as it appears within these pages.

The author and the publishers wish to express their gratitude for permission to quote copyrighted material from screenplays of the Marx Brothers' films to:
—David L. Loew, for A Night in Casablanca
—Metro-Goldwyn-Mayer Inc., for excerpts from the following Metro-Goldwyn-Mayer Inc., motion pictures:
A Night at the Opera © Metro-Goldwyn Mayer Corporation, October 29, 1935. Renewed © Metro-Goldwyn-Mayer Inc. (successor to Metro-Goldwyn Mayer Corporation), October 30, 1962.
A Day at the Races © Metro-Goldwyn Mayer Corporation, June 10, 1937. Renewed © Metro-Goldwyn-Mayer Inc., June 12, 1964.
At the Circus © Loew's Incorporated, October 10, 1939. Renewed © Metro-Goldwyn-Mayer Inc. (formerly Loew's Inc.), October 10, 1966.
Go West © Loew's Inc., December 11, 1940. Renewed © Metro-Goldwyn-Mayer Inc., December 14, 1967.
The Big Store © Loew's Incorporated, June 17, 1941. Renewed © Metro-Goldwyn-Mayer Inc., June 20, 1968.
—MCA Entertainment, Inc., for excerpts from the following motion pictures:
Cocoanuts, Animal Crackers, Monkey Business, Horsefeathers, Duck Soup

ACKNOWLEDGMENTS

There is a dangerous myth in circulation that a book is an independent effort, while film is a corporate enterprise. I would like to insist that a writer is as dependent upon the contributions of others as any artist in any medium, though some are less ready to admit it than others. Among those who share the credit on this project are Mr. Jim Morrow, whose perception and wit have served as a fount of inspiration here and forever; Miss Lindsay Doran, who kept the author alive when the world didn't seem to care particularly; Dr. Howard Suber, who nurtured the undertaking from a pile of old chestnuts into a pretty formidable oak and performed roughly the same task on my ego; and the following people, for assistance and encouragement real or imagined: Joe Adamson (author of the author), Michael Barlow, Susan Marx, Bill Marx, Trevor Black, Robert Cushman, Pauline Kael, Betsy Cahall, Pat Kolker, Ann Schlosser, Mrs. Arthur Orloff, Nanci Matcheski Hayes, David Shepard, Don Strachan, Vernon Harbin, Richard Dyer MacCann, William K. Everson, George Stevens, Jr., Bob Epstein, Lou Stoumen, E. J. Allan, Vince diBona, the late Marvin Borowsky, Colin Young, the staff of the Library at the Academy of Motion Picture Arts and Sciences, the MGM Script Department, all those who granted me interviews, including Harry Ruby, George Folsey, Arthur Sheekman, Morrie Ryskind, Robert Pirosh, Nat Perrin, Mrs. Herman Mankiewicz, D. A. Doran, Willy Clar, and, not least among them, Sid Kuller and Irving Brecher, who were much nicer to me than I was to them—and, not least of all, Mr. George Seaton, who provided the initial boost at a time when I had not the slightest intention of writing a Marx Brothers book. To this day, Mr. Seaton has no full conception of how coincidental that first meeting in his office really was. I was looking for the mail room.

The author is all gratitude toward the American Film Institute and the University Film Association, which provided fellowships enabling the project to be completed.

The author and publisher also wish to thank Universal Studios and Metro-Goldwyn-Mayer, two sinking ships which, in their frantic effort to stay afloat, have granted permission to reprint dialogue created forty years ago by the talented men they have forgotten how to employ, for prices that were only moderately outrageous.

CONTENTS

i

of their holocaust

Willed without witting,
Whorled without aimed.
In the name of the Former,
And of the Latter,
And of their Holocaust.
Allmen.

—James Joyce, *Finnegans Wake*

HEAVEN KNOWS WHAT

Cedric Hardwicke is my fifth favorite actor, the first four being the Marx Brothers.—George Bernard Shaw

I feel deprived practically every time I go the theater. It isn't going to be the Marx Brothers tonight.
—Walter Kerr

The worst they might ever make would be better worth seeing than most other things I can think of.
—James Agee

There are other funny men. There are other musicians of accomplishment. There are other fantastics. What makes these great clowns is this combination of fun and fantasy with something else, a mixture of worldly wisdom and naivete, of experience but also of an innocence never altogether lost, of dignity and absurdity together, so that for a moment we love and applaud mankind.—*The Times* (London)

I am a Marxist, of the Groucho sort.—Anonymous revolutionary in Paris, 1968

There has never been a book on humor written by a funny man. George Meredith's essay on comedy was so dreary I don't think anybody but the proofreader ever got through it all.—Arthur Sheekman

Rational people are sometimes very nice, but they get to be frightfully dull when they try to explain things like what makes us laugh. Arthur Sheekman is one of the Marx Brothers' better writers, and he should know. Some day he must write a book on the subject, and then his statement wouldn't be true any more, and then he *wouldn't* know, and we'd be back where we started.

When in the past intellectuals railed on against the movies, it was always on the grounds that movies were somehow "beneath" the other arts because they made their appeal to basic emotions and feelings rather than to the cerebrum. They would point out with some superiority that the Gunfight and the Chase were more popular than the Metaphysical Argument, thereby proving that movies could do nothing important. This idea rests on the notion that there is something base about anything basic, and that feelings and drives are "beneath" the intellect. Ever since the gun was fired at the audience in *The Great Train Robbery*, film has been a medium where mood and sensation were more important than any ideas. It is a matter of intensity and the power to haunt, not simply visualization and the presence of the image. It is the advantage a silly film like *King Kong* holds over a brilliant film like *Before the Revolution.*

The early days of the American Motion Picture were fortunate in coinciding with an Age of Heroic Comedy—a time when comedy, which had traditionally labored under Aristotle's delusion that glory was reserved for the figures of tragedy, came to be used to glorify a personality at the expense of the whole world. What set Chaplin, Keaton, Fields and the Marx Brothers apart from their forebears was that they became epic characters, and it was their surroundings rather than their persons that wound up being ridiculed.

Hardly does one open a newspaper or read a magazine any more without somehow encountering the Marx Brothers—not simply a movie of theirs playing somewhere or a nostalgic account of their "hilarious hijinx," but as a *metaphor.* They have permanently entered the English language, like Don Quixote and Napoleon, as a mythic embodiment of some vital aspect of our own being. This might explain why people are still showing, and writing about, and memorizing dialogue from, their *bad* movies. Their bad movies at least remind you how good they are in their good movies. And their good movies tell you something about yourself that is still being told when all the punchlines have become familiar.

In a dishonest world, honesty is amusing; in an indirect, discreet world, directness and indiscretion are a riot; in a world full of compromises, going to extremes is hilarious. In a world where everybody explains things, people who confuse the issue are a panic.

BIRTHMARX

CHICO: 1887

The first child of Sam and Minnie Marx was born on March 22nd in New York City and named Leonard, and he was a restless Aries who lived so fast he could hardly keep up with himself.

The image he left behind in colleagues' minds is best described by Irving Brecher: "Chico was a delightful character who could never remember his lines and was more interested in what horse was going to lose that day, so he could get his money on it." Chico couldn't rest until he had a bet on one horse in every race that might be running that day in every state in the union, and sometimes he spent more time on the phone making long-distance calls than he did in front of the cameras making the money that was paying for them. In what George S. Kaufman called "an odd combination of business acumen and financial idiocy," he could arrange some of the most enviable deals in the history of show business and then blow all the money before the picture was released and have to go out hustling again. He could lose $10,000 in one afternoon at the track and never flinch. Likewise, $10,000 could fall into his lap, and he'd come out just as flinchless. "If I lose today, I can look forward to winning tomorrow," he used to say, "and if I win today, I can expect to lose

Sam Marx and sons.

tomorrow. A sure thing is no fun. Groucho and Harpo like sure things, but there's no fun in security." It is hard to avoid the feeling that the main attraction for Chico in being a motion picture star was the chance to play for high stakes.

The chronicle of his childhood is a series of hairbreadth escapes and escapades revolving around his frantic unceasing search for some sort of action. At a young and impressionable age he knew a household eternally occupied by at least one penny-ante poker game, and when the obsession for card playing grew powerful enough in his own veins he felt compelled to pick up whatever was handy and hustle it down to the pawnshop to keep himself going. A prodigal whiz at the business of memorizing and multiplying imposing and impossible figures, he preferred to use his talent in making odds rather than in multiplying fractions, and he made a much bigger impression on his grammar school than it did on him. After he graduated from the sixth grade his short-lived job at a lace store proved hardly more compatible. His pay check rarely lasted the trip home, and once he was home he simply found himself something to hock that would barely last him the trip back again. He couldn't even make a simple delivery for his father, a simple tailor, without losing the trousers of a custom-made Easter suit to some fellow hustler and then recouping his losses by hocking his father's shears. In one of his films, he and Harpo are discovered checking into a hotel with an empty suitcase. Groucho asks him if he realizes his suitcase is empty. "That's all right!" he says. "We'll fill it up before we leave."

Growing up in a melting pot's tenement district in the heat of the Migration to America, young Leo avoided trouble by adopting an Irish or German or Italian or whatever accent was necessary to dodge hostility. Even when playing nightclubs in his old age, he thought of his audience in terms of ethnic stock. "We didn't think there would be anyone there but the Cohens and the Levys," he said of performing one Ash Wednesday, "but when I looked out at the tables I saw nothing but the McCarthys and Raffertys." Once when a misinformed new neighbor asked him what he did for a living, Chico, not used to the question, decided to announce that he was a smuggler. The neighbor looked startled. "Nothing big," Chico assured him. "Just Mexicans."

"Isn't that dangerous?" asked the neighbor, getting worried. He shrugged. "Just for the Mexicans."

Shortly afterward, he dashed over to the neighbor's house with a Mexican gardener, trying to see how long the guy would believe this story. "Look!" he said, beaming. "You can have him cheap! I've retired!"

As a performer, Chico comes off just great if you'd only compare him to your uncle Ernie or your brother Fred. It is too readily conceded that he is the least of the three Marx Brothers. He may be almost consistently outclassed by whomever he shares the spotlight with, but he would be sorely missed if he were not there. Writers who saw the brothers in live performance have generally agreed that he was invariably the most sympathetic of the three characters to any theater audience. As Irving Brecher describes it: "Harpo was off on a cloud somewhere, he appealed most to the children. Groucho was the Enemy of the Republic, he appealed to the sophisticates—but there aren't many of those. The favorite was always Chico." Usually he comes across more as an extroverted entertainer than a comic artist. Morrie Ryskind, a long-standing friend, recalls performances Chico put on in Ryskind's living room for little kids gathered around the piano that could rival anything he did on film. And he was less critical of written material than either Groucho or Harpo, generally concerning himself less with the quality of his lines than the quantity of them. Writers soon learned to give him plenty of yeses, nos and whats so that when he added the lines up he had as many as Groucho did. His only method of demonstrating that a line didn't meet his approval was to let it slip from his mind. His comic style has been described as an "irrelevant vehemence, which makes it seem that he is chagrined by something but has forgotten what it is." It is probably his dialogue.

Chico walked with a determined forward lean, as if he always knew just where he was going next, although in most cases he probably didn't. Inheriting his mother's self-confidence, he could barge his way into any poolroom in the country and line up suckers for pool, suckers for cards, suckers for bets and any number of easy lays. He could round up booking agents, theatrical exhibitors, movie producers, and even, when Harpo needed a

tonsillectomy, find a cut-rate cutthroat who tried to sell him etchings while the incision was healing.

In Hollywood, Chico entertained friends by taking them out to dinner at Chasen's, reserving ringside seats at the American Legion fights, and then taking up an enormous double suite at the Ambassador Hotel and throwing a bacchanal involving every big-time gambler and every good-time girl within hailing distance. According to Sid Kuller, one of his writers, "Chico had more fun than Groucho, Harpo, Gummo, and Zeppo put together."

At the Friars Club, a favorite hideout for card-crazy showmen, Chico once watched a good friend getting bilked by a gang of obvious sharks. He pulled his friend to one side and warned him that his opponents had a set of signals that was certain to leave him out of the running and that he'd better quit the game. Thankfully, the guy retreated and suffered a loss of only $1,800. The next day he walked in and discovered Chico blissfully playing on with the same bunch of crooks. The friend pulled Chico aside and warned *him* of what was going on. "Oh, sure, I know," said Chico. "I just wanted to see if I could beat them, signals or no signals."

It didn't take long for him to get a good solid reputation for being a sucker. Weasels with a hot tip to unload always knew he'd fall for it and would chase him all the way to the back door of the sound stage to con him into it. When he ran out of tips and games and race horses, he'd stand on a street corner and make bets on whether the next passing license plate would be odd or even.

Writing a check to Heywood Broun for gambling debts, Chico prudently instructed him not to try cashing it before twelve o'clock the next day if he wanted it to go through. Broun followed the advice and waited till twelve, but it still bounced. "What time did you cash it?" asked Chico accusingly. "Twelve-o-five," declared Broun self-righteously. Chico shook his head. "Too late."

"There are three things that my brother Chico is always on," Groucho was known to remark. "A phone, a horse, or a broad." His trailer on the film set was used mainly for seducing purposes, and he would arrange for his girls to be hired as extras, just so they'd be handy. As long as any pretense of propriety was abandoned, everybody, even his wife and his daughter, gave up showing any outward sign of objecting. His actions may have been totally obnoxious and to some people immoral, but he himself was wholly without blame. "That's his life," Groucho said of him shortly before his death. "He can't change it. Our mother and father couldn't change it. If he made ten thousand dollars a day, he'd spend ten thousand dollars a day. It's better he doesn't make so much, then he won't wear himself out spending it. He's always happy. In fact, he sleeps better than I do." With Chico, one of the most supremely unfrustrated of all living beings, there came none of that tension and uneasiness so familiar to those who don't respond to their bodies' demands quite so readily.

When Chico died in 1961, he was eulogized by a rabbi with the phrase "He did not have an evil or a mischievous thought in his soul." It must have *seemed* like a nice thing to say.

HARPO: 1888

Adolph was born November 23rd and, with a tranquility known only to Sagittarians and the second-born, quickly resigned himself to the general unruliness of the Fates and thought no more about it for seventy-five years—gleefully accepting with little undue agitation whatever came his way. Little agitation at all, in fact. Due or undue. Practically none.

Characteristic was the fatalist awareness that the nice wrist watch he'd been given for his *bar mitzvah* wouldn't last long before it was hocked by his big brother, and characteristic was the simple solution: He just took the hands off the dial and knew it was his forever. Years later, when his watches were in no apprehensible danger, he'd keep them eternally set at twenty after twelve and boast, "I haven't wound this watch in three years!" In one of the films, Chico is pestering Harpo to take care of business and get to work, and Harpo stands there dreamily and shoves peanuts into Chico's mouth.

"Most people have a conscious and a subconscious," he said of himself. "Not me. I've always operated on a subconscious and

Harpo in the production of *Yellow Jacket* in which he appeared with Alexander Woollcott.

Harpo and Susan Fleming, shortly after their wedding.

Harpo in make-up on the set for *Horsefeathers* with Amelia Earhart.

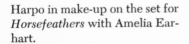

a sub-subconscious." Ben Hecht recalls that Harpo had only to float into a room full of people, and his relaxation, contentment, charm, and good will would contaminate the assemblage. The best time to try to understand this man is when you're sound asleep and the cosmic forces deep inside your consciousness are in total command. As soon as you wake up and start worrying about where you have to be today and remembering something you did yesterday and wondering what will happen to you tomorrow, then you and he have nothing in common. When Harpo was called as a witness in a government investigation of Joseph Schenck, he couldn't recall anything about a trip he had taken to Mexico on Schenck's yacht only five years before, not even whether he was married at the time. The only evidence he could supply the court was that his total earnings in card games had been $7,827.

On the screen, Harpo's actions bespeak an ethereal freedom that is immediately recognizable as something we know nothing about. With or without his musical instruments, he strikes a responsive chord of sweet rhyme and no reason, profane as it might seem to the complexities and ambiguities we are used to facing.

There are times when he is doing nothing more than acting out preposterous hyperboles of emotions we all go through every day. Harpo doesn't become pleased: Every muscle, tendon, and ligament in his soul arches into a static paroxysm of glee. He never gets annoyed: His entire existence crystallizes itself into a sullen nucleus of resentment. When he isn't exaggerating the familiar, his actions have no explanation at all. And they don't want one.

To hear Harpo tell his life story in the book written by Rowland Barber, you would think he wandered through his salty boyhood of gang fights, hostile police, meatless meals, irate landlords, roughhouse saloons, painted women, murderous madams, fast-moving swindlers, killers, and thieves in the same serene state of semi-delight he later lavished on the Algonquin Hotel and his grapefruit ranch. One can only guess that this is the inevitable reflection of light on darkness, but one of Barber's impressions that can never be escaped is that Adolph's free-associational habits bore only blood relation to his brother's dynamic restlessness. He lounged around the tennis courts and chased wild balls, he filled his delivery routes with detours, he sat and listened to tales of Germany and learned magic tricks from his aging grandfather.

And one of the best diversions from these diversions was to stand in front of a cigar store and watch a self-absorbed cigar wrapper named Gookie. In the back room of this cigar store congregated a claque of card sharks that often included Leo and Frenchie (Mr. Marx) himself, but Adolph got his kicks standing at the store window watching the cigar wrapper. Gookie was a humorless little man who constantly went around grumbling to himself about something. He could wrap cigars faster than anyone in New York, but when he did his eyes crossed, his tongue rolled up and blocked off his mouth, and his cheeks puffed out from all the air that couldn't get out of his mouth. He couldn't have *known* he was wearing such a grotesquerie every time he rolled cigars or he would have quit the business on the instant and driven a cab. Yet he must have been somehow dimly conscious of it, because when Adolph had fully mastered all its subtleties and pounded on the glass to demonstrate this talent to him, Gookie bellowed and roared and chased him up the street for it. But this was only so much encouragement to do encore after encore, day after day, and no matter how many laughs he got from brothers, friends, and the boys in the back room of the cigar store, Gookie never seemed to appreciate it. Adolph continued getting laughs from that face till the end of his life ("Strangers abruptly confronted with it," according to Alexander Woollcott, "are credibly reported to be heard for weeks thereafter screaming in their sleep"), and, though Gookie probably never lived to see them, there wasn't a single Marx Brothers movie that went by without at least one silent tribute to New York City's finest cigar wrapper.

George Burns has attested that offstage Harpo would go on doing anything for a giggle. "There was nothing he wouldn't dare to do," recalls another friend. "Jump up on the desk, swing on the chandelier, climb up the window . . ." Harpo was in costume in front of a hotel in Baltimore waiting for nothing in particular when a stately woman emerged from a taxi. Without a word of warning or introduction, he scooped her up in his arms, raced

In the first year of the new century, young Harpo is given his bar mitzvah.

into the lobby, ran up to the desk clerk and shouted, "Register us both!" He was being carried up a mountain in Amalfi in a canvas chair drawn by two natives when he tired of being pampered and plopped one of the natives in the chair and carried *him* up the mountain. He was getting a polyp removed from his throat and had been administered a local anesthetic when the doctor, picking up his probe and preparing to charge down the orifice, was scared off by a gargantuan wild-eyed stare on the face of his patient. Again and again the doctor resumed his concentration, gathered up his instruments, and proceeded to plow ahead, and again and again the doctor emerged from the stare a broken man.

By the time he married Susan Fleming in 1936 (or 1937— even *he* didn't know) and adopted four children, he settled down at El Rancho Harpo in Palm Springs to an almost disgustingly happy existence. He gave up partygoing and gadding about, and spent his time painting, playing the harp, and watching comedy shows on television. (Anything besides comedy put him to sleep. He'd wake up in time for the credits and say, "That's the worst show I ever saw.")

Harpo's social circles consisted almost exclusively of witty marathon talkers, for whom he became an amused and eternally receptive audience. Even at Hollywood's Hillcrest Roundtable of comedians, he was the only member who wasn't always busy trying to top everybody else. He didn't do anything, in fact, but sit there and listen and smile. He was convinced that being amused and eternally receptive was his chief claim to popularity among witty marathon talkers, but this wasn't entirely true. "You don't have friends like he had without giving as well as taking," as Sid Kuller pointed out. Ben Hecht, one of the "friends like he had," commented that "he says he's a listener, but once you get him started he can talk for seven hours straight." ("I don't talk; I listen," insists Harpo, in an autobiography that runs 650 pages.)

On the set, Harpo simultaneously baited and abetted the orgiastic recalcitrance of his brothers by spending most of his time off in one corner nourishing his soul with harp rehearsals. Often he exasperated his arms this way, and since his scalp was annoyed by that inescapable red wig, a director would have to do nothing more than have one of the nearby girls sit and massage his head and arms for a while to keep him in one place all day. He played his comedy as he played his harp: by doing whatever seemed comfortable and with little regard for all the restrictions laid down by people he didn't know.

A shine comes into the eyes of people who recall Harpo Marx that can scarcely be equaled by the one they reserve for their own mother. When Harpo died in 1964, a stunned Hollywood populace searched through its memories and impressions for words strong enough to recall the experience of knowing the man, and found none. There are some things that can't be captured in words, and Harpo Marx is one of them. Those spoken about him before or after his death reflect only a shadow of the awe he inspired:

Harry Ruby, writer for the Marx Brothers: "He was one of the sweetest human beings that ever was."

John Guedel, producer of "You Bet Your Life": "He always believed the best of a man until he was proven wrong—and then he gave him the benefit of the doubt."

Samuel Goldwyn: "Harpo Marx was one of the gentlest human beings I have ever known."

Red Skelton: "His happiness was reflected in his voice."

D. A. Doran, producer at MGM: "From the way Groucho talked, he gave the impression that he knew a lot of things. Harpo knew something he wasn't telling."

Groucho Marx: "He inherited all my mother's good qualities—kindness, understanding, and friendliness. I got what was left."

As for Harpo, his best summation of himself was: "I am the most fortunate self-taught harpist and non-speaking actor who ever lived."

Even the time-entrenched cliché "Rest his soul" fell foully upon the lips. Harpo had a soul that reached out and touched everyone he knew or came in contact with, and it is almost impossible to imagine it at rest. At peace, of course, always. But at rest, never.

COLLECTION OF HARPO MARX

GROUCHO: 1890

Possibly the greatest of all the insidious frauds of civilization is this idea that the mind is a logical organ. People who consider themselves irreproachably rational can stand in a room exhibiting a picture of Washington crossing the Delaware and denounce a foreign enemy for breaking a Christmas truce; they can subscribe to a religion that believes in three gods in one for one day in seven; they can see themselves threatened daily by dissidents who demand to be treated equally and dissidents who are tired of being treated all the same, and then defend freedom of speech by clamping down on anyone who tries to speak out. To say that something "doesn't make sense" is to imply a criticism of the thing, yet all it really indicates is that it is part of the general scheme of things. Rationality is one of the more recent additions to the cumbersome mental baggage, and as a newcomer it is deeply mistrusted by all the staid and respectable instincts like aggression and propagation and self-preservation, who were there first and aim to keep it that way. In any crisis or tight situation, logic can be counted on to be consulted last, except in movies, cheap novels, and TV shows. The concept of Rationality is not much more than an unseen ideal, like Justice, Perfection, Immortality, and the Public Servant. The mind *really* works in patterns that go something like this:

> He had taken his watch out of his pocket, and was looking at it uneasily, shaking it every now and then, and holding it to his ear. "Two days wrong!" sighed the Hatter. "I told you butter wouldn't suit the works!" he added angrily, looking at the March Hare.
> "It was the *best* butter," the March Hare meekly replied.
> (Lewis Carroll, *Alice in Wonderland*)

> "What's all this?" said Baby Puggy. (All *what* never seemed to occur to her to explain, and if she was satisfied, what the hell are you kicking about?)
> (Robert Benchley, "The Menace of Buttered Toast")

> JACK: How you can sit there, calmly eating muffins

when we are in this horrible trouble, I can't make out. You seem to me to be perfectly heartless.

ALGERNON: Well, I can't eat muffins in an agitated manner. The butter would probably get on my cuffs. One should always eat muffins quite calmly. It is the only way to eat them.

(Oscar Wilde, *The Importance of Being Earnest*)

When I was your age, I went to bed right after supper. Sometimes I went to bed right before supper. Sometimes I went without my supper and didn't go to bed at all!

(Kalmar and Ruby, *Horsefeathers*)

What do you think of the traffic problem? What do you think of the marriage problem? What do you think of at night when you go to bed, you beast?

(Kaufman and Ryskind, *Animal Crackers*)

The sentences of Groucho Marx, like our vast, ambitious mental enterprises, lose their way, fail to accomplish what they set out to accomplish, and are proud of it. Groucho is the vicious outsider who knows that all your pontificating is going to come to nothing and is dead set on beating you to it.

He was born Julius Henry Marx, so he went through his whole life calling himself Groucho. Born into a family of poker fans, he refused to find card playing anything but a bore. Blessed with two pool-cue, pinochle, and parlor-trick experts for big brothers, he decided he wasn't interested in that. Surrounded by illiterates, he excelled at all things literary and turned into a first-class student. By nature a serious and reflective person, he went on to become one of the world's greatest comedians. Since it went against his Libra grain to be anything but obeisantly polite and considerate, he became adept at the rude and slashing insult.

The mind of Groucho Marx was always working, but it just wasn't about to be told what it should be working at. All you had to do was pressure him into doing something, and you could be certain his nimble brain would conjure up an overriding compulsion for its opposite. The greater the encouragement to mingle in a crowd and crack funny jokes, the greater would be his natural inclination to go off in a room by himself, play the

Groucho with one of his carefully chosen favorite people, his brother Harpo.

Groucho (center) with Gummo (left) and a friend named Vic Harris (right).

guitar, read a book and worry about something. Usually you couldn't get a good gag out of him until he was encased away in a cathedral and surrounded by obsessionist zealots who were guaranteed not to be amused—like the time he attended a spiritualists' meeting and answered a call for questions to the Great Spirit by standing up and asking, "What's the capital of North Dakota?"

Unrecognizable to all but friends when he walked the streets without his moustache, he got his kicks out of ad-libbing whole comedy routines for the benefit of people who thought he was just a strange little man. A very distinguished-looking maître d' stopped him on his way into the dining room of one of Los Angeles' more prestigious hotels and said, "I'm sorry, sir, but you have no necktie."

"Don't be sorry," Groucho told him. "I can remember when I had no pants."

"I'm sorry," the maître d' repeated, doing his best to pretend that nothing had been said, "but you cannot enter the dining room without a necktie."

"Who makes these rules that men have to wear ties? Some little guy sitting upstairs in a T-shirt?"

Then in the middle of the dining room Groucho saw a baldheaded man and shouted, "Look! You wouldn't let me in without a necktie, but look at him! You let him in without his hair!"

Sometimes he'd go into restaurants and refuse to admit that he was Groucho Marx, to avoid getting the special treatment he felt he didn't deserve. "My name is Johnson," he'd say, and then, indicating his family: "This is Mrs. Johnson and these are the little Johnsons. I'm a plumber and I'm in town for the plumbing convention." When this got a reception not quite akin to that afforded royalty, his wife would nudge him and badger him into telling who he really was. "My wife wants me to tell you who I *really* am," he'd repent sheepishly, and then stoutly declare, "My name isn't Johnson, it's Smith! This is Mrs. Smith and these are the little Smiths. And I'm not really a plumber, I'm in dry goods."

Groucho had less fun pulling practical jokes than he did pulling impractical reactions to practical situations. Like the salutation he chose when an impulse seized him to answer the telephone in a general's office while on a USO tour during the war: in a falsetto imitation of every receptionist in the history of the switchboard, he yodeled, "World War Two-oo!"

Groucho stood right on the edge between masochism and misanthropy, and he remained edgy all his life. Nothing suited him, and if it suited anybody else, he would keep nagging about it until it didn't.

One of the great causes of tension in Groucho's life rose out of having an astounding reputation as a comedian without having a temperament particularly suited to performing. The hyperactive spark of the extrovert simply was not in him, and appearing on stage before thousands was more apt to give him stage fright than exhilaration. "As a lad," says Groucho, "I don't remember knocking anyone over with my wit." He didn't even *want* to go into show business in the first place; what childhood aspirations he had were centered on the medical profession, and there were times in later years when he wondered if he'd done the right thing. He knew damn well that the only reason he wore that painted moustache was to give him something to hide behind, and to stand up in front of a crowd and show off his timidity bothered him even more.

Of the three brothers, it was Groucho who most highly valued a stable existence and a comfortable home life, even though each of his three marriages went down the chute sooner than any of the others' did. He preferred the company of his children to the company of most of the grown men he knew, and usually considered their opinion of one of his shows at least as important as any of the others offered up to him. Eddie Cantor once found Groucho in a department store chasing his giggling four-year-old daughter up and down the escalators and making wisecracks to amuse passers-by. He treated his offspring approximately the way he treated everybody else in the world: He spoke loudly and carried no stick at all. He improvised parodies for bedtime stories, lavished attention on them like talcum powder and made threats he didn't have the heart to carry out.

And movie-making showed up approximately 463rd on the list of things that amused and fascinated him. He rarely had any confidence in either the director or the producer (if he liked one, he was certain to resent the other). He worried about every line before he had the nerve to deliver it (Norman Krasna was on the set a lot, and Groucho would keep turning to him and saying, "Think of something funny"). His brother Chico spent too much time on the phone talking to bookies (though Groucho spent nearly as much talking to investment counselors). Nine o'clock in the morning was too early for the comic muse to operate (and getting up that early aggravated his insomnia). There was no john within three miles of the sound stage (he figured the building designers had just assumed actors were not human). None of the technicians knew what they were doing or even cared whether they knew (his definition of overtime was that all the stagehands were paid four times what they were worth instead of twice; but whenever six o'clock showed up he deliberately blew his lines so that everybody would get overtime). His opinion of the television complex was even lower: "No matter how individualistic a spirit you are, the networks will tame you" was his dour summation.

Far more satisfaction than any of the performing arts could afford him was derived from sitting down and writing something—and without all that fuss. His first book didn't come out until 1930, but it was his brilliant manipulation of words that got him that oft-resented stature as a comedian in the first place. In one of his many magazine articles, he describes how a campaign sprung up to run him for President. "Naturally I was touched," he says, "but only for five dollars, and that came later." At the Marx Brothers Retrospective held at the Museum of Modern Art in New York he was asked why he didn't pay much attention to revivals of his old films. His only comment was "I'm allergic to nostalgia." When a middle-aged teacher came on his quiz show and claimed she was "approaching forty," Groucho asked her "From which direction?"

On paper or in person, he is able to make the silliest pun or the most senseless non sequitur sound like it *must* have meaning. Checking into a hotel, he might pester a desk clerk over the telephone by getting outraged that he had been delivered a bucket of ice and no skates with it. The clerk would argue as best he could that they never send skates up with their ice, and he

At the Circus: waiting for the cameras to roll.

Groucho and Harpo on their last film together, *Love Happy*, 1949.

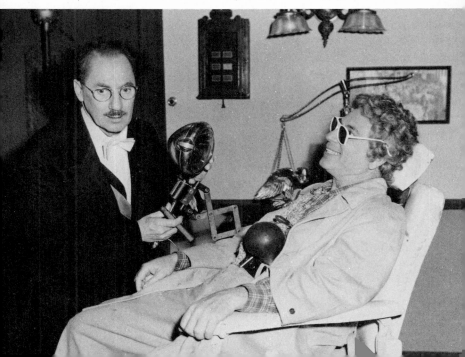

would argue, "I *always* get skates over at the Plaza." When presented with a tree surgeon on the TV show, he greeted him with "Tell me, Doctor, did you ever fall out of a patient?"

The key achievement of Groucho's aberration has been the training of his mind to come up on the spur of the moment with the line that you or I think of the next week or two months later. "I have a hair-trigger mind," he has said. "Not a very good one, but it works kind of semiautomatically." With the result that most of the time he makes his remarks before he gets a chance to hear them. He probably was not aware of everything he was saying when a "You Bet Your Life" contestant stated she had thirteen children and could explain it only by proclaiming, "I love my husband!" "I like my cigar too," said Groucho, "but I take it out once in a while."

He was capable of voicing a responsible and original opinion on any given topic, but it wasn't uncommon for comedy to creep into his comments without any apparent volition on his part. Discussing television commercials, Groucho made the observation, "About midnight the depilatories, the deodorants and the cathartics sneak in. All I can say about these products is that their commercials are more offensive than their users. It must be pretty generally accepted that no one with good taste stays up at twelve o'clock at night."

It was no less common for comment to creep into his comedy, apparently just as uncontrollably. Like anybody with a perceptive and analytical mind, Groucho saw that the only way to react to the world at large was in horror. He managed to be cynical without being bitter, and only the sincere joy he received from getting laughs out of people saved him from being called a nasty old wretch by anybody but outsiders. When the radio version of "You Bet Your Life" won the Peabody Award, he could freely admit that he had never heard of George Foster Peabody and then go and make a remark ("It's a good thing the guy died, otherwise we couldn't have won any prizes") that would have been greeted with a stunned silence followed by cries of outrage if anybody else had tried to get away with it. Once a clergyman came on his television show glowing and declared, "Groucho, I want to thank you for all the enjoyment you have given the world." Groucho shot right back, "And I want to thank you for all the enjoyment you've taken out of it." He made a jab at the show-off in every showman when somebody asked, at one of the parties George Gershwin was fond of holding for the purpose of performing a medley of George Gershwin tunes, "Do you think Gershwin's melodies will be played a hundred years from now?" "Sure," said Groucho. "If George is here to play them."

His comments about his own profession seem to derive from several decades, not of rationalization but of observation. "The first thing which disappears when men are turning a country into a totalitarian state is comedy and comics," he insisted once. "Because we are laughed at, I don't think people really understand how essential we are to their sanity."

GUMMO: 1897

ZEPPO: 1901

Little brother Milton and baby brother Herbert were affable fellows and decent actors with good senses of humor. However, being an affable fellow and a decent actor with a good sense of humor just makes you look like a jerk when you're sharing the stage with three great comedians.

Being a funny guy seems to be an inevitable part of being born a Marx Brother. But the circumstances that take over after that and turn you into a great comedian are less easy to come by. All the brothers professed a wish to get out of show business if they ever got a chance, but Gummo is the one who took it when he got it. As for Zeppo, many of his associates feel that his was the case of a man of talent going the way of most men of talent: to waste. "You put a fellow in decent clothes among three fantastic clowns and he *can't* stand out," as Harry Ruby claims. When *Animal Crackers* was in rehearsal, the producer asked Zeppo if

Gummo, flanked by big brothers Chico and Harpo, sometime in the 50's.

Zeppo.

All five Marx Brothers.

he couldn't get more variety into his part. Zeppo answered, "How many different ways are there to say 'Yes'?" The only time he was given any other sort of thing to say was when Groucho fell ill and suffered an appendectomy while *Animal Crackers* was in Chicago. Zeppo took over Groucho's part and a stand-in took over for Zeppo. Groucho sat in the audience while recuperating and discovered to his glee that his baby brother could match him point for point in delivery, if not in originality, and stayed out of the show for two weeks to give him his chance.

Zeppo took after the gambling side of the family and was also fond of pulling practical jokes like walking up to total strangers and yelling, "Hey, how are you? How've you been? How's the family? I've never seen you before in my life!"

Although James Agee recommended Zeppo to posterity as "a peerlessly cheesy improvement on the traditional straightman," most critics were fond of assuming that acting was of no concern to him and consequently that treating him fairly could be of no concern to them, and they wrote of the fourth Marx Brother as of a fifth wheel. Finally, fed up with being handed shoddy material and degrading writeups, he left the act and built up an agency with Frank Orsatti. During the war he invested in an engineering plant that was making airplane parts and safety devices. By backing inventions and toying with some himself (he recently invented a wrist watch that measures the heartbeat and sets off alarms when the heartbeat maladjusts), he managed to continue a wealthy man without publicly having to humiliate himself forever.

Gummo sold ladies' apparel while all four brothers were having their great successes, and that suited him fine. (That is to say, being off the stage suited him fine; not ladies' apparel, which did him no justice.) When it became three brothers and even greater successes, he joined Zeppo and became their manager, which he remained long past the dissolution of the team. In 1953, acting as spokesman for Groucho when he underwent surgery, Gummo told newsmen, "Groucho's surgery is so minor that he even thought about doing it himself, but couldn't find anyone to hold the mirror." He was sitting in a restaurant with Groucho when the latter started to play Philosophical Celebrity and sighed, "There are really two Groucho Marxes." "Oh, yeah?" said Gummo. "How come I'm only getting commission from one?"

Fourth Marx Brothers are always welcome but never essential. When MGM did without them altogether, they billed what was left as "Groucho Chico Harpo MARX BROTHERS," with the suggestion that this was really all there was to it in the first place, that what they were presenting was—mind, body, and soul—the Marx Brothers.

ii

antiquity

> Why do you say this thing is new? The dreams of men are older than the contemplative Sphinx, or garden-girdled Babylon, and I fashioned this thing in my dreams.
>
> —H. P. Lovecraft, *Dreams and Fantasies*

3 Marx Bros. & Co.

Recently excavated poster shows Groucho (center), Gummo (above, left) and Harpo (above, right) in *Fun in Hi Skule*.

THE NIGHTINGALES c. 1907–1910

FUN IN HI SKULE 1910–1913
"An Artistic Screamingly Funny Howling Masterpiece"

MR. GREEN'S RECEPTION 1913–1914

HOME AGAIN 1914–c. 1919
"The Greatest Comedy Act in Show Business;
Barring None"

The misty dawn of the Marx Brothers lies shrouded by the wild fancy of those who were not there and the faulty memories of those who were. The written remains of what transpired are few and paltry, each one written solely for the purpose of contradicting all the others. The truth, if it ever existed, has gone through its customary transformation into something more easily digested by the human mind.

It befell at the time of the Turn of the Century—which, as we all know, was a gay and innocent time, long before death and taxes and wars and Communists and Brussels sprouts and capital punishment—that Minnie Marx, a German immigrant whose father was a magician and whose brother was the second half of a comedy team called Gallagher and Shean, took a fancy to the notion of turning her gay and innocent children into singers and putting them on the dirty and wicked stage.

The Kingdom of Vaudeville was at that time ruled over by the rival princes Keith and Orpheum, and under these stood an infinite array of lesser potentates called Managers. These were cruel and petty tyrants, who delighted in tormenting without mercy all performers who fell within their grasp and inflicting upon them harsh punishments for things they didn't do and stiff fines for causes made up on the spur of the moment. (This was a habit they passed on to their children, who all grew up to be junior-high-school teachers and lunchroom monitors.)

Julius and Milton Marx were the original Three Nightingales (a feat which they accomplished only with the aid of Lou Levy or Janie O'Riley or whoever the fates occasioned), but as time passed Adolph, Julius, and Milton became the Four Nightingales (with or without one or two of the others), and together they faced such a string of abuse as would rank them among the most courageous boys who ever lived. They faced theaters only recently converted by missionaries from men's clothing stores, and still not without their share of men's clothing. They faced stages scarce seven cubits by two—and often not even stages, but unstable benches at one end of a hall. They faced dressing rooms that were euphemisms for the back yard of the theater. They faced salaries that were half what they pretended to be, and sometimes were spared the worry of facing a salary at all.

Typical was the night in Mississippi when they were making an appearance at an open-air theater, replete with open-air dressing room, and only a plague's throw from the swamps of Louisiana. There was a makeshift make-up lamp on the shelf, and it acted as a beacon for parasitical insects the world over. The small troupe, finding itself served up as a meal to the ravenous arachnids, screamed plaintively for the Manager. Said Manager, ever eager to please, produced two smudge pots a-smudging, and hurried the swollen and infected Nightingales out of the clutches of the murderous insects and into the clutches of the murderous audience. However, the minstrels found jeering, catcalling, and like abuse much curtailed that evening, as the theater had caught fire due to the influence of the smudge pots, and the audience restricted its activities to running away and screaming absurdly for the intervention of the gods. Whereupon Adolph, Julius, Milton, and Lou Levy repaired to the ruins of the dressing room to discover that their wardrobe and their personal possessions were no more. But all was not lost. They soon divined, to their immense relief, that the Manager, together with the collected

Groucho (left) and Harpo (behind his left elbow) are all that's readily identifiable in this ancient Coney Island photograph.

The Four Nightingales endure a brief metamorphosis into the Six Mascots: from left to right, Aunt Hannah, unidentified extra, Groucho, Gummo, Minnie and Harpo.

THE SIX MASCOTS

spoils of the evening, had escaped injury and was at that moment many miles away, in perfect safety and comfort.

At length it was time to strike back. It came to pass that necessity forced our Nightingales into Nacogdoches, Texas, where it chanced that a runaway mule distracted the attention of the assembled, so that they departed from the theater, caring little for the wondrous sight of the Human Nightingales. "Truly," said Julius to Adolph, "this is the last in a long series of straws." And they were instantly seized by demons. When the audience returned to the theater, they found there not four inept songbirds as had once occupied the stage, but Four Boys Possessed. A burlesque took place of all that had previously transpired: the songs, the theater, the Manager, the state of Texas, the dingy town, the audience, the universe, Grover Cleveland—none was safe from ridicule. At the close of the ceremony, the boys anticipated their destruction at the hands of the crowd either by Tar or by Feather, but much to their astonishment they beheld a scene of great merriment and rejoicing, and the applause went on through the afternoon and far into the night.

They were Nightingales no more.

It was a wild, bounding, boundless, violent, disordered, post-adolescent act that the Marx Brothers hit vaudeville with, week after week, town after town, manager after manager, boardinghouse after boardinghouse, for fifteen years. It was a roughhouse act to play to roughhouse audiences in roughhouse theaters; it sent Chico running up and down the aisles, Harpo riding up and down with the curtain, and everybody climbing up and down the backdrop; it consisted of kicking, slapping, fighting, shouting, funny lines, unfunny lines, elaborate shenanigans, simple slapstick, and music, music, music. Tenors sang, sopranos sang, and even Groucho sang, and Harpo and Chico hit sour notes, labored through chord progressions, kicked the harp, fussed with the piano stool, and gave all impressions they couldn't play their instruments, and audiences went nuts every time they found out they could. Often they violated their written material in deference to hilarious improvisations, and often they violated their written material in deference to pretty dull improvisations, and in time they learned to play their audience like another instrument, to generate excitement and build excitement to hysteria, to stick to the routine when they needed to and to take off whenever they got the chance. Witnesses swear that they destroyed props, back-drops, costumes, and sometimes promoted physical damage to the theater.

Harry Ruby, one of their later writers, still remembers being startled by the experience. "It was a completely different kind of humor!" he insists. Groucho would sit there listening to the aria of some buxom operatic, and then tell her, "When you've finished with that, will you take the air?" He would patiently wait through almost all of his brother's harp solo and then interrupt him with "Play softer. We can still hear you."

"We'd never *seen* anything like this before!" says Mr. Ruby. Little wonder. What the brothers did was simply set up a situation and then, without bothering to provide any reason, destroy it. When literary devotees gather to drown inspiration in a sea of analysis, you will hear a lot of talk about a mysterious thing called "motivation." This boils down to the idea that for every-thing a character does, we should be given a nice, neat reason why he did it. If there is no motivation, we won't understand the action.

Right around this time, Mack Sennett's Keystone Comedies were making mayhem and destruction very popular. There was nothing novel about the Marx Brothers doing *that*. But the Keystone Comedies were still motivational comedies. Like all comedies before them, they very carefully established plot lines, situations, mistaken identities, hostile rivalries, frustrated inten-tions, fallen dignities, and all the other stock motivations, before anything was allowed to happen. Nobody pushed a pie in a man's face until he had seen that man trying to steal his wife. Nobody chased anybody or knocked anybody down unless that person had made him good and mad. And the cops *would* have driven straight along the road if they *could* have.

The Marx Brothers bothered with none of this. They did what they pleased and gave no reasons for it. They became the type of character whose motivations we never understand and whose actions make perfect sense. Their mother kept telling them they shouldn't do anything that hadn't been written for them. But we all know how young men react to what their mother tells them.

"We always played to ourselves, never the audience. Sometimes we got to laughing so hard at ourselves we couldn't finish," insists Groucho. Once Harpo found a cockroach crawling across the stage, and all four Marxes got down on their knees and made bets about its progress. There is a limit to how far filial loyalties will go, and beyond that limit stretched a rather strange attitude toward a profession and a rather novel idea of entertainment. The conventions of stage comedy were not Commandments, imposing cromlechs to be questioned only by Monarchs and their Ilk, but puny artifacts, to be called upon if handy but otherwise only to be kicked over and destroyed, like the scenery.

Stan Laurel begged for his chance to get up on the boards, and when he got it he played every gesture and every expression as straight as he could make it. W. C. Fields practiced juggling with his feet till his legs bled, and he didn't bring one change into his act without weeks of rehearsal. The number of times that Eddie Cantor took an interest in the crawling of insects on the stage can be counted on the fingers of one ear.

But when were they ever seized by demons?

The schoolroom routine was the easiest way for comedians to get started. Gus Edwards was such a big hit with his school act that now there were hundreds of them. After several years in vaudeville, they could make up a school act without even thinking. Which is just what they did. Harpo blacked out some teeth, put on a ratty red wig, and stuck a sand bucket over his head and he was Patsy Brannigan, the standard bumpkin. Groucho put on a German accent and became Mr. Green, the customary angry teacher. A young Hebrew boy could hardly be done without, and this role was taken by Gummo. Like every other comedian, they started out by doing imitations of every other comedian.

GROUCHO:	Why were you late?
HARPO:	My mother lost the lid off the stove, and I had to sit on it to keep the smoke in.
GROUCHO:	If you had ten apples and you wanted to divide them among six people, what would you do?
GUMMO:	Make applesauce.
GROUCHO:	What is the shape of the world?
HARPO:	I don't know.
GROUCHO:	Well, what shape are my cufflinks?
HARPO:	Square.
GROUCHO:	Not my weekday cufflinks, the ones I wear on Sundays.
HARPO:	Oh. Round.
GROUCHO:	All right, what is the shape of the world?
HARPO:	Square on weekdays, round on Sundays.
GROUCHO:	What are the principal parts of a cat?
GUMMO:	Eyes, ears, neck, tail, feet, etc., etc.
GROUCHO:	You've forgotten the most important. What does a cat have that you don't have?
GUMMO:	Kittens.

Eventually a second half to the routine developed, and that was called Visiting the Old School Ten Years Later. All the characters from *Fun in Hi Skule* would reappear at a party given in Mr. Green's honor, and they would sing songs and stuff. (Minnie had this idea her sons were musicians and she couldn't get it out of her head. She also had a fixation for "class." It wasn't enough that the act was funny; it had to have class. There were roses pinned to the backdrops, and an original song called "Peasie Weasie" cost $50.) While this was happening, Mr. Green grew a large black crepe moustache and let his hair show rather than cap his dome with a false scalp, and a gathering storm of prewar resentment against anything German caused him to drop his accent altogether. At the same time, with the help of friendly advice and critical acidity, Patsy Brannigan saw the wisdom of leaving all the talking to his brothers, who had less trouble enunciating, and depending more and more on acrobatics and

Groucho in the back row with the girls, Chico and Harpo front and center.

magic tricks to steal attention. Slowly and almost reluctantly, but in the end inevitably, he adopted a silence pristine and inviolate, and only after he stole a horn off a taxicab and stuck it in his belt did he allow himself even the most incommunicative of sounds. One week they were in San Francisco, and he bought himself an old used raincoat to protect himself from the climate. One good rain, and the raincoat fell apart at the seams and buttons. One good look at the sight of the old raincoat, and Patsy had a new prop.

As the costumes grew more outlandish, three individual spirits grew more distinct, and three characters began to grow from inside those spirits. One became a monologuist because he thought and read and talked a lot; one became a renegade immigrant because he was a renegade who had a fascination for immigrants; one became a pantomimist because making faces and doing stunts was his idea of a good time. One more became a pseudo-straight man because he stammered over the big punchlines and wasn't particularly interested in the whole idea. Together they became a divergent unity, because together they were divergent brothers.

The troupe was on the brink of dismemberment when *Mr. Green's Reception* wore out its welcome in every major, minor, and one-horse town in the country, and finally Uncle Al Shean, after two rather depressing attempts to get friends to write a new act for his nephews, sat down with a piece of brown wrapping paper fresh from the butcher's and wrote *Home Again* himself. Groucho, whose medical ambitions were getting the best of him, was swearing he'd never look another Theater Manager in the eye again and had to be coaxed back with a heavy barrage of great lines that nobody could resist. Chico, whose enthusiasm for the team's perpetuation *ad infinitum* was rivaled only by his mother's, was told to go ahead and ad-lib things. Harpo was advised not to say much of anything.

As *Fun in Hi Skule* had become *Mr. Green's Reception,* so *Mr. Green's Reception* metamorphosed into *Home Again.* In the new act, the musical second half remained, but the schoolroom prelude was replaced by a scene on the docks—to be more specific, according to an observer (S. J. Perelman) who saw the thing in 1916, "the Cunard dock in New York, an illusion conveyed by four battered satchels and a sleazy backdrop purportedly representing the gangway of the *Britannic.*" A mass of people (sixteen) get off the ship (walk in front of the backdrop), and Mr. Green mingles with the crowd, saying goodbye to them all and rattling off a monologue that begins, "Well, friends, next time I cross the ocean I'll take a train. I'm certainly glad to set my feet on terra firma. Now I know that when I eat something I won't see it again." The speech includes some local New York humor ("This must be the Far Rockaway boat." "How do you know?" "I can smell the herring.") that was a total mystery to Midwestern audiences. Gummo, pretending to be Mr. Green's son, punctuates the monologue with wisecracks of his own, and

To
Harpo
and
Susan 7/25/38

From
Uncle Al
at The age of 36

Uncle Al Shean.

finally Mr. Green announces, "Nowadays you don't know how much you know until your children grow up and tell you how much you don't know."

Patsy Brannigan and Leo the Wop show up among the crowd and start stealing lingerie off the female passengers. Leo says to Mr. Green, "I'd like-a to say goombye to your wife." Mr. Green says to Leo, "Who wouldn't?" Mr. Green tells everybody on the dock to be sure to come to his party. A cop comes on and explains that some of the ship's silverware is missing. He accuses Patsy but finally decides he's innocent; he shakes his right hand and the silver drops from Patsy's left sleeve. (Harpo got such a big laugh with twelve knives that he jacked it up to twenty-four. The longer it went on, the bigger was the laugh, and so finally it became an endless cascade of cutlery climaxed by a coffee pot, and a simple gag had become a routine. This got to be such a standard bit that when Harpo was being introduced and people asked him what his act was, he'd tell them, "I drop knives.")

Shortly after the party scene starts, Gummo comes out and says to his father, "Patsy Brannigan the garbage man is here." Groucho says, "Tell him we don't want any." When Harpo and Chico enter, they start climbing over couches to sit in ladies' laps, and guzzling the water out of the goldfish bowl and then swallowing the goldfish.

"The plot structure," according to Mr. Perelman, "was sheerest gossamer: vague reference was made to a stolen chafing dish, necessitating a vigorous search by Harpo of the corsages of two showgirls." Eventually Groucho gets tired of being annoyed by these two rambunctious guests, and when they start chasing a girl around the room he gives up the fight and joins them. They start leaping on one another's backs, climbing over the piano, rolling over the couch.

From here on out, the course of events was anybody's guess.

But the day that will never be forgotten is the day that Groucho, Harpo, Chico, and Gummo decided to call themselves Groucho, Harpo, Chico, and Gummo. It occurred during a poker game when four guys named Julius, Adolph, Leo, and Milton, and a monologuist named Art Fisher were making jokes about Knocko the Monk, a comic-strip character, and about how his popularity had infected vaudeville with a plethora of Knockos, Blockos, Bippos, Zippos, Bangos, and Whangos. Fisher was dealing, and he cracked, "Here's a lead card for Harpo." Hahahahaha. Julius was temperamental enough to be Groucho. Heh heh heh heh heh. Leo was always chasing chicks; he could be Chicko. Heeheeheeheehee. Milton wore gumshoes; he could be Gummo. Hohohohoho.

Then they decided it was *fun* to be Groucho, Harpo, Gummo, and Chicko. Why be anything else? They tried to get themselves on the program that way, and a clumsy typesetter dropped the k out of Chicko.

And so it had come to pass. Julius, Adolph, Leo, and Milton had become Groucho, Harpo, Chico, and Gummo. Not just for their show-business careers, but forever. They would never again be real people, they would always be myths. They would never again be ordinary men, they would always be lunatics. They would never again be reality, they would always be comedy.

And the Host of Eternal Abstractions—Pinocchio, Captain Nemo, Little Black Sambo, Natty Bumppo, Sergeant Bilko, Victor Hugo, Marco Polo, Cagliostro, Punchinello, Valentino, Brando, Satchmo, Ivanhoe, Cyrano, Cisco, Pancho, Argo, Nero, Metro, Pharaoh, Apollo, Dido, Tito, Pluto, Zorro, Pizarro, Othello, Belasco, Fiasco, Ringo, Gringo, Alamo, Psycho, Yojimbo, Vertigo, Picasso, Salammbo, Inferno, Colorado, Antipasto, Arms Akimbo, Casino, Bingo, Bongo, Tango, Nympho, Flamingo, Espresso, Rococo, Heigh-Ho-the-Derry-O, and Green-Grows-the-Briar-O— looked down and smiled.

THE CINDERELLA GIRL 1919
"A Merry Melange of Mirth, Melody, and Music"

The Marx Brothers' first attempt at a "legitimate" musical show was written on commission by Jo Swerling, with music by Gus Kahn, and based on not much more than Chico's unswervable confidence and unshakable desire to do a "legitimate" musical show. It had a halfhearted story and a stack of halfhearted backdrops and a row of rotten chorus girls in rotten costumes. It played for three days in Battle Creek, Michigan, at the height of a flu epidemic that was decimating the country like the Plague. The city's schools and churches were all closed, but Minnie managed to talk the mayor into letting the theater open, so long as only every other seat and every other row was occupied. An audience showed up, but not a whole audience, and everyone in it was antiseptically hooded and masked like refugees from The Ride of the Clan, and everyone in it feared for his life if the fellow next to him so much as breathed. Nobody was in much of a mood for laughing, which put the stars not in much of a mood for making jokes, which put everybody in even less of a mood for laughing. The epidemic was so contagious it killed the show. When the script failed, they tried self-admitted improvisation. When improvisation failed, the flu began to look pretty attractive. When *Cinderella Girl* failed, it was back to vaudeville.

HUMOR RISK c. 1920

I'll bet you didn't know the Marx Brothers made a silent movie. That's because nobody's ever seen it. When movies were silent, they could be made very cheaply, and if you could get a few thousand dollars and a camera together it was worth trying at least once. Each of the brothers put up $1,000, and so did two friends, Al Posen and Max Lippman, and so did the author, Jo Swerling again (you'd think they'd learn). The film was shot in Fort Lee, New Jersey, in between shows (they were then doing four a day) in a vacant lot near the vaudeville theater. Interiors were done in a studio on Tenth Avenue in New York. The Marx Brothers abandoned their stage characterizations far enough to allow Harpo to play the love interest and Groucho, in the manner of burlesque melodrama, to play the villain. Mildred Davis, soon to become famous with Harold Lloyd, was the leading lady and played opposite Harpo, who made his entrance sliding down a coal chute. Groucho was thwarted in the end and trudged off toward the horizon in the last shot with a ball and chain on his foot.

Fascinating as this film would be to antiquarians today, there weren't enough of them around at the time to guarantee it any success. Nobody who looked at it could summon up the remotest degree of enthusiasm (except, of course, Chico), but nothing was certain until it was screened for an audience. Screening it for an audience, however, required summoning up a theater owner who could summon up a remote degree of enthusiasm, and nobody could do that, not even Chico. Finally, somewhere in the most godforsaken outposts of the Bronx, Chico dug up some good-natured fellow who agreed to show it once, at a Saturday matinee.

Everyone involved slunk down to the theater that Saturday and consoled themselves with rationalizations about the innate comedic perceptivity of all young children. Having convinced themselves of this, as it turned out, only made things worse, for the instant the picture flashed on the screen every kid in the house reacted as if he'd been let loose in a museum. There was hooting, running, name-calling, and paper-airplane throwing to be done and nothing about to distract them from it.

Whereupon the Marx Brothers saw to it that *Humor Risk* and all remnants of its memory were destroyed, if only to keep silent film fanatics from saying it was the best movie they ever made. If you want to find out anything about it, your best bet is to get hold of one of those kids.

I'LL SAY SHE IS 1923–1925
"The Laughing Revue"

The war was over and it was time for the Twenties. The last straight laces of the Victorians were finally being broken, and the land was being purified of Puritanism. Ankles were being bared, and then calves, and then knees, and sexual freedom was roaming the streets again for the first time in centuries. It was as good a time for rebellion as it was for moral indignation, so the genteel life that was good enough for Grandfather wasn't good enough for anybody else any more. The country folk headed for the city and the city folk headed for Europe, and those who didn't head anywhere sat around and said dirty things about America's values. The war had turned "glory" and "virtue" into dirty words; now the cynicism of Ernest Hemingway, H. L. Mencken, and F. Scott Fitzgerald was the smart thing.

Like any period of disruption, the Twenties were very big on art and literature. Inspiring things were being done in every field, and for comedy fans there were the screen, the stage, and the humor magazine. People in the market for a laugh were treated daily to *Judge, Life, Vanity Fair, The New Yorker, The Ziegfeld Follies,* Bert Lahr, Ed Wynn, Willie Howard, W. C. Fields, Charlie Chaplin, Buster Keaton, Harold Lloyd, Larry Semon, Stan Laurel, Marc Connelly, Stephen Leacock, Heywood Broun, Franklin Pierce Adams, Eddie Cantor, Jimmy Durante, Bert Wheeler, Billy Bevan, Andy Clyde, Jack Pearl, Sam Bernard, Ring Lardner, Robert Benchley, Dorothy Parker, George S. Kaufman, Will Rogers, Joe Cook, Joe Penner, Joe Jackson, Joe E. Brown, Frank Tinney, Eddie Buzzell, Ted Healy and the Stooges, Fanny Brice, E. B. White, Donald Ogden Stewart,

Corey Ford, Oliver Herford, Robert Sherwood, Don Marquis, Frank Sullivan, Raymond Griffith, Reginald Denny, Ben Turpin, Clyde Cook, Harry Langdon, Dave Chasen, Al Jolson, Zasu Pitts, Marie Dressler, Irvin Cobb, Jack Benny, Ben Bernie, George Jessel, Chic Sale, Montgomery and Stone, Gosden and Correll, Smith and Dale, Weber and Fields, Clark and McCullough, Moran and Mack, Burns and Allen, and, of course, Groucho, Harpo, Chico, and Zeppo.

Zeppo, who had developed a proficiency for not singing, acting, juggling, dancing, telling jokes, or doing somersaults that was almost uncanny, was shanghaied out of high school just to make sure there were still Four Marx Brothers when Gummo left. Gummo left to be a soldier, but, when he was through being a soldier, said he was through being an actor too. Zeppo was named "Zeppo" to avoid confusing him with Gummo.

I'll Say She Is was a potpourri of old gags, old routines, somebody else's music and dance numbers, scenery left over from a decade's fiascos, costumes left over from worse, and a title that had somewhat less to do with the show than I did. It was an underground production thrown together out of spit and desperation when the Marxes needed a show to appear in and a producer needed someone to appear in his show, and it was financed by a pretzel-salt manufacturer whose concubine was destined for stardom and had no talent and wanted a chance to prove it. She danced gamely, the Marx Brothers did their routines routinely, and everyone stood in front of the worn-out backdrops and felt silly. And there were delusions that all this would play on Broadway.

Chico's restless ambition was shooting for the Big Time, and New York's fabulous vaudeville showhouse the Palace Theater didn't look big enough anymore, so he was trying to talk his brothers into Broadway. He was also trying to talk Broadway into his brothers. Neither listened. What he wanted was a musical comedy, but what he settled for in *I'll Say She Is* was a revue.

The standard format for one of these things was a line of dancing girls coming on at the beginning to indicate that the show was starting and to give people time to get to their seats and finish their conversations, followed by the star comic (comics) coming on and doing a short skit to introduce himself (themselves), followed by toe dancers and adagio dancers and ukulele plunkers coming on one after another, interspersed with appearances by the star comic (comics) again, until finally the end would come and there would be a big comedy sketch featuring the star or stars or sometimes everybody, and the chorus would come on again and sing, "It was nice having you to see our show, but now we're afraid it's time to go, tra la la, the end!" and they would all take curtain calls and go home to bed.

In other words, a revue was just like a vaudeville show. Except that it played on Broadway.

At least that was the promise held out to the star comics when Joseph M. Gaites remodeled his two productions *Love for Sale* and *Give Me a Thrill*—each of which had died a death matched only by the other—and held the hybrid out as a chance for the Marx Brothers to do their old numbers and to act out some new skits by Will Johnstone.

Will Johnstone was a cartoonist for the New York *Evening World* (his forte was to take an actual news item and string out a series of jokes about it) who had been trying for years to get out of cartooning and write a few theatrical hits (just like the Marx Brothers had been trying to get out of vaudeville and make it into Broadway) but had found his spurts of inspiration too inconsistent to come up with anything that held together from beginning to end. By now he was in his late forties and still struggling for a smash—though he was so lighthearted about his struggling that he was not even much of a success at being a failure. Will Johnstone wrote the new material and the lyrics for the songs that his brother Tom wrote the music for in the show that Gaites called *I'll Say She Is* for want of anything better to put on the marquee that Jack built.

The opening scene is in a theatrical manager's office into which in steady succession parade Zeppo, Chico, and Groucho, each one promising to knock any audience dead with his imitation of Joe Frisco (a buck-and-wing dancer and singer of the time), and then lapsing into his Joe Frisco imitation and then being ushered out of the office. The last of these failures is succeeded by Harpo, who hands the agent a business card and watches the *agent* do the Joe Frisco imitation. A solemn ballet act by a team of girl dancers is immediately followed with its burlesque by the Marx Brothers, all dressed as tramps and swooping gracefully from one leering pose into another. There is a courtroom scene where they make puns on legal terms, play poker, and give Harpo a chance to drop knives. In both of these scenes the brothers get their effects by working together disparately, all four of them doing different funny things at the same time and ending up at the same climax in a different way.

There were twenty-four scenes in *I'll Say She Is,* including all the singing and dancing acts, the harp and the piano, and one serious romantic ballad interrupted by Harpo, zealously tugging across the stage a large cable to whose nether end was affixed himself, and the finale was a forty-five-minute purported representation of Napoleon and Josephine exchanging farewells one eventful night before a battle. Groucho, costumed ornately as Napoleon, clanks around his lady's bedchamber endearing himself with aphorisms like "Jo, your eyes shine like the pants of a blue serge suit." He leaves for the battlefield every once in a while, and keeps tromping back insisting that he's forgotten his sword or something. Every time he disappears, one or two or three of Josephine's lovers climb out of the curtains or the closet or the chandelier and carry on an exchange equally tender. Harpo even makes one impassioned attempt at breaking Josephine's arm. Then at every reappearance of the Emperor, they duck back into whatever hiding place is convenient (the room is full of them). Napoleon eventually suspects something. He says, "Jo, you're as true as a three-dollar cornet." He equips himself for battle by slipping on some garters and proclaiming, "Now metal can never touch me!" (in mock of a current advertising slogan boasting that Somebodyorother's garters never allowed metal to touch the wearer's skin). He hears a martial refrain offstage and remarks, "The Mayonnaise! The Army must be dressing!" He leaves with the declaration, "I'm off! And if I leave you here alone I *must* be off!" At the instant of his departure the room is again crowded with lovers. At the instant of his return the room is again chaste and pure. Now he's really suspicious. He produces his snuffbox and gaily sprinkles pinches of snuff about the furtive corners of the room, chanting all the while, "Come out, come out, wherever you are!" Chico and Zeppo emerge from the furniture, exploding. Harpo emerges from under the bed in a gas mask.

Josephine maintains her loyalty. "I am true to the French Army!" she declares.

"Thank God," says Groucho, "we have no Navy!"

The Napoleon sketch was a product of the combined energies of Will Johnstone and Groucho Marx and was dreamed up by the two of them during intermission at Broadway's *Chauve-Souris*. It came as a topper to a long evening of laughter and song that knocked its audiences out or put them to sleep, depending on what city it was playing in. After this had gone on for nearly a year, its stars began to grow restive over the alleged promise to hit Broadway. An imposing round of threats, protests, and angry notes began. In vain did the producers aver that half their engagements flopped like mashed potatoes, that the show was all roughhouse and no wit, that cosmopolitan audiences had discerning tastes, that it was late in the season and nobody would pay much attention.

Somebody must have lost a big game to Chico, because the promise was finally made good. When the Casino Theater was left vacant by somebody else's overambitious leap into Broadway, Gaites arranged with Shubert and got the theater and spent about $200 making over the costumes and the scenery into something only moderately disgraceful. The Marxes spent one last anxious week on the road, working after every show till early in the morning ironing out old gags and making up new ones. The promise had become a threat: Once their bluff was called, they realized they were no less worried than the producers.

On May 19, 1924, a freak fluke guaranteed lifelong notoriety for the four headliners of vaudeville. The first-night audience of *I'll Say She Is,* consisting chiefly of old fans who cheered and whistled at every revival of a favorite routine, went in knowing they were going to like the show and came out knowing nothing more. What critics were likely to be gathered in their midst, however, couldn't be trusted to be anything beyond third-string novices and apprentices concerned less with the virtues of the show than with the standards of their craft and the opinions of their superiors. The whole idea of *I'll Say She Is* was to make the Big Time, but there was little hope that the Big Time Critics were going to make *I'll Say She Is*.

On May 19, 1924, a dramatic show that had begun to attract important attention was scheduled to open, side by side with a slipshod side show with a shady past starring some damned acrobats called Julius, Adolph, Leonard, and Herbert Marx (their real names were being suppressed at the moment to preserve some kind of dignity). The Big Time Critics got themselves ready for the dramatic show, received tickets for the side show for their cubs, cleaned their tuxedos, broke appointments, and set aside Thursday evening for the theater. Then the play failed to open. Its first night was postponed a week.

On May 19, 1924, a hostile five mingled with a receptive five hundred and faced an onslaught of comedy that nothing had prepared them for. The New York *Times* later said, "They were not much of a surprise to vaudeville patrons, but there are four or five people in New York who rarely go to vaudeville and they all write reviews for the newspapers and so the boys were discovered again."

On May 20, 1924, began a spreading of the Word that was to go on through the summer, into the fall, through the next year, and probably into the next century. New York's most sophisticated crowd couldn't stop talking about these unsophisticated comedians. It started with the reviewers, Alexander Woollcott, Heywood Broun, John Corbin, Percy Hammond, George Jean Nathan, and went on to FPA, Frank Sullivan, George S. Kaufman, Herman Mankiewicz, *Judge, Vanity Fair, American Mercury,* and every other with-it periodical present, until it became the smart thing to do to know all about the Marx Brothers. People invited them to their parties, asked them to speak on the radio, introduced them into their poker circles, quoted them on the streets and in their columns, and, soon enough, found out that their names were Groucho, Harpo, Chico and Zeppo, and started spreading *that* around.

May 20, 1924, marks the beginning of the Marx Brothers Proper, for now they were accepted. But why should this be? Why should literate, well-polished intellectuals go crazy over slapdash slapstick? Why should a lot of tuxedoed gentlemen get any kind of kick out of watching a lot of buffoons running around and being silly? The men inside knew, and their tuxedos couldn't deny it. There are some aspects of being human that are as lasting as the stars. And none are more lasting than the stars of bedlam.

TOO MANY KISSES 1925

A lot of things happened to the Marxes during their stay in New York as celebrities. Groucho bought a big Studebaker and tried to buzz it around the block during the matinee of the day he bought it. He ended up stranded in the thick of New York traffic dressed as Napoleon, while soloists covered for him with hundreds of unrequested encores. Chico got himself thrown in jail one night for insulting a policeman who had the nerve to protest when he crossed the street against the lights. But Harpo got himself in the movies.

Nothing much was doing that first summer, and Harpo wandered over to Hollywood and wormed his way into a Richard Dix comedy called *Too Many Kisses*. Like *Humor Risk*, this is one of the Great Lost Films, but from all existing reports it will stay great only as long as no one finds it again. Richard Dix is sent to France by his father because his father thinks he's paying too much attention to girls. (His father doesn't know much about France.) Some confusion has arisen here, due to the fact that, while it's been generally understood to be France the boy is sent to, some indignant Spaniard wrote in when he saw the movie and complained about the treatment of "my people" on the screen. (Perhaps the Spaniard didn't know much about France either. Maybe he hadn't been to Spain in a while and thought it was France now. Maybe he couldn't read English and thought the reason everybody was acting French was to make fun of Spaniards.)

Harpo played a village idiot in wherever the hell the story took place, and he didn't get to do very much because it was only a light romantic comedy rehashing all the old boy-meets-girl-naïve-villager-vs.-sophisticated-American-revolution-in-the-streets-make-fun-of-Spaniards-by-acting-French gags. Nevertheless, he was very excited when the movie came to town in March and went around and told all his newfound sophisticated friends about it, and they went down one night in a theater party to see it. "We sat there waiting for me to come on and dominate the screen," Harpo recalls, "and nothing much happened at all for a couple of reels."

As luck would have it, the studio had decided that Harpo's face-making was not quite up to the standards set by Richard Dix and had used him only once, as a cutaway. Harpo was sitting in the theater watching the movie and he bent down to pick up his hat. Suddenly he flashed on the screen peeping through a door. "Look!" said Minnie. "There you are!" And when he looked up he was gone. For five more reels it was Richard Dix.

It was beginning to look like movies and the Marx Brothers were not made for each other.

THE COCOANUTS 1925–1928

No doubt about it, the Marx Brothers had made the Big Time. Their next show was produced by Sam Harris and written by George S. Kaufman with music by Irving Berlin. They didn't come any bigger than that. Sam Harris, an ex-partner of George M. Cohan's, was an effervescent little man who never had a bad word to say about anyone until 1933, when he declared, "Hitler is not a very nice fellow." Sam Harris had a grasp of show business that was intuitive rather than analytical, so he naturally knew no rules and did everything right, and naturally had trouble articulating what he wanted from people and always got it. When *Once in a Lifetime* was gasping its last gasps out of town, it was Harris's oblique remark in the middle of a stumbling critique, "I wish that this weren't such a noisy play," which prompted Moss Hart to perform the toning-down rewrite that put the show across. His oblique remark in the middle of preparations for *The Cocoanuts*, "What you need here is your Weber and Fields scene," nearly prompted George Kaufman to desert the production.

At his peak, Kaufman was Broadway's pinnacle of sophisticated wit—or the cold-soup negativity that passed for wit in sophisticated circles. *Of Thee I Sing* and *You Can't Take It with You* are examples of his perception and cleverness that are remotely stunning. *Stage Door* is an example of his wise-ass snappishness that is enough to send you up the wall. Kaufman, who customarily wore his legs wrapped around each other and his arms wrapped around his head, sat upstairs in his house on 63rd Street in New York and got no kicks out of anything but all-day writing sessions and nerve-racking stage productions. He exhausted his collaborators (who numbered among them Marc Connelly, Moss Hart and Edna Ferber—*Cocoanuts* was one of the very few plays he worked on alone) with his compulsive working habits. At this time he was drama editor for the New York *Times*. Even after he became a millionaire he maintained the position, just to keep himself busy.

And Weber and Fields were something far beneath him. But the Marx Brothers seemed to be beyond him. The plan was to build a whole musical-comedy play around them, and many of the crucial elements (the characterizations, the comic style, and even some of the routines) were already there to start with. But how were you going to mingle the conventions of polite comedy, romantic comedy, situation comedy, or *any* form of conventional comedy with the impolite, unromantic, anti-situation, unconventional farce of the Marx Brothers? That problem had never been faced before. None of the serious elements in a play with the Marx Brothers could be taken seriously, but if they weren't damn good they'd be a shameful contrast to the brilliant comedy they were supposed to be supporting.

But a musical play was what the Marxes wanted, not another series of sketches. Kaufman's work satisfied them. When he sat on a bare stage and read them *Cocoanuts,* a satire on the current land boom in Florida, Harpo and Chico were so pleased they fell blissfully asleep.

Cocoanuts fared badly in its out-of-town tryouts. According to one witness, the show was hilarious, and it was only an obstinately Philadelphia audience that kept the theater in silence. At one point Groucho even gave up the effort and walked up to the footlights and ad-libbed an unrelated monologue. When that didn't work either, he scanned the audience for some object suitable for ridicule. As soon as he spotted Alma Gluck, a famous opera and concert-hall soprano, he got down on one knee like Al Jolson, shot his arms out, and proclaimed, "*Oy!* Alma Gluck!" That made Philadelphia more sullen than ever.

But just to spite Philadelphia, New York welcomed its local boys home and let them carry on with their foolishness all night without discouragement. The production polish of the new play, after *I'll Say She Is,* was stunning. (There were washlines that compared favorably with the production of *I'll Say She Is.*) The New York *Times* even mentioned "costumes of such brilliance that the eye fairly waters." The songs were impressive, too, though Berlin failed to come up with a single hit tune for the thing. By reviewers' testimony, the first-night audience felt a letdown through most of the first act but got such a kick out of the second that they left with no complaints. There were grumbles here and there that they never reached in this show the frantic peaks of the first, but grumbles like that are part of the routine whenever you're presumptuous enough to try and have a success twice. Even among Marx Brothers, and even as late as the Fifties, the sentiment was expressed that nothing they ever did could beat the fast and furious *I'll Say She Is* and that wonderful Napoleon scene. *Cocoanuts* favored a more sedate lunacy and even seemed ill-disposed toward getting the Four Marx Brothers all on stage at the same time. What Groucho could do with Chico or with his newfound female straight man, Margaret Dumont, and what Harpo and Chico could do when he was gone, were now the main points of interest. Suddenly finding oneself sophisticated and accepted does have its pratfalls. But the Unwritten Law was still anarchy, and anarchy was still strictly enforced.

That no two performances of *Cocoanuts* were ever the same has become part of the canon fodder of Marx Legend. Morrie Ryskind served a brief cut-and-rewrite apprenticeship on the out-of-town run of *Cocoanuts,* and once the show settled down in New York, he was alerted to its progressive sea-change into things foreign and unknown. "You should see *Cocoanuts* sometime, Morrie," said Kaufman to Ryskind one day. "It's not what we wrote."

For one thing, Harpo could put in a gag anywhere he felt like it. This was where he picked up the blonde-chasing business, and he did it right in the middle of Groucho's scene with Margaret Dumont, for no reason clear to the audience, or even to Groucho. Or even to Harpo. He just asked one of the chorus girls if she'd run across the stage so he could run across after her honking his horn. Then it would be up to Groucho to come up with a comeback, like "First time I ever saw a taxi hail a passenger," or "The nine-twenty's right on time. You can always set your clocks by the Lehigh Valley."

For another thing, Groucho had a neurosis about getting a laugh every second he was on the stage. Sometimes he'd make puns on lines that already were puns to start with. Sometimes he'd make jokes about the show and the performance rather than the situation. Sometimes the idea of delivering the proper build-up to a laugh line would bore him, and he'd sail right on into the punchline without bothering with anything beforehand to explain it. This was as often perplexing as it was funny.

For yet another thing, it got to be quite dull to stand up and do the same routines eight times a week for months on end. Every star has his own reaction when he is faced with the prospect of being amusing night after night with material that fails to amuse him. Some of them leave after a few months and let the show go on without them. When Orson Welles was starring in his own Mercury Theater productions, he would alternate performances of unmatched brilliance with performances of equally unmatched sloppiness. When Laurence Olivier and Anthony Quinn were through playing Thomas and Henry in *Becket*, Olivier played Henry and Quinn played Thomas. And in a musical comedy the liberties that could be taken ran even greater gamuts. Al Jolson was known to bound on stage when his show was half over and say, "Well, I'll tell you how the story comes out: the fellow gets the girl. Now, shall we go on with it, or do you want to hear me sing?" And he wouldn't go on with it, he'd just sing for the rest of the night.

The Marxist approach was to take the methodical structure they were given and carefully render unto it a chaos. This wasn't out of keeping with the nature of the show, of course; audiences came expecting it. And the more they expected it, the more they got it. Eventually this got to be good for business, too. People who had already seen the show came back again to see what had happened to it now. So did George Kaufman. He looked at this play that had his name on its credits and went backstage and muttered, "Hey, somewhere in the second act I think I heard one of the original lines."

Soon Kaufman held a rehearsal, and *Cocoanuts* went back to "what we wrote" again.

The Marx Brothers' second Broadway hit ran 377 performances, including a revamped summer edition where Kaufman wrote new dialogue, Berlin wrote new songs, and everybody sent their costumes to the cleaners. After that, they followed the customary beneficent procedure of allowing the rest of the country to see what had been delighting New York for so long and played in all the major cities of America for two seasons in a row. The story of *Cocoanuts* doesn't even end here, but for the time being let's all pretend it does.

ANIMAL CRACKERS 1928–1930

Although *Animal Crackers* was the first full-fledged play Morrie Ryskind had his name on, he had spent the last few years worming his way into columns with cute sayings, and into magazines with clever verse, and onto the writing rosters of Broadway revues with comedy sketches. Although his aspirations headed him toward the Great White Way, Ryskind was soon to become one of Hollywood's favorite people for turning plays and novels into screenplays (*My Man Godfrey,* for example). But right now he was one of George Kaufman's favorite collaborators and one of the Marx Brothers' favorite comedy writers.

Sam Harris was handling production again, and Kaufman and Ryskind agreed to write the book together, so the Marxes took off for a European vacation and left everybody else behind to do the dirty work. It turned out to be one of New York's hottest summers, and the two writers sweated through every day for three months in one miserable corner of Kaufman's house writing another unromatic comedy. The formula that paid off so well last time was called into play once again, so that the Marxes came off, as Gilbert Seldes pointed out, "not as a team but as four individual comics," and so that every once in a while, as Morrie Ryskind pointed out, "that fellow that nobody cared about made love to that girl that nobody cared about."

Irving Berlin didn't write the music for the new show. Groucho had his eyes on Bert Kalmar and Harry Ruby and had even gone up to see them at Waterson, Berlin, and Snyder, the music company they worked through, and told them he thought the two song writers and the four brothers would make an ideal couple. Kalmar and Ruby, who performed in their songs some of the most imaginative comic distortions of convention and reality, were also two of the most shameless perpetrators of 1920s Romantic Piddle. Kalmar and Ruby wrote songs like "Show Me a Rose and I'll Show You a Girl Named Sam," and they also wrote songs like "I Wanna Be Loved by You, Boop-Boop-a-Doop." Bert

Kalmar was once a vaudeville headliner as a dancer, and Harry Ruby was once Harry Rubinstein, an itinerant song-plugger, nickelodeon pianist, and trolley-car conductor with Harry Cohn. Kalmar and Ruby had been making what might be called a decent living as song writers until they sat down one day for a laugh and knocked off a sentimental ballad called "Who's Sorry Now?" They didn't want the song released, of course, because it was just a joke and if anybody took it seriously it could prove damaging to their career. But the song was released without their permission, it turned into one of the biggest hits on Broadway, and they became the hottest team in the song-writing business for the next two decades. They went on turning out lightweight sentimentality alternating with brilliant absurdity for years, having apparently learned their lesson from "Who's Sorry Now?" that the line between popular romance and absurd nonsense is almost indiscernible.

The Marx Brothers back from vacation after two smash successes were not people easy to deal with. It was plain to them now that audiences who came to see a Marx Brothers show came to see the Marx Brothers and not to see the show. They had no doubt they were in for another hit, and they were just as apt not to show up as they were to clown around all day if they did show up. This got Kaufman sore as hell. He didn't have to put up with this! He was ready to stomp off and engage himself in worthier activities, and, but for the remonstrances of cub Ryskind, who really *did* have to put up with this, would have thought it over on the way out. The geometrically expanding stock market, too, was no efficiency booster, as tidy sums were becoming untidy fortunes daily and overnightly, and the perpetrators of this comic masquerade—writers, actors, librettists, all—were beginning to look at it as little more than seed for the Big Harvest. Story conferences kept degenerating into quibbles over points and margins. Groucho had the *Wall Street Journal* with him every minute and gave out hot tips to all his friends. Chico was on the phone with his broker as often as with his bookie. Sam Harris would have complained, but he was too busy keeping up with the gossip.

As it turned out, the three weeks of clowning hadn't gone to waste. Enough work had gotten done to get a good show in good shape by the time Philadelphia was scheduled to look at it, and everybody but Kaufman (who, as usual, had found something else to be busy with) was there to see a resounding success resound.

The drudgery that good comedy requires was drudgery even when Marx Brothers comedy required it, which is probably why the outsized prankishness that attended it was so welcome. The morning directly after opening night, the crew assembled to perform the accustomed pruning ritual that accompanies opening nights good and bad. There was some rephrasing to be done on Groucho's speeches, and Groucho was there. There were some sacrifices to be made among the straight lines, and Morrie Ryskind was there. There were sixteen bars of music needed for a bridge, and Harry Ruby wasn't there.

"Hey," said Sam Harris. "Anybody know where Ruby is?"

"I don't know where he is," said the orchestra leader.

"I don't know where he is," said Bert Kalmar.

"I don't know where he is," said the Little Red Hen.

"I know where he is," said Groucho. "What teams are playing?"

"What *teams* are playing?" said Harris. "What the hell does that mean?"

Groucho and Sam Harris consulted a paper and found out that the New York Giants were playing the Philadelphia Phillies. Then they got in a car and drove down to the ball field to watch Harry Ruby, all dressed up in a New York Giants costume, working out with his favorite baseball team.

Like everybody with a great talent in one area, Harry Ruby had a consuming interest in another. Since he had eked out a career in show business, he made an arrangement with some of the teams to let him join in on practice sessions. If he had become a professional ball player, he would have spent all his spare time hanging around backstage.

But he was proud of the uniform he had on, and the professional bat in his hands, and the swell fellows he was playing ball with. He saw his friends sitting in their car watching him, and he stood in his privileged position on the ball field and waved to them. It never occurred to him that his friends might be a little annoyed. It never occurred to his friends, either. They sat in their car and laughed their heads off.

Kaufman and Ryskind had gotten themselves in trouble by trying to make one too many decisions about how the show should be run. They had made up their minds that the harp solo and the piano solo were getting to be worn-out devices and that *Animal Crackers* could do without either. They had therefore included in the play their conspicuous absence. The troupe hadn't been in Philadelphia two weeks before Harpo came up to Morrie Ryskind with something on his mind. "Well, Morrie," he said, stalling, "they love the show, all right, but, well, it seems to me it needs something, in the second act somewhere, you know, maybe what they'd like is something aesthetic."

Aesthetic? Where was Harpo Marx getting a word like aesthetic? "What do you mean by aesthetic, Harpo?"

"Well, I don't know, maybe a little more music or something. We don't have very much music."

"No, this is a book show. That's perfectly on purpose."

"Yes, I know, but—"

"Look, Harpo, what do you want?"

What Harpo wanted, simply, was to play the harp. He said it as if it were an experiment, as if he'd just try it once and see how it worked. Ryskind agreed to let him try it, but he knew what it meant.

Or he thought he knew. He hadn't counted on Chico storming up to his hotel room two hours later and demanding to know "What's this about Harpo playing the harp, huh? That sonofabitch touches that harp just once, and I'm gonna do my piano number!" Before anybody else had a hell of a lot to say about it, the harp and piano solos were right back in the act where they belonged.

The piano routine belonged at the beginning of Act Two, right after Groucho's big monologue about exploring Africa. It was punched up with some comments from Groucho's corner, and eventually Groucho, Harpo, and Chico worked out a whole new scene around the piano, playing football with Harpo's coat, making puns on popular song titles and burlesquing the "Anvil Chorus."

They were still in Philadelphia tinkering with this scene when it occurred to Groucho that he still didn't have enough cracks to make while Chico was playing the piano. He mentioned it at dinner with Morrie Ryskind one night, so Ryskind mulled over his stew for a while and finally came up with a line that Groucho thought was great. He trundled back to the theater for the performance, chuckling contentedly to himself, confident that *that* line would do its job, even if everything else failed. When the time came for the piano routine, he braced his vocal cords and let his line out loud and clear.

Nothing came back, not even an echo. Now he had to say *something*. He looked out over his unenchanted audience and told them, "Well, that'll teach you one thing. Never have dinner with Ryskind." One of the most useless bits of advice ever given to an audience.

As usual, when they came back into New York people loved the show just the way it was, and as usual the way it was came out every night a different show. But if the Marx Brothers were not constantly testing the limits of what they could get away with, it would have been a different show anyway. Groucho was fond of making his entrance (being carried in a coach by four natives) with one or both of his small children in his lap, and never letting on what *that* gag might be. At one point all four brothers performed a number called "We're Four of the Three Musketeers." Eventually it was agreed among them to do the song without the verse. The next week they managed to get through without the chorus. Without the verse or the chorus, the little patter in the middle ("Eenie!" "Meenie!" "Miney!" Honk!) seemed rather lonely. And rather puzzling to the crowd. Harry Ruby ventured backstage one evening to inquire as to why such obscene license was being taken with his material. "*You* go talk to those crazy men," said Sam Harris. "*I* can't do anything with them." So Harry Ruby talked to those crazy men, and they finally leveled with him and told him, "Look, Jew boy, mind your own business." That was small comfort.

Kaufman's luck was the same when he launched an attack one Wednesday afternoon after an especially dispirited matinee. Groucho answered back with a phrase that was growing immensely popular among the criticized: "Well, they laughed at Edison, didn't they?"

"Not at the Wednesday matinee, they didn't!" answered Kaufman.

And Miss Dumont, who had come back for more punishment, was getting her share. She was absolutely shocked by the indignities this band of ruffians delighted in afflicting her with backstage, like pulling chairs out from under her or putting frogs in her bath or goosing her every time her backside was turned. And the more shocked she was by the indignities, the more they delighted in them. Once she came to the theater gushing to all the ladies about a marvelous new slip she had bought for herself, and it occurred to Harpo that if she was so pleased with it perhaps she'd like to display it to the house. During their scene together he pulled an old prank from *Home Again* and slipped the thing right out from under her dress. Miss Dumont held back her tears until she got offstage.

Not even the Marx Brothers were safe from the Marx Brothers. In the middle of Harpo's harp solo, Groucho chose to dredge up from the depths of his memory an old scandal that had kept the newspapers in gravy for weeks about four years previous. A name that one hears every day and then forgets forever sounds totally out of context with the world when it comes back again, and the minute Groucho called out curiously, "I wonder whatever happened to Rhinelander," there was set off in the theater such a whoop of hysteria that Harpo had to stop playing until everybody calmed down enough to hear him.

But the story that veterans of *Animal Crackers* most often love recalling is the story of the Great Bathrobe Intrigue. It seems that as far back as Philadelphia, Sam Harris, George Kaufman, Morrie Ryskind, Bert Kalmar, Harry Ruby, Zeppo, Chico, and Harpo had all chipped in $10 and given Groucho a beautiful $80 bathrobe on his birthday. As one birthday followed another, the nine men fell in league and gave each other $80 bathrobes every time. When Harpo's birthday came around, Morrie Ryskind managed to find a very handsome, elegant robe for only $70, which fit him perfectly and looked just great.

"Nuts to that!" said Harpo, and the two of them went back to the store and found a garish, awful-looking thing for $80 and bought it. Harpo felt "It's not the gift but the principle of the thing."

When it came time for Ryskind himself to celebrate his Golden Day, there were kinks to be ironed out. Groucho could only come up with $7 because the stock market was doing funny things. Chico could only come up with an IOU because his last poker game had been even funnier. Finally Ryskind was asked to chip in a share. They told him it was for a worthy cause.

By the time January 27, Harry Ruby's birthday, looked imminent, the gang was tired of bathrobes. All eight parties of the allegiance got together and decided it was time to make a break from tradition and ignore Ruby's birthday altogether. ("We didn't tell Harry," says Ryskind, "preferring to surprise him.")

Ruby, too, was beginning to feel that perhaps the idea had worn thin. For just that reason, he felt it was his duty to remind all his friends of their obligation. From January 13th on, the company received every day a telegram announcing TWO WEEKS UNTIL HARRY RUBY'S BIRTHDAY or ONLY TEN DAYS LEFT BEFORE HARRY RUBY'S BIRTHDAY or HARRY RUBY'S BIRTHDAY IS FOUR DAYS AWAY.

He even brought it up with Groucho one day in his dressing room. "Well, Groucho, how is it going?" he said.

"How is *what* going?" said Groucho.

"You know what I mean. I'm talking about the birthday present."

"Well, that's a funny thing," explained Groucho. "You know what happened? I called a meeting of all the fellows just to take care of that. And everybody's for it except me."

"Really?"

"Yeah. We've reached a deadlock."

"Now, wait a minute! That's not a funny thing. I've shelled out a lot of money for everybody else's birthday. What's the idea?"

"Harry, I did all I could. I honestly called the boys together with every good intention and we talked it all out and everybody's for it except me. That's just the way it is."

Came January 27th. It was a Saturday. Harry Ruby showed up at the matinee. He was dressed very well. He had his acceptance speech in his jacket pocket. He was already practicing feigned expressions of joy and surprise. Nothing happened.

Harry Ruby showed up at the evening performance. He was still fingering his acceptance speech. He was still thinking, "Maybe they're kidding and they're going to come out and give me a big beautiful robe and all of my friends will be there to see it." Nothing happened.

Bright and early Monday morning each of the guilty parties received an official-looking letter from Mr. Ruby's attorney announcing Mr. Ruby's intention to sue for breach of contract, alienation of affections, and an $80 bathrobe. Still nothing.

There was a scene early in the second act of *Animal Crackers,* shortly after the piano routine, in which Groucho presented to Margaret Dumont an enormous chest he had supposedly brought back from Africa and announced that it contained diamonds and emeralds and other such joys. On this Wednesday at the matinee it also contained one Ruby. No sooner was the presentation speech out of Groucho's mouth than Harry popped up out of the trunk and said, "Where's my bathrobe?"

Once again the audience was mystified. So was Groucho. Harry climbed out of the chest and stomped offstage before Groucho could think of a funny answer.

Ruby claims that any other comedy star would have killed him for pulling a trick like that on the stage in front of a paying audience. But Groucho was very good about it. "That was a clever stunt you pulled," he told Harry. "That was very funny. How did you think of it?"

"Where's my bathrobe?" said Harry.

"Look, Jew boy, mind your own business," said Groucho.

It was still small comfort.

THE COCOANUTS 1929

Sound had come to motion pictures. People who tried to argue whether this was a turn for the better were drowned out by the cacophony of sputters, whines, gurgles, hisses and thumps emanating from all the better movie screens. A honeycombed hierarchy of technicians, actors, writers, directors, producers, agents, managers, distributors, exhibitors, executives, and presidents set up in the flourishing days of silent pictures now had to accommodate itself to a whole new medium without falling apart.

Nobody in the movie business knew much about sound. Nobody in the sound business knew much about movies. Everybody in both businesses resented everybody in the other. Nothing was finished on time. Microphones were hidden in vases and corsages. Monk's cloth was hung on the walls as if it were soundproofing. Noisy flies drowned out the dialogue of great actors. Casts and crews of thousands were kept waiting for hours while repairmen fiddled with bad connections. People from the telephone company were in executive positions in the studios. Cameramen were being told they were making too much noise and shut up in a box. The box had a glass window on one wall to let the camera see, but it couldn't have any kind of window on any wall to let the cameraman breathe or it would have defeated its purpose. Cameramen fainted of suffocation.

No method had been developed yet for dubbing extra sounds onto the sound track. So if you wanted a musical background for a scene, you had to bring a whole orchestra onto the sound stage and have them play while the cameras were running. The prospect of cutting the sound track when you cut the film had everybody stumped. (It was never even clear from one minute to the next whether the sound was going to go out to the theaters on the film or on a separate disc.) That meant that if you wanted to cut to a closeup in the middle of a sequence, you had to have two cameras going so you could leave your sound track alone. (It also meant that you were never sure how wide the image on the film was going to be, since the sound track crowded one-tenth of the frame off the film and the disc didn't. So there was no way of knowing whether anything on the left side of the picture was going to show up on the screen or not.) If you wanted to have three different shots in the sequence, you had to have three cameras going. If you wanted to cover the sequence in any kind of decent way, you had to have five cameras going. That, in turn, meant that when you lit the set, you had to light it in some strange way that would be appropriate for five different cameras pointing in five different directions. (*Gentlemen of the Press* needed seven.)

Admiral Byrd once allowed himself in those primitive days to be subjected to one of these battalions of mechanism, and the equipment broke down and the whole day was spent trying to figure out what was wrong with it. The admiral kept asking what the problem was and nobody could tell him anything. That annoyed him. He stood on the sound stage and hollered, "If this was *my* outfit, I'd sure as hell know what was wrong!" People had to have more patience than Admiral Byrd to handle sound motion picture equipment in 1929.

So it was chaos *before* the Marx Brothers arrived. But the studios were scouring New York for stars who could talk, making it somewhat inevitable that Chico would run across somebody who was interested in the Marx Brothers.

The deal was first attempted by the head of their agency, William Morris. He arranged with Walter Wanger of Paramount for a three-film contract at $75,000 a film. When Wanger took the cheery news that he was getting all four Marx Brothers and the rights to their hit Broadway play for $75,000 to Adolph Zukor, head of Paramount, Mr. Zukor offered to spit in Morris's eye. The compliment was not returned, but Morris's son showed up the next day to see if he could smooth the matter out, and he brought Zeppo along to indicate his good intentions. Morris, Jr., hardly got a word in edgewise. The show belonged to Zeppo, who furnished Zukor with ten minutes of "Tonight Show"-type remarks to the effect that Mr. Zukor was the one showman in the world and that when he, Zeppo, gave a thought to what Mr. Zukor had done for Mary Pickford and, by inference, the entire motion-picture business, it inspired him to a violent quaking and an uncontrollable shivering; but he hoped that Mr. Zukor would excuse such behavior for what was, after all, the greatest moment of poor Zeppo's miserable existence. Once having cemented the relationship in this fashion, he went on to say, "Mr. Zukor, all our lives we've worked to perfect this one show. It's a big hit. All our jokes are in it, everything we've ever done. We're willing to make a picture for you, give you all our material, all our services, and all those marvelous gags—the whole thing for one hundred thousand dollars." Wanger, who was also present, jumped a foot or two when he heard that the price had gone *up* in hopes of luring the buyer. But Zukor hadn't even noticed. He was still grinning from one ear to the next over the "one showman in the world" part. He was, in fact, unable to figure how such a juicy offer had happened to be turned down. He reasoned that it must have been stupidity on the part of one of his subordinates. "Walter," he said, "what's wrong with that?" The job was done. And there are those who say Zeppo Marx *wasn't* born to be an agent.

Conveniently, Paramount had equipped its Long Island studio for sound recording, so it was possible for the Marxes to keep going strong on Broadway every night and still leave afternoons and late mornings free for daytime moonlighting, a practice being taken up greedily by Alice Brady, Rudy Vallee, Eddie Cantor and every other performer who had two contracts waved in front of his face. Since nobody had any great ideas about remodeling *Cocoanuts* into anything but what it was on the stage, things were never going to get very hectic in the Scripting and Rehearsal departments. The Marx Brothers had been reciting *Cocoanuts* dialogue and acting out *Cocoanuts* routines long enough for *Cocoanuts* to be imprinted on their cerebral cortexes as a permanent behavior pattern. All they had to do was get them on film and they had several thousand more dollars to play with. This was going to be an interesting new experience.

George Folsey, *Cocoanuts'* cinematographer, had been battling the problems of sound for the last year and a half, in short subjects and features, and by now was just as good as anybody at coming up with excuses for solutions. In the same year he was director of photography for Rouben Mamoulian's *Applause,* and the problems he faced on that one usually kept him up half the night.

Cocoanuts had great stars, a guaranteed script, good production, and a top-notch cinematographer. All it needed was a capable director and it was home free.

Now, Robert Florey was a capable director. A young Frenchman born in Paris, he had been assistant and assistant director for a range of talents from René Clair and Max Linder all the way to Al St. John and some Swiss comedian called Wilhelm Gfeller, and had directed sophisticated comedies in

America since 1925. In 1928 he attracted a lot of attention by making *The Life and Death of 9413—a Hollywood Extra* together with Slavko Vorkapich and Gregg Toland for only $93. This clever one-reel experimental film was fashioned out of cigar boxes and an erector set in Vorkapich's kitchen, and its ingenuity and impressionistic style amused a lot of people. The fact that it was made for $93 knocked them silly. Florey was well educated in France and Switzerland and spoke English beautifully. He understood film-making, he understood theater, and he understood comedy. He had a lot of impressive credentials, all right. Just one problem. He didn't understand the Marx Brothers. He didn't think they were funny.

You would think if there was *one* qualification a Marx Brothers director would have to have, that would be it. You wouldn't even think it would be terribly difficult to find somebody who had it. I know of at least a hundred. But somebody was looking at Robert Florey's record when he gave him the job and not at Robert Florey, so he directed *Cocoanuts*.

More sympathetic was Joe Santley, an ex-child star and leading man, who is listed as co-director but didn't really do much more than help design and work out the filming of the elaborate song and dance numbers. (Which are done with tricky angles, Busby Berkeley fashion, a procedure later employed by Busby Berkeley.) At least he *got* the jokes, but since he wasn't supervising the production, this was not only of no benefit to anybody, it actually succeeded in messing up the sound track every once in a while.

You see, it wasn't bad enough that the equipment would break down four times a day. Even when it was working perfectly, Santley or the make-up girl or some visitor to the set would start giggling whenever one of the Marx Brothers made a move, or the third cameraman would get so intrigued by what Groucho was doing he'd forget to pan over to Harpo. Strictly speaking, there should have been no need for a rehearsal or even a run-through, but eventually it got so that if they didn't act out each scene at least once for the crew, everybody would fall down laughing while they were doing a take. And ad libs were no help either. In one scene Groucho was at the hotel desk calling,

"Front!" when it occurred to him that it sounded like he was calling a dog named Front, so he jumped down to his hands and knees and peered out from behind the desk and called, "Here, Front! Here, Front! Here, Front!" But to the man who was doing his closeup, he simply ceased to exist. The cameraman peered around with his closeup lens back and forth across the set and up and down the wall and the floor and finally found Groucho's head behind the desk just as he was getting up, so he had to wander around all over the set again to get back where he started from. "The poor man," says Folsey. "He went out of his mind." When they did the scene a second time, they retained the ad lib but had everybody prepared for it. This time (and this is the shot you see in the film) the cameraman was so intent on following the move that he started panning away prematurely twice before Groucho even did anything.

To his credit, almost, Florey made no attempt at halting the string of improvisations. To him any difference that might crop up between the way a scene was done one time and the way it came out the next was decidedly peripheral, if it was apparent at all. He didn't even do anything to correct the mistakes. Whatever happened, his reaction was always the same: "This is funny?" The only Marx Brother he took any interest in was Harpo, and this took the form of sitting around with his face in his hands trying to come up with new silent gags for him to do. He finally made a telephone out of chocolate and had him eat it, and put Coke in the inkwells and had him drink it. What he did not do was think of an interesting way to insert them in the sequence as it had been played out several hundred times already, so now they stick out like silent thumbs.

But the Marx Brothers were out to have all the fun they could. Harpo kept badgering Florey for French lessons every time he heard French being spoken, and he kept badgering George Folsey (whom he insisted on calling Bob) for a belt for his horn. "Hey, Bob, lend me your belt, will ya?" he said one day, and Folsey slipped off his belt and gave it to Harpo, and Harpo wore it all the way through *Cocoanuts* and *Animal Crackers,* and Folsey never saw it again as long as he lived.

Between the director and Groucho there was practically no

communication, except that every day around noon Groucho would start heckling Florey about letting them go to lunch before the vultures ate all the rolls. Groucho didn't care much for French lessons; what he got his real kicks from was listening to the cameramen running around rattling off a whole string of shop talk he'd never heard before. Groucho would catch Folsey tossing off vernacular like "Get a broad and stick it over there" (referring to a two-bulbed, diffused light called a broad), or "Put some silks on it" (silkscreens), and he'd stop him and ask him what he was talking about. Folsey would then patiently explain to him, as technician to actor, that when he said, "Let's get a kicker in here" he was asking for a boost in the amount of light on the subject, and when he said, "Break the neck of that baby down," he meant to shorten the neck of the stand under the baby, or face light. And he would just about get finished with his explanation in time to hear a whole comedy routine elaborated around it solely for his benefit. It took Folsey quite a few explanations and any number of comedy routines before it occurred to him that Groucho was just using him as a straight man and didn't have the slightest interest in knowing what his jargon really meant. But by then he couldn't even say, "Let's put some silks on that broad," or "Why don't you break her neck down?" without being made to look ridiculous for having said it. One day a crewman asked if the leading lady needed more fill light around the eyes and Folsey made the mistake of saying, "Aw, no, I'll get a baby into her before the day's over." That did it. Groucho had Folsey on the five-yard line for the rest of the afternoon.

As the reluctant Frenchman remembers the experience, Groucho was making comedy routines out of everything and never stopped talking. About Zeppo he remembers only two things: 1) he was always the first of the four to show up, and 2) he was always late. Zeppo was usually the only one good enough to hang around in a convenient place when the cameras weren't running. Harpo was always roaming into a nearby projection room where his harp waited for him, or falling asleep in his dressing room. Groucho headed for the phone and squared things with his broker. Where Chico went was anybody's guess. Eventually the crew got pretty good at locating the others, but

Chico could be up on the roof, down in the cellar, over on the next sound stage watching Jimmy Durante, or, most likely, in the girls' dressing rooms. When a scene was over he'd ask if they'd be needing him in the next half hour, and if anybody was foolish enough to say no, he'd be gone all day. During one frantic search for the missing fourth, Morrie Ryskind, who stayed with the picture all through shooting to keep an eye on the script, responded to a hunch and called the New York Bridge Club. "Is Chico Marx there?" he asked. A polite voice answered, "Yes, but he can't come to the phone right now; he's playing a hand."

And the technical problems that were faced reached pretty bizarre proportions. When a lawn was needed for the auction scene the studio went and bought a whole truckload of grass mats, the kind they use on cemetery plots before the lawn fills in. But Folsey knew that artificial green wasn't going to show up as the medium gray that would be taken for green because it didn't contain all the yellow pigment common to natural grass. So he had the carpenter shop donate a barrel of wood shavings to the cause and sprinkled the shavings in among the grass in the grass mats and then he got another barrel of shavings and painted them all *purple* and sprinkled them in too so that it wouldn't look too light. They couldn't just go outside and photograph a lawn; they had to have a parade of grass mats dressed up with yellow and purple shavings to masquerade as a lawn.

Even little pieces of paper were causing troubles. *Cocoanuts* features an abundance of notes, charts, diagrams, and even, in the Groucho-Chico encounter, one large table-sized map. Not a one of them could be unfolded near a microphone without such an onslaught of crackles, rustles, and pops infecting the sound track that it sounded like the place was burning down. It took any number of drowned-out punchlines, cameras turning on and turning off again in disgust, and hunting parties sent out searching for Chico again, before it occurred to anybody that if they soaked the paper in water for a while it wouldn't make any noise. So now, for reasons we keep waiting to hear explained in the dialogue, every piece of paper that appears in the film is limp and soggy like it's just been retrieved from a kosher brine barrel.

George Kaufman happened by every so often to watch them

Robert Florey with the Marx Brothers. COLLECTION OF HARPO MARX

all struggle and to pick up material for his satire of the Talkie Scare, *Once in a Lifetime*. Rouben Mamoulian checked progress periodically, too, especially when they were shooting the dance numbers. When Florey and Santley set one of their cameras up in the catwalks and shot straight down at the chorus line, Mamoulian was genuinely moved.

The problems weren't even all technical or logistical. Not many films like *Cocoanuts* had ever been made before, so everybody went around making rules about how it ought to be done. "You people from the stage, you don't understand," Joe Santley would say to Morrie Ryskind. "In a motion picture, you've got to show the audience where everything is coming from. Now, this point here, where the music is supposed to start up during the dialogue . . . Where does the music come from?"

"What do you mean where does the music come from?" Ryskind would say back. "Where does the music *ever* come from? The guy says to the girl Something is on my mind and the girl says Really? What is it? and somebody in the orchestra hits a note and they sing. That's where the music comes from."

Santley disagreed. "No, no," he said. "Motion picture audiences won't accept that." So he hired sixty guys with instruments to sit in a bandstand and *look* like they were playing music so that everybody would know where the music came from. Unfortunately, what with having a whole orchestra on the set to provide the music in the first place and getting the dialogue and singing to be heard at just the right volume above the music and everything, the directors neglected to take any pictures of the sixty guys in the bandstand. So they sat there and got paid for the day, but the audience *still* never found out where the music was coming from. "Nobody gave a damn, of course," says Ryskind.

Shortly after shooting began, Walter Wanger, the man in charge of production, had similar words of wisdom to impart to Groucho. We can picture the scene: Mr. Wanger, sitting at his luxurious desk in the middle of his luxurious office, has his luxurious secretary usher Groucho in. Groucho, without his moustache, resembles a cynical bookworm who grins with his teeth clenched; he enters and sits, stage L. His chair is not very luxurious. He does not look very comfortable. He crosses his legs uneasily, with the air of one who does not want to cross his legs.

Mr. Wanger speaks first: "Mr. Marx, I've been in this business a long time." That, right there, should be enough to disqualify him from passing judgment on things, but Groucho bravely holds still. "Movie audiences [Mr. Wanger continues] are not going to accept a painted moustache. They want everything authentic. Everything authentic. You'll have to go back to the crepe one you used in 1916."

Groucho does not move. The fact that Chaplin's moustache

never fooled anybody floats into his head, but, no, he remains stoically silent.

Mr. Wanger again, now with the mock eloquence befitting his stature: "Oh, and that's something else. We can't have you talking directly to the audience, as your habit was on the stage. Theater audiences are well aware that they are only watching a show, but a man who sits in a movie house likes to think that what is happening on the screen is real. So we have to take certain precautions. You understand."

Groucho rises slowly, with the deliberation of one who is thinking it over. He falls down, with the air of one who has forgotten to uncross his legs. He rises again, somewhat more cautiously. "You, sir, are a schlemiel!" he snorts, and exits. If the set designer is kind enough to provide a spittoon by the door, Groucho uses it on the way out.

Single spotlight on Wanger, who has buried his face in his hands and is sobbing softly. Slow curtain.

Imagine! Wanger actually spoke as if he knew what he was doing! Why, the movie makes it perfectly clear that *nobody* knew what he was doing!

Cocoanuts exists. It is the earliest surviving record of Marx Brothers comedy that we have at our disposal. As such, it is as enigmatic and baffling a remnant from a dead civilization as the Great Sphinx. Were the Marx Brothers really like this? Posterity's first glimpse of Groucho is at the age of thirty-eight, Harpo is forty, Chico forty-two. At that age you would expect them to be rather set in their ways. You might even say their peak years are past. But Groucho's delivery can claim none of the power and pungency we come to know him for later on. And Chico's lines don't sound funny when he says them; they just sound belligerent. Harpo alone emerges triumphant, an angelic devil and a demonic angel, floating in and out around this darkling plain, performing unimaginable gags, making faces both ghastly and transcendental, reminding the world that all the problems of sound recording are of no concern to *him*. This film leads us to believe that there can be no doubt as to who is the star of the Marx Brothers. If it weren't for Harpo, those three brothers of his who sound so unsure of themselves would never have gotten anywhere.

They are watered punch and the play is weak tea, but trying to judge either on the basis of this movie is like trying to judge a painting by a Xerox copy. It is indeed a filmed play in the worst sense of the word. Or words. The play isn't even filmed very well. The cameramen can't keep people in frame whether they happen to be Marx Brothers or not. When Harpo drops things from his sleeve, the floor is just out of camera range, so we never see them. Groucho has to call them out as they fall ("What's this? A grape-fruit! A coffee pot!"), or we'd never know there was anything but a noise. Characters are forever stopping in the middle of sentences to figure out the next word they're going to say, and nobody seems very concerned when Groucho and Margaret Dumont break in on each other's dialogue, or when person after person makes an overexplained entrance and an unexplained exit, or even when references to a 4:15 train turn it into a 4:30 train and back again.

The limit is when Chico completely forgets his lines in the prison escape scene and has to make up new ones as he goes along. Chico is trying to tell Bob Adams that Polly Potter is going to get married if he doesn't hurry up and break out of jail. When Bob Adams asks him who is going to get married to her, all Chico can say is "Polly" again. Finally, Oscar Shaw, who is doing his best to play Bob Adams, realizes that Chico is never going to get the line right and blurts out, "Do you mean that Polly is going to marry Harvey Yates?" (Chico has said nothing to give him that impression.) "Yeah," says Chico. "That's right."

The wisdom of setting these comedy routines down in the middle of such appalling romantic contrivance appears just a little questionable. This really isn't a play at all: It's still just a series of short scenes, one following another only because they can't all come at once, and the best excuse it has for a finish is so it can end. Whatever topical appeal the Florida land boom may have had in 1925 is wholly lost to us now, so the satiric element is worn to zero. The "plot" is "resolved" by a mysterious "man with a black moustache" who has a lot of money to buy the hero's architectural plans with and also restore Groucho to solvency, but his arrival out of nowhere is never heralded on the screen. I bring all this up only because most of the time and all of the attention of the film seem to be directed at the songs and dances and heroes and villains, and the Marx Brothers are made to look like four saps who litter the scenery (in other words, like conventional comedy relief). One of the greatest things about the Marx Brothers is their ability to dominate their films, but here the overwhelming preponderance of the film is genuinely depressing. It's as if they thought an audience entering a theater with "the Marx Brothers" on the marquee couldn't bear to sit through any more than five minutes of them at a time.

The near-unknowns who played Bob Adams and Polly Potter on the stage are replaced by a famous romantic team of the 1920s, Mary Eaton and Oscar Shaw, who actually got top billing, and in this movie deserve it. An awful lot of time is spent discussing their problems, and an even awfuller lot of time is spent singing a song called "The Skies Will All Be Blue When My Dreams Come True." Irving Berlin didn't have a hit song in *Cocoanuts,* and that was it.

BELLBOY:	We haven't been paid in two weeks and we want our wages!
GROUCHO:	Wages? Do you want to be wage slaves, answer me that.
BELLBOYS:	No.
GROUCHO:	No, of course not. Well, what makes wage slaves? Wages! I want you to be free. Remember, there's nothing like Liberty, except *Collier's* and the *Saturday Evening Post.* Be free, my friends, one for all, and all for me, and me for you, and three for five, and six for a quarter.
ZEPPO:	Pardon me. Couple of telegrams for you, Mr. Hammer.
GROUCHO:	There you are, business is beginning to pick up already. Now, if you gir—boys will only be calm. . . . Uh-huh. "We arrive this afternoon on the 4:30. Kindly reserve two floors and three ceilings."

Must be mice. "If we like your property, we will immediately buy it." See that? Things have started our way already.

BELLBOY: Who's it from?

GROUCHO: Western Union. And they've got a lot of money, too. On the 4:15, eh? Well, I'll take the bus down myself.

ZEPPO: Here's another one, Mr. Hammer.

GROUCHO: See? We're gonna be stuffed by tonight. This hotel will be so crowded that we'll be turning away thousands of people. "If there is another hotel in Cocoanut Beach, cancel our reservation." I knew it, it was too good. Wait a minute—"P.S. Aunt Fanny had an 8-pound boy, can you come to the wedding?" You see, everything is all right, boys. Everything is all right. You're all invited to the wedding of Aunt Fanny's 8-pound boy.

BELLEBOYS: By the time Groucho gets to make an entrance and go through a monologue, the less patient of us have gone home. In his first scene he is accosted, as manager of the Cocoanut Hotel, by the most unconvincing set of bellboys in the world and asked for their wages. Not only are they incapable of making up their minds whether to be boys or girls, they aren't even sure whether they want the money or not. Groucho's eventual response to the complaint is "Forget about money. Don't think of it, just forget about it, because you won't get it anyway," and that seems to mollify them. They throw up their hands and go into a silly dance. Which would probably be hilarious if it *looked* like it made sense (Groucho is certainly capable of pulling off more outrageous façades than that), but he is so apologetic about it that his absurdities just don't hold water. But they are enough to hold the bellboys. These bellboys must be thicker than water.

DUMONT: What in the world is the matter with you?

GROUCHO: Oh, I . . . I'm not myself tonight. I don't know who

I am. One false move and I'm yours. I love you. I love you anyhow.

DUMONT: I don't think you'd love me if I were poor.

GROUCHO: I might, but I'd keep my mouth shut.

DUMONT: I'll not stay here any longer and be insulted this way.

GROUCHO: Aw, don't go away and leave me here alone, you stay here and I'll go away.

DUMONT: I don't know what to say.

GROUCHO: Well, say that you'll be truly mine, or truly yours, or yours truly. Can't you know that I'm . . .

DUMONT: Will you keep your hands to yourself!

GROUCHO: Come on, I'll play you one more game! Come on, the three of you! Oh . . . Can you come down a little bit? Just think, tonight. Tonight! When the moon is sneaking around the clouds, I'll be sneaking around you. I'll meet you tonight under the moon. Oh, I can see you now, you and the moon! You wear a necktie so I'll know you.

LOBBYING: For a hotel that isn't doing any business, this place has a very busy lobby. Groucho's harangue about Florida land values delivered to Margaret Dumont has the same air of feeling sorry for itself as his excuses to his bellboys. Even when he is saying hilarious things like "Take the alligator pear. Take all the alligator pears and keep them, see if I care. Do you know how alligator pears are made? No, that's because you've never been an alligator, and don't let it happen again," he doesn't sound very happy about saying them, and we grow curious as to why he is bothering. Harpo and Chico make their entrance here, and the four brothers stage a magnificent minute trying to introduce themselves and simply slapping their extended hands around, leaning on each other and honking horns, and chasing themselves all over the lobby. This very soon degenerates into some disorganized horseplay being played against no particular horses, and some clever gags being lost in a dispirited shuffle. Groucho says there are no vacancies but plenty of rooms, and he and Chico quibble over whether to take rooms or vacancies. A man stops Chico and asks him what time are the trains to Philadelphia and Chico tells him, "Once a week, sometimes twice a day," while Harpo reaches under the man's overcoat and whisks off his jacket. Chico tries on the jacket but decides it's too big; it needs something taken out. They take out the wallet. There is one unspeakable spot where a woman who has stuffed a handkerchief in her bosom turns to go, and Harpo leans softly over and steals it *back* from her, with his *teeth, after she has turned away!* This, of course, can't be done.

After that, the lobby is vacated, and it is Groucho and Margaret Dumont once again, this time pretending to be lovers of some sort. Groucho makes a few rather hopeless puns and stumbles over his words as if he couldn't control his own mouth.

This is a fascinating scene for anybody who wants to catch a stale glimpse of vintage Marx Brothers. Here's Chico, who is not above any trick in the book and openly admits it, and here's Harpo, whose compulsive pilfering shows off his talent for sleights of hand that must rank him somewhere between a circus clown and a magician, and the characters are familiar only by face. Groucho, too, is a different Groucho from the Groucho he becomes. Here he isn't even *trying* to be as biting and acidic as he is in the thirties. Though he comes off as a more versatile actor in this Jewish comedian characterization, he also comes off as a less forceful comedian, and less forceful for Groucho is less effective.

But what this scene inevitably tells us about the Marx Brothers is something not especially worth knowing: that at this point in their lives they feel very uncomfortable about playing to a silent house.

———

BREAK ON THROUGH: The Doors of the world, like its Words, Telephones, Opera Hats and Respectful Gestures, exist not to be utilized but to be toyed with. The Napoleon scene was bound to inspire repercussions, and this is just the first in a series.

The terribly uninteresting man and woman who are plotting a robbery have decided they need to have somebody witness other suspects on the night of the theft, so the woman entices

COLLECTION OF HARPO MARX

each of the Marx Brothers up to her room and then calls the detective. There is a door joining her room to Margaret Dumont's and two doors into the hall and one door into a closet, and as soon as the Marx Brothers get there they all seem terribly concerned about hiding from each other. When one goes into the next room to hide from somebody or other, the next guy has to go into another room to hide from him.

Strange that a movie that couldn't be made until the sound track was invented should let the scene least dependent on dialogue get away with being its best scene. Except for the knocks and the slams, this is good old precision-timed silent comedy, and the only dialogue involved is contained in quick exchanges like "Did he go?" "Who?" "Anybody."

Just to diversify the merry-go-round, Harpo dives under the bed, and then he Australian crawls across the floor, spewing water into the air like a whale. Eventually he comes to port in Margaret Dumont's room, flops down on her bed, and gestures for her to join him there. ("Certainly not!" she reacts, as if there were even a particle of reality in the suggestion.) When the detective finally does show up, he doesn't scare anybody. Groucho even makes a special trip out of his closet to walk around behind him. Groucho risks being caught in his own hotel to follow the man who's looking for him into the room of the woman he should be looking for instead of Groucho. Imagine.

GROUCHO: Now, uh, in arranging these lots, of course we use blueprints. You . . . you know what a blueprint is, huh?

CHICO: Yes, oysters.

GROUCHO: How is it you never got double pneumonia?

CHICO: I go around by myself.

GROUCHO: You know what a lot is?

CHICO: Yeah, it's-a too much.

GROUCHO: I . . . I don't mean a whole lot, just a little lot with nothing on it.

CHICO: Any time you gotta too much, you gotta whole lot. Look, I explain it to you. Sometimes you no got enough-a too much, you gotta whole lot, sometimes

you got a little bit, you no think it's enough, somebody else maybe think it's-a too much, that's a whole
lot too. Now, it's a whole lot, is-a too much, a too
much is-a whole lot—same thing.

GROUCHO: The next time I see you, remind me not to talk to
you, will you?

CHICO: All right . . .

GROUCHO: Come over here, Rand McNally, and I'll explain this
thing to you. Now look, this is a map and diagram
of, of the whole Cocoanut Section. This whole area
is within a radius of approximately, uh, three-quarters
of a mile. Radius. Is there a remote possibility that
you know what radius means?

CHICO: That's-a WJZ.

GROUCHO: Well, I walked right into that one. It's gonna be a
cinch explaining the rest of this thing to you, I can
see that.

CHICO: I catch on quick.

WHY A DUCK?: The Marxes can get away with substituting
insanity for motivation only so long as they keep up the insanity.
When the humor falls to the level of lead-balloon puns, and the
energy cools to the level of a bored business conference, we have
to start asking the old embarrassing questions. Why doesn't
Groucho throw Chico out of the hotel if he knows he's not going
to pay his bill? Why is he so intent on using Chico as a shill if
Chico is too dumb to grasp the idea? Why does he say, "I can let
you have three lots watering the front or I can let you have three
lots, uh, fronting the water," if it should obviously be said the
other way around? Why do they photograph it all in one stupid
shot from one stupid angle? Why? Why? Why?

The auction scene, where Chico predictably screws up
Groucho's plans, has a different problem. It's perfectly obvious
what's going to happen, and we can all see it coming. So whatever comedy the scene might have is going to be dependent on
some great timing or wonderful delivery. And Chico just stands
up there and acts malicious.

It is at this point that our attention is asked to be centered upon Margaret Dumont who discovers her necklace missing and Bob Adams who is unjustly accused, while the comedy breaks down and gives up. It is hard to tell which we are less interested in.

THE LITTLE BREAK: The eloquent effortlessness that Harpo uses to get Bob Adams out of prison is surpassed only by the cumbersome elaborateness of his preparations. We *saw* him steal the key from the detective, but when he walks up to the cell he's carrying a ton of tools. He makes noises and sight gags with them (he smashes his hand with the sledge hammer twice, both times on purpose) before he gets around to opening the door with the key. Once Bob is out, Harpo locks himself in (apparently on purpose again), but breaks out very quickly by removing one of the bars. Now, he must have known he could do that before he even stole the key.

Nor does Harpo perform his thievery for anything but amusement. He derives his greatest pleasure from giving back what nobody noticed he had taken. This scene, where poor Bob Adams stands between Harpo and Groucho, to find personal possessions being lost on one side and the point of his sentences being lost on the other, loses a lot of its theatrical effectiveness when it is photographed and you realize it could be tricked up. You just have to keep informing yourself that it isn't.

GROOM: I feel highly honored, but I'm afraid, uh, I'm not much of a speechmaker. Nevertheless, Mr. Hammer, it was very nice of you to call on me.

GROUCHO: You must call on me sometime.

GROOM: I was just about to say . . .

GROUCHO: Yes, come up and see my flowerbeds.

GROOM: What I intended to . . . say was . . .

GROUCHO: I want you to see my pansies.

GROOM: Well, uh . . .

GROUCHO: I have short pansies and long pansies.

GROOM: I was just going to say that . . .

GROUCHO: Next spring I'm going to get some early bloomers.

GROOM: As I was about to say . . .

GROUCHO: There seems to be a steady stream flowing in and out over there.

GROOM: I wouldn't dream of taking up any more or, more of your time. I merely wanted to thank you all . . .

GROUCHO: Yeah . . .

GROOM: And, uh, as I said before, I hadn't intended to make a speech at all.

GROUCHO: Well, you certainly succeeded!

PUNCHY: It appears there's nothing the most clumsy technical malfunction can do to destroy a scene with all three Marx Brothers in it. And this one has all four. (Zeppo was in the auction scene, but he didn't say or do anything. He appeared briefly in the lobby scene, but he disappeared just as briefly. Here he comes to the party and says Groucho will be there soon and, sure enough, Groucho walks right in. Big part Zeppo gets in this picture.)

The party isn't much, but once the guests gather around the festive table and celebrate the occasion with a lot of thudding dull speeches, we get as good a Marx Brothers scene as we could hope for under the circumstances. Groucho's speech is aimless on purpose. He even borrows a few clichés from Gothic tales and the Rotary Club to spice it up. Margaret Dumont chants hers like it was a church-choir solo. The groom stands up and can hardly even get three words out without each one being jumped on like it was a defenseless rabbit. And no matter who is talking, he hasn't finished his first sentence before Harpo makes a big point out of rising slowly, allowing a behemoth peeve to overcome his face, and exiting engulfed in a wince. Each time he returns, he is slightly more tipsy, and each time he leaves he is noticeably more peeved. Finally he sits down with Chico and performs the grandest bit of filching in the whole film. He steals the scene.

But once again they get carried away with the story, and the heroes and villains spend five or ten minutes on technicalities, interrupted by a cutaway to the Marx Brothers (a *cutaway* to the *Marx Brothers!*), before we are allowed the relief of a fadeout.

Mary Eaton sings, "The skies will all be blue when my dreams come true," and we are greeted with a shot of the Paramount mountain and cloudy skies. It is a very appropriate sort of ending.

Looking at *Cocoanuts* today, you would expect it to be received in 1929 as one of the Great Disasters of the Year, like the Stock Market Crash. But you would be failing to take into account the breath-taking effect of hearing a synchronized sound track. It may *look* ineluctably clumsy, but it talked! it sang! it danced! All of the first sound movies looked clumsy. (Few things on this earth are clumsier than Alfred Hitchcock's *Blackmail*.) That apparently had nothing to do with it. Even at its original preview length (two hours and twenty minutes) *Cocoanuts* was a great hit with movie fans, talkie fans, Marx Brothers fans, musical-comedy fans, and even critics. No matter what pot shots they may have leveled at the sound quality ("Brobdingnagian heads seem to be served with Lilliputian lung-power," the New York *Times* pointed out) or the photographic difficulties (*Outlook* reminded us that a silent film camera could encompass castles, landscapes, and unruly mobs with no apparent strain, while a sound camera is helpless in the face of twelve chorus girls) or the "sappy musical comedy plot" (as *Life* called it, noting that "Mary and Oscar sing at odd moments throughout the picture and it doesn't help a bit"), everybody loved the movie itself and called it a good show (everybody, that is, but Groucho's son Arthur, who was now seven and stomped out on its premiere because there was "no shooting" in it). Some theaters found *Cocoanuts* so popular they booked it three or four times during its first release and got away with calling it "The funniest picture ever made." One theater in Los Angeles actually brought it back for ten return engagements. Within a few months it had grossed two million dollars.

So where has all the magic gone? Can it be the chopped-up second-generation dupes that are all we have to call *Cocoanuts?* Can it be bad sound transferral that has lost for us the sarcastic edge of Groucho's voice and the amiable edge of Chico's? Can it be the degree to which we can tolerate yesterday's notions of romantic pleasantry?

Hardly. When the Marx Brothers first saw the film in a Paramount screening room, they were filled with such wrath and dismay at this pallid version of their classic show that they asked permission to buy back the negative and have it destroyed like *Humor Risk*. Luckily for their pocketbooks, the request was denied. When *Cocoanuts* showed up at one of those exclusive Hollywood parties in 1939 in the presence of Morrie Ryskind and Irving Berlin, they both devoutly wished it had never been invited. Try showing it to any audience now. Good heavens.

THE AMERICAN FILM INSTITUTE

ANIMAL CRACKERS 1930

Animal Crackers didn't stay on Broadway as long as *Cocoanuts* did, but it still stuck around long enough to become routine. Harpo used to play poker with the boys at the Algonquin, run down to the theater just in time for his entrance, and go back to the game the minute the show was through. He had his walk from the hotel to the theater so closely timed, in fact, that when the New York City pedestrian laws went through their periodic revision and decided to forbid denizens to cross against a red light, it made him a second or two later than he was supposed to be and he almost missed his cue.

Harpo's entrance, in a full suit and dapper top hat and cloak, was customarily followed by a bubble-blowing routine, in which Groucho asked for strawberry and Harpo blew a red balloon. This one night, however, he reached under his costume for the balloon and didn't find it. This seemed odd, but the explanation was not long in coming. When the butler showed up to take Harpo's hat and coat—at which point his whole suit was to fall away and leave him standing in a swimming suit—there was no swimming suit. In the rush of being late he had forgotten to put it on, and the suit fell away to leave Harpo standing in a supporter and his shoes. He didn't catch on right away that anything was wrong, since the actors around him were so good at expressing shock every night at the sight of the bathing suit that when they now expressed *real* shock at the sight of *no* bathing suit the difference was not readily apparent. It took a few embarrassed moments of hushed silence and frantic gestures before he glanced down and ran offstage, and before anyone had the presence of mind to pull down the curtain. Groucho soon roused a rather stunned audience by telling them, "Tomorrow he's not wearing anything, so get your tickets early." When Harpo reappeared he was wearing his swimming suit and crimson makeup. He was applauded mightily.

Presently *Animal Crackers* left Broadway, and the Marxes spent a few weeks at the Palace at some phenomenal sum before the show started its trip across the country. *Animal Crackers* hadn't been on tour very long before each of the brothers started getting desperate notes from his respective broker telling him to quick send money or he was in trouble, and then notes saying he was in trouble, and then notes saying he was wiped out. Harpo lost everything he had and still needed $10,000 to cover debts. In Pittsburgh Zeppo took him to meet a friend on his riverboat gambling house and they humored him into giving them the $10,000 out of sport. Groucho got so depressed he just sat in his dressing room one night and refused to go on. When he finally did condescend to walk on stage, he started making profit-and-margin jokes until he could get it off his mind. He could see the

Harpo was at the peak of his croquet mania right around this period.

A rare still of Chico on a movie set.

days coming when, as he described it, "the pigeons were feeding the people in Central Park." It wasn't time for the Twenties any more.

Paramount talked over the next film with Morrie Ryskind, and they decided to do a little more cutting before shooting started this time and somewhat less afterward. Ryskind was sent along on the tour with the script in his lap, and for two weeks he performed ruthless incisions wherever audience enthusiasm flagged. On the basis of what was left, he fashioned a screenplay for *Animal Crackers* that was knit more tightly than its perfunctory parallel for *Cocoanuts*.

Directing was going to be a bit more tight, too. The iron fist of Victor Heerman was imported from Hollywood to render these services. Heerman's major directing jobs were in the hard-drama category (*Rupert of Hentzau* in the silent days), but there had been a time when he wrote and directed for Mack Sennett. Mr. Heerman began to see, however, that he was going to have to function chiefly not as a comedy craftsman, since the comedy was all created, but as a drill instructor. The studio heads filled him in thoroughly on the goings-on behind *Cocoanuts*, and Heerman took a solemn oath on the production schedule that such goings-on were not going to go on behind *Animal Crackers*. To sustain for himself a general degree of directorial control, he made two major moves. First, to make things easy on himself, he assigned an assistant director to each Marx Brother and made him responsible for his whereabouts. Second, to make things easy on the assistant directors, he had four small cells constructed on the sound stage and chained the Marx Brothers into them and told them to stay there. No kidding. And no aimless wanderings, no harp rehearsals, and no six-no-trump bridge hands.

To the Marx Brothers, this was a very funny idea. They made jokes about it for days. After a week and a half, however, when the gag began to pale somewhat and Heerman showed no sign of letting up, the reaction grew relentlessly more sullen. As the weeks wore on and the humor wore thinner, the reaction grew more sullen and more relentless, but they stayed right in those cells till the end of the picture, whether there was anything funny about it or not.

Heerman handled all aspects of the production with the same kind of discipline. He was met with a steadily mounting efficiency from the technical crew, who had by now faced all the problems sound could ever present them with at least once, and when something broke down they were almost always able to figure out what was wrong with it.

Lillian Roth and Hal Thompson were presented with the thankless task of playing The Girl and Guy Nobody Cared About. Lillian Roth was a tempestuous starlet who had just given Cecil B. DeMille a lot of trouble with *Madame Satan* and was being sent out East to the Marx Brothers to be taught a lesson. She burst into tears when she heard the news.

Shooting had already started by the time Miss Roth got to New York. What she saw she described as "one step removed from a circus." Though the Marxes may have been chained to the set once they got to it, there was nothing guaranteeing that their arrival would be free from vexation. Chico had to be called on the telephone before he could be counted on to be awake. Whichever one of them showed up first would find out the others weren't there and disappear until they were. By the time each of them had done this once or twice the assistant directors would get to work trying to convince each one of them that the others were waiting for him.

Animal Crackers still went over budget and over schedule. It still had a heady share of aches and grievances and a good overdose of chaos. But it also had a fighting chance to be a really good translation of a stage show into a filmed stage show.

Animal Crackers is. All the uncertainty and confusion have vanished with the early signs of spring. The pockets of comedy are so sure of themselves that they are almost intimidating, and even the romance has been raised to a level that might be called negligible. (Roth and Thompson are not quite so starched as their *Cocoanuts* counterparts; it's almost fun to watch Lillian Roth clown around in a part she can't bring herself to take seriously. "He'll get to the bottom of this!" she intones ominously at one point, as if she were telling a story on "Romper Room." The more she mangles her lines, the more we wonder what prompted the Brilliant Playwright George S. Kaufman to write them.) Groucho even gets to sing the deservedly famous Kalmar and Ruby song "Captain Spaulding," which later became his theme song on "You Bet Your Life" and forever.

The comedy gets most of its kicks out of making polite society of the Twenties look ridiculous. As polite society of the Twenties has died out as an institution but not as a frame of mind, it's still a joy to watch it look ridiculous. The dialogue, partly because its target is an affected sophistication, reaches a level of literacy and wit that later Marx Brothers efforts can't hope to rival. It also reaches the most violent forms of verbal dislocation the mind can grapple with. A sentence will contradict itself before it is quite out of its speaker's throat. "Why, you're one of the most beautiful women I've ever seen, and that's not saying much for you," Groucho will say to Margaret Dumont. Or, when there is some dispute about who took a valuable painting and its owner snorts, "Maybe there was no painting," Groucho agrees with him: "That's right, maybe there was no painting. I saw it." It seems perfectly natural that the words "I feel that the time has come" should be followed by "the walrus said," even though no Lewis Carroll reference or walrus appears in the picture before or afterward. Groucho even gets away with facing the camera after a perfectly terrible line and insisting, "Well, *all* the jokes can't be good! You've got to expect that once in a while!"

Groucho's seemingly spontaneous and genuinely thought-provoked delivery meshes nicely with Kaufman and Ryskind's incisive ellipses and solipses of logic. They sound like anything but contrived jokes. Morrie Ryskind tells the story of his sister reading the *Animal Crackers* script the afternoon before the play opened. After the performance she remarked, "If I hadn't already read all those lines, I'd swear Groucho was making them up as he went along." Some people see the movies today and still get that idea. But comedy like this *can't* be made up as you go along. Writers deny that the very famous Marx Brothers improvisations and ad libs were ever anything more than marginal, and we can

From *Animal Crackers* on, a blond wig was deemed more appropriate to the medium of black-and-white film than Harpo's customary flaming red.

comfortably assume that, even when Captain Spaulding and Roscoe Chandler confuse each other's names, it's all been well planned, timed, and rehearsed.

It was still necessary, remember, to go through the scenes once or twice before the cameras started in order to get a giggle-free take. What made the Marx Brothers great performers was their habit of messing this up by getting bigger laughs on the fourth rehearsal than they did on the first. The number of Harpo gags in *Animal Crackers* that are out-and-out repeats from *Cocoanuts* (blowing bubbles that turn out to be cigarette smoke, handing everybody his leg, dropping knives, wrapping himself around Chico, forwarding his pocket when somebody tries to put something into his own) and are probably out-and-out repeats from *I'll Say She Is* and *Home Again* tell us a lot about how much diversity was expected of a performer before packaged entertainment. (Joe Jackson did nothing but his bicycle routine for generations.) The fact that they are twice as funny the second time tells us a lot about Harpo.

A word should be said for the set. There are glossy futuristic wall panels and stairways pretending to be Margaret Dumont's house. They are not always framed in fascinating ways, but every time they are they create a great image of dynamic austerity that is just asking to have a shambles made of it.

ENTRANCING: Zeppo—eternal harbinger of Groucho—gets to show up at Margaret Dumont's party and tell all the guests that Groucho is going to show up soon. Groucho shows up. (Gotta say one thing for Zeppo: He's accurate.) Groucho sings that he only came to say he has to go. Chico shows up and explains that even though he couldn't come tomorrow because that was too soon, he'll charge for not playing yesterday because his rates for not rehearsing are too steep to be afforded. Groucho thinks Chico looks alike. Harpo shows up and starts firing off Groucho's guns. It promises to be a swell party.

GROUCHO: Pardon me while I have a strange interlude. Why, you couple of baboons! What makes you think I'd marry either one of you! Strange how the wind blows tonight. It has a tintity voice, reminds me of poor old Moslin. How happy I could be with either of these two, if both of them just went away! Well, what do you say, girls? What do you say, will you marry me?

DUMONT: But, Captain, which one of us?

GROUCHO: Both of you, let's all get married. This is my party. Party! Party! Here I am talking of parties. I came down here for a party, what happened? Nothing. Not even ice cream. The gods looked down and laughed! This would be a better world for children if the parents had to eat the spinach. Well, what do you say, girls? What do you say? Uh, are we all going to get married?

LADY: All of us?

GROUCHO: All of us!

LADY: But that's bigamy!

GROUCHO: Yes, and it's big of me, too. It's big of all of us, let's be big for a change. I'm sick of these conventional marriages! One woman and one man was good enough for your grandmother, but who wants to marry your grandmother? Nobody. Not even your grandfather.

STRANGE ALLUSION: Groucho is standing there talking innocently to Margaret Dumont and one of her guests, explaining to the two ladies how pleasant life would be if they all three got married to each other. Suddenly the ladies freeze and go out of focus while Groucho strides moodily to the camera and delivers a sultry monologue to the effect that he doesn't want to marry either one of them and that the wind is blowing very strangely tonight. He strides back, all set to take up plans again. They don't appear to have heard him. This goes on three whole times, with speeches about parents eating their children's spinach and shares of stock going up and down dusty corridors. The speeches come to an end when Groucho runs away with a whole troupe of chorus girls. Both ladies appear very flattered.

This parody of *Strange Interlude* is a bizarre thing to insert in a show that is supposed to be a play itself. What is striking about the Groucho character is his resolute honesty in the face of two-faced hypocrisy. Here he seems to be wearing two faces on his sleeve and showing one of them only to us. If we are somewhat baffled by the persistent refusal of the characters in *Animal Crackers* to be insulted when Groucho insults them, this scene may give us a clue. People with two faces presume that *nobody* means what they say.

CHANDLER: Well, I've alway tried to do what I could, especially in the world of art.

GROUCHO: Art. Well, I don't know how we drifted around to that, but what is your opinion of art?

CHANDLER: I am *very glad* you asked me!

GROUCHO: I withdraw the question! This fellow takes things seriously, it isn't safe to ask him a simple question. Tell me, Mr. Chandler, where are you planning on putting your new opera house?

CHANDLER: Oh, I thought I should like to put it somewhere near Central Park.

GROUCHO: I see. Why don't you put it right in Central Park?

CHANDLER: Could we do that?

GROUCHO: Sure, do it at night when no one is looking. Why don't you put it in the reservoir and get the whole thing over with? Of course, that might interfere with the water supply, but after all we must remember that art is art. Still, on the other hand, water is water, isn't it? And East is East, and West is West, and if you take cranberries and stew them like applesauce, they taste much more like prunes than rhubarb does. Now, uh . . . Now you tell me what you know.

MEET ROSCOE: Roscoe W. Chandler, the art connoisseur, isn't really such a bad guy. There is an easy temptation to throw a stereotype in the Marx Brothers' way and let them mow him down as a foregone conclusion. The Chandler character as played by Louis Sorin (who must be one of the best straight men a fellow ever had) is a different case. He seems to be a man with whom sitting down and talking for a couple of hours would not be an altogether oppressive experience. The swiftness and apparent unconcern, then, with which Harpo and Chico and then Groucho reduce him to cottage cheese comes more as a tribute to them than an ignominy to him. What can a man do when he is up against somebody who takes a check from him and bounces it on the floor to prove it's no good? And any fool can steal a tie or a handkerchief, but how do you cope with somebody who cops the birthmark off your forearm? And *you* just try and carry on a routine, professional, self-important conversation with some clown whose train of thought keeps jumping its track and hopping onto side rails. Groucho charges at Chandler with the silliest absurdities in such a grand aggressive way that it's impossible to challenge them. Like when he proposes the eight-cent nickel: "Think what that would mean! You could go to a newsstand, buy a three-cent newspaper, and get the same nickel back again. One nickel carefully used could last a family a lifetime!" Chandler finds himself accepting the notion. "I think that is a wonderful idea," he tells Groucho. "Then there can't be much to it," Groucho answers him. "Forget about it." What can you do?

HANDS ACROSS THE TABLE: Everyone gets so excited over Groucho's affairs with Margaret Dumont they forget what great things can happen when Margaret Dumont confronts Harpo. This is certainly one of those Great Things, and it reminds us that there is not another comedian or comedy team in existence that can provide sparkling, ingenious verbal comedy and then turn around and be hilarious in pantomime. Only the visual humor, however, is able to pour on laughs in an unending stream like this scene does and clobber us with one gag without waiting for us to catch our breath from the last one. Harpo engages in a series of frenetic attacks on Margaret Dumont's person for reasons he never bothers to make particularly evident, and after he is through giving everybody his leg, clambering all over them, and assuming grotesque expressions of ferocity, he and Chico coerce Miss Dumont and her friend into sitting and playing bridge with them.

Now, four people seated around a bridge table being photographed from ten feet away *should* be the dullest thing since toast. It's Harpo's concept of the rules of bridge that keeps everybody hopping. When he is not happy with a card he tosses it in the air or rips it to pieces. Once Margaret Dumont has raised the bidding on spades, he switches hands with her. ("Why, I haven't a spade in my hand!" she exclaims with surprise. "All right, we double," acquiesces Chico.) At no point is it ever clearly decided which suit is trump, but Harpo manages to take every single one of the tricks, half of them with the ace of spades. ("Ace of spades . . . ace of spades," Chico laconically calls them out. "He plays a good game.") We almost feel like applauding Miss Dumont and her friend for their obstinate refusal to see their opponents' second face, even though that's the only one they're showing. Harpo and Chico lay their cards on the table before the game ever starts, but out of sheer politeness the ladies won't look at them until it's all over.

GROUCHO: I was sitting in front of the cabin, when I bagged six tigers.

DUMONT: Oh, Captain!

GROUCHO: Six of the biggest tigers . . .

DUMONT: Captain, did you catch six tigers?

GROUCHO: I bagged them. I . . . I bagged them to go away, but they hung around all afternoon. They were the most persistent tigers I've ever seen. The principal animals inhabiting the African jungle are Moose, Elks, and Knights of Pythias. Of course, you all know what a moose is, that's big game. The first day I shot two bucks. That was the biggest game we had. As I say, you all know what a moose is? A moose runs around the floor, eats cheese, and is chased by the cat. The Elks, on the other hand, live up in the hills, and in the spring they come down for their annual convention. It is very interesting to watch them come to the water hole. And you should see them run when they find that it's only a water hole! What they're looking for is an Elkohole.

NONSENSE: Groucho's monologue about exploring Africa is full of lines you've heard before ("One morning I shot an elephant in my pajamas. How he got in my pajamas I don't know") and lines you never want to hear again ("I was sitting in front of the cabin, smoking some meat. There wasn't a cigar store in the neighborhood"). More fun than this are his instructions to Chico the pianist ("Play 'Somewhere My Love Lies Sleeping' with a male chorus"), or his comforting words during the power failure ("Captain! The storm has put the lights out! And you can't see your hand before your face!" "Well, you wouldn't get much enjoyment out of that").

Harpo startles a lot of people when he reacts to situations in a perfectly appropriate way, because he does it with such an outsized hyperbole of that appropriate way that it hardly even seems human. One might expect him to show some defiance to the man who is chasing him from the room, and to get a certain smug satisfaction out of that defiance. One would *not* ordinarily expect him to flip out both lips in a flippant bubble of a pout, and then make over his whole face into a gargoyle of glee. No less startling than his hyperboles are his wholly *non-sequitur* reactions. "Hide!" Chico hisses to him perfectly clearly. Harpo goes to the middle of the room and stands on his head.

And in the eye of the cyclone is poor Margaret Dumont, who acts as if she is in charge of three clever and infinitely unruly children. Her Mrs. Rittenhouse character is not as stuffy as her Mrs. Potter of *Cocoanuts*. Sometimes she seems to let herself enjoy all this nonsense. Her only definite reaction is to roll her eyes heavenward periodically to indicate that there is nothing on heaven or earth that can be done about this. And there isn't.

ZEPPO: "In care of Hungerdunger, Hungerdunger, Hungerdunger, and McCormack . . ."

GROUCHO: You've left out a Hungerdunger! You left out the

Groucho with Louis Sorin as Chandler (left) and Margaret Dumont as Mrs. Rittenhouse (right).   UNIVERSAL

main one, too! Thought you could slip one over on me, didn't you, eh? All right, leave it out and put in a windshield wiper instead. I tell you what you do, Jamison. I tell you what. Make it, uh, make it three windshield wipers and one Hungerdunger. They won't all be there when the letter arrives, anyhow. "Hungerdunger, Hungerdunger, Hungerdunger . . ."

ZEPPO: ". . . And McCormack."
GROUCHO: ". . . And McCormack."

ZEPPO: "Gentlemen, question mark."

GROUCHO: "Gentlemen, Question Mark!!" Put it on the penulti-
            mate, not on the dipthonic. You want to brush up
            on your Greek, Jamison. Well, get a Greek and
            brush up on him!

ZEPPO: "In re yours of the fifteenth."

GROUCHO: I see.

ZEPPO: Now, uh, you said a lot of things here that I didn't
            think were important, so I just omitted them.

DUMONT: Well! . . . Whoa, Captain! Good gracious! Oh, my!

GROUCHO: So . . . you just omitted them, eh? You've just
            omitted the body of the letter, that's all. You've just
            left out the body of the letter, that's all! Yours not
            to reason why, Jamison! You've left out the body of
            the letter! . . . All right, send it that way and tell
            them the body'll follow.

ZEPPO: Do you want the body in brackets?

GROUCHO: No, it'll never get there in brackets. Put it in a box.

———————————————

THE BODY IN BRACKETS: There is a common assumption that
Zeppo = Zero, which this scene does its best to contradict.
Groucho dictating a letter to anybody else would hardly be cause
for rejoicing. We have to believe that someone will be there to
accept all his absurdities and even respond somewhat in kind
before things can progress free from conflict into this genial
mishmash. Groucho clears his throat in the midst of his dictation,
and Zeppo asks him if he wants that in the letter. Groucho says,
"No, put it in an envelope." Zeppo nods. And only Zeppo could
even try such a thing as taking down the heading and the salutation and leaving out the letter because it didn't sound important
to him. It takes a Marx Brother to pull something like that on a
Marx Brother and get away with it.

Most comedy routines consist of jokes strung out on some
logical premise. When two Marx Brothers get together, they
make use of the same kind of jokes but they string them together
on a logic of digressions. Most of us end up off the track in spite
of ourselves, but Marx Brothers *set out* to do it. They proceed
with their irrelevancies intently and resolutely, and there is a

strange flourish of triumph when they have reached the end and gotten nowhere. "I want you to make two carbon copies of that letter and throw the original away," Groucho tells Zeppo. "And when you get through with that, throw the carbon copies away. Just send a stamp, airmail. That's all. You may go, Jamison. I may go, too."

AN OLD SPINACH CUSTOM: Well, we're back to Weber and Fields again. Groucho and Chico must be the strangest comedy team on record. Groucho, who has been tossing off hilarious one-liners all evening, is suddenly playing straight man to a very ordinary dialect comedian and trying to get laughs from his reactions to the punchlines. Chico will make a very sad pun. Groucho will grab himself by the ear and yank himself onto the table. After all the great Groucho–Chico confrontations of the Thirties, it is an odd phenomenon to find that the archetypal scenes that inspired them, in this and *Cocoanuts,* are so dreadfully unamusing. What is even more odd is to discover, after the familiar exchange about searching everyone in the house for the painting and if it isn't there we'll search the house next door and if there isn't a house next door we'll build one, has been hailed by every film text in the brief, discouraging history of film texts as if it were the only absurd thing the Marxes ever said (and usually quoted wrong to boot), to discover after all this that the way it comes across in the movie is simply not very funny. Either the show has run out of energy or there is just nothing that can follow the bridge scene and the stuff at the piano, but by the time Groucho is through sending a stamp airmail, the whole enterprise is as good as over.

Reviewers of *Animal Crackers* had little to say other than that the play was on film now and that audiences were going into hysterics over it. (One described the reaction as "the kind of laughter that pours over every minute or two in a wild burst and between bursts trickles on its own momentum.") Everything they had been unhappy with *Cocoanuts* about (the story, the singing, the dancing) was kept to a minimum, so that griping was all over now. The picture is dominated by the Marxes almost in totality, and that tickled the lot of them. Reviews dwelt chiefly on nice things to say about the Marx Brothers and general expressions of awe. It is a mystery, then, why recent critics have consistently compared this unfavorably to *Cocoanuts,* since it is approximately five times the better film.

Animal Crackers served as a prime source of inspiration for all the Marx Brothers films after it, and many of its gags and situations turn up in disguised form later on, especially in *Horsefeathers* and *Duck Soup,* which Kalmar and Ruby wrote the screenplays for.

But it's not as if they had made a movie yet. There is still the uncomfortable feeling that a powerful spirit is waiting to be released, that the disruption and excitement of which they are capable have yet to be realized. The prime virtue of *Animal Crackers* is that it has preserved for all time what was thought to be an ephemeral entertainment. By the time sound film was perfected something began to happen to physical reality that no one had really foreseen and that few people were aware of even yet. Nothing was transitory any more. It was possible to record *anything* for posterity.

Posterity had never before been one of the chief concerns of the performer. He was forever providing amusement for the moment and nothing beyond but a legend. Posterity was a problem for playwrights and philosophers and inventors. Their work would last. Only gradually did people adjust to the fact that now everything—the inflection of your voice, the smoothness of your gestures, the total impact of your personality—could become a contribution to civilization whether anybody wrote it down or not. Records and silent films were incomplete. Now there was *nothing* left out. If sound motion pictures had existed in 1603, the great actor Richard Burbage would be one of the immortals of the arts, like Shakespeare, instead of one of those alien shadows out of history, like Cheops.

Animal Crackers reaffirmed the awareness that some things are as lasting as the stars. And now one of those things was the Marx Brothers.

iii

nothing but amok

We might justly be considered "odd" by the world; yes, even crazy and dangerous. . . . Whereas we believed that we represented the will of nature to something new, to the individualism of the future, the others sought to perpetuate the status quo. Humanity—which they loved as we did—was for them something complete that must be maintained and protected. For us, humanity was a distant goal, toward which all men were moving, whose image no one knew, whose laws were nowhere written down. . . .

—Hermann Hesse, *Demian*

COLLECTION OF HARPO MARX

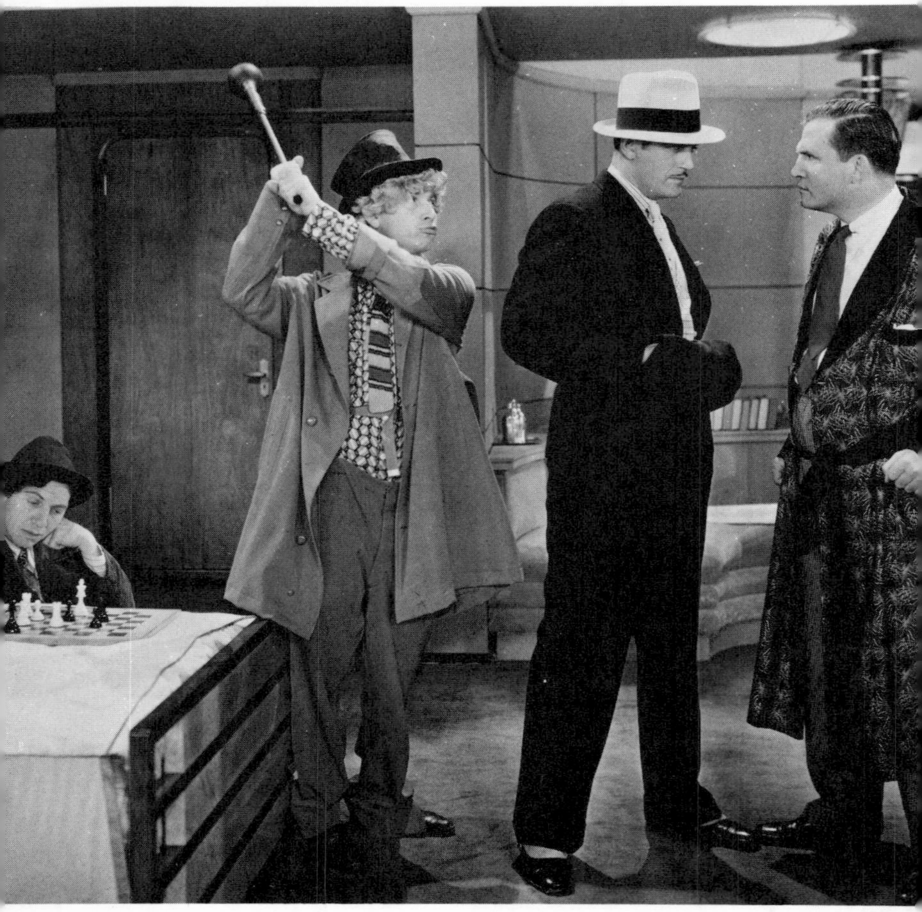

MONKEY BUSINESS 1931

There's no point in even discussing this picture unless we take the effect of *mood* into account. There was a mood dominating the early Thirties that affected everything that went on; it clearly outstripped whatever influence anything else may have had, like the weather, or politics, or religion, or even sex. In its deeper moments it might have been termed despair. On good days it worked its way up to discouragement. Very often it was the basic reflex reaction of hunger. The Great Depression was an economic term, but it was also, inadvertently, a pun. Everyone had his brighter moods, of course, but they usually kept them locked away in a chest until some day when they could use them. The Movie Industry was kept busy turning out images of spectacle and wealth to drug people, like Novocain, into losing track of what their lives were like. As for coming up with a clue to how to go out and face those lives, it wasn't much help.

Typical of Thirties comedy was the desperation of Laurel and Hardy, the sneering malevolence of W. C. Fields, and the simple wish-fulfillment of Frank Capra and his *Mr. Deeds Goes to Town*—not to mention the multi-directed *If I Had a Million*, the wish-fulfillment film for all time. The common theme seemed to be that the money and property demons had gotten us into this mess, and if we can make them look silly for an hour and a half we won't feel quite so victimized. Which is just why the money and property demons put up the capital to finance *Mr. Deeds Goes to Town* and *If I Had a Million*.

Apparently one of the most inviting aspects of writing a history of the Marx Brothers' career is the opportunity to brush off their first three original films in one subordinate clause. "After they made *Monkey Business, Horsefeathers* and *Duck Soup*" is the usual line—as if to say, "Once they finished their tea and had a few crumpets with jam . . ." And yet, whenever a critic discusses "the films of the Marx Brothers," he is describing precisely these three pictures, or whichever one of them he has happened to see recently. All three films, which bear a great family likeness to each other on account of common paternity, are possessed of an upsetting combination of the bizarre and the mundane that makes them stand out, not only in relation to the more conventional Marx films following and preceding them, but the whole pile of Hollywood oatmeal surrounding them. Like the Tenniel drawings for *Alice in Wonderland,* they have the essence of something antiquated, buried, and exhumed, mixed with the taste of worlds unknown. They bear faint resemblance to the program fillers we are used to seeing, and in moments of success or failure there are sparks of a rarely echoed brilliance that trigger infinity.

Our story begins in the last days of 1930, near the end of the frenzied, two-and-a-half-year spate of *Animal Crackers* (all good Marx Brothers stories begin at the end) as it finished its tour of the country and sat in the Bronx waiting to die. New York, once the home of childhood memories and the Big Time, was now a sad reminder of a Wall Street Waterloo, a daily grind, and a dear departed mother. The thrill of appearing on Broadway had worn itself down to a nub, and the nub was only a slight nervousness before the curtain went up and a desperate glance at the population of the balcony to see how much longer the show was going to last. There did happen to be a few offers floating around that had less of a pallor to them. One was for an appearance at the Palace Theater in London, performing the greatest of their old vaudeville specialties in Charles H. Cochran's International Vaudeville Show. This foreign entanglement would get them not only out of New York but out of *Animal Crackers.* Next, a radio network offered to star the Marx Brothers in a series. On top of that, there was still the third commitment in their Paramount contract, to be met the next spring, and nobody as yet had the shade of an idea what *that* was going to be. Groucho, conducting the team's business from his dressing room (usually while dressing), contacted Will Johnstone, a man with all the wrong background, and appointed him writer for the series.

"Why me?" asked Johnstone, naturally. "A radio series is something I've never tackled."

To which Groucho replied something like "Well, that's one reason. If you think of any others, call me."

Shortly before their departure for London, a card arrived backstage billowing with huzzahs and hosannas ecstatic enough to turn even Groucho's head. He returned the card to its sender, S. J. Perelman, before the second act began and requested his presence after the show. He knew Perelman only foggily, acquainted with his cartoons and things from the pages of *College Humor* and *Judge*, and with *Dawn Ginsbergh's Revenge*, the small anthology of his work to which Groucho himself had contributed a dust-jacket blurb. ("From the moment I picked up your book until I laid it down, I was convulsed with laughter. Some day I intend reading it.") Perelman, as a young cartoonist of promise, had progressively worked his way up to a position where the editors of two magazines thought he was worth big money but where the editor of neither magazine had it. "A deep cleft, reminiscent of the Rift Valley in East Africa, appeared between my eyebrows about the first of every month," he recalls. "I started receiving a trickle of letters from the bank that soon grew into a cascade. Perhaps, its officials hinted delicately, I would like to transfer to some bank that had facilities for handling smaller accounts. Maybe I didn't need a bank after all, they hazarded, but merely a loose brick in the fireplace." Perelman would make a likely collaborator for the radio engagement: Like all the best writers of Marx Brothers comedy he came of Jewish stock, he originated in New York City, he was one of their more devoted fans, and he had considerable talent in some other field.

When Groucho had Perelman and his wife Laura cornered in his dressing room, Perelman stuttering at the prospect of confronting a boyhood legend, Laura blushing because the boyhood legend was still in his underwear, and because other boyhood legends in their underwear were dashing in and out of the room, he delivered the assignment.

"I've never worked on a radio script," Perelman ventured.

"Really?" said Groucho. "That's great! I can't imagine two people worse equipped for the job!"

On the basis of such encouragement, Perelman and Johnstone encountered each other the next day. There was little they could do, in terms of facing their task, but say hello, shake their heads at each other, grin congenially, kid around, tell funny stories, suggest that the Marx Brothers were like stowaways on an ocean liner, laugh that off, shrug their shoulders, and go home.

Lunchtime at the Astor was the hour appointed for the two to walk in, enthrall the Marxes with their ideas, and sign important contracts with the radio people. When it grew alarmingly clear there was damn little enthrallment to look forward to ("We expected to be pistol-whipped and summarily flung into Times Square"), they agreed to throw themselves at the mercy of the court jesters and keep their fists clenched.

Before they were allowed to say anything, they waited uneasily through a series of interruptions. Chico kept excusing himself and going to the phone to call the race track. (If business engagements were going to keep him away from the race track, then the race track was perfectly justified in keeping him away from the business engagements!) Harpo kept leaping up from the table without *bothering* to excuse himself and starting aimless conversations with blond ladies (without bothering to excuse himself for that, either). When one or the other or both were actually sitting down with attention to spare, they were using it up on Groucho and his prattle about the stock market. Johnstone, who was familiar with all this, waited patiently for the prime moment for an edgewise word and then blurted out, "Stowaways on an ocean liner," and grimaced.

Whereupon four things happened in a succession too rapid to document:

1) All four faces lit up spontaneously and hid themselves in conference.

2) It was decided that this was a *great* idea for a movie. "No, no," said the writers. "This was an idea for a radio series."

3) Perelman and Johnstone were rushed across the street

and up the stairs into the New York office of Paramount boss Jesse Lasky, who was corralled into signing them up for outrageous weekly sums and, since there was nothing to restrict production to Long Island any longer, sending them to Hollywood.

4) Railroad tickets were purchased to get the writers and their wives briskly transported to Paramount Studios before the week was out.

By the time they recovered their senses they were passing through Denver.

But Groucho's mind was not at rest. Under sane conditions it was the *producer's* business who wrote the script for a movie, but the Marx Brothers were one of the few cases in Hollywood history where the task of choosing authors was considered too hopeless to leave to anyone but the actors. Fortuitous couplings of active minds with parallel big-city backgrounds bred rabid Marx Brothers men, and Groucho's knack for spotting them was in the realm of no executive. One evening the stage doorman (a lovable old fellow named "Pops") presented Groucho with a small skit written especially for him and Chico. The skit was accompanied by a letter on the stationery of one of New York's larger theatrical agencies, prattling on in grandiloquent prose of no restraint to describe the talents of the struggling young law student who wrote the skit. The law student was Nat Perrin, who had written nothing else of any importance, except, interestingly enough, the letter. Mr. Perrin had not even *done* anything else of any importance except, interestingly enough, steal the stationery. Perrin's only show-business experience, in fact, was in the Borscht Circuit, that notorious string of resort hotels in the Catskills and the Poconos that served as a shacking ground for thousands of liberated couples and as a rigorous training ground for people like Moss Hart, Danny Kaye, Phil Silvers, and Dore Schary, who provided entertainment for the spooners with material they had stolen from Broadway. Perrin had an itch to get into *real* show business, but one lucky connection with the Warner Brothers publicity department had proved unprofitable because he had looked too disappointed when they told him what the salary was going to be. Now he was working his way through law school running orchestras and staging shows, and he was trying again.

Groucho liked the skit he wrote. There was no way to put it in *Animal Crackers,* but maybe we could get this guy to do special material for Chico in the movie. There had been no call, up to now, to find a new writer for this purpose, but it did seem a shame to pass over somebody who would have been perfectly good for it if there *had* been. Besides, he was losing confidence in those other fellows. What did they know about writing a movie script, anyway? They had been signed up for a different reason—because they didn't know anything about writing a radio script. "Meet Chico tomorrow at the Paramount office," he said, and Chico had a gag man.

Now it hardly seemed fair to Groucho that *he* didn't have a gag man. He resented the special attention his brother was getting. His good friend Arthur Sheekman came to his mind. Sheekman was a columnist from Chicago who was bright enough to get people like Fred Allen and George M. Cohan to write his column for him, and when he once had the temerity to approach the Marx Brothers' press agent to try applying Groucho to the same task during *Animal Crackers'* run in Chicago, he got to meet Captain Spaulding, became fast friends with him, and by this time was one of the two or three people in the world who the misanthropic comedian could put up with for over an hour. He helped him with his column, and together they wrote comedy sketches for a Broadway revue called *Three's a Crowd,* until finally Groucho decided that Sheekman was too good for Chicago and sent him the telegram which, in Sheekman's own words, "lifted me from local to world-wide obscurity." Before he knew it, he was out of the rat race in Chicago and into the Good Life in New York, writing "Coming Next Week" trailers for MGM. And this is where Groucho hunted him up, slaving over *The Big House* and *Let Us Be Gay,* when he approached him with the idea of becoming a gag man.

Meanwhile, outside the office of a Mr. Russel, one of Paramount's East Coast representatives, Chico and Nat Perrin were having a roundabout argument over salary. Every time Chico came up with one figure, Perrin came up with another topic. Finally Chico settled with himself for $100 a week. Perrin said that was fine but, in light of past experience, decided not to press it. He said it didn't matter; he said it wasn't important. ("If they'd offered me six dollars, I'd have taken it.") To Chico the financier this was the height of apathy. "What's the matter with you?" he said. "Don't you *care?*" Now there was a chance of losing this deal by not being anxious *enough* about money. Getting into the movies was like getting out of the draft. The floors of all the offices were carpeted with eggshells.

When they entered the office, a Mr. Russel had a large piece of paper on which he was writing things down. "How much does this man get paid?" he asked. Perrin was on the verge of saying, "Whatever you think is right," when Chico flatly declared, "One hundred dollars." Without looking up, a Mr. Russel wrote "$100" on his large piece of paper. Slowly, Perrin realized that it made no difference to anyone present whether he got $100 or $1,000. Swiftly, they signed the papers and left the office. By the time he got to Hollywood and found out *all* writers were getting at least $750, he felt decidedly put-upon.

Then there was Harpo. Not having a gag man clearly didn't bother *him,* so Groucho took it upon himself to break his reading habits and take a look at the funnies, where he turned up a cartoonist named J. Carver Pusey, a mild-mannered newspaperman who did a strip called "Little Benny," about a boy who couldn't talk. Pusey got himself signed up with Paramount too. All three men were instructed to board the Santa Fe for Los Angeles the minute the Marxes arrived home from London.

And so, with no less than five writers contracted to write their movie for them, the Marx Brothers felt secure.

Now we cut back to Hollywood, where Perelman, thoroughly appalled all the way across the country by his prolific partner (Johnstone insisted on doing water colors of every vista that came into view, besides getting three weeks of comic strips finished in three days, all with a hand shaken by a rocky roadbed and three crocks of illegal applejack), now stepped off the train to be appalled anew, by what he later described as a land of "Moorish confectionaries, viscid malted milks, avocado salads, frosted papayas, sneak previews . . . studio technicians, old ladies studying Bahaism, bit players, chippies, upraised voices extolling the virtues of various faith healers or laxatives . . . the city of dreadful day. . . . Bridgeport with palms. . . . A metropolis made up of innumerable Midwestern hamlets . . . an unalloyed horror . . . a hayseed's idea of the Big Apple . . . everything about that city's murders had the two-dimensional quality of American life . . . viewed in full sunlight, its tawdriness is unspeakable; in the torrential downpour of the rainy season, as we first saw it, it inspired anguish. . . . After a few days I could have sworn that our faces began to take on the hue of Kodachromes, and even the dog, an animal used to bizarre surroundings, developed a strange, off-register look, as if he were badly printed in overlapping colors."

Hollywood in 1931, before civilization, pollution, and inhibition set in together, was a mad town, mad in its extraordinary ability to inflate all the most limited concerns into the most unlimited obsessions; mad in its freedom from taboos, so that everybody could be liberated enough to imitate everybody else; mad in its exorbitant outgrowths of piddly thoughts. Los Angeles has always been famous because whatever it displayed, it displayed it prodigiously, just as it now displays the industrialist's disrespect for the balance of nature prodigiously.

Don't ever let anyone tell you that Hollywood is anything but a land of make-believe, where pink clouds billow, fairies dance, and the sun always shines. Because that part about the fairies is true. The film industry itself is no more crass or commercialized than, say, the insurance business or the plumbing-goods trade. The fact that the studio czars resisted anything out of the ordinary in their relentless drive for homogenized entertainment, or that they couldn't regard the screen as one huge canvas because they regarded the audience as an overgrown Kansas, is circumstantial evidence. There is no reason to believe that the studio executives ever offered the artists under them any less deference or respect than the Betty Crocker Kitchens offer their great cooks.

In a typical studio move, Perelman and Johnstone were given an "office" (i.e., bare room) in one of those dust-colored tenement buildings which, in oppressive disregard for environmental psychology, house most of the non-production work done inside the studios. Why there should be any necessity for working inside the studio at all is rather puzzling. The whole place seems to have been regarded by its barons as one large factory— or, worse, one large office building—where all the elements of production were assembled in one place and set working. And this is the way dreams were made. Bad dreams.

Film-making in the Thirties was the realm of the producer, and (once in a while) the star, and (almost never) the director. The producer dictated policy, made crucial time and money decisions, decided who should do what and how he should do it, and supervised the aggregation of contributions into the amalgamation of a movie. The only hope for transcending the murky atmosphere of Hollywood lay in the appointment of a producer with a brain in his head and a heart in New York, a producer who could be big brother, rich uncle and second cousin to the Marx Brothers. The heads of Paramount—a pack of furriers, ex-prizefighters, and penny-arcade owners—had made a decision of striking perspicacity: they assigned Herman J. Mankiewicz to the production of the Marx movies.

Herman Mankiewicz, a Promethean wit bound in a Promethean body, one of the most entertaining men in existence, for those fortunate mortals who knew him personally, was called the "Central Park West Voltaire" by Ben Hecht, who used to start arguments with him on subjects on which they were in complete accord, just for the sake of engaging in scintillating satirical discourse for hours on end. A blunt speaker in a world of word-mincers (he was once fired from Columbia Studios for making a remark about Harry Cohn's ass), he seemed always in a position where his talents exceeded the importance of the job he was given, and his gambling debts exceeded the salary he was given for the job. It was as a screenwriter that the studios kept him busiest (his script for *Citizen Kane* was turned into the greatest American film of three decades), but when the screenplay form proved too confining for his genius he was made a producer, and when he proved too disorganized and uneven-tempered to be a producer he was made a writer again. A former collaborator of George S. Kaufman, Dorothy Parker, Heywood Broun, Robert E. Sherwood, and Marc Connelly, a former writer for the Chicago *Tribune,* the New York *Times,* the New York *World, Vanity Fair,* and *Saturday Evening Post,* and *The New Yorker*'s first drama critic, Mankiewicz could rarely bring himself to take a movie script seriously; he was less fond of doing his best work on them than he was of completing an eight-week assignment in the last three weeks and then telling himself it wasn't his best work. His attitude toward his own job allowed him to keep his underlings enmeshed in an atmosphere of jovial informality. ("It was always fun to come into Mankiewicz's office," one writer recalls. "You could hear the noise as you were coming to the door. You never heard any noise from any other producer's office.") He had a greater respect for the Marx Brothers, in fact, than he had for movie-making, and was even known to go to costume parties dressed as all of them. (He also had a respect for nonsense in general, as evidenced by *Million Dollar Legs,* the insane W. C. Fields comedy he produced and half wrote with his brother Joseph.) His regard for the Marxes stretched back to *I'll Say She Is,* to the glorious age of Broadway in the Twenties, to the days when Groucho would come to Mankiewicz's home and ask Mrs. Mankiewicz, "Can Herman come out and play?" Mankiewicz was a large man who ate a large lunch and belched all afternoon. He had no intention of being an arduous taskmaster, but he knew what working with the Marxes was like. "This is an ordeal by fire," he told Perelman and Johnstone. "Make sure you wear your asbestos pants."

So the virgin scenarists were able to apply their talents with no regard (in fact, with evident distaste) for their surroundings. Mankiewicz had instructed them only to "proceed as fancy dictated" and to leave him alone for the next six weeks. Dispensing with the triumph of "virtue" and the overthrow of "wickedness," the *de rigueur* Hollywood morality, they set to work making villains out of film convention's heroes and virtues out of its vices. Day after day they worked themselves in and out of stitches concocting the first original Marx Brothers film.

No matter how many different sensibilities and different personalities applied themselves to the problem of writing Marx Brothers comedy, it always came out sounding distinctly like Marx Brothers comedy. Nearly everyone has a streak or two of the right buoyant aggressiveness in him, and it became simply a matter of coaxing it out. (Financially, though, it was always a rather foolhardy venture. Suppose the comedians didn't like the script. Common practice with a rejected screenplay is to sell it to some other star. Can you imagine anybody else in the *world* being able to use a Marx Brothers script? Fortunately for the screenwriters of America, Hollywood was otherwise rife with interchangeable personalities.) But for the first time, there was cinematic mobility to contend with. A scene change was now permitted whenever mood, action, or whim dictated. Part of the problem with *Animal Crackers* and *Cocoanuts,* as movies, and especially as Marx Brothers movies, was that they held still too long. Without deliberation or even deliberate action, this was dispensed with, and *Monkey Business,* truer to the spirit of things, takes place all over an ocean liner.

The Marxes, simultaneously, were boarding the *Paris,* in New York, for London. (This is cinematic mobility right here.) Groucho at the last minute decided to take his whole family along and impulsively reserved for himself the ship's royal suite, a monstrous three-bedroom, one-piano affair, which fairly stunned his brothers, each of whom thought *he* was the spend-thrift of the family. The bon voyage was attended by the New York Giants and Harry Ruby, who sang encores of his new song, "Three Little Words," until Groucho was thoroughly seasick.

Harpo and Chico took to the *Paris* night life immediately, but Groucho refused to have anything to do with it, even to the point of declining an invitation to dine with the captain because he was in no mood to wear a tuxedo. "Tell the captain he's a lousy driver," he instructed a messenger. "He's got no right to leave the bridge just to have dinner." The captain, of course, thought that was a very funny answer and made an appointment for eight o'clock. When Groucho's wife showed up alone, she explained to the captain that her husband wasn't feeling well. As if this poor excuse for an excuse didn't give *itself* away, Groucho came in fifteen minutes later wearing a business suit and sat at another table. His wife got up and danced by with Harpo (who was wearing a tuxedo) and insisted that he go to the captain and apologize. This he did, by saying, "I wasn't really sick. I just told her to tell you that because I didn't feel like putting on a tuxedo."

Hardly had 1931 begun before the Marx Brothers were at the Palace Theater and being received with vociferous joy.

But the London winter turned out to be a trial, especially when a determined poker fiend kept Harpo and Chico grinding through game after game one night till nearly daybreak. Their fingers began going numb *before* they ran out of firewood, and once that had happened, they started splintering all the furniture and heaving it into the flames. By the time their diehard friend had gambled away everything he owned, he found himself sitting on his own bare floor staring at his own bare walls. Harpo and Chico reimbursed the man for his losses and his furniture, left him inhabiting the most unfurnished flat in London, and retreated to a taxi, where they told the driver, "Take us to the warmest restaurant in town."

While in England, the Zeppo Marxes purchased some Afghans. An Afghan is an ungainly creature that looks like the issue of a llama that married a poodle. It's just what Zeppo Marx *would* purchase.

Abruptly, in the middle of their stay, the Marxes cabled Paramount. By now their lack of confidence in their own talent discoveries had broadened into open hostility, and they told the studio to get rid of those two incompetent neophytes and hire somebody who knew what he was doing. Jesse Lasky, now in Hollywood, read the telegram, smiled softly, showed it to Perelman and Johnstone (who did *not* smile) and burned it. So much for executive decisions.

On Saturday, February 14, the Marxes arrived back in New York. They told the press that they would have stayed longer, but the American newspapers took so long to get to England that they couldn't keep track of the stock market. Groucho found the customs procedures something worth complaining about, and he said so. "How about the Pilgrims?" he asked newsmen. "Were they bothered by all this landing card and visa business? Did a guard stand on Plymouth Rock waiting for them?"

By the time he got to filling out his Declaration of Purchases form, he was angered to the point of belligerency. His answers read:

NAME:	Julius H. Marx
ADDRESS:	21 Lincoln Rd., Great Neck, Long Island
BORN:	Yes
HAIR:	Not much
EYES:	All the better to see you with
OCCUPATION:	Smuggler

LIST OF ITEMS PURCHASED OUT OF THE UNITED STATES, WHERE BOUGHT, AND THE PURCHASE PRICE:
                    Wouldn't you like to know?

When he was through with that, he turned to his wife and asked her if she still had the opium on her. It was then that his entire family was herded into two vast rooms and stripped mother naked, while every item of clothing and luggage was fine-tooth-combed. Even at that point, the only thing that kept him quiet was the undeclared watch that he was hiding in his mouth.

Now a quick dissolve back to Hollywood, where Perelman and Johnstone were informed the following Monday that their pleasant six-week sabbatical had run its course, that there was to be a public recitation of their joint project that very Friday evening at the Roosevelt Hotel and that it had better be good. This didn't worry them (*they* thought it was great), but for the sake of a good impression they spent the week burnishing the dialogue with cinematic horseradish: they inserted irises, pans, tilts, dissolves, Jackman shots, Dunning shots and "even, at one point, specified that the camera should vorkapich around the faces of the ballroom guests." Slavko Vorkapich, the montage editor and film theorist, would definitely not have been pleased to discover himself turned into a verb that day.

And now (cinematic mobility again) the Marxes descended on New York, closed up their houses, rounded up their gag men, and took the train to Hollywood. On board, haply, was Morrie Ryskind, on his way to Goldwyn's to script Eddie Cantor's *Palmy Days*. There would emerge from the transport at every stop an entire enclave of comedians and writers who would play catch at the station, amuse passers-by, heckle strangers, and then hop back on again.

And with that they entered Hollywood. On the subject of their various assaults on the staid, stolid movie world, which has always been the same since, limitless fictions abound. When William Wilkerson of the *Hollywood Reporter* got off the train at Barstow to take a private plane into Los Angeles, and took with him a couple of the Marx Brothers who were getting tired of the train, a whole legend sprang up wherein the Marxes dumped Harry Ruby out of the plane at the airfield and then sent vague and conflicting telegrams to Paramount announcing their arrival for two and a half hours before turning up at the wrong place. Another story is that they once tackled a Paramount executive, took his pants off, and threw them out the window. Yet another is that it was Ernst Lubitsch they tackled, and that they wrestled with him on the ground for some length of time until they lost interest and got up and walked away.

When told all this, Nat Perrin could only shake his head as if to change the subject and mutter, "No, they were more amusing than that."

"They were practical men," says Arthur Sheekman, "not idiots."

All the same, there was a difference. The Marx Brothers made films that were direct outgrowths of their personalities, while most stars had personalities that were direct outgrowths of their films. They didn't say what they were told; they came in and told their writers what to tell them to say, while most stars made their whole livelihood out of being a mouth. And they continually said what came to mind, whether it was some kind of gag or a caustic remark, while Hollywood was full of people who wouldn't have said what they thought even if they had thought of anything to think. No wonder people were surprised. "There was no such thing as a star having four heads," says Perrin. For the most part, there was no such thing as a star having any heads at all.

Groucho's distaste for the Hollywood pleasantries was evident right away. He never attended premieres, shrank from performing at parties, resisted swimming pools, openly refused to leave a footprint at Grauman's Chinese Theater, signed autographs "Charlie Chaplin" or "Mary Pickford," and once, when asked to emcee a series of "impromptu" performances at an important social function, insisted on stripping the event of all its dishonesty by announcing to the world which props each performer had happened to bring with him that evening. Chico's attention was centered more on the horse race at Santa Anita than the rat race in Hollywood. And Harpo, situated strategically in the thick of the fru-fru at the Garden of Allah, one of the most column-conscious dens of thunder thieves in the state, blithely slept through all the excitement so he could be at the studio in the morning. The closest association any of them had with their unnatural habitat was the Comedians' Roundtable at the Hillcrest Country Club, where they could fight for their very reputation with the likes of George Burns, Jack Benny, and Georgie Jessel. This was home!

Right off they proved themselves a little startling when they rolled up their sleeves and got personally involved in the preparation of their first movie, and this was when they had hardly gotten off the train. At eight-thirty that Friday night, February 20, 1931, Perelman and Johnstone showed up at the Roosevelt, by now somewhat intimidated by the whole ordeal ahead of them. Since both were equally ill-equipped to handle a dramatic reading, the only fair way to choose lots was to flip a coin. The lot it fell to was Perelman's, whose "only Thespian flight heretofore had been a minor role in a high-school pageant based on Pocahontas." As the audience slowly gathered, each writer lost another ounce of the confidence that had been steadily accumulating since they had gotten the job. The first to show up, forty-five minutes late, was Herman Mankiewicz (they knew he was a genius; he could see through *anything*), accompanied by Joseph (he was a professional screenwriter; he'd be full of professional criticisms), followed by Zeppo with his wife and Afghans ("the dogs had eaten the upholstery of a Packard roadster that afternoon"), and Harpo with a couple of blondes he had picked up at dinner (he didn't even look interested), then Chico and his wife (who brought a wirehair that started fighting with the Afghans), then Groucho and *his* wife (Groucho was never satisfied with anything), then Sheekman, Perrin, and Pusey (gag men, eh? That's how much confidence they have in us!), then all *their* wives and pickups (what is this, a *show?*), then a lot of other people that nobody seemed to know (who the hell invited *them?*), and finally a few Paramount officials (whose very profession it was to be miserly with their enthusiasms. Great!). By the time he started reading, he was facing a gathering of twenty-seven people and five dogs. His trepidation had blossomed into a full-flowering fear. How could a full-length 126-page script dashed off in six weeks by a couple of cartoonists ever crack more than a condescending smile out of these staunchly entrenched Ionic pillars of the industry?

"Go ahead, man! Get a move on!" Groucho called. That was encouraging, too. Perelman, with the pleading look of a basset hound in his eyes, turned to Johnstone. Johnstone was, for all intents and purposes, dead.

And so Perelman read their script. To this day nobody remembers what was in it (except the vorkapich) or how good it actually was. For one thing, it was being read so badly it was hard to tell. ("At times my voice faded away altogether and I whispered endless pages of dialogue to the unheeding air.") For another, there were those in the crowd to whom a good script would have meant the end of a job and a return to New York, and they didn't *want* to like it. And the Marx Brothers would only naturally refuse to be happy with anything not up to par with the final versions of *Animal Crackers* and *Cocoanuts*. The only laugh aroused in the entire evening was inspired by a descriptive passage concerning a clock placed in the belly of a nude. Readings of scripts are never particularly effective, anyway. All the timing is lost when you have to identify the speaker of each line, and none of the action is very clear until it can be acted out. And a *bad* reading to a tired, semi-hostile audience, most of whom had disembarked from a dusty, four-day railroad ride scant hours ago, had little going for it but impermanence.

Harpo fell asleep. Half the crowd, including the dogs, followed his example.

"But Perelman went on reading," says Sheekman. "Valiantly, I thought. I would have shot myself on page twenty-five."

Only the dreadful silence that celebrated the turning of the last page was needed to wake the audience up again. Once it was over, nobody was at a loss for something to say, but, as is customary, each dreaded voicing the first opinion, for fear of being rudely denounced as the minority by everybody else. Finally, Chico turned and addressed Groucho. "What do you think?" he asked.

All eyes were on Groucho as he lit his cigar and masticated its nether tip contemplatively. What he said, of course, was the typical "It stinks." Yes, everyone in the room agreed, their various opinions could be adapted to fit that one.

And so it was, girls, dogs, big men, small men, gag men, and even yes men said "No!" and vacated the room—leaving Perelman and Johnstone just as incredulous as when they had been rushed into Jesse Lasky's office in the first place.

They need not have mourned. Not only were they paid handsomely for their seven weeks' work, but their script was so bad that they would have to be paid just as handsomely for another five months, until they worked it up into something presentable. By now the cozy twosome had turned into a club. Every day there would gather different combinations of the same gang of thugs: Perelman, Sheekman, Perrin, Johnstone, Pusey, Harpo, Groucho, Chico, Mankiewicz and sometimes even the director, a tall, lanky fellow named Norman McLeod. And sometimes Zeppo. Every day the shouting, bargaining, improvising, compromising, and mob warfare would continue. And this, for five months, is how *Monkey Business* was written.

Every day Sheekman would grapple with Perelman over the inclusion of esoteric literary dialogue. Perelman was cultured and Joycean enough to be able to make puns on words like the German *Morgen,* for morning, and J. P. Morgan. Wouldn't *that* have been hilarious? "I think we draw the line at German puns," commented Sheekman. (Though this didn't stop them, four years later, from putting one in *A Night at the Opera.* When informed that Signor Lassparri is worth $1,000 a night as a singer, Groucho responds, "A thousand dollars a *Nacht?*" Nobody gets it.)

And every day Mankiewicz would grapple with Sheekman over Sheekman's incorrigible insistence on having a plot in this movie. Not only did he want a gangster plot to get in the way of all the shenanigans, he even wanted to *start the picture that way,* so that when the Marx Brothers came on screen they would break the established mood and look even funnier than usual. To all this Mankiewicz said unprintable things. His attitude toward plots was very simple. "If Groucho and Chico stand against a wall for an hour and forty minutes and crack funny jokes, that's enough of a plot for me," he said. The producer dictated policy.

Amid the bargaining, poor Pusey got lost. His ideas, most of them physical maneuvers for Harpo, were not the sort of thing that could be hollered across the round table, nor was he much of a hollerer. He would quietly contact Harpo and softly gesticulate his new idea to him, or he would sketch it out, cartoon-fashion, and display it in silence. Harpo would nod congenially. It was soon obvious he wasn't adding much to the din, and after ten weeks he went back home. For a time, there was an ex-vaude-villian named Solly Violinski in his stead, but there didn't seem to be much point in that, either.

Amid the bargaining, little Nat Perrin got shuffled around a bit, too. He was surrounded by people who were loaded with experience in some field or other, and all he had was an education. As reverently as show-business people spoke of this commodity, they didn't seem to think much of anybody who never played the Orpheum Circuit. Ostensibly hired for the express purpose of doing Chico lines, he soon found such formal stratifications broken down entirely in the excitement of creation, and material was being written by one gang of writers for another gang of comedians without much concern for categories. As a specialist in the dialect area, his most specialized contribution was the incidental invention of the phrase "Atsa fine, boss," which Chico inexplicably fell in love with and used constantly for the rest of his filmic life, whenever he couldn't think of the line he was supposed to say.

Chico remorselessly continued to play cards, establish contacts, and make his mysterious phone calls in the midst of every harangue. So long as they were writing lines for him, he was happy; his presence in the room exerted all the influence he needed.

Amid the bargaining, a lot of the Marx Brothers' recent trip to Europe seems to have found its way into the screenplay. The idea of Groucho making wise-guy remarx to the captain becomes a whole comedy routine. The rigamarole of standing in line and going through customs is turned into a fitting background for a routine the Marxes did in *I'll Say She Is:* doing imitations, one brother after the other, of a famous singing star. (During *Animal Crackers'* stay in New York, Maurice Chevalier had invited the brothers up on the stage during one of his shows, and they had shown their appreciation by doing a succession of Maurice Chevalier imitations. So, right in the middle of the fussing with the passports, comes a succession of Maurice Chevalier imitations.) When Groucho and his family journeyed to the Continent, he and his son Arthur saw a Punch-and-Judy show on the streets of Paris. In *Monkey Business,* a Punch-and-Judy show on shipboard becomes a big sequence for Harpo. When the Marxes' ship docked in New York and Groucho made his acid observations about the Pilgrims to the press, the president of a ladies' fashion-wear corporation was also interviewed and made several important announcements to the effect that Paris would always be the center of fashion and that therefore there would be no future for an American ladies'-wear university. The revised script of the new movie finds this poor fellow lampooned in the form of a female opera celebrity who gets badgered by Groucho.

The second script for *Monkey Business* had no trace of the first, except for that old shred of a notion about stowaways on an ocean liner. The second script was written chiefly by Perelman and Sheekman, with sight gags by Johnstone, contributions by Perrin, and intrusions by Groucho, Harpo, and Herman Mankiewicz. After hundreds of gatherings, regroupings, and sessions of raconteur wit, everybody met on the sound stages (where there was more shouting space) and started working things out. At this point the comedians did most of the inventing, the director started to take control, and everybody else just sort of coached. Here was the chance to practice timing and delivery, work out the logistics and the mechanics, make up some more gags for Harpo, and see what the film was going to look like. Here was the *only* chance, in fact, to get it ready to be photographed. A few weeks on the lot had to take the place of months in Philadelphia.

Around this time, people started to notice that shy, introverted fellow who was directing the picture. Although the Marxes bore, almost by default, the responsibility for locating writers, the choice of a director was on a different plane entirely, and they left that up to the studio. Norman McLeod was a small-town lad from Michigan, the son of a minister, the holder of advanced degrees from the University of Washington, a university light-heavyweight champion, a pilot in the Great War—in other words, an all-American hero, until he went to the big city and spent nine years drawing cartoons on Al Christie comedies. (Silent comedies, desperate for laughs, often resorted to putting funny cartoons on the subtitles.) He had directed *Taking a Chance*, and his script for *Skippy* had been made into a film starring six-year-old Jackie Cooper. That was the career of Norman McLeod. The idea of assigning him to *Monkey Business*, which was already manned with neophytes, could only have been, in light of the Marxes' unprofessional attitude toward cooperation, with a malicious eye on his boxing experience.

McLeod almost fit right into the studio director mold: He was an intelligent, agreeable coordinator who understood his particular field (comedy), had no distinctive style of his own (he is what the style fanatics call "a competent craftsman") and didn't make trouble. The great achievements of his career were all accomplished by dominating a film with somebody else's personality, as in *Road to Rio*, Danny Kaye's *Secret Life of*

Walter Mitty and W. C. Fields's first great sound film, *It's a Gift*. McLeod felt that the Marx Brothers understood *Monkey Business* better than he did, and rather than get indignant, grow imperious or interfere, he just held the rudder, called "Janie . . ." when he got confused (Jane Lauring, the cutter, was on hand during shooting to guarantee continuity between the three cameras) and weathered their stormy sea with tranquility.

(One of the few exceptions to this practice occurred during the shooting of the party scene. Harpo was to be annoying a crowd of people, and McLeod decided they should react by laughing at him. Sheekman started fighting again. He said they should react by being startled, shocked, anything but amused. "No, no," McLeod admonished. "If they don't laugh, the audience won't laugh." Another of those laws of comedy that have nothing to do with anything funny. One whole day was spent shooting footage of the people laughing, and it all had to be thrown out.)

McLeod's manner was customarily so subdued that his speech was only slightly louder than his breath. ("I'm as quiet as a mouse pissing on a blotter," he used to say.) Even his hushed tones had an authoritative quality about them, so that they would often overtake the set of the film he was directing, until the loud disorganized business of movie-making came to be conducted in near silence. The story goes that one studio guard, awed by the atmosphere, was watching an empty McLeod set during lunch hour and couldn't even answer the phone out loud.

Between the quiet minister's son and the boisterous tenement underdogs there developed a tension in approach which comes out on the screen looking like the very embodiment of that "quietly noisy relaxed intensity" Edward Albee tosses off as a joke in *Who's Afraid of Virginia Woolf?* There is a disorderliness with its own sense of order and a staccato rhythm meshed with cinematic timing. McLeod could no more control the Marx Brothers than anybody else could, but they listened to what he said. The Marxes, after all, never pretended to be artists (a good thing, too, or they would have been drummed out of Hollywood), but they did pretend to have a point of view. What they needed was a director who didn't. There had to be somebody who could take this myriad melange of contributions and make a movie out of it; everybody else was too worried about his own little gags. (This was a good thing, too. Did you ever *see* four people battling for control of one whole production and trying to get it to come out all of their own ways at once? Not to mention *ten.*) McLeod kept himself quietly in the background and put it all together.

The cameras were rolling by midsummer. By this time Nat Perrin, who had received word that he had passed his bar exam, might have returned home to a tidy practice and an orderly life had not Mankiewicz recommended him to MGM for Keaton's *Sidewalks of New York,* thereby cultivating a healthy career that hasn't quit since.

Also about this time, two federal agents showed up at Groucho's rented home in the Hollywood hills and demanded that he pay for that undeclared watch. Hunted down at his own door like a common criminal, Groucho realized he had learned an important lesson. "I'll never buy anything at Dunhill's again," he swore to the G-men. "The place is obviously full of stool pigeons."

Sheekman and Perelman were still around to invent enough fresh dialogue to keep Groucho amused through the weeks of shooting, and Johnstone hung on to come up with funny things for Harpo. Only once before had the Marx Brothers preserved on celluloid something that hadn't proved itself seaworthy outside the sound stage, and *Humor Risk* had not been an experience particularly worth recapturing. Just as with *I'll Say She Is,* they found themselves involved in a whole unfamiliar game, and, just as with *I'll Say She Is,* they were worried. They began to exercise not restraint but caution. Last-minute changes were introduced and tried out before the final take. Groucho would get on the phone every half hour toward the end of the day and keep dinnertime postponed until they had gotten through some knotty problem, and then they would keep working at it until it was time to get on the phone again and postpone his daughter's bedtime. Lines were rejected because they were "old" or "tired"—not that the outside world had heard them even once, but simply because they had been in the script for so long that everybody

On the *Monkey Business* set: "Macko" is Norman McLeod and "Echo" is Charles Barton, the assistant director. LARRY EDMUNDS BOOK SHOP

was sick of hearing them. Lines that the lighting crew had heard in rehearsal didn't strike them as funny by the time there was film in the camera, so they were thrown out in favor of some new lines that would break them up again. Nobody rested, nothing stood still.

By this time sound was being handled with *some* proficiency. You could cut whenever you wanted to, and the camera was out of its little box and being shrouded in blankets or jammed into saxophone cases to keep it quiet, but it was allowed to do its job and follow the action again. Sheekman noticed that "on shooting a film, half the time seems to be given to readjusting the lights." Johnstone found himself as fascinated by the hilarious technical jargon as Groucho was, and he ran back to New York as soon as the film was finished and recorded such pearls as "All cooking!" "Stewing!" "O.K. for sound!" "Up to speed!" and "Get a gobo!" in one of his comic strips.

Slates now differentiated between a SOF (Sound on Film) shot and one that was to be taken MOS (which stands, believe it or not, for Mit-Out Sound).

Monkey Business is the only film on earth good enough to give us a glimpse of Frenchie Marx, Father of All Marx Brothers. He appears twice: once on the ship, before the interview with the opera celebrity (who is forthwith referred to as "Madame Frenchie") and once on the dock, while his sons stand in front of him and wave at the camera. He is a genial, dapper gentleman who looks pleased by everything that goes on. According to all reports, he flew into hysterics every time a Marx Brother moved a muscle, and often had to be ushered, helpless, out of screening rooms when their rushes were showing.

Monkey Business is also the first film ever made in which the love interest is handled by Zeppo Marx, presumably to keep things all in the family. (And to give Zeppo something to do. "As a favor for having been good and quiet for so long," as one reviewer said.)

It is also the first Marx Brothers film which, in compliance with Groucho's wishes, does without Margaret Dumont.

To McLeod can be attributed the air of easy fantasy that colors the film (he was one of no less than four cartoonists engaged in the project), the light, apparently effortless atmosphere in which the madness all takes place, and the smooth integration of this whole pack of divergent loose ends. Directorial control is most evident in certain shots: the scene of the saxophone improvisation, for instance, where spontaneous applause bursts out of nowhere, or the great single shot of Harpo riding the puppet's wagon down the ship's hallway, wearing a mask on the back of his head, honking his horn.

But, true to form, it is *their* personality that comes through. The movie is all theirs, there are more comedy routines than can be recorded, at least one of them is doing something every minute, and when there are two or three at once there are unexpected cuts to the other one, busy with something else. The bitterness of Depression sarcasm, the non-stop comedy of a platoon of gag men, the (aforementioned) cinematic mobility, and the incredible cartoon quality of some of the images are all added to the established non-pattern of the Marx Brothers to create a willy-nilly, pell-mell film. Considering it was just about everybody's first movie, it had no right turning out so good.

Monkey Business was released toward the end of 1931, the same year as Charlie Chaplin's sweet and lovely *City Lights*. The difference is obvious right away. *Monkey Business* is riddled with a mood of unabated rebellion and out-and-out revolt. Chaplin, like most film-makers, appeals to our sympathies. *Monkey Business* appeals to our drives.

VIEW FROM THE FORWARD HATCH

GROUCHO: I want to register a complaint.

CAPTAIN: Why, what's the matter?

GROUCHO: Matter enough! Do you know who sneaked into my stateroom at 3:00 this morning?

CAPTAIN: Who did that?

GROUCHO: Nobody. And that's my complaint. I'm young, I want gaiety, laughter, hotcha-cha! I wanta dance! I wanta dance till the cows come home. . . .

CAPTAIN: Just what do you mean by this?

GROUCHO: Another thing, I don't care for the way you're running this boat. Why don't you get in the back seat for a while and let your wife drive?

CAPTAIN: I want you to know I've been captain of this ship for twenty-two years!

GROUCHO: Twenty-two years, eh? If you were a man you'd go in business for yourself. I know a fella started only last year with just a canoe. Now he's got more women than you can shake a stick at, if that's your idea of a good time.

CAPTAIN: One more word out of you and I'll throw you in irons!

GROUCHO: You can't do it with irons, it's a mashie shot. It's a mashie shot if the wind's against you, and if the wind isn't, I am! And how about those barrels down below?

CAPTAIN: Barrels?

GROUCHO: Yeah, I wouldn't put a pig among those barrels.
CAPTAIN: Now, see here, you . . .
GROUCHO: No, not even if you got down on your knees. . . .

What's more fun than a barrel of Marx Brothers? *Four* barrels of Marx Brothers!

The mere act of hauling themselves on board a ship and hiding out in the hold without booking passage is not presumptuous enough. They must sing rousing choruses of "Sweet Adeline" and write insulting notes to the captain. And most actors would be satisfied with an entrance. The Marx Brothers have to have a fanfare. The camera sits and admires the forward hatch, listening to the last chorus of an ancient song booming from its innards, and straightaway dollies in lovingly on four kippered-herring barrels; then out pop the Marx Brothers at the end of the verse like four lampoonish jack-in-the-boxes, grinning and bowing in smug recognition of their own efforts. When the dialogue starts up, it's pretty soggy by comparison, but after that head start it hardly matters. No matter what it is they happen to say, the sound of their voices just gives their Puckish Pageantry another dimension.

Hardly are two lines exchanged before Groucho kicks off a series of gripes about his living quarters. When Zeppo thinks he hears somebody coming, Groucho *hopes* it is the captain so he can tell him what he thinks of his ship. The kippered herring may have spoiled, but the comedy is very fresh today.

Finally, like all hopeful young stowaways, they are discovered (but not before they've had a few laughs at the expense of the crew), and they dash off to unleash their maniacal fury on the unsuspecting passengers of the ship. Running, galloping, sliding, hula-hooping, and roller-skating their way around the deck, they set off waves of disturbance among the perfectly ordinary denizens of the ship's hallways, all of them drab, dull, and unimaginative enough to have actually paid their fare.

Straight off the difference is apparent. In *Cocoanuts* and *Animal Crackers,* they were four men in funny clothes who were perfectly satisfied to crack jokes and do silly things. Here they are

ruthless gnomes from another realm. On Broadway, they were strapped down by all the restrictions prosperity and the stage bring with them; in *Cocoanuts*, Groucho was even burdened with running a Florida hotel. The glory of *Monkey Business* is that all four of them run nothing but amok.

Split up, they find various targets to inflict themselves on, each instilled with the idea that he has not only as much right on the ship as any of the paying passengers but a great deal more. Groucho makes good his promise to wreak vengeance on the captain for the rotten life he's had for two days in a barrel. "Are these your gloves?" he says, interrupting the uniformed officer in the middle of a premeditated boast, "I found them in your trunk." Groucho browbeats the man for five merciless minutes, and then in a moment of unwilling condescension offers him his gloves back. When the captain is so nervy as to accept, Groucho starts in again. "You *would* take them, wouldn't you?" he says, as if he knew all about the man, and then shouts, "Keep away from my office!" for a parting shot as he disappears into the captain's office. All the while the captain reacts less with rage than with an unsettled incredulity. He hasn't just been insulted; he's had his whole world view invalidated.

After that, the scene in which Groucho and Chico share the captain's lunch is doubly outrageous. Groucho, who has just confessed to spending the cruise in the hold, breaks into the captain's quarters, takes the one remaining chair at the table, and orders the captain to give his to Chico. The captain, reflecting the popular view of figures of authority, is an officious, dim-witted person who tries to run a taut ship but hasn't got a taut in his head; gradually it gets through to him that these hungry fellows might be the stowaways; ominously he announces his intention to begin to suspect them, while they sit there and eat his lunch. "One of them goes around with a black moustache!" he declares, glowering at Groucho. When Groucho makes a halfhearted funny reply, the captain is even good enough to repeat the straight line and give him a chance to come up with a better answer. Apparently this is all so new to him he has no idea how to cope with the situation.

Harpo eludes the first mate by crashing a puppet show disguised as a puppet. He plays Punchinello to a hand-made Judy, and soon it becomes hard to tell the real puppets from the unreal Harpo—so hard, in fact, that his pursuer, Tom Kennedy, begins to feel that *he* must be part of the show too. By the time he catches sight of Harpo, he has lost sight of what he's supposed to be doing, and he jabs Harpo's rear end mischievously with a pin to get a laugh out of the audience. At one point the captain grabs Harpo's leg and begins to pull it. Tom Kennedy runs around behind him and pulls Harpo's leg too. Then Harpo runs around and pulls Harpo's leg. That's when you realize it's not Harpo's leg. It's Harpo pulling their leg.

Another of the officers, sending his subordinates off to "look up on B deck" for the stowaways, lets Harpo and Chico shave off his moustache, right from under his nose.

The first twenty minutes of *Monkey Business* is four comedians and a boat full of straight men. Like any code of accepted behavior, the drab routine of the ship makes no allowance for such free-spirited renegades. They tend to disregard routines, show them up for what they are, and snafu their functions beyond repair. And so, like any code of behavior, it demands nothing more urgently than to hunt them down.

DON'T SHOOT

ALKY: I'm wise! I'm wise!

GROUCHO: You're wise, eh? Well, what's the capital of Nebraska? What's the capital of the Chase National Bank? Give up?

ALKY: You . . .

GROUCHO: Now, I'll try you on an easy one. How many Frenchmen can't be wrong?

ALKY: I know . . .

GROUCHO: You were warm, and so was she. But don't be discouraged. With a little study you'll go a long way, and I wish you'd start now.

ALKY: Do you see this gat?

GROUCHO: Cute, isn't it? Santy Claus bring it for Christmas? I got a fire engine!

ALKY: Listen, mug . . . do you know who I am?

GROUCHO: Now, don't tell me. Are you animal or vegetable?

ALKY: Grrr!

GROUCHO: Animal.

ALKY: Get this . . . I'm Alky Briggs!

GROUCHO: And I? I'm the fellow who talks too much. Fancy meeting you here after all these drinks!

ALKY: Wait a minute!

GROUCHO: Sorry, I can't stay. The captain's waiting to chase me around the deck.

And so, in a very brief span of time, the fire is going, the pump is primed, and the stage is set for a climax. What follows, Groucho's confrontation with the gangster Alky Briggs, is one of the six or eight priceless gems left to the world by these spasmodically brilliant comedians.

Alky is having a vicious argument with his wife, Thelma Todd. Groucho, hunted by Tom Kennedy, charges in with some dry cleaning in his hand, a perfect stranger, and says, "Pardon me while I step into the closet." As no conceivable reaction would be adequate, they ignore him altogether. Only after Alky leaves does his wife, sharing some of the attributes of the captain, allow her gradually dawning awareness of his presence to evolve into something resembling suspicion. "What are you doing in the closet?" she demands. "Nothing," whispers Groucho softly. "Come on in."

They engage in one inning of ring-around-the-closet in order to get to know each other, he punning and extemporizing by way of introduction, she playing along with abandon (having had no abandon to play along with ever since she got married). Then, just as her sorrows are half drowned, she rescues them again and lays them dripping on the table for his commiseration and sympathy. More puns. "I want life, I want gaiety, I want music!" she screams, enumerating exactly the wild desires Groucho rattled off five pages ago to a disinterested captain. They both find themselves, Bonnie-and-Clyde fashion, in the middle of an early-Depression rut. Before they get around to dancing, they stretch things out delectably by feigning reticence, arranging settlements and finding in their absurdities loopholes of logic—in other words, by making an afternoon of it.

Having established a perfect rapport, Groucho moves in to culminate the affair with a well-aimed kiss and finds monogamistic morality standing in his way. Angry monogamistic morality. With a gun. When he opens his eyes, there stands Alky Briggs, ready to do him in.

Now, how many alternatives does a situation like that offer you? Groucho utilizes twenty-three out of a possible none. Caught redhanded, staring down the barrel of death, no physical or logical escape at his disposal, his first response is to rebuke his adversary. Referring to the intrusion as "an outrage," he explains indignantly that he is "not in the habit of making threats" but that his immediate response is going to be "a letter about this in the *Times* tomorrow morning."

Brigg's only answer is "You won't read it. 'Cause I'm going to lay you out pretty."

Well, it's in the bag! Groucho is up against a sitting duck! Not only is Alky Briggs a gangster, stuck in the role of a gangster, accustomed solely to gangster situations and gangster responses, but he is a *movie* gangster, choked in the dust of gangster clichés and doomed to go on mouthing the same inane gangster words forever. It's not hard to beat an opponent like this; all it takes is a little versatility. Groucho begins babbling nonsense; he utters a long string of homilies, vagarisms, and *non sequiturs;* his voice goes up, his voice goes down; he wanders back into the closet, he ducks out of it again; he changes the subject, he changes the object, he changes the preposition. Realistically, of course, he could be gunned down in a minute. But by the rules of the cinema, the victim has to deliver the proper lines first. He can't be shot until he's said, "Don't shoot! Don't shoot!" or "Lay off, Alky, it's not what you think!" So there stands Alky, delivering cliché after cliché, waiting for his cue, and off goes Groucho on a whirlwind of nonsense, leaving him stunned.

That's the Marx Brothers for you, coupling jokes one after the other like railroad cars. You find yourself stuck at the crossing fascinated, unable to do anything but watch them all roll past. How many ways can there be to stall when somebody's got a gun at your head? Groucho must have smart answers for everything, some of them funny because they integrate so perfectly with the situation, some of them funny because they don't relate to anything at all.

In all their best sequences, the Marx Brothers have this quality of insistent consistency, where the wisecracks keep coming and won't stop, where the puns and the sight gags battle for attention, where the illogic carries you along with its seeming logic and then dumps you in alien territory and walks away, where the real crosses into the unreal and then back again so often that you doubt your own sanity less than you mistrust it.

These moments, rare though they are, are magic; there are few moments on film that can match them and none that can top them.

WONDER IN ALICELAND

GROUCHO: Now, there are two fellas trying to attack you, aren't there? And there are two fellas trying to defend you. Now that's 50% waste. Now why can't you be attacked by your *own* bodyguard? Your life'll be saved and that, uh, that's 100% waste. Now whaddya got? You've still got me, and I'll attack you for nothing.

HELTON: Say, what're you gettin' at?

GROUCHO: I anticipated that question. How does an army travel? On its stomach. How do you travel? On a ship. Of course, you're saving your stomach. Now that same common sense . . .

HELTON: I don't think you realize who . . .

GROUCHO: Oh, I realize it's a penny here and a penny there, but look at me. I worked myself up from nothing to a state of extreme poverty. Now what do you say?

HELTON: I tell you what I say, I say . . .

GROUCHO: All right, then it's all settled. I'm to be your new bodyguard. In case I'm going to attack you, I'll have to be there to defend you too. Now let me know when you want to be attacked and I'll be there ten minutes later to defend you.

Well, there's not much *Monkey Business* can do any more to top all that. It doesn't even try. It's content from here on in to amble along at the carefree, savage, quietly noisy pace it had originally established. By now nobody the madmen meet is any match for them, the captain and the crew have given up trying to find·them, and the two gangsters whose rivalry they get mixed up in are perplexed into submission. They are four demons in a land of dullards; they are spice in the lives of men who will go to their graves unseasoned. Before they contrive to slip off the ship unscathed and unpunished, one of the gangsters is given a dia-

tribe on the absurdity of bodyguards; a man is flipped over on his head for having mentioned a frog in his throat; a serious chess game is not only disturbed but carried away from its players into another room; two passengers have their pockets picked and are given surrealistic alibis; a man with a heavy beard is leaped upon, on the grounds that he must be somebody else in disguise; and *everybody's* sense of decency and decorum is disrupted enough to spoil the afternoon. To spoil it, that is, for Decency and Decorum fans.

And consider the use of the camera in this scene. It turns into Harpo.

At one juncture they decide they will get past the guards with a fake ID. If they steal somebody else's passport, then all four of them will have to claim to be the same person. This is not quite preposterous enough. So they steal the passport of *Maurice Chevalier!* Now they not only have to claim to be the same person, they all have to claim to be somebody that not a single one of them could possibly be! They can't seriously expect that to work. They are openly doing it only to cause trouble. Harpo, for instance, leaps in unrestrained enthusiasm at the well-stacked, carefully sorted official papers on the table in front of him and commences flinging them madly in all directions at once, wrenching, by way of revenge, the most profound primordial chaos out of a rather silly excuse for order.

By their very nonentity in the course of the story, all the characters in opposition to our heroes have become—through the logic of film—the faceless "they" that you always read about and complain about but never meet. Well, here they are, visible, nondescript, and perfectly useless (and all played, fittingly enough, by Hollywood extras). All they do is what they are supposed to do, while the Marx Brothers are busy seeking out excitement and inciting hysteria. The contrast is evident in every shot. To Aristotle's famous apothegm "Moderation in All Things," the Marxes have an antidote: "Go to Pieces." Decency and Decorum become a rival comedy team.

THE PARTY OF THE FOURTH PART

ALKY: Keep your eye on Helton. We're gonna grab his daughter and take her to the old barn.

GROUCHO: Old barn! A fine tinhorn sport you are! With all the good shows in town, taking a girl to an old barn! Huh!

ALKY: Once we get ahold of that girl, he'll take orders from me. And believe me, I'll show him . . .

GROUCHO: Enough of this small talk, where's your wife Lucille?

ALKY: Would you . . . Sh! Someone's coming. I'll be back.

GROUCHO: All right, be back next Thursday and bring a specimen of your handwriting. And above all, don't worry.

ALKY: Aaah!

ALKY: What are you doing out here? I thought I told you to spy on Helton.

GROUCHO: I *did* spy on him.

ALKY: What was he doing?

GROUCHO: He was spying on me.

ALKY: Did he see you?

GROUCHO: Naw, I was too foxy for him! All he could do was spy on me!

This is beginning to look like *Home Again.* They get off the boat and head straight for a party. Like *Home Again,* though, this serves less as a story line than as a succession of situations. The Party, as a Marx Brothers motif, stretches back to *Mr. Green's Reception* and was used in both their Broadway plays. It is the perfect setup for a burst of welcome insanity: the deadly affair that is supposed to be fun and never is. In this one, there are no headlong dives into divans or piggy-back chases, but Harpo and Groucho do succeed successively at various extravagant attention grabs, both of them knowing full well they are surrounded by a pack of died-in-the-womb time-consumers with a cigarette in one hand and a drink in the other standing around trying to think of something to say, and that anything they can do will come as a relief. The fact that some of the gags are pretty good is almost incidental.

Harpo makes several surprise appearances, not the least of which is as a train to a stately madam's gown. Later, for no good reason, he is seen crossing the lawn on a bicycle with a carnation suspended in front of it. The girl he is chasing is, rather justifiably, screaming. Groucho makes his entrance stalking around the room in a hilarious 270° pan. When he gets to one corner of the room by walking past all the others, he stands on a couch and commands the attention of the entire assemblage. "A lady's diamond earring has been lost," he announces. He holds up a diamond earring and looks at it. "It looks exactly like this." He looks at it again. "In fact, this is it!" And with that, he bounds away.

Groucho spends most of his time on the back porch playing parodies of back-porch histrionics with Thelma Todd. The gangster business is brought in just enough not to intrude. Even the harp and piano solos play rather nicely. Chico wants Harpo to play "Sugar in the Morning," a running gag that has run all the way over from *Animal Crackers*. Joe Helton announces with a horror that his daughter has been stolen. Groucho, taking it all with a grain of mustard, suggests a full-scale picnic in the old barn, and in the mob that rushes out the door Harpo leaps on a dowager's back and Chico exclaims, "I wish *I* had a horse!" and the comedic charm and directorial control that have so fully enchanted us in this picture escape with the rest of the crowd.

THE OLD BARN

This first in a series of regrettable attempts to provide a Marx Brothers movie with a climax demonstrates the key problem the others either fall prey to or manage to ignore: chiefly, it is that a film going nowhere in particular feels pretty sheepish about itself by the time it doesn't get there. Their plays didn't have this problem, since nobody expects visceral excitement from the last scene of a play. But here there are two tasks that must be

COLLECTION OF HARPO MARX

faced: The plot must be settled, and it must be done with a high-intensity action scene. This always seems to be too much for the script writers, who have been working along with no discipline or structure all through the film and have done very well by both. Suddenly everything looks like a strain; the comedy that has sprung naturally from nothing at all seems at a loss for inspiration when presented with a point of departure.

Zeppo fisticuffs it out with Alky Briggs while Harpo and Chico "keep score" and Groucho calls out silly comments from the loft. And then, to finish it all off, to provide us with the final statement and put a capper on the evening's entertainment, what do they give us? Zeppo, in a far shot, being congratulated by Joe Helton for saving his daughter, and Groucho pitching hay furiously to one side. "What are you doing?" Helton turns and asks him. "I'm looking for a needle in a haystack," he answers. Fade out. End title. List of Players.

This? We're left to find our way back into the world by ourselves? How can a film of such strength and determination purport to end in such a limp-wristed, arbitrary gag? It looks like the ultimate in the blueprint routine—they have forgotten what movie they started out to make. They simply close with a show of disgust. Now that the film is over there is nothing left to believe in any more.

"Everybody," says Groucho Marx, "thinks he's an individual and everybody else is nothing." *Monkey Business* is the cinema's strongest expression of that belief. It establishes the Marx Brothers once and for all as the artists of anti-art—that is, while the conventional role of the artist is to impose order on the chaos of life, the Marxes take what order there is in life and impose chaos on it.

In any other comedy about stowaways, the gags would all be about *hiding* from the captain and *eluding* the first mate, not directly confronting them and telling them what you think of them right to their face. According to Harpo, "People all have inhibitions and hate them. We just ignore them. Every man wants to chase a pretty girl if he sees one. He doesn't—I do. Most people at some time want to throw things around recklessly. They don't—but we do. We're sort of a safety valve through which people can blow off steam." Into a world of hungry bread lines and depressing headlines, a world of rules and conventions, a world of stoplights and picket fences, burst this beloved safety valve. *Monkey Business* became one of the biggest hits of the season.

Most of the critics responded with some enthusiasm, but nothing unconditional. *Time* magazine said Harpo was "still the funniest as well as the most versatile Marx," and the New York

Times said, "Groucho carries the show." Both Mordaunt Hall of the New York *Times* and Harry Evans of *Life* pointed out that the movie was full of perfectly awful puns and that somehow the perfectly awful puns were funny. *Life* (then the name of a humor magazine) said that its reviewer would "promptly go into hysterics when Groucho and Chico Marx pull puns that we would never see printed in this magazine if we could help it." *Variety* noticed the constant action and the fast pace and went on to call it "ridiculous throughout and apparently striking the right note at this period." Damn right!

London was less happy. The British *Saturday Review* called it "an antidote for these troublous times," but insisted that it added up to nothing more than foolishness. It called the harp solo "again the real success of the film." So much for the *Saturday Review!*

But over here, all was peaches. Paramount, happy with the receipts, signed the brothers on for two more films, this time at $200,000 per film. The Marx Brothers, happy with the laughs, made more films like it. Though they were never again to make a movie so cluttered with gags and situations, *Monkey Business* established the precedent, in form and style, not only for their later productions but also for the director's—whenever the studio had something offbeat to do during the next several years, they gave it to McLeod.

Many elements in *Monkey Business* pop up in the later Marx films. The jealous husband returning to find Groucho with Thelma Todd (*Horsefeathers*), the stowaways idea (*Night at the Opera*), the gags from the doctor routine (*Day at the Races*), and the bodyguard business (*Big Store* and *Night in Casablanca*) are the most obvious examples.

But *Monkey Business* finds its clearest descendant in a routine Chaplin once admitted he had always wanted to do. "Then there's the gag," he said in a 1957 interview, "about the man who goes to a very pompous dinner party. Everything goes wrong for him. The butler gets his name wrong; his neighbor at table drops butter on his coat; the serving maid pours soup down his neck. He suffers it all with a smile and polite reassurances: 'Oh, please don't bother—it's quite all right.' Then finally, after the last indignity, he goes berserk, runs wildly round the room, breaking the china, scaring the guests, and, at last, setting fire to the place."

This is the routine that the Marx Brothers spent their lives doing. Except, of course, that Marx Brothers movies all begin just after the last indignity has been inflicted.

HORSEFEATHERS 1932

Horsefeathers brings up the problem of *approach*. Now, if you were listening closely to the words instead of just reading along and nodding your head, you would be impelled at this juncture to ask, "Wait a minute! How does a film like *Horsefeathers* bring up a problem like approach??" And then I would come up with some *non-sequitur* answer such as, *Horsefeathers* brings up that problem by being a film about college professors. It pretends to make fun of college and the whole stuffy state of mind that presides there. This makes it a rather odd thing to watch *Horsefeathers* today, because today college professors *like* the movie. They call it "surrealistic." You mustn't mind the college professors for saying this. They enjoy doing things like that, for it gives them a feeling they have accomplished something. It is a no doubt well-intentioned attempt to give the Marx Brothers some legitimacy. This is a little like converting the savage to Christianity. Are you doing the savage a *favor?*

A rational examination of surrealism leads one to the inescapable conclusion that surrealism and Marx Brothers comedy are simply not in the same category.

Surrealism as a school was intended as an assault upon the bourgeois sensibility. *Horsefeathers,* the most surrealistic of all the Marx Brothers films, was perpetrated by people just oozing with bourgeois sensibility. (It is a picture of Lincoln that Harry Ruby displays in his home, not a print by Dali.) Surrealism as a

COLLECTION OF HARPO MARX

school was searching for a new reality beneath the conscious mind, in dream states or in bizarre acts of fate. The Marx Brothers were smugly satisfied with the reality we have now. (The errant destruction of the game of bridge in *Animal Crackers* was accomplished by a bunch of guys just nuts about the game of bridge.) Surrealism as a school was dedicated to what André Breton called "the true functioning of thought, in the absence of all control by the reason." That should be enough to cinch the matter right there, except that Groucho once claimed that the Marx Brothers were after "the overthrow of sanity, to give the brain a chance to develop." This is why I enjoy putting surrealism and Marx Brothers comedy in the same category.

Of course, if you're going to expand the definition of the word "surrealism" just far enough to include absurdist comedy and the Marx Brothers, then there's no reason not to include Norse myths and Saxon tales in the definition, as they seem to be just as committed to the overthrow of sanity. Then again, you must consider William Blake and Hieronymus Bosch. They weren't surrealists either. This line-drawing game can become awfully complicated, but if you just *pay attention* to what's being said, it will become very clear that what the surrealists had in mind was the *demolition of categories*, not the creation of just one more. So much for rational examinations.

It seems reasonably worth noting that the surrealists, generally, as a bunch, indicated a rather strong preference for the idea that the Marx Brothers were the greatest thing since peaches and cream. Philippe Soupalt, who used to walk into cafés yelling, "Everybody switch drinks!" and stop people on the street and ask them for the address of Philippe Soupalt, had friendly words about *Horsefeathers* when it came to France with its subtitles on:

> The comedy of the Marx Brothers lifts us out of reality by exaggerating our peculiarities and aggravating our habits. The real quality of the Marx Brothers and of their extravagant, excessive comedy remains human. They are exactly like ordinary people and act just as we should act if social regulations did not prevent us from behaving in that way. I

believe that, though most films rapidly go out of style, this satiric comedy will make us laugh for a long time to come.

He was right, of course, depending on your definition of "ordinary people."

Antonin Artaud was another surrealist writer and thinker, and when he saw *Animal Crackers* he went bananas. "If there is a definite characteristic, a distinct poetic state of mind that can be called *surrealism*," he said, "*Animal Crackers* participated in that state altogether. The poetic quality of a film like *Animal Crackers* would fit the definition of humor if this word had not long since lost its sense of essential liberation, of destruction of all reality in the mind."

I see. He has decided that *Animal Crackers* is surrealistic, but it isn't humor. It's a good thing we consulted one of these guys, isn't it? Maybe if we consult a film aesthetician about *Horsefeathers,* he'll tell us that it is aesthetic but it isn't a film.

It was an affinity like this that prompted Salvador Dali to write a Marx Brothers script. Salvador Dali had always felt that he and Harpo were kindred spirits, and when at last he first came to the West Coast, to prove it he made a barbed-wire harp tuned with spoons (spoons would have been apropos if Harpo dropped spoons, but he didn't drop spoons, he dropped knives, that's why Dali used spoons) and covered with Saran Wrap, and presented it to Harpo and his wife, who were so pleased that they stuck it in a remote corner of the house and finally threw it away. Kindred spirits though they were, Dali and Harpo soon found that they were totally unable to communicate, since Dali at the time didn't know English. This problem was solved by conversing through Dali's wife, who didn't know English either.

When asked in recent years about the script, Dali grew furious and began beating pigeons with his cane. "No one would *dare* to do Dali's script!" he expostulated, exasperated. Dali had learned English since we last met him.

When asked if there wasn't someone who could find affection for the script, his countenance softened. "Harpo liked it," he said.

Well, Harpo *didn't* like it. *The Marx Brothers on Horseback*

Harpo immortalizes Salvador Dali.   COLLECTION OF HARPO MARX

Salad was full of such characteristic Marx Brothers touches as
flaming giraffes dashing around in the background and flower
gardens blooming forth out of easy chairs. The script was out-
lined in a series of sketches, Harpo's admiration for which he
demonstrated by having them hanged in his living room. The
sketches depict:

    1) An eyeball with twenty-three arms.
    2) A large pair of lips that looks like a couch (or a couch
that looks like a large pair of lips).
    3) Thirty-six arms asleep on a sofa.
    4) Groucho as the Shiva of Big Business, answering ten

Two of Dali's sketches for "The Marx Brothers on Horseback Salad."

telephones with six arms. (Dali liked his Marx Brothers well armed.) One of the lines is busy with an ice-cream soda.

5) Harpo with an apple on his head and his hair full of some sizable crustacean. His harp has a large tongue on it instead of spoons. For some reason, Harpo seems to be playing the harp.

The script was of no visible good and could no more be played than the barbed-wire harp tuned with spoons instead of knives. It had no plot, no logic, no consistency, none of the conventional elements that are unnecessary to Marx Brothers movies. It was absurdity but it wasn't comedy, and, like Dali's script for *Un Chien Andalou,* nothing in it held true long enough to be ridiculed. Harpo was very pleased with the whole affair, got a big kick out of Dali and all the arms, and struck up a lasting friendship that lasted until Dali went home. When Harpo died, he left the script to his beautiful wife, Susan, who, to this day, has lost it.

Surrealism has a way of creeping up on you when you're not really looking for it, or dropping in for the weekend like an uninvited guest. Most days it turns up in the newspaper. You may search the world over to find surrealism, only to discover it in your own back yard. Shakespeare intended his plays to be more or less realistic, but what could be more surreal than a mad Scotsman killing his king and reciting iambic pentameter in the middle of the night to get over the fact? You would almost expect Lady Macbeth to come on stage and say, "What the hell are you doing reciting iambic pentameter at *this* hour?"

For that matter, what could be more surreal than Minerva springing fully grown from the forehead of her dad? Or Beowulf suddenly finding a magic sword on the ground while fighting a battle a hundred miles under water with a vicious monster's *mother?* Or three Oriental kings traveling hundreds of miles at the behest of a star in the sky, only to arrive at a manger, where they leave gifts to the baby being born because they have somehow got the idea he is a Great Teacher, but they don't stick around to hear what he has to say? People of all ages have employed legends, myths, fantasies, religions, and other absurdities to free themselves for brief refreshing moments from the shackles of the humdrum. Nobody really believes a giant lumberjack pals around with a big blue ox, or that skeletons dance in graveyards, or that Neptune broods in the ocean. Nobody even *wants* to believe it. Nobody said they *had* to believe it. But people will remember these things longer than they'll remember that Lincoln is the capital of Nebraska, which they *do* believe. We have a fascination for utter transcendent unlikelihoods that we are not likely to shake, so long as we are human (which should be for at least another few weeks). If we don't get enough of them in our daily life, we make them up in our sleep. Reason, logic, and reality, like calcium, thiamine, and riboflavin, are things Nature never intended us to have a steady diet of.

Now, it is my firm opinion that you've got to watch out for people who call Marx Brothers comedy surrealistic. They can't be trusted. It's *true,* I've decided, but anybody who thinks he must go around saying it can safely be classed as one of The Faceless They. They're like the people who want to explain what makes us laugh. I'm telling you, those rational people will stop at nothing! Once they've set out to explain something, they keep at it till the job is done! The purpose of surrealism, and the purpose of laughter, is a *subjective* purpose. As soon as you've classified it and objectified it, you've killed it. But that won't stop them if they're dedicated.

I should also point out at this time that when Eugène Ionesco, French absurdist playwright and author of *The Bald Soprano,* was asked to name the greatest influence upon his work, he spoke the names of Groucho, Harpo, and Chico Marx. Ionesco was not, strictly speaking, a surrealist, but helped originate a movement called the Theater of the Absurd. Can you call the writers of Theater of the Absurd "surrealists"? *There's* a question to keep you up at night!!

Writing for the Marx Brothers was like no other experience Hollywood had to offer. Norman Krasna, a screenwriter who was a friend of Groucho's but never happened to write a film for the team, has pointed out that, once Hollywood's writers recognized the existence of the Marx Brothers, comedy writing could never be the same again. The Marxes' *non-sequitur,* helter-skelter approach to dialogue meant that the cute and careful contriving of

situations, the tame spacing of punchlines that once characterized comedy writing were beginning to be doubted as articles of
faith. The absurdist strain had entered film comedy as an acknowledged debt to Groucho, Harpo, and Chico.

Harry Ruby affirms that when you sat down to write a script
for these clowns, you went about it like nothing else in the course
of human events. To prepare material for comedians he alternately describes as "iconoclastic" and "*meshuggeneh*," one, he insists, finds oneself going through mental contortions unrecognizable even to schizophrenics. The results of Kalmar and Ruby's
efforts in this direction (*Horsefeathers* and *Duck Soup*) are
without a doubt the weirdest things even the Marx Brothers ever
tried to do—even weirder when you hold them up next to
Kalmar and Ruby's efforts in other directions: their Wheeler
and Woolsey or their Clark and McCullough scripts, where all
the cute and careful contriving is right there where it should be.
Horsefeathers and *Duck Soup* almost look like parodies of everything else Kalmar and Ruby wrote. Oh, here and there you might
find a surrealistic flash, as in *Kid from Spain*, where Eddie
Cantor tries to cross the Mexican border by proving he's a
farmer, and tries to prove he's a farmer by producing a snapshot
of a field. "What's that?" asks the border guard. "That's a picture
of my cow eating corn," replies Cantor. "Well, where's the corn?"
"The cow ate it all." "Where's the cow?" "Well, you don't expect
him to stick around when the corn's all gone, do you?" But somehow Eddie Cantor just doesn't convey the feeling of a hallucination.

And the plot of *Kid from Spain* is too pat. It is one of those
stories where the hero gets himself into some goshawful predica-
ment and has to spend most of the footage getting himself back
out. Ever since *I'll Say She Is*, the Marx Brothers seemed almost
adamant about structuring their performances episodically.
When Chaplin or Keaton (or almost anybody) made features,
they *used* the stories as something to *help* them sustain audience
interest. The Marx Brothers insisted on working *against* their
story, as if it were some sort of referee.

The combination of lunatic dialogue and haywire plotline
resulted in a game that nobody but the Marx Brothers would

play. Mostly, as Ruby attests, because nobody else could pull it off.

A hallucination, as a rule, is not easy to work with. Ask the writers and directors of the Marx Brothers films and the other people who tried their hand at getting along with them. They'll tell you. Ask Herman Mankiewicz's wife.

SARAH MANKIEWICZ: It was like a three-ring circus. I was always screaming, somebody was in back of me, goosing me, they would throw me around, on chairs, on the desk, and they were absolutely wild. Physically manhandling me!

It was pretty orderly when it actually got down to the shooting. It was serious, and they rehearsed, they knew their lines, they knew what they were doing. They were rather meticulous about their comedy.

Ask Teet Carle.

TEET CARLE (Paramount publicity agent): They were wild . . . no doubt . . . oh, gosh . . . wild, wild, wild, wild. Groucho particularly. It was almost impossible to say something to Groucho that he didn't make a laugh out of it. For instance, I went up to him one day—and this would happen a lot— "I have a boy here from Dayton, Ohio . . ." And he said, "I once had a boy in Dayton, Ohio. I wonder whatever happened to him. I must write my first wife."

GEORGE FOLSEY (cinematographer): Groucho just made a joke out of everything. Everything you said to him! They were never uncooperative. I had no problem with them. Technicians *expect* actors to be kind of nuts and impossible and inefficient. D. A. Doran said, "There are three kinds of people: men, women, and actors." You make a picture with Red Skelton, and you can go out of your mind. He's on all the time, and he's very funny. That's the kind of people they are.

HARRY RUBY: We knew the Al Jolsons, the Sophie Tuckers, the Belle Bakers, the Avon Comedy Four. And then along came the Marx Brothers, and they were different from any other people in the business—*entirely different!* Different from anything there ever was in show business!

GEORGE OPPENHEIMER: I found writing for the Marxes spiritually and mentally grueling.

SID KULLER: Every comedian can become exasperating or frustrating, not just the Marx Brothers. The creation of comedy is a painful experience.

S. J. PERELMAN: As far as temperaments and their personalities were concerned, they were capricious, tricky beyond endurance, and altogether unreliable. They were also megalomaniac to a degree which is impossible to describe.

LEO McCAREY: They were irresponsible and I couldn't get them all together at the same time—one was always missing.

MORRIE RYSKIND: If they showed up, you were lucky.

ARTHUR SHEEKMAN: They did nothing to disrupt the picture. I saw *Monkey Business, Horsefeathers* and *Duck Soup* in production, and I never saw them hard to locate. There seem to be conflicting legends going.

GEORGE SEATON: They didn't disrupt the picture, but they kept the set happy. The Marxes would make jokes and ease the tension.

NAT PERRIN: They were very funny guys, but they weren't Katzenjammer Kids. They were pretty reasonable.

ROBERT PIROSH: They were reasonable and helpful.

LEO McCAREY: They were completely mad.

IRVING BRECHER: There is no basis in the assumption that they ran wild and that the pictures just happened to get made. No, really, Groucho will be the first one to tell you that they weren't making up the pictures as they went along.

MORRIE RYSKIND: I don't think there was an excessive amount of improvisation. Basically, the Marx Brothers shows were written.

HARRY RUBY: Sometimes you'd walk in, and they're doing something that you didn't even write!

IRVING BRECHER: They may have occasionally done a tiny bit of changing under the eye of the director, but they never ran wild. As a matter of fact, it took a long time to prepare scripts for the Marx Brothers, because they *wanted* everything down on paper. I devised all the business comedy in *Go West* and *At the Circus.*

SID KULLER: To say that you worked with the Marx Brothers and that you wrote every single line and piece of business is patently untrue and unfair. You've got to have a lot of gall and guts and great imagination to say that.

IRVING BRECHER: That doesn't mean that Groucho didn't occasionally have a line to add to a scene . . . and Harpo would occasionally add a thing to it.

ROBERT PIROSH: A lot of what went on the screen was their material.

HARRY RUBY: In a Marx Brothers picture there was no law and and order. Anything went. Harpo might be sleeping . . . over there; and the other fella might be playin' a trombone in the middle of the thing; and Chico might get up and disappear—say, "Folks, do you mind, I want to, um, I want to go down and get a Coca-Cola," and *not* come back. . . . You never knew how they were gonna come in, how they were gonna dress, what they were gonna do, what they were gonna say. They were just amazing.

IRVING BRECHER: They are not exactly organized performers.

EDDIE BUZZELL: The truth of the matter is that no one can "handle" a Marx Brother. It isn't that they don't know any better or are obstinate. But theirs is a non-conformist sort of comedy.

HARRY RUBY: Do you want to know how to write a Marx Brothers comedy? You're running around the room like this. . . .
—We'll have a girl come in.
—A girl?

—Yeah, a girl.

—Well, so what?

—What do you mean, so what?

MORRIE RYSKIND: I'd be crawling along the floor, saying, "What can Harpo do here?" That kind of thing.

SID KULLER: Working with the Marxes was more than a job, it was a real intellectual experience.

S. J. PERELMAN: It took drudgery and Homeric quarrels, ambuscades and intrigues that would have shamed the Borgias.

NAT PERRIN: I couldn't say I remembered any such thing. There may have been a lot of talking at cross-purposes and very little listening, but I think that was fairly normal for the way comedies of that period were being put together.

HARRY RUBY: It was a different kind of writing! You had to write a different kind of humor!

ARTHUR SHEEKMAN: It's harder working for an extremely intelligent group of people, because they each have their own notions and their own style. It's easier working for a comedian who isn't terribly bright, he does what you ask him to do. And with three or four sensitive and intelligent comedians, there's bound to be concern about whether this one or that one has too little to say or whether his material is inferior to the next man's.

S. J. PERELMAN: I did two films with them, which in its way is perhaps my greatest distinction in life, because anybody who ever worked on any picture for the Marx Brothers said he would rather be chained to a galley oar and lashed at ten-minute intervals than ever work for these sons of bitches again.

SID KULLER: I can never think of them in any terms but happy terms.

NAT PERRIN: I had more fun on their films than I had on the other films I worked on, very definitely.

ARTHUR SHEEKMAN: Well, what's fun? If you work hard on a scene and it comes out funny, you feel you've had a good

time. If the scene doesn't work out, you want to shoot yourself.

IRVING BRECHER: It was a great experience for me, particularly
because they were such great artists. I'd say I enjoyed working with them; it gave me a great deal of satisfaction.

HARRY RUBY: It was a memorable experience. It was the greater
part of my life, it was the greater part of Bert Kalmar's life.

LEO MCCAREY: I didn't like it.

So the Marx Brothers were impossible to work for and a lot
of fun; they did a great deal of improvising and followed the
script exactly; they were extremely crazy and were very serious
men; they were just like every other actor except they were completely different; and they were totally chaotic performers who
did everything they were told. That ought to settle things.

One actress did a skit with the Marxes on radio, and she has
testimony which bears out some of these impressions and contra-
dicts all of them:

The Marx Brothers seemed calm. They stayed calm until
about three hours before air time on the last day. Then Chico
began to brood. He called his brothers and me into a huddle
and dropped his voice to a near whisper, although everyone
else had left for the dinner break.

"We're doing the wrong script," he confided. "It isn't
funny. It isn't *funny*."

"Oh, I don't know," said Groucho, and sat down in the
front row of the auditorium. Harpo, standing on the stage
beside Chico, said nothing.

"Even this one is better," insisted Chico, pulling some
wrinkled pages from his pocket. Slowly and somberly he read
every line of a ten-minute skit, his brothers listening gravely.

"There," he said morosely when he'd ended. "Isn't that
funnier?"

"Oh, I don't know," said Groucho.

Harpo said nothing.

Chico turned to me.

"What do *you* think?" he asked.

"I don't like it," I said. "There's no part for me."

"I hadn't thought of that," he replied with real concern.

Groucho cleared his throat. "I think we'll stick to the first script," he said. "We'll cut the last four lines in the first scene —and segue right into Josephine." He rolled his eyes and flipped his brows at me. "Fine talk!" he added.

"But it's not *funny*," said Chico doggedly.

They had reached a stalemate.

"Groucho is right," said a firm voice.

Harpo had spoken. Chico immediately stuffed the papers back in his pocket and the crisis was over.

The atmosphere before the show was relaxed but serious. Each Marx brother knew that he was flanked by two expert laugh-getters. It made for confidence.

Harpo and I stood alone in the wings, watching the show. Seconds before his entrance he turned to me.

"Think you could find a hammer?" he whispered. "A big one?"

I scurried off to a stagehand and borrowed an enormous one.

"Listen," Harpo said when I returned. "If I put it in my pocket, sit down at the harp, and then take it out—*will that be funny?*"

It was funny, all right. He sat down by the harp, touched the strings, and a look of wild consternation spread across his face. When he pulled out that lethal-looking hammer, the audience convulsed.*

Now, wait a minute! If Harpo wanted to do a gag at the harp, why hadn't he thought about it at least *once* beforehand? And whence did this mysterious second script arise, to appear suddenly in Chico's back pocket? If Chico wanted that other script so badly, why hadn't he said something sooner? You might also notice that Groucho can muster no serious enthusiasm for anything. Neither the accepted script nor Chico's renegade version receive his approval; they only get more or less severe forms of disapprobation. It would not seem calculated to promulgate good will.

---

* Mary Jane Higby, *Tune In Tomorrow* (Ace Publishing Company, New York, 1966).

Perhaps somebody ought to get this straight from the pro-verbial mouths of the proverbial horses—and this is just what somebody on a Los Angeles newspaper did when the proverbial horses were still making films during the Thirties:

QUESTION: Why do you hold story conferences?
GROUCHO: Usually to rewrite what we've done before.
CHICO: And to play tennis afterwards.
QUESTION: What happens at the conferences?
CHICO: We write the story quick and finish with a bridge game.
QUESTION: Does Harpo attend?
CHICO: Not until after we've had the preview.
HARPO (playing the ocarina): Peep, peep!
GROUCHO: Chico isn't really there, either. He's usually talking on the telephone.
QUESTION: Do you think audiences are quicker to "get" a funny point now than before?
GROUCHO: Before what?
QUESTION: Oh, just before.
GROUCHO: Yes. They've heard the same jokes so often they know when to laugh.
QUESTION: Does the same gag get over in all parts of the country?
GROUCHO: It has for the last ten years.
CHICO: Every place but in the theater.*

That ought to settle things.

The actual story of *Horsefeathers* is, on the surface, pretty routine. Bert Kalmar and Harry Ruby were in New York when they got the request to do the next Marx Brothers picture. "What's it about?" they asked. "I don't know," they were told. (The Marx Brothers had given up the stage and decided to keep on making movies until somebody made them stop. It was not that the love of film was in their hearts, as they were by tradition

* Philip K. Scheuer, "Three Marx Brothers Interviewed" (Los Angeles *Times,* June 13, 1937).

a live-performance act and the necessary detachment of the medium kept them one step removed from their audience and their best performance, or that they wanted the money very badly, as they all had plenty of money except Chico, who had none at all, but they had arrived at that time of life when they hungered for a "soft racket." They called film-making a "soft racket" because it was achingly tiresome and remorselessly exhausting, but once the work was over you didn't have to act it out again for every audience in the world until they were sick and tired of it and sick and tired of you and you had to admit you agreed with them; you could attend to your cabbage-trimming and cribbage-kibitzing while the show played to standing ovations on every continent without you. Groucho didn't believe in rushing headlong into production, however; he had definite thoughts about having second thoughts, so he firmly insisted that the Marx Brothers rush headlong into production only once a year, to avoid swamping theater chains with spool after spool of Marx Brothers footage and to avoid rushing headlong into oblivion. So the Marx Brothers made only one film a year, even in 1932, which was mapped as an all-out year for Paramount, who called it Paramount's Paramount Year, which it wasn't.)

Kalmar and Ruby spent some weeks in New York with S. J. Perelman, H. J. Mankiewicz and all four Marx Brothers, collecting vague ideas into amorphous organization, before they took off without Perelman and, on the seventeenth of January, journeyed westward to California for the fourth time in their screenwriting career, whereupon Kalmar and Ruby, like just about everyone who journeys westward to California, settled there for the rest of their lives. (S. J. Perelman, who was elevated, by his work on *Monkey Business*, from the lowly role of struggling cartoonist to the exalted role of struggling screenwriter, still stayed as far away from California as he could. Perelman, one of the great comic essayists of the age, had this brief recurring flirtation with screenwriting, but they never got serious about each other. During the early Thirties, writing for Wheeler and Woolsey and so on was his chief source of livelihood, and as late as 1956 he was writing for as formidable a production as *Around the World*

NOTHING BUT AMOK **175**

in 80 Days, but these are neither his nor filmdom's great accomplishments. According to Perelman, "Writing for the silver screen, like herding swine, makes the vocabulary pungent but contributes little to one's prose style. Unhappily, I had few qualifications for Hollywood: I was immoderately slothful, had no facility for salesmanship or apple-polishing, and possessed a very low boiling point. Faced with hallucinatory tasks like transferring *Sweethearts* into a vehicle for Jeanette MacDonald and Nelson Eddy or distilling a scenario from *How to Win Friends and Influence People,* I became inarticulate and disputatious by turns, a square in a hole full of round pegs. As my shortcomings grew obvious to management, I was given more and more leisure, and lacking the agility to wash windows or harvest oranges, I was forced back willy-nilly to my embroidery hoop." Whatever that means.)

In Los Angeles at the end of the line, Kalmar and Ruby spent some more weeks transforming the amorphous organization into a fuzzy outline, harrowed at every turn by four Marx Brothers and Herman Mankiewicz, a ruthless gang of hard-headed independents who habitually turned a granite ear to the game of Simon Says that constituted Hollywood and weren't going to accept anything without an argument. (One of the first major script conferences for *Horsefeathers* Ruby remembers with especial delight. It started out with that heart-warming invitation, "Whaddya got?"

"I think we got an idea."

"Oh, yeah? What's your idea?"

"Groucho is a college professor."

Granite ears.

"Yeah? What about it?"

"Well, of course he goes against all the rules. And Harpo is a dog catcher. Now in the first scene . . ."

Zeppo was worried enough to ask, "What do I do?"

"What do *you* do? Will you *wait* a minute, Zeppo? We haven't got—"

"All right! All right! I know what happens! I get to announce Groucho at a party again!"

"Zeppo, will you shut up?" said Groucho, with the pretense of quelling this quibble. "Every time you open your mouth, you make less sense than when you *don't* open your mouth."

"In the first scene—"

This was Chico's cue to interrupt the interruption. "Hey, we came to listen to the man, let's listen to the man."

"Better yet, let's *not* listen to the man," retorted Groucho. "Not listening to Harry Ruby is a liberal education."

And this is the way it went on for months.)

Harry Ruby tells the story of the way Vince Barnett confounded things during the final writing stages. Vince Barnett used to pick up jobs as extras and others (he is the funny little illiterate secretary in *Scarface*), when he wasn't pursuing his normal vocation, which was playing an insulting waiter at parties, functions, and special occasions. (Hollywood is the only place in the world where gagsters gather in such numbers that such a demand for insulting waiters is created that one man could fashion a whole career out of it.) In this fine old profession, Barnett was following in the footsteps of his father, a legendary figure in the trade, often referred to by Groucho as "Old Man Ribber."

When the script was nearly finished, Kalmar and Ruby ventured to volunteer another reading, and the Marx Brothers and Co. agreed to assemble in the studio commissary and pass judgment on it.

Suddenly—before the writers have gotten very far, before anybody has even had a chance to interrupt—there comes a disgruntled German dialect floating across from the next table.

"Cheesus, fot kinda chonk is zis?"

The reading deteriorates. There is silence. Maybe he's talking about the food. The Marx Brothers make no reaction. The reading continues. "Now, in the next scene . . ."

"Who rot zis gobbitsch? Did somebody get *pate* for zis?"

Silence again.

"Maybe ten dollas zey give zem, huh?"

"Hey," murmur the writers to their companions. "Who the hell is *he?*"

"I don't know," says Harpo genially. "He's in the picture, I think." Vince Barnett *is* in the picture. He is going to be an extra in the speak-easy sequence. Harpo is right.

"Well, why does the fact that he's in the picture have anything to do with giving him the right to criticize our dialogue?" Vulnerability is at a feverish enough pitch when you're trying to display your own handiwork to a passel of granite ears.

"Oh, don't say anything, Harry." This is the Marx Brothers *avoiding* a scene. "He's a nice guy." They seem to be getting more complacent as the writers get more enraged. The fact that he's a nice guy has probably less to do with anything than the fact that he's in the picture.

"Nice guy!? Nice guy!?" they finally explode. "What's this nice-guy stuff? If we did that to you, would you call *us* a nice guy?"

At the point where Bert Kalmar is making plans to get up and go slug the fellow, the time has come to call off the whole charade, introduce Bert and Harry to Vince Barnett and shake hands all around. Bert and Harry get to know Vince Barnett and he turns out to be a nice guy.

Arthur Sheekman doesn't believe this story, and he tells another one. Sheekman is called in after the script is written to finish a few touches and supply some last-minute hyperboles. In his version of the story, it is the first day of shooting and they are doing the speak-easy sequence, when Vince Barnett walks up to Sheekman and tells him the script for this scene is lousy. This does not especially upset Sheekman for two reasons. First, he has previously been warned that Barnett is a professional heckler and that he's going to say a lot of things he doesn't really mean because somebody has paid him to. Second, he didn't write the script for this scene. He is so singularly unperturbed by the incident that he raises an outrageous fuss. "I suppose you could write funnier stuff!" he proclaims. "I suppose you've written something funny at some point in your life!"

Barnett, looking slightly wounded, tells Sheekman, "Don't give me any of that. You start hounding me, and I'll tell everybody about that extra girl." He is referring to an affair Sheekman once had with an extra. "One more word and I'll tell everybody about her!" But this is Hollywood, and the threat of that revelation distresses Sheekman even less.

"Oh, I suppose you think *you're* funny. Do you think *you're* funny? You're wrong. You better stick with that dog." Barnett is with a dog. "That dog is talented. Without that dog, you're finished."

Whereupon Skeekman goes back to the business of thinking up funny lines for Groucho, and Barnett goes off in a corner to lick his wounds. Later in the day, Chico approaches Sheekman and lets him in on the inside information that somebody has hired Barnett to do this. The struggling writer receives this news with equanimity and a friendly smile. He does the same thing when Harpo tells him the news and the same again with Groucho. Finally Zeppo, who isn't even in the scene, shows up and informs Sheekman that there's a trick being played on him, and by then it isn't even much of a trick any more.

This goes on for three days. Barnett tells Sheekman his script is full of cheap jokes and makes oblique references to his shady past, and Sheekman tells Barnett he doesn't know what he's talking about and doesn't have as much talent as his dog. No matter what Barnett says to Sheekman, he can't churn his bile for all his life is worth, and no matter what Sheekman says to Barnett, he strikes him to the heart. Herman Mankiewicz comes up to Sheekman and tells him he's being joshed and he shouldn't take it seriously. Sheekman smiles. Kalmar and Ruby approach him in secrecy and tell him the same thing. So do Rodgers and Hart, who are working on another film across the lot. People from all over the Paramount studio come to watch this battle of wits on the speak-easy set for *Horsefeathers*. Total strangers approach Arthur Sheekman and tell him in a confidential whisper, "Do you know what? That fellow over in the corner is Vince Barnett. He's making nasty remarks about that script you wrote because somebody paid him to do it. I just thought you should know."

"Oh," Sheekman says to them, his smile dimming.

At the end of the third day, everybody decides the joke has gone far enough, and they introduce Arthur Sheekman to Vince Barnett and shake hands all around. Sheekman never does tell Barnett that he was in on the trick from the beginning, as by this time he is so annoyed by the whole thing that he hates the guy.

Because *Monkey Business* was such a success, Norman McLeod was given the privilege of directing the Marx Brothers again. Some privilege! Because *Monkey Business* was such a success, the Marx Brothers gave themselves the privilege of doing whatever they wanted. All the uncertainties they faced before seemed hardly worth facing again, and their characteristic unruliness was corroborated. Success was approval and liberty was license, and now they were off and running.

Will Johnstone came out from New York again, so he and Harpo spent all their time in another room or home at Harpo's house making up dog-catcher jokes to rival the ones in the script. The combined imaginations of Bert Kalmar, Harry Ruby, Will Johnstone, and Harpo Marx managed to come up with sight gags that called not only for some tricky special-effects contrivance (it was Kalmar and Ruby's idea for a panhandler to make the simple request, "Say, Buddy, could you help me out, I'd like to get a cup of coffee," and for Harpo to respond by reaching into his coat pocket with his accustomed ease and transcendental dexterity and pulling out a *steaming hot* cup of coffee. It was Johnstone's and Harpo's idea to have telephones and slot machines spewing forth quarters to accompany his invasion of the speak-easy) but for a plethora of animals (and their concomitant care and feeding) which included a seal (who chased everybody all over the set), a pig, a duck, a cat, three horses, a dead fish, and a half platoon of dogs (including Harpo's personal dog Kayo).

And Groucho's endearing habit of throwing out perfectly good dialogue and replacing it with more perfectly good dialogue was now backed up by a whole committee of silent-picture gag men, who sat in an office with Arthur Sheekman as their chairman responding to any pangs of doubt Groucho might have recourse to feel while the cameras were turning. When, once in a while, something good came of this, Sheekman would take it to Herman Mankiewicz, who would take it to Groucho, who decided that not much good was coming of this and called it off.

And Chico was no help to matters by breaking some ribs and fracturing a knee when he and a real-estate person smashed cars a few weeks before production was supposed to start.

COLLECTION OF HARPO MARX

The Marx Brothers wouldn't have Norman McLeod to kick around any longer.

Rivalries and camaraderies among the writers ran their usual and unusual gamuts, including a foot race between Harry Ruby and Arthur Sheekman staged on the football field while the final scene was being shot. This was quite a big thing, as Harry Ruby was always the athlete of the bunch and Sheekman actually beat him. Sheekman still recalls the victorious day. "It seemed important at the time," he says.

The usual fussing about the harp and piano occurred, with the usual result that they were included in the festivities, much against the better judgment of everybody. (By now this had been going on for twenty years. But public demand kept it going on for over twenty years more.) Groucho got his revenge in the course of the film, however, by turning to the camera at the beginning of the piano number and announcing how disgusted he was. He also did what he had carefully refrained from doing all through the Twenties: perform resolutely on his favorite instrument, the guitar, for the first and last time in any movie—presumably to show his brothers how silly they looked. It worked. In the next film there was no harp and there was no piano.

And Zeppo? Why, he had no reason to worry about what he would be given to do. He got to play the romantic lead; that precedent was already established. And, since *Horsefeathers* was a musical comedy, the romantic lead would have to sing. So Zeppo sang. This is probably why 1933, which was *not* Paramount's Paramount Year, found him announcing Groucho at a party again.

So, entrusted with the job of directing the directionless, was a man distracted. Poor McLeod was beginning to lose interest in maintaining the directorial control of *Monkey Business*. He was engaged in a battle for his life. He found himself lost on his own set, surrounded by animals, gag men, clowns, and insulting waiters, left with all the decisions made by everybody else, occasionally goosed for his efforts, and tragically ill-equipped to cope with raving mania quadruply personified. (Big-city restlessness and underdog rage are not bred fruitfully in Michigan.) There has never been a director able to tolerate more than two pictures with the Marx Brothers. McLeod, in fact, was the first director in the history of the motion picture ever to hold *that* long a record. By the time *Horsefeathers* was finished, he wanted no part of them ever again, and he restricted himself to ordinary run-of-the-mill fantasies like the Topper films and Paramount's *Alice in Wonderland*.

———————

The script for *Horsefeathers* bears an unusual resemblance to the movie, though they're not exactly twins. Drastic changes occur in instances of Harpo, where the gags originally intended for him turn him into such a silly and insipid character that he could almost be mistaken for Harry Langdon. Almost none of the Harpo gags in the script have found their way into the film, and of the two whole sequences originally intended for him, two of them have been thrown out. The first, in which his stubborn donkey causes a traffic jam and Harpo stumbles around making dumb mistakes like climbing on a woman's back instead of the donkey's and being dragged through the windshield of his truck, is replaced by a much better Johnstone–Harpo routine where he causes the traffic jam on purpose, and his enigmatic nonchalance dumfounds an angry cop. The second—in which he rotates the DOGCATCHER sign on his hat to read KIDNAPPER when he grabs a couple of girls and throws them into a nearby store, and then switches it back to read DOGCATCHER when dogs won't let themselves be caught by a kidnapper, and then switches it to KATNIP-PER when he kidnaps a kitten, and then switches it to DOGCATCHER again when the third girl he grabs turns out to be pretty awful—is not replaced at all, and was apparently photographed and finally excised. The climactic ride to victory in a chariot fashioned out of a garbage wagon is one of the more inspired substitutions.

And while bad Harpo gags were being exchanged for good, good exit gags were being exchanged for nothing. The classroom scene was intended to end with Harpo and Chico beating Groucho in a pea-shooting fight and dragging him out on a stretcher while he moaned, "Bury me near a radio. I don't want to miss Amos 'n' Andy." Now the scene just fades out, unconcerned, in the middle of the pea-shooting. A scene in Groucho's office originally ended with the three of them chasing a seal,

Harpo carrying a secretary out of the room, Chico carrying the chair, and Groucho hanging a sign on the door reading: "Out to Lunch, or No Smoking." Now they just run after the seal and we don't even get to find out if they catch him. The scene in which Connie Bailey falls out of a boat and into the lake no longer ends with Groucho leaping into the water and saving a duck. Connie Bailey sloshes around for a while and then she fades away. It's not as if they didn't have good endings for these scenes. They seem not to have wanted them. It is partly these noncommittal, what-the-hell fadeouts, in place of the snappy laugh finishes we are used to seeing, that are responsible for the strange, willy-nilly atmosphere of this film.

And several of the other changes merit question marks. Groucho was so worried about the quality of the verbal humor that the changes he brought about were not very frequent and didn't make a hell of a lot of difference and were not nearly so constructive as the ones made by Harpo, who didn't let these things bother him. What gets the ax includes some treasures:

ZEPPO: But you can't pick up football players in a speak-easy. It's unethical.

GROUCHO: It is, eh? Well, I'll nip that in the bud. How about coming along and having a nip yourself? Or better still you wait here, and if I'm not back in two days get a couple of bloodhounds and we'll put *them* on the football team.

PROFESSOR: The absorption of oxygen into the blood is taking place every moment of our waking and sleeping hours.

GROUCHO: Excepting February, which has twenty-eight, and every leap year one day more.

PROFESSOR: Any questions?

CHICO: What's got four wheels and flies? A garbage wagon! Ha!

JENKINS: Come out of there and I'll beat you to a pulp.
GROUCHO: If that's your best proposition, I'll stay here.

And included in the film, but chopped after previews, was the following interchange between Groucho the college president and Chico the Prohibition bartender:

GROUCHO: How much do you get for a cake of ice?
CHICO: Well, you see, if you wanta Scotch ice, that's seven dollars a cake. If you wanta rye ice, that's nine dollars a cake. For champagne ice, we get thirteen dollars and twenty cents.
GROUCHO: What's the twenty cents for?
CHICO: For the ice.

Least comprehensible of all omissions is the bit in the football-game climax, where the Marx Brothers steal the referee's whistle and stand in a line and act innocent when he comes to get it back. Groucho gives it all away by blowing the whistle, and the referee grabs it from him, telling him, "You can't do that, even if you are the president." "Aw, what's the good of being president," asks Groucho, "if you can't even blow a whistle?"

Added at the rehearsal juncture were most of the nonsense and hogwash that ends up in Groucho's classroom lecture, and one of the best lines in the film—Groucho's assessment of what it's like to crawl into a barroom on your hands and knees: "That's no way to go into a speak-easy. That's the way you come out."

When *Horsefeathers* had its first public screenings, the insecurity Groucho was fond of feeling turned out to be securely grounded in reality. Groucho and the writers were discouraged to find some of their favorite lines getting nowhere near the response expected of them. Harry Ruby's gag, "I'd horsewhip you if I had a horse," which has remained one of Groucho's favorites for years (and which, like every good line in the movie, people insist on attributing to Perelman), was received with chuckles. Another of Ruby's lines, referring to an Eskimo ("Two thousand dollars for ice?! I can get an Eskimo for two hundred dollars and make my own ice"), was granted a greeting no more spectacular. "Why that didn't get a howl, I'll never know," sighed Groucho. Harry Ruby himself feels that audiences of the time just weren't expecting that sort of dialogue. "The kind I like is too esoteric," he claims.

Well, *Horsefeathers* is esoteric enough to beat the band. Sometimes it's hard to tell *what* response it expects from us. *Horsefeathers* is a Hollywood musical-comedy romance that isn't a Hollywood musical-comedy romance, it is a series of April Fool's jokes that throws logic to the winds of March, a succession of digressions on no point at all, a progression from whim into whimsy, a chain of the unexpected with all the links missing. Its writers were more at home with *Duck Soup*, its director was more at home with *Monkey Business*, and its stars were more at home with *Animal Crackers*. Call on *Horsefeathers* sometime, and nobody is at home, and that is its random and disordered charm, its tragic flaw and its comedic reward. If you collect enough insanity in one place, the s will fall out.

The rebellion and momentum of *Monkey Business* are gone; the characters of *Horsefeathers* are not stowaways or outlaws: They are in no danger and can do whatever they want. The question we ask of them now is not "How did you get away with that?" but "Why on earth would anybody want to *do* such a thing?" The actions of *Horsefeathers* are like the sentences of *Animal Crackers;* no sooner do they make up their mind where they're going than they change it and shoot off somewhere else. The title of *Horsefeathers* is from a Barney Google cartoon of 1928.

Horsefeathers' director of photography, Ray June, was singled out by Lewis Jacobs as one of America's better cameramen. In *Horsefeathers* he actually succeeds in getting one pleasing image or two, but most of the time his camerawork is characterized by a lot of aimless panning and random framing that simply makes the movie look like it was shot in a hurry. Ray June was apparently just as baffled as everyone else. Some of the sets threaten collapse.

There are, here and there, scattered throughout the world, funnier films than *Horsefeathers,* but there are none, anywhere, more winningly quixotic.

I'M AGAINST IT

GROUCHO: You're a disgrace to our family name of Wagstaff, if such a thing is possible. What's all this talk I hear about you fooling around with the college widow? No wonder you can't get out of college. Twelve years in one college! I went to *three* colleges in twelve years and fooled around with *three* college widows! When I was your age I went to bed right after supper. Sometimes I went to bed *before* supper. Sometimes I went without my supper and didn't go to bed at all! A college widow stood for something in those days. In fact, she stood for plenty!

ZEPPO: There's nothing wrong between me and the college widow.

GROUCHO: There isn't, huh? Then you're crazy to fool around with her.

ZEPPO: Aw, but you don't . . .

GROUCHO: I don't want to talk to you again about this, you snob. I'd horsewhip you if I had a horse! You may go now. Leave your name and address with the girl outside, and if anything turns up we'll get in touch with you. . . . Where you going?

ZEPPO: Well, you just told me to go.

GROUCHO: So that's what they taught you in college. Just when I tell you to go, you leave me!

Introductions are always awkward, it seems, and *Horsefeathers* tackles the problem of introducing Groucho to an unsuspecting audience by assuming that we all know what's going on, that we just got finished watching *Monkey Business,* that we have all suffered the last indignity together, that the overthrow of reason is an established fact.

On February 9, 1713, the Vice Chancellor of the University

of Leipzig, who was H. L. Mencken's great-great-great-great-grandfather but was not aware of it at the time, stood up before the entire faculty and student body of the University and, in a carefully written speech couched in official-sounding Latin phrases, denounced the teaching of anything so unscientific as Newton's Law of Gravity, denounced all the students for being students, and denounced the professors for teaching them to be students. Oddly, the assemblage grew unsettled.

In 1932, Groucho does the same thing at Huxley College, but not without denouncing himself for doing the denouncing. The auditorium stage is peopled with capped and bearded fogies in flowing robes and grizzled chops (a stereotypecast image left over from the Sunday comix and high-school teachers' terror tactics) who have appointed Groucho Marx, of all beings, to be head of their establishment. (Their logic for this choice has been thrown to the winds along with the rest of the logic and their reason for the decision has been overthrown as part of the overthrow of reason.) Groucho denounces the discriminating taste of the faculty, belittles them, pulls their beards, and makes them look silly. Naturally, they respond by acting flattered. They congratulate him. They gush. Is this a satire on incompetence in the halls of higher learning? Not much, because the satire hasn't gotten anywhere before it turns into an auction, and the auction turns into a scolding, and the scolding into threats of adultery, which is the cue for a song, which is the cue for another song, which becomes a lecture on prudence, which becomes a lecture on non-prudence, becomes critical to the plot, becomes critical of the dialogue, becomes dig, becomes jig, becomes mourning, becomes elections, becomes a pumpkin at midnight, becomes the first song again. All this within five minutes without changing locale.

Now we can see that the next hour affords us two options: We can either let these freelance pot shots at the world take us on a trip down choppy moonlit waters into vertigo, or we can summon up all our critical faculties and walk out of the room.

THE PASSWORD ROUTINE

CHICO: Who are you?

GROUCHO: I'm fine, thanks, who are you?

CHICO: I'm fine, too, but you can't come in unless you give the password.

GROUCHO: Well, what is the password?

CHICO: Aw, no! You gotta tell *me*. Hey, I tell what I do. I give you three guesses. . . . It's the name of a fish.

GROUCHO: Is it Mary?

CHICO: Ha ha! Atsa no fish!

GROUCHO: She isn't, well, she drinks like one. Let me see . . . is it sturgeon?

CHICO: Ah, you crazy, sturgeon he's a doctor, cuts you open whenna you sick. . . . Now I give you one more chance.

GROUCHO: I got it! Haddock!

CHICO: Atsa funny, I gotta haddock too.

GROUCHO: What do you take for a haddock?

CHICO: Wella, sometimes I take-a aspirin, sometimes I take-a Calamel.

GROUCHO: Say, I'd walk a mile for a Calamel.

CHICO: You mean chocolate calamel. I like that too, but you no guess it. Hey, whatsa matter, you no understand English? You can't come in here unless you say sword-fish! Now I give you one more guess.

GROUCHO: Swordfish . . . I think I got it. Is it swordfish?

CHICO: Hah! At's it! You guess it!

GROUCHO: Pretty good, eh?

In Scene 1, Zeppo sends Groucho to the speak-easy to get football players; in Scene 2, Groucho shows up at the speak-easy looking for football players. That's it! That's the beginning and the end of cause and effect in this movie! It was only put in there to tease you.

In Scene 1, Groucho's song is called "Whatever It Is, I'm Against It," and the second verse—which is a different song—is called "I Always Get My Man." Then, as soon as Zeppo comes up with a plan, Groucho is *for* it—and he goes to the speak-easy and gets the wrong men. That's more like it.

Groucho arrives at the speak-easy with stately aplomb and full attire, dropping his dignity whenever dignity is called for and exercising his dignity when there is no use for it at all, to meet his first challenge as president of Huxley College (and the outrageousness of his being in that position is confused by the outrageousness of a man in that position being in this position): to battle his way past a speak-easy door without knowing the password. His weapons: only the tools and devices of the English language. Soon the battlefield is strewn with sentence fragments, mangled metaphors and broken chains of association. Was ever clash of Moor or Saracen more gruesome?!? Chocolate Calamel?— Atrocity!

And so it goes, from one knowing the password and making the other one guess, to both knowing the password and congratulating each other, to neither knowing the password and both sitting outside on the sidewalk. Arbitration and bargaining reach the stalest mate possible.

When Harpo encounters the despondent pair outside the speak-easy, he is introduced as Chico's partner. (Like all icemen, Chico has a dog catcher for a partner.) Unarmed (without English), Harpo bypasses all this squabbling and makes it into the speak-easy without a fight. Once there, the place surrenders to him. So does the sequence, and though his brothers make futile stabs at reclaiming it, nobody ever hears them, or the sounds they appear to make, while Harpo is stretching his luck across the room, hitting the jackpot at a slot machine, a pay telephone, and a trolley conductor's change belt, one after the other. No device is ever a match for him. On that fateful day when machines move in and take over the race, the Harpos of the world will be flitting around fitlessly pulling out plugs.

Harpo dances an ethnic jig for the bartender, when anyone else would let a laconic "Scotch" suffice. (He makes the gift of speech look like a prosaic thing to have to go through life with.) When he passes a table of card players and one of them says, "Cut the deck," you *know* what's going to happen, but you know just as well that it *couldn't* happen, and then lo! an ax appears before them, and *thonk!* the halves are scattered to the four corners of the room. And they were sore annoyed. (Not afraid. Not the least bit startled. Just annoyed. They seem quite tired of having people chop their cards in half.)

When Groucho and Chico entered, they were crawling on the floor, which, Groucho explained, was the proper way to leave. Now, when they do leave, they run out shouting the password. This is perfectly appropriate. It allows us to see which direction this film is going: backwards.

REASON PUDDING

GROUCHO:	Where would this college be without football? Have we got a stadium?
PROFESSORS:	Yes.
GROUCHO:	Have we got a college?
PROFESSORS:	Yes.
GROUCHO:	Well, we can't support both. Tomorrow we start tearing down the college.
PROFESSORS:	But, Professor, where will the students sleep?
GROUCHO:	Where they always sleep. In the classroom.
SECRETARY:	Oh, Professor. The Dean of Science wants to know how soon you can see him. He says he's tired of cooling his heels out here.
GROUCHO:	Tell him I'm cooling a couple of heels in here. Where were we? Oh, yeah. How much am I payin' you fellas?
PROFESSORS:	$5,000 a year. But we've never been paid.
GROUCHO:	Well, in that case, I'll raise you to $8,000. And a bonus. Bring your dog around, and I'll give him a bonus, too.

Each Marx Brother has his own form of comedy. Zeppo is at his funniest when he opens his mouth and sings. It has taken forty years, of course, for the full humor of this to come across.

For a normal comedian this may be bad timing, but for a Marx Brother it's immortality. Almost every crooner of 1932 looks stilted and awkward now, but with Zeppo, who was never very convincing in the first place, the effect crosses the threshold into lovable comedy. "I think you're wonderful!" he oozes charmingly to Thelma Todd, and we *know* he never met her before shooting started.

When he launches into Kalmar and Ruby's song "Everyone Says I Love You" (which people are rumored to have *liked* in 1932), the scene shifts to Harpo, who finishes it up whistling. He then performs his pantomime specialty with a cop, where he displays a respect for rules and regulations rivaled only by his reverence for machines and passwords. For a finish Harpo locks his adversary into the wagon with the rest of the dogs.

What nobody in this film seems to have caught on to yet is that it all takes place in a college, where supposedly intelligent people exchange ideas and develop thoughts. They haven't even *tried*, with the single solitary exception of Groucho's secretary, who sashays into his office with news of the impatience of the Dean of Science in the next room, and chooses to express it intellectually. "The Dean," she announces, "is furious! He's"—are you ready?—"waxing wroth!" Only Perelman would think "waxing wroth" was a way for anybody to say "He's angry."

"Oh," says Groucho, giving her everything she deserves, "is Wroth out there, too? Tell Wroth to wax the Dean for a while!"

Then Chico and Harpo clamber in (the Dean of Science is refused admittance, but an iceman and a dog catcher have no problem) and proceed to deliver the ice. (Ice in a professor's office is hidden stealthily behind a picture on the wall, plainly based on the concept of reversible slang: If diamonds can be referred to as "ice," then ice must *be* diamonds.) Harpo picks up a book of his father's life and throws it on the fire. Chico makes some bad jokes and useless puns. When we next see Harpo, he is *shoveling* books into the fire. He does this because there is plainly a fire in the fireplace. They all exit, following a seal.

FUN IN KOLIJ

GROUCHO: As you know, there is constant warfare between the red and white corpuscles. Now then, baboons, what is a corpuscle?

CHICO: That's easy. First is a captain, then is a lieutenant, then is a corpuscle.

GROUCHO: That's fine. Why don't you bore a hole in yourself and let the sap run out? We now find ourselves among the Alps. The Alps are a very simple people living on a diet of rice and old shoes. Beyond the Alps lies more Alps and the Lord Alps those that Alp themselves. We then come to the bloodstream. The blood rushes from the head down to the feet, gets a look at those feet, and rushes back to the head again. This is known as auction pinochle. Now, in studying your basic metabolism, we first listen to your hearts beat; and if your hearts beat anything but diamonds and clubs, it's because your partner is cheating, or your wife. . . . Now here is a most unusual organ. The organ will play a solo immediately after the feature picture. Scientists make these deductions by examining a rat, or your landlord, who won't cut the rent. And what do they find? Asparagus! Now, on closer examination . . . Hm! This *needs* closer examination. In fact, it needs a nightgown. Barivelli, who's responsible for this? Is this your picture?

CHICO: I no think so. It doesn't look like me.

I know! I know what you're going to say! There's nothing plausible about a seal in a professor's office, and it doesn't make sense. You might just as easily argue that a seal isn't a natural inevitable result of everything that's gone before. We all know we'll never see an arctic seal in a professor's office, just as we know we'll never see a green sunset or the planets of Betelgeuse or an honest encyclopedia salesman. That doesn't improve the situation. What is the plausible but the most inexhaustible source of the commonplace?

Some day somebody will explain why the road to greater happiness is filled with such unhappy things as biology lectures. The professor stands there and talks about respiration as if he were talking about life, with the resigned tone of voice that must make it a chore for even him to listen to what he is saying. Somewhere in the classroom is maybe one person who will learn about this stuff if it kills him, and if it kills him enough he'll become a professor.

Horsefeathers' idea of college is all speak-easies, dog catchers and football, and its idea of a college professor must rank somewhere between Captain Hook and the Sheriff of Nottingham on the believability charts. Robert Greig plays the professor in this scene, and he gives the part all the shallow and incompetent treatment he gave the part of the butler in *Animal Crackers*. A professor who confuses the quest for knowledge with the possession of it is being played by an actor who confuses playing a part with reciting dialogue.

The professor is honored by the presence of a belligerent Groucho, who delights him with the presence of two eager young students (Harpo and Chico, who have not been in the room a full minute before they have started running around, making time with the coeds, and fighting with each other over chairs). Soon Groucho and his brothers understandably tire of the presence of the professor, and once old Life-in-Death is ushered out of the room and the ghastly alabaster sign of decay is clattered to the floor ("Take that, you numbskull!"), things can start happening.

Groucho confuses himself with a corpuscle and goes on its journey, he shows us the Alps that lay stretched between the pancreas and the small intestine, and he finds a horse who reminds him of Zeppo. For reasons not clear even when explained, Groucho finds it useful to admonish Harpo with the old "As you grow older, you'll find you can't burn the candle at both ends!" routine. It takes Harpo perhaps a third of a second to produce the candle burning at both ends which he keeps in his

inside pocket. Groucho, stunned, is forced to recant. ("I knew there was *something* you couldn't burn at both ends.") The president of a college has been shouted down by a mute.

Harpo and Chico, who have stolen the professor's cap, gown, and beard, pep up the lesson with whatever charts and diagrams they have handy, and when they run out of charts and diagrams they pep up the lesson with a pea-shooting match. Groucho fires right back, but they are too much for him and down he goes, elucidating von Steinmetz to the very end.

That's two down. Champion the plausible and the commonplace for just one second and you're doomed.

THE ICEMAN LEAVES ME COLD

GROUCHO: Are you Miss Bailey? Come, come! One of us is Miss Bailey, and I'm not!

GIRL: I'm Miss Bailey, and who are you?

GROUCHO: I'm Professor Wagstaff. Who are you?

GIRL: Miss Bailey!

GROUCHO: Ah, then you *are* Miss Bailey! Thought you could slip one over on me, didn't you? Listen, Madam, you've got to give my son up.

GIRL: Give him up?

GROUCHO: You *can't* take him from me! He's all I've got in the world, except a picture of George Washington crossing the Delaware.

GIRL: But, Professor, I . . .

GROUCHO: Whatever you say is a lie! He's only a shell of his former self, which nobody can deny. Whoopie! I tell you, you're ruining that boy, you're ruining him. Did my son tell you you have beautiful eyes?

GIRL: Why, yes.

GROUCHO: Told *me* that, too! Tells that to everyone he meets! Oh, I love sitting on your lap. I could sit here all day if you didn't stand up.

In a man's college years, there arises only one impulse stronger than the impulse to throw the professor out the classroom window—and here, in this scene, in Connie Bailey's bedroom, we shall examine that impulse. Like all the other scenes in *Horsefeathers,* this opens with harmonious monotony and proceeds capriciously into dynamic bedlam: a scene that starts out resembling domestic comfort closes with everyone dashing back and forth and Groucho flying through the air and thudding to the ground.

In his tranquility, Jennings, the rival of everybody, gets as far as the coatrack, where he takes his coat, and—bingo!—Harpo the household imp appears (whom nobody in the room is perceptive enough to see) and commences scurrying about, doing Jennings' kissing for him and attending to his daffodil (Jennings keeps a daffodil in the collar of his coat). Groucho's entrance, heralded by the absence of a knock, is forecast by a worried Zeppo, fearful of his father's wrath. (Groucho's off-screen image somehow becomes the Apotheosis of the Puritanical Victorian. On screen, of course, he turns into the usual bundle of self-contradictions and fripperies. One wonders how his son is capable of deciphering enough of his babble to understand that he is angry.) His first deed, once in the room, is to make a vicious stab at an introduction. He reaches into his vest, pulls out nothing where a calling card should be, shows it to Connie, and *puts it back.* (He knows he hasn't shown her anything but his thumb and forefinger. He knows he has made things just less clear than they were before. But if he had it to do all over again, he'd do it the same way. Material objects are unimportant and it's the gesture that counts.) No sooner has he done that than he is on the couch making love to Connie Bailey (you remember Connie; she's the one he's been telling Zeppo to give up), then, as soon as he is caught with her, starting in on Zeppo again, this time for taking her away from him, then announcing his plans to marry this girl he's just met and telling his son to leave, then saying no, I'll leave with you, then *not* leaving with him but closing the door after him, then leaving a light in the window *to await his return*—all in the space of perhaps one breath (interrupted only by Harpo, who delivers the ice). Groucho goes on to make a series of exits and entrances, each time putting on and taking off his rubbers (a rather crude visual pun) and putting up and taking down his umbrella (cruder and more visual) to prepare himself for the rain outside (there's no sign of rain outside) and alternating doors with Harpo (whose mission with the ice will let nothing stand in its way, not even Connie's not wanting any), and, finally, having to share his spot next to Connie with Chico. (You're going to ask when Chico came in. I just don't know any more.) Everyone goes through with the part he's been given as if it were inexplicable, inescapable, ineradicable, and inevitable. Fate. Chico sits uninvited on the couch, Groucho sits unquestioningly beside him, Harpo stomps through with the ice, drops it out the window, and leaves. There could be no argument.

The Marx Brothers seem determined to strip the bedroom situation of all its anxieties, and even though this is the fourth version of this scene—running around shutting doors on each other and ducking into closets and hallways and coming in and out of various positions on the couch—the excuses and intrigues to rationalize it all have been peeled away. Though what is left is pretty impotent as far as plotting is concerned, it is enticing enough comedically for the erection of a whole entrance-and-exit orgy, and everyone just goes in and out for the sheer joy of doing it again.

Harpo's adventures alone with Connie are no less a sideshow: he does headstands in Connie's lap and makes faces at her and hides beneath her on the couch; Groucho asks directions of her and watches assorted arms point in three directions at once (he comes looking for sex and gets a brahma); the rubbers find their way to Harpo's feet (they never *get* there, they're just there) and when Groucho can't locate his own feet he replaces the rubbers on Connie's feet again (he thinks Harpo's feet are Connie's feet); and in the middle Chico's piano grinds the whole thing to a halt, just to bring us out of our reverie.

The television people have removed from the print the scene with Harpo but left in the scene with the piano. Television people have a strange idea of good taste.

GAMES COMEDIANS PLAY

CHICO:	You gotta brother?
FOOTBALL PLAYER:	No.
CHICO:	You gotta sister?
FOOTBALL PLAYER:	Yeah.
CHICO:	Wella, you sister she's a very sick man, you better come with us.
FOOTBALL PLAYER:	Yeah? What happened to her?
CHICO:	She hadda accident in her automobile.
FOOTBALL PLAYER:	Ah, she has no automobile.
CHICO:	Wella, maybe she's-a fall offa horse, I no look very close. Come on, we take you in our car.
FOOTBALL PLAYER:	You will, eh? Well, I have no sister.
CHICO:	That's all right, we no gotta car. Come on.

It goes on and on. The next in our series of picaresque episodes finds Groucho in the locker room, and Groucho finds Chico in a locker, crouching down calling numbers to himself. ("I'm practicing secret signals" is his only justification. I suppose *you* could do better.) The two lapse into some banter about a chauffeur who doesn't have anything to do with the story, which doesn't have anything to do with the story. What makes the Groucho–Chico routines funny is that they have nothing to do with the story, but this routine doesn't even have *nothing* to do with the story.

Then Connie goes after Groucho to get the Huxley team's signals. (Why, that's the first place I'd look if I wanted a football team's signals—the coat pocket of the president of the college.) When Groucho discovers that's what's on her mind, he drowns her in the lake like his guitar. She cries out for a lifesaver. Guess what he throws her. Just guess. She meets a very sad end.

The big football-game climax is like the climax to *The Freshman,* but not enough. Watching Harold Lloyd trying to play along with the rules is very amusing, but the rebels of *Animal*

Crackers were better off playing football around Mrs. Rittenhouse's piano. Even in a scene which is a bad idea, funny things keep happening. Groucho goes to a microphone in the middle of the game and announces the birth of twins to an unseen Mrs. Moscowitz. The Marx Brothers worrying about a football game can't look like anything but a copout, but the Marx Brothers performing a copout can't even look like a *real* copout.

Will Cuppy once described Philip II of Spain as a man who "was famous for never having any fun—he thought having fun was a waste of valuable time, so he spent twelve hours a day in his office making memoranda on little pieces of paper. Many years later these memoranda were carefully collected, classified, tied into packets, and thrown out." Here and there, *Horsefeathers* gets around to making this comment about college professors. But for the most part, *Horsefeathers* is a film that is three generations and a half continent removed from anything that has to do with college. This might have some relation to the fact that it is a film made by a lot of people who never went there (namely, Kalmar, Ruby, and all four Marx Brothers). Part of the success of *Animal Crackers* and *Night at the Opera,* after all, hangs on their ability to come up with credible arsenals of opposition strong enough to provide a contrast. The best that *Horsefeathers* can come up with is junior high school.

However, if they *had* set their scene squarely in the college situation of 1932, it wouldn't have much to do with colleges today. Even what is taught there has changed, all the way from the laws of physics to the "important" writers of literature. Only frustrations, fantasies and final exams remain constant.

Horsefeathers' commercial success was almost necessarily a letdown after the trails blazed by its predecessor. Critical reception ranged chiefly from cool to lukewarm, and reviewers, calling it "forced" and "inadequate," were adept at providing superficial reasons for its disappointments: Harpo should never be photographed in closeup, Groucho should have given classes in sex education, and other such verbal popcorn.

Forsythe Hardy, in Edinburgh's short-lived *Cinema*

Quarterly, had similar criticisms, calling it nothing more than a collage of "mad moments and expert wisecracks . . . the madness lacks a method and the picture a plan," thereby sizing up all its virtues and calling them a vice. Film criticism has been known to change its mind, too. Almost as often as the laws of physics.

In London, though, the *New Statesman and Nation* had other things to say. Allowing that the comedy bits amount only to "a series of cul-de-sac," it applauded the Marxes' consistent refusal to make any appeal to sentimentality and pointed out that their nonsense makes subconscious sense. "They gave the old *motif* a new twist," it said, "when they introduced the psychological disturbance that is caused by seeing something that is mad and aimless . . . something which, if not utterly disconnected, depends for its connections on the workings of the unconscious."

Turns out old Philippe Soupalt, the surrealist lunatic, was right; we *do* still laugh at *Horsefeathers,* forty years after it was made. There was no logic to what he was saying; all that prattle about "ordinary people" didn't make much sense. The other reviewers were much more logical when they took the movie apart and carefully told us what was wrong with it. But, like anything with only logic to hold it together, their criticism fell to pieces and washed away, while the movie is still there.

The world is a different place than it was in 1932, and nothing looks very much the same, but college professors still talk as if there is something you could know for certain, and myths and dreams and fantasies and absurdities are still considered one of those extraneous sides to human nature, that we could do without and really will one of these days, although somehow they keep popping up and calling themselves "surrealism" or something and causing trouble.

So *Horsefeathers* has nothing to do with the reality of college, just like it has nothing to do with the reality of anything else. It is nothing but a mock of the world we know, nothing but a myth that makes another myth out of objective reality.

All our desperate attempts to make sense out of things are doomed to failure sooner or later. Every certainty a man can invent is certain to be contradicted by some other certainty.

Like all certainties, this is not true. And if it were true, it would contradict itself.

DUCK SOUP 1933

Duck Soup raises the question of *intent,* and it does that mostly because as the film progresses it becomes a point of befuddlement just what anybody was *intending* by any of it. Marx Brothers movies and plays, as we have already seen ample evidence to demonstrate, have tended to become opportunities for the personalities of the Marx Brothers to wreak themselves on various aspects of the world. Part of the reason *Duck Soup* is such a great comedy is that it is the result of a clash between the comic personalities of the Marx Brothers and another comic personality equally prodigious. Now, a clash of personalities isn't *necessarily* going to result in a great movie. But if all the personalities involved are comic geniuses, that seems to help.

First, there was the Marx Brothers. By 1933, the film colony was getting used to having a few of them running around loose and even got a furtive thrill out of catching sight of them here and there. One encrusted matron was sure she recognized the Marx Brother out of make-up who was lounging with Eddie Cantor at the Brown Derby and saw to it that he recognized her. "Are you *Harpo Marx?*" she almost insisted.

"No," snorted Groucho. "Are you?"

Louella Parsons should have known what to expect when she came to call on the little imps at the studio one comfortable afternoon to gather up some tidy witticisms for her millions of readers. What she got was a dirty old crack about Louella Parsons that she couldn't even print without making herself look stupid.

And William Randolph Hearst's reaction must have been

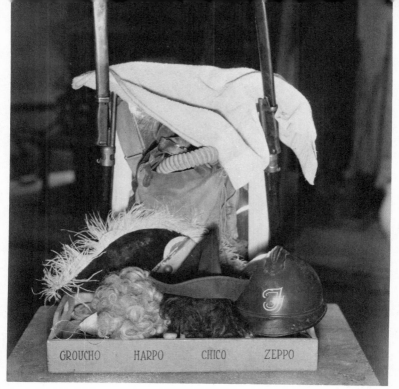

GROUCHO   HARPO   CHICO   ZEPPO

something less than surprise when he invited Harpo up to San Simeon, his personal museum of the remnants and mementoes and triumphs and failures of civilizations dead and buried, and arose one fine morning after a snowstorm of Ice Age fury to discover that ten of the more statuesque marble nudes in the West Courtyard had been gallantly defended against the cold with the finest furs of his female guests.

Paramount Pictures, too, was forced to adjust to the reality of their existence. The day they infiltrated the hallways shortly after daybreak and shuffled all the name plates on the office doors, so that officials and executives spent half the morning getting their appointments wrong and making unwelcome new friends, was remembered by many and excused by even less. Just as fondly cherished was their habit of pausing in the midst of exit-and-entrance conferences with set designers to look at each other and declare (taking their cue from the word "exit"), "Oh! Exit!" and exit.

Groucho, Harpo, and Chico allowed all their serious business to be handled by Rachel, a convenient secretary whom they kept encased in an office high atop some old degenerate stairs suspended over a real-estate firm. Groucho would call her once every hour or so and say, "What's new, Rachel?" so that she could say, "Nothing, Groucho," and he could hang up. Harpo, whose only religion was that he didn't believe in stairs, would whistle to Rachel from the street to let down her basket, so that he could take care of all the really important things on the curb of Beverly Drive. Harpo, whose memory for girls was about on a par with his memory for everything else, had Rachel keep a little black book for him, to keep track of which ones were worth taking out again. Rachel's prime duties, in fact, were keeping track of girls for Harpo, books for Groucho, and bridge fourths for Chico, and just generally keeping track of the office, so *that* load was off their minds.

Now and again, however soothed they were by the balmy tropics of California, a yen would blossom for the slush and soot of grotesque old New York, and one day, while Harpo and Charlie Lederer were lounging around San Simeon with nothing much to do but recline amid the relics and shadows of our forgotten ancestors and contemplate the cumulonimbi in the California sky, it entered their head to revert back to the Mystic East and drop in on their old friend and fellow croquet-player Alexander Woollcott, whom they hadn't seen in a sloth's age. Without pause, then, they proceeded by limousine, airplane, seaplane, rented car, and rowboat (in that order) to the island of Neshobe, where they reverted to aboriginal nakedness, leaped out of the bushes, and said, "Boo!" Woollcott, who was playing croquet, said, "It's your shot now, Alice." Having accomplished their original intention, they proceeded by limousine, airplane, seaplane, rented car, and rowboat (not in that order) back to Hearst's Xanadu, to resume swallowing dragonflies and staring at five-thousand-year-old naked women.

Groucho, sporting one of his favorite hobbies, the game of tennis, jumped through the hoopla surrounding the Beverly Hills

Tennis Club's grand opening of a new clubhouse and ignited the nice America vs. England match they had planned for him (pitting Ellsworth Vines and Groucho Marx against Fred Perry and Charlie Chaplin) by sparking Chaplin's annoyance into burning rage every other minute with his suitcase and his wisecracks. Chaplin, who took his tennis as seriously as he took everything else, was determined to grit his teeth and sweat at the palms. Groucho, who also took his tennis as seriously as he took everything else, showed up with twelve rackets and a suitcase, as if he were going to swing through twelve rounds of tennis and then take off for Madagascar. When Chaplin asked, less out of concern than irritation, what in God's name might be contained in that suitcase, Groucho answered, in effect, that those tennis players proficient enough to carry suitcases were rarely so foolish as to give away their contents. But he finally did give away its contents, after two rounds of straight unfunny tennis, when it developed that the contents were a picnic lunch, which Groucho spread out all over his portion of the court, and gave away generous portions of it to his opponents. This only prompted the unappreciative Chaplin to rise to the heights of his temperament and threaten apoplexy. "I didn't come here to be your straight man!" he protested. That's what *he* thought.

Another one of Groucho's hobbies was not going swimming in his back-yard pool. He specifically kept no swimming pool in his back yard for just this purpose. Groucho remained entrenched in a tradition where pool was something you did in your cellar, but he was quick responding to invitations to help fill somebody else's pool with people, like when film director Archie Mayo, who was in the process of moving in across the street, happened to make the neighborly remark, "Any time you want to drop in, drop in," before he chugged down the street to attend to some matter he really had his mind on, and hardly had he turned the first corner before Groucho, twelve-year-old Arthur, and six-year-old Miriam were lollying and gagging about the Mayo pool. This was a very genial arrangement to just about everybody, except Mrs. Mayo, who had been informed neither of the invitation, nor of her neighbor's identity, nor of what Groucho Marx looked like out of make-up, and who suddenly loomed up from out of the foliage to find three complacent strangers in her back yard, and who could only gasp in astonishment, in vain hopes of scattering the group. Groucho, charmer that he was, never bothered to mention that they had been properly invited, but only glared at her resentfully, as if she were The Lady from Shanghai, and filled her in on the information that they were three strangers who had happened into her back yard. The good woman, in her shock and disbelief, was unable to come up with any objection on a level beyond "Scat!" and "Shoo!" while Groucho, in his amusement, was making perfectly ordinary conversation like "As long as I'm going to swim here, I wish you'd see that the water is heated. It's a little too cold for my blood." This sent Mrs. Mayo nearly to the point of popping, so she bustled next door to call the police to put a stop to all this.

Then, upon Mrs. Mayo's return to the yard and entry into the house, Groucho strolled, dripping, into her new home behind her, followed by his two obedient children. The sight that greeted his eyes was a series of opulent walls and staircases but no furniture as yet, causing him to remark that he considered it mighty strange to see a family putting a pool in its back yard when it couldn't even afford furniture, but that he had grown to expect such things of Hollywood folk. His hostess then showed her true colors by turning livid with rage, purple with anger, white with wrath, and blue in the face, all at once, and she remained that way until the police showed up in prosaic black and white to haul this vagrant away. They asked for his name and he, staunchly refusing to be intimidated by propriety, told them it was Julius H. Marx, which was perfectly true, and they were on the verge of shoving him and his litter in the squad car when he mentioned that he had some certified identification across the street in Groucho Marx's house, and once he said the secret word they let him go scot free.

But they didn't let Harpo go, and they dragged him all the way to the police station the day he dressed up as Kaiser Wilhelm. It was perfectly legitimate, of course. He was going to Marion Davies' costume party, and you're *allowed* to put on a costume when you go to a costume party, and Harpo had gone all the way—all the way to fifty pounds of headgear, moustaches, noses, chins, emblems, medallions, ceremonial weaponry, straps, belts, buttons, knee boots and full martial whoop-de-doo. He had gone so far, in fact, that it had become impossible to take the mess off, so that even though he won second prize and nobody at the party ever guessed who he really was, it had become a test of the limits of human endurance just to carry it all around, and besides, his eyes got tired holding the monocle. At length, Charlie Lederer fixed him up with a convenient ride with a jim-dandy couple who were friends of his, who were too smashed to carry on with the party any further, though they weren't so smashed that they couldn't continue smashing each other in the face for a while in the back seat on the way home. Harpo, situated between them, paid a heavy price for their inaccurate fire, and eventually, bored with bearing the brunt of their battle, he pulled the visor of his spiked helmet down. The chauffeur let him know that this went on every other night in the week and advised him not to worry about it, even when they chased each other into the house and raced around slamming doors and breaking things. The chauffeur calmly shut off the motor, put out the headlights, closed up the car, and—still telling Harpo not to worry—vanished into the night, never to be heard from again.

Harpo sat there, stunned, immobile, realizing that nobody was going to take him home to the Garden of Allah, and, further, there was no way to *get* anybody to take him home to the Garden of Allah, and, even further, he couldn't take a taxi or a trolley or a bus or a train because the false pockets on his costume left him no place for a wallet. He would have to hitchhike. He could still hear the chauffeur's disembodied voice echoing in his ears. "Don't worry about it." It was a shame the chauffeur couldn't hear *his* voice, which, even though it reverberated roundly through the hollows of his helmet, was only a pale, indistinct shadow of itself by the time it emitted from the visor that was now jammed shut.

The joyriders on Sunset Boulevard were a privileged bunch that Saturday night, for, if they only looked out of their windows, why, there was old Kaiser Wilhelm, a-hitchin' a ride with his thumb out. Though many of them laughed to see such a sight, nobody stopped to give Mr. Wilhelm a lift, nobody except the police, who gave him a lift all the way to the police station, opened his visor with a crowbar, made faces at him and closed it again. It was the vagrancy charge all over again, but when he said the secret word, "Harpo," nothing happened. Could he prove he was Harpo Marx? No. Did he have his papers with him? No. If they called Marion Davies, could she vouch for the fact that Harpo Marx had attended her costume party? No. Nobody ever found out who he was, and he hadn't even been invited in the first place. Hadn't even been invited!? Vagrancy, impersonating Kaiser Wilhelm, and illegal entry.

The only recourse left was to have them call his big brother Chico. Aroused in the middle of the night from a deep round of cribbage, Chico only naturally assumed that Harpo was at a strange version of a party and the only reason anybody could possibly have for asking Chico Marx if he had a brother named Harpo was some sort of question-and-answer game. Yes, he said, he had a brother named Harpo, and started thinking up funny answers for all the other questions, dredging up childhood memories and indulging in sly in-jokes and arcane references to whorehouses they had played piano in, jails they had been thrown in, and movies they had made. Harpo Marx turned out to be a red-haired, cross-eyed mute who was last seen in Gloversville, New York, where he had been arrested for vagrancy and illegal entry.

Whoever it was the Beverly Hills police had on their hands now, he was in real trouble. Vagrancy, illegal entry, escaping from the Gloversville jail, impersonating Kaiser Wilhelm and *impersonating Harpo Marx.*

That was more than too much to bear. How could you respond to being arrested for impersonating yourself? There was just nothing to do about that but fall asleep. And only when Charlie Lederer came to bail him out did he see any use in waking up again.

———————

Then there was Leo McCarey. It finally dawned on the Marx Brothers that for once they ought to choose their own director. One day they happened on the realization that they were going

to need somebody who could say something more than "Janie
. . . " to them. The most likely prospect in the vicinity, the Marx
Brothers made it known, was that gracious and charming young
Leo McCarey, who politely refused the whole idea.

McCarey's film career had gone from birth to maturity in the
few years since he had graduated from USC, and simply working
for Hal Roach for five years and coming up with the idea of
teaming Stan Laurel and Oliver Hardy together and then supervising all their early films (and by McCarey's definition "supervising" the films is to be translated as "making" them) was
enough to establish for him a reputation as one of the only
creative individualistic directors there were, at the tender age of
thirty-four. Word had even gotten as far as the Marx Brothers,
and you couldn't impress the Marx Brothers with a branding
iron. Unfortunately, word of the Marx Brothers had also gotten
as far as McCarey. Norman McLeod probably took him aside once
or twice and showed him his bruises.

McCarey had a habit of dominating every film he directed,
in ways that were spontaneous, graceful, and various. Sometimes
he did so much improvising at the rehearsal stage and even on
the sound stage that the actors were never sure exactly what was
happening. Sometimes his constant pantomimes in the course of
his conversation were infectious enough to show up on film being
performed by his actors. (Many of Stan Laurel's familiar mannerisms, in fact, were originally familiar mannerisms of Mc-
Carey's. The director had a "Let's go have a beer" gesture and an
"Anybody want to play tennis?" gesture that friends and associates haven't shaken even yet.) Sometimes he sat around playing
the piano or telling stories to the crew until he had an idea for a
scene, and then he'd proceed ahead at his own convenience
through lunch or past suppertime to get it done while his enthusiasm was up, and underlings got used to the idea that things
went on only when McCarey felt like it and gave up trying to
question the procedure. When visions of sacrificing all this control to look for a missing Chico danced through his head, he let it
be known that there were other things to do.

McCarey was the type who was more amused by the subtleties and frailties of human behavior than in hyperbolic parables

of man's innate lunacy; light, romantic comedy was more to his liking than hard, clanking buffoons. Two of his most choice achievements as a comedy director—the two-reel Laurel and Hardy silent *Big Business* and the Cary Grant–Irene Dunne divorce comedy *The Awful Truth*—are delighted comedic studies of the heated passions and cool tensions in the steady rise and fall of true human conflict. McLeod's most choice achievements as a comedy director came from being fairly agreeable to just about anything his comedy stars wanted to do.

Part of what made McCarey a great director was that he had a particular style to impart to his productions, but how was he going to impart it to the Marx Brothers? Part of what made McLeod a great *Marx Brothers* director was that he had no particular style at all.

———

Then there was the idea of a political satire. And that's where the question of intent comes in. *Duck Soup* has been called a political satire in as many languages as Europe can muster, and often enough to lead one to believe it was the Marxes' answer to Chaplin's Hitler satire, *The Great Dictator*. (Typically, their answer comes seven years before the question.) But if you go back and ask the guys who *made* the picture, they don't seem to have been thinking of that at all. Leo McCarey says only that "it kidded dictators." Harry Ruby gets almost indignant when you ask him and says, "We wrote shows and movies for only one purpose: Entertainment. That is all there was to it!"

Arthur Sheekman disavows the mantle of satirist somewhat more reluctantly: "Comedy is best when you upset stuffy people or notions, but that doesn't mean that you start out with social criticism. Comedy almost invariably turns into criticism of some kind, and Marx Brothers comedy is criticism of everybody who is pretentious."

"This whole business of social significance is nonsense" is the personal pooh-pooh of George Seaton, and one of the real studio favorites. Hollywood seems convinced that there is a hard core of intellectuals lurking in the shadows, all set to riddle movies with Freudian symbolism and social significance, and if they're not stopped it'll mean the end of us. Dare to suggest that either of these insidious poisons has anything to do with your liking of a movie, and the whole town is sure to hate you for it.

Nat Perrin, however, tells us, "It is possible that whatever satire is there kind of crept into it because that was the way the men involved thought." That's more like it. Groucho's recent remarks on Vietnam may shed some light on this topic: "It would be different if we were fighting a just war, if there is any such thing," he says. "If I were a youngster, I wouldn't march into the firing lines with any bravado. I would go to Canada or Sweden or hide or go to jail. If I had a son twenty years old I'd encourage him to evade the war. He has a right to his life." Even more recently, United States Attorneys thought hard before deciding not to file a criminal complaint against Groucho for making the statement "The only hope this country has is Nixon's assassination."

Let us now remember that George Kaufman and Morrie Ryskind—who didn't work on *Duck Soup* but wrote *Of Thee I Sing*—which really *was* a political satire—would never let the Marx Brothers make a movie out of it for the specific reason that it wouldn't be a political satire any more by the time they were through with it. Let us also remember that Morrie Ryskind was expelled from Columbia University six weeks before he would have graduated because he wrote an anti-war editorial for the *Jester*. And that Mr. Ryskind now does a conservative column for the Washington Star Syndicate, where he writes anti-anti-war editorials.

This raises the question of intent all over again. It is a strange line of reasoning that presumes, simply because you did not *intend* to do something, that you did not in fact do it. It's always been popular with little kids accused of breaking something, but it never caught on in the courts. How pleasant it would be if one could drive onto Los Angeles' complicated freeway system and, by simply not *intending* to go to Santa Monica, not go there. But if one finds oneself at the end of the line staring at the ocean, perhaps it would be best to try figuring out where you are and how to get back to civilization again.

Duck Soup was prepared amid an atmosphere of ruin, disruption, and veritable collapse. Not only was Hitler taking over Germany, but Roosevelt was closing the banks in America, Paramount was tottering near bankruptcy, and financiers were flitting in and out of the picture like moths. Groucho was spearheading a movement to form a Screen Actors' Guild, which was only going to benefit the majority of Hollywood actors who were not movie stars, and was only going to alienate everybody else. Zeppo was getting ideas about going into business as an agent, and when Gummo moved out from New York the two were actually talking seriously about it. Then Frenchie Marx went to the hospital, and, after flirting with the nurses for a while, breathed his last. There was even an earthquake in Long Beach.

And the next thing you knew, Groucho and Chico were in New York doing a radio show, like they were supposed to do in the first place instead of making all those movies. Groucho and Chico played two lawyers named Beagle and Shyster, and, as Groucho's character claimed for himself both top and bottom billing, the name of the law firm was Beagle, Shyster, and Beagle. The show went over with just about everybody except a real lawyer named Beagle, who claimed that strangers were continually calling him up in the middle of the night to say, "Is this Mr. Beagle? How's your partner, Shyster? Snicker, Snicker! Guffaw, Guffaw! Click!" Reasoning that the best defense was no offense, radio's favorite Beagle changed his name to Flywheel.

The half-hour episodes were written alternately by Arthur Sheekman and Nat Perrin and by George Oppenheimer and Tom McKnight (the latter of whom was signed up at a urinal). Due to the very nature of Marx Brothers comedy, the writing took more time and more punchlines than writing for any other comedian would take. The writers labored practically every day and night on the enterprise, frantically compiling old jokes and incorporating them into each other and desperately striving for new ones.

Approximately one half of the Marx Brothers' appeal is contagious over the radio and that goes for Groucho and Chico too. Though it must have seemed like a sound idea, the radio program was too much of a sound idea to work: Standard Oil of

New Jersey canceled the show after twenty-six weeks, although insidious gripes and grievances in the Middle East were said to have had something to do with it. Other sponsors who dropped Groucho and Chico for reasons of diminishing market or troublesome raw materials included American Oil and Kellogg's Corn Flakes. "If you're hungry some morning," says Groucho, "you might try this combination."

And the next thing you knew, Groucho and Chico were back in Hollywood again.

There is good reason to believe that the only cause McCarey had for even pretending to undertake the project was the steadily accumulating evidence that it was never going to be completed. Besides that, he was getting close to the end of his contract, and when the showdown came he just wouldn't bother to renew. He met with all the Marxes and all the writers and a whole barrage of Herman Mankiewicz and found the gang very pleasant and agreeable, just so long as nobody brought up the subject of movie-making. So, for three weeks, many darts were thrown at dartboards. Many contests were held, many wagers were won and lost. The only real bugaboos in this grand setup were Kalmar and Ruby, who had this idea about rival duchies and parliaments and spies and wanted to hash it over.

"When are you going to learn to mind your own business?" they'd be told. "You'll never get anywhere, Harry. You'll never amount to anything."

This left Kalmar and Ruby to function as a sort of Lewis and Carroll and blaze the trails of this maniac expedition by themselves. Rufus T. Firefly was born. Sylvania. Freedonia. The plans of war. A hostile diplomat named Trentino.

Once the throwing of darts got to be a bore, the Marxes chanced to turn their fancy to matters of moment. "Say, we've got a picture to do," they informed the writers one day. "Paramount's putting a lot of money into this, you know. We're going to have to stop fooling around."

Bert and Harry nodded politely.

"All right, now, we're going to have an important meeting, you hear? I know this is asking a lot of you fellas, but we want this picture to be one of our biggest hits, and we'd like to go over each of the scenes with you. Could you please come in tomorrow morning at nine-thirty?"

"But we *always* come in at nine-thirty."

"Well, then, come in at eight-thirty."

What could this mean? Kalmar and Ruby sat up in their respective beds all night holding their heads in their respective hands. And everybody *did* come in at 8:30. Everybody but the Marx Brothers. When they didn't come in at 9:30, yesterday's quibbling began to look academic. By 11:30 it was downright marginal. And when they *did* show up at a quarter to twelve, what was their attitude? Apologetic petulance? Paternal condescension? Nonsense. Utter indignation! All expectations of apologies were roundly disappointed and sent home to bed.

"Where were *you*?" they fumed.

"Where were *we*? We were right here."

"How do you like that, they were right here! We go out of our way to have a meeting, and they just sit right here!"

"Well, wait a minute . . ."

"Look, Harry, we're making a picture and spending a lot of money, and when we say nine-thirty we mean business."

"Well, wait a minute, Groucho. Where were you guys?"

"Why, RKO!"

"RKO?? We're not making this picture for RKO!"

"Don't change the subject!"

It didn't take the writers long to see that they were never going to get anywhere until they tried enlisting reinforcements. Grover Jones, one of the most confirmed Hollywood natives in sight, was usually occupied scripting Westerns, like *Stampede* and *Gun Smoke,* and little homey affairs like Paramount's *Tom Sawyer* and *Huckleberry Finn,* and he specifically asked for the opportunity to be assigned to the Marx Brothers unit, involved in the production and attendant on all script conferences. After two weeks of dealing with the Marx Brothers, he walked out. Another Paramount contract writer, Kean Thompson, entered the scene, and, like Grover Jones, he went out of his way to request the *Duck Soup* assignment, and, like Grover Jones, he began to take part in the daily activities, and then, like Grover Jones, he disappeared after two weeks and couldn't be found again.

Then the Marxes decided to follow the example set by Grover Jones. It seems they had been dickering for some time with the front office and the William Morris Agency over the profits from *Monkey Business*. The whole thing started when the agency complained they never received their share. The Marxes apparently felt they didn't *deserve* a share. (We'll never know just what it was they said. The agency asked that it be stricken from the record on the ground that it was "frivolous.") Then, expectedly performing the least expected, *they* sued the *agency*, claiming that the share the William Morris people *did* get on *Cocoanuts* and *Animal Crackers* was too high, because of some underhanded deal they had made with Paramount. Supposedly, the deal violated the Marxes' contract, but they could never prove that, because Paramount kept shifting the contract from one subsidiary to another and it never held still long enough for anybody to read it. Finally, by March of 1933 the Marx Brothers' steadily mounting annoyance reached a pique. They marched out of Paramount Pictures and into the warm, loving arms of old Sam Harris, through whom they formed Marx Bros., Inc. By April they were sitting in New York merrily issuing stock. By May they were taking on the whole Paramount mountain in a lawsuit.

McCarey, sensing that the conflict had grown so steeped in the acrid that a reconciliation was hopeless, renewed his contract after all. Therefore, at approximately that very moment, the Marxes, to McCarey's horror, settled every single tiny problem and returned to the studio. (The lawsuit was resolved by deciding that "the plaintiffs reserve the right to make a claim against the bankrupt estate of the defendant, if an accounting of the proceeds of the film shows that they have any." Personally, I don't see how talking like that is going to solve a thing.)

And now that the fighting was over, it was time for the fighting to resume. McCarey knew what he was in for, and he knew what he was in up to. Sheekman and Perrin came home from New York (the two bewildered novices who had met on a train were now writing Goldwyn musicals and had become a pretty reputable team, even when they weren't writing for the Marx Brothers), and McCarey set them to work on Kalmar and Ruby's first draft, not only dropping more gags into the stew but, now that McCarey was really going to direct the film, getting a little of McCarey into the screenplay, and playing up the *Big Business*-like passions and tensions of true human conflict in Groucho's squabble with Trentino. A few of the bigger giggles from the expired radio show found convenient niches in the story line, among them a line about shadowing a man all day Shadow-day, and another about a riddle in the middle of a courtroom whose admonition ("That's irrelevant!") turns out to be the answer. Sheekman found the old Plow Routine (the bit where you are about to ask somebody a favor and then envision the fellow refusing you and then get so indignant about his refusal that when you finally see him you smack him in the face before he even gets a chance to say anything) a convenient way to rile up Groucho over nothing in particular and get the war scene started. McCarey brought the boys over to his Malibu beach house to work, where they could think straight.

There was even employed, for one incredibly brief period, another gag man, in the form of Eddie Kaufman, a very pompous and nice little man who smoked big cigars and collected letters and signatures. Kaufman babbled continually through writing sessions, on the assumption that if his voice was heard he was contributing somehow. He later became a producer at RKO. Strangely, Kaufman never got around to walking out. He hardly even had a chance to walk in.

But before they were finished they had the brothers to answer to. They soon reached the point where everybody just ran around making up gags about no matter what and squeezing them somehow into the picture. The assemblage jammed together in great hordes and small claques and tried all their jokes out on each other again, but by this time they were all of them hardened veterans, which means that none of them laughed. As Groucho remembers it, the only sure way to test a gag was to try it out on Zeppo. If he liked it, they threw it out.

Groucho tried enlisting the aid of a seasoned non-professional one day on the way to the studio. He asked a service-station attendant what he thought of his new joke about a man who stuffed spaghetti with bicarbonate of soda, thus causing and curing indigestion at the same time. He got a slightly pained expression and a full tank. It was only months later, after the movie was finished and previewed, that the attendant explained how funny he thought the gag was but that he hadn't been able to summon up a grin that particular morning because a toothache was bothering him. So much for *that* audience. (The gag later popped up in a completely unlikely context in *Night at the Opera.*)

By the middle of July a final script was finished, and by the time rehearsals were over it was half gone. McCarey shared the viewpoint that a script for the Marx Brothers was about as definite as a treaty for the Indians. Like most of their directors, he preferred Harpo to the verbal comedy that proliferated endlessly and made a nuisance of itself, and as usual, nearly every bit of business written for Harpo in the script was replaced with something better by the time it was filmed. McCarey gave Harpo some prankish consistency by coming up with a pair of scissors for him to snip off the end of everything he sees with. McCarey went around engendering enthusiasm for the picture by telling everybody one of the lines from the battle scene. "They fought this whole war with laughing gas!" he'd say and fall to the floor in a fit. (Much as it seems to have amused McCarey, it never excited an audience and it left the movie after the first preview.)

McCarey's eagle-eyed mind seized on one small script reference to Chico as a peanut vendor. He sought out Edgar Kennedy to play a lemonade vendor, brought Harpo in as Chico's partner, and for a couple of days the four of them improvised and shot, Hal Roach fashion, some dandy comedy routines whose only connection to the plotline was by extension.

The Marxes soon found that they weren't so charmed as they had expected to be by the constant attempts of this man they had gone to such lengths to get to direct their movie, to really *direct* their movie. They knew he was a talented man, but they hadn't quite expected him to insist on the fact.

The insertion of familiar silent-comedy bits, for instance, was taken as an affront to their sensibility. "That idea of snapping your fingers went out with the Keystone Kops," Groucho muttered. Harpo was malleably receptive to just about anything McCarey wanted to do, but none of them was specifically sure just where it was going to get them.

Then, in a fit of *auteur*, McCarey just went and threw out one of the major scenes of the film—a sequence taking place in a theater, which included not only a tango scramble after Freedonia's plans of war (resembling the football-signals complications in *Horsefeathers*) but an expansive production number involving the dictatorial ambitions of Groucho ("Of course you're all aware/A King must have an heir/Someone to pass the family name along/Will someone tell me where/I'll ever get an heir/If a King can do no wrong!") and a couple of gags that would have seen their day as classics had they been allowed to live ("You haven't been still a moment since you've been here. You act as if you had neurosis." "I no gotta new-rosis. My uncle he's got a flower shop—he's-a gotta new-rosis."—"If his Excellency doesn't get here soon, he'll miss the whole performance." "He's-a not missing anything. He's backstage with the girls." "Backstage with the girls? What could he be doing there?" "Well, he *could* be playing solitaire, but I don't *think* so"). It was replaced, instead, by an improvisational field day involving Harpo and Chico stealing the plans of war from Margaret Dumont's safe and reviving vaudeville's classic mirror routine. Nobody was sure what to make of that. Including the writers. Harry Ruby walked onto the sound stage one vacant afternoon and found Groucho and Harpo recognizing each other as mirror images of themselves. He began to get the impression that his own haphazard script had been heltered and skeltered all over the halls. This, naturally, is the way everyone *thinks* comedies must be made. But Ruby knew better.

"What scene is that?" asked Ruby, just to kick things off.

"This is the scene where they break into Mrs. Teasdale's house," Harpo explained to him.

"Oh, *that* scene!" said Ruby. "Uh-huh."

DUMONT: The plans of war are gone. . . . They were taken right from under my nose.

Harpo with Leo McCarey.

Between takes.

GROUCHO: A fine place to keep the plans of war! Who was with you?

DUMONT: The Secretary of War.

GROUCHO: What was he doing under your nose? What a fool I was to trust you—to listen to your siren song.

DUMONT: But—

GROUCHO: You gratified your selfish whims, while nations tottered, dynasties rocked and the world plunged headlong into a chasm of chaos and oblivion—I've read worse than that in three-dollar books. In fact, that's where I got it.

CHICO: That's fine, now we gotta the plans—we take them right over to Trentino.

GROUCHO: Hands up!!!

CHICO: Hey, you no got-a gun.

GROUCHO: Who *said* I had a gun. Keep your hands up and I'll get one. . . . I'll be back in five minutes.

CHICO: Wait a minute. . . . Can you use a knife?

GROUCHO: Well, a knife isn't as good as a gun but this is no time to be choosy. Now—hand over those papers or I'll blow your brains out. You double-crossers—you traitors. You'll be court-martialed for this. You know what this is? This is treason—and you know what treason is?

CHICO: Sure, my uncle he's-a got-a hundred and sixty-five *treason* his back yard.

And Mr. McCarey's self-indulgent habit of working when he felt like it was frustrated by certain self-indulgent habits on the part of his stars—among them the recurrent practice of popping up when the mood of the moment impelled them to and otherwise wandering off to where fate led them, as well as turning rehearsals and shooting days into unwarranted gag sessions, all of this complicated by a clause in their contract which insisted that, no matter what happened, no shooting of any sequence was to be begun after the hour of six in the afternoon. "Read my contract" became the standard defense after the day had been whittled away to nothing in this fashion and McCarey had tried to start things up again too close to sunset. (Chico, who could be counted on to arrive late, would always try to leave early, on the flimsy pretext that "it's after quitting time in New York," and would refuse to be convinced of the irrelevance of this fact.) Such intrusions on his prerogative were not intended to cement new friendships, and McCarey was on the verge of gathering up whole armies to march into battle against them when it occurred to him that the simplest way to chastise his antagonists was to pull the same trick on them. So one day he got all four of them together, started working a scene over until it got good and late, excused himself to go make a phone call, hopped in his car and went home to his wife and dog. An assistant stood around and made excuses for him, and while McCarey was curled up contentedly watching the hour approach six and dreaming of indignant Marx Brothers, the Marx Brothers were anxiously watching the hour approach six and dreaming of short fuses and the Fourth of July. Their combustion point had threatened arrival and found no sign of discouragement, when the assistant decided that he had to make a phone call too, and advised the comedians to go ahead and rehearse without *him.* He ducked behind a corner and giggled and chortled for a moment or two, and by the time he had recovered his composure and found his way back, the omnipotent hour of six was looming ominously on the horizon and Chico's facial muscles were fairly twitching in anticipation. "Gee, I'm sorry to keep you waiting, fellas, but I had to talk to Leo on the phone," the assistant rather breezily let them know. "He's home in bed, and he wanted me to tell you he's recovering nicely and has every expectation of being here bright and early tomorrow morning to direct this scene for you."

What a wet match that turned out to be! They couldn't even walk out in anger. They couldn't even get angry at anybody. They couldn't even come back with "Read my contract." All they could come back with was "Hell!" and things like that. Leo McCarey was the only man on earth who could teach the Marx Brothers a lesson and come out of it with his life. But you'll notice he planned the gag so he'd be miles away from them when the punchline came.

———

Margaret Dumont was popularly demanded back into the game. Groucho admitted that dropping her was one of his less inspired inspirations, but one feels his heart must have been warmed by some of the other exclusions: the harp and piano solos, any hint of a love interest (Kalmar and Ruby created a romance between Zeppo and Raquel Torres, but McCarey went ahead without it), and even the mundane melodic ditty, "Keep on Doin' What You're Doin'," which Kalmar and Ruby later put in a Wheeler and Woolsey picture.

There are some exclusions that are regrettable. Probably for Hays Office reasons, the sight gag couldn't be used wherein Harpo, displaying a tattoo of an outhouse on his chest, is slapped on the back by Groucho, causing the door of the outhouse to swing open and a little hand to reach out and shut it again. The replacement (a live dog barking out of a tattooed doghouse) isn't quite so ingenious. Also unused is Groucho's habit of taking a rabbit from his hat every time he exits or enters a room. Or the opening exchange in the battle scene: "Your Excellency, the enemy is approaching! They are only a stone's throw from here!" "So that's their game! Very well, we'll throw stones too. Go out and get me an armful of stones." Or Groucho's answer to the problem of some evidence of treachery: "I know how to solve this mystery: I'll get a small glass slipper and go from house to house and when I find the girl whose foot fits the slipper I'll go in the house and you'll never see *me* again." There were apparently so many gags flying around that they could afford to lose a few in the shuffle.

But Arthur Sheekman was standing by to come up with stand-ins. Not dreamed up till the last minute were such witticisms as "Go! And never darken my towels again!" And the plea of a helpless man trapped in a bathroom: "Let me out of here, or throw me a magazine!"

In fact, when the gags flew, they flew in all directions, just to provide local color and local off-color.

"What's my character in this picture?" asked Harpo one day.

"What's your *what?*" asked Mankiewicz. When things got too serious, he was uncomfortable.

"My character." Harpo was being plagued by pleas from

Alexander Woollcott, who was going around calling him the greatest pantomimic artist since Chaplin, to perform in the Soviet Union, and his head was turned in a neat 240° arc. "I can't play this part unless I know what my character is."

"Aw, hell," said Mankiewicz, "you play a middle-aged Jew who goes around picking up spit."

It was Bert Kalmar who wondered, "Well, do you think they'll like it?" during a screening of the rushes.

Chico was definite. "Like it! Look, they'll piss!"

"No doubt about that," said Groucho. "But will they *laugh?*"

A female lead was hard to find, and selection was still in progress when Chico volunteered, "I don't like that one."

"Why not?" he was asked.

"Oh, she's old and has big tits."

"I resent that!" huffed Mankiewicz. "My *mother* is old and has big tits."

The title was no easy matter, either. *Duck Soup* is actually the name of one of McCarey's Laurel and Hardy pictures, but that's no justification. Groucho, who claims he can understand every one of their titles but *I'll Say She Is*, explained it all with the following recipe: "Take two turkeys, one goose, four cabbages, but no duck, and mix them together. After one taste, you'll duck soup the rest of your life."

Shortly after the film opened, it was revealed that there really was a Fredonia and it was a town in New York. Its mayor felt obligated to address a letter to Paramount saying, "The name of Fredonia has been without a blot since 1817. I feel it is my duty as Mayor to question your intentions in using the name of our city in your picture." Groucho felt it was *his* duty to write back, "Your Excellency: Our advice is that you change the name of your town. It is hurting our picture. Anyhow, what makes you think you're Mayor of Fredonia? Do you wear a black moustache, play a harp, speak with an Italian accent, or chase girls like Harpo? We are certain you do not. Therefore, we must be Mayor of Fredonia, not you. The old gray Mayor ain't what he used to be."

"The most surprising thing about this film," McCarey recalled later, "is that I succeeded in not going crazy." He succeeded admirably. Less innocent bystanders were stunned by the managerial finesse that McCarey assumed in handling his obstreperous comedians and maneuvering them through the many harrying details of a large production.

Duck Soup features the one and only musical performance on record of all four Marx Brothers together (a ridiculous mock-whoopee that includes lines like, "You got guns, we got guns, all God's chillun got guns," and manages to lampoon at one time Hollywood musicals, patriotic hoopla, glorified violence, team-spiritualism and football rallies), which is beautifully and filmically choreographed and is yet another example of directorial prerogative, as there is no trace of it in the final script. *Duck Soup* is centered around an admirably compact and workable story, considerably more complex than *Monkey Business*' and less of a plotpourri than *Horsefeathers*', a story which is told not in images, not in words, not in music, but in gags, some of them good, some of them bad, some of them priceless, but enough of them so that the plot doesn't have to be handed over to some rancid Romeo to sweat out in agonizing scenes that neither we nor he are much interested in, in order to "hold the picture together." *Duck Soup* holds *itself* together. *Duck Soup* is characterized by Kalmar and Ruby's characteristic fanciful absurdity, which deals with motivation and story line on its own terms or not at all; it features some of the most playful performances on record, not only from the Marx Brothers but from all the supporting players; everyone seems to be not only comfortable in his part but downright cozy. (They look too busy, anyway, doing sight gags and making faces, to be conscious of the fact that there are cameras trained on them.) (Speaking of cozy, it also features Harpo's love of animals bordering on sodomy. He wanted to attack an old ladies' home in *Animal Crackers*, he was hitting the hay with a heifer in *Monkey Business*, and now in *Duck Soup* he finally makes it to bed with a horse.) It features the devil-may-care cutting of Leo McCarey, who seems to have been more interested in spontaneity than in continuity. (If the actors don't shift position from shot to shot, the sun does. When two good shots don't match, McCarey's answer is to put them together and let them fight it out.)

Duck Soup juggles logic and defies gravity, it is outrageous, it is ridiculous, it is funny, it is savage, it is silly, it is a symphony in gagtime, composed by an army and orchestrated by one man. McCarey had fought back and won. He had even been gracious and charming enough not to turn it into a Leo McCarey film.

The political slant that *Duck Soup* inevitably adopts is one in which international diplomacy becomes a gangrenous display of blunders, madness, egotism and tomfoolery. This is a point of view that still has its advocates. Ever since 1933, in fact, politicians have selflessly dedicated themselves to upholding its truth.

There are political satires and there are political satires. *Duck Soup* is neither.

NOBLE SAVAGE

DUMONT: Oh. I want to present to you Ambassador Trentino of Sylvania. Having him with us today is indeed a great pleasure.

TRENTINO: Thank you, but I can't stay very long.

GROUCHO: That's even a greater pleasure. Now, how about lending this country $20,000,000, you old skinflint.

TRENTINO: $20,000,000 is a lot of money. I'd have to take that up with the Minister of Finance.

GROUCHO: Well, in the meantime, could you let me have $12 until payday?

TRENTINO: $12!?

GROUCHO: Don't be scared. You'll get it back. I'll give you my personal note for ninety days. If it isn't paid by then, you can keep the note.

The Marx Brothers have always seemed somewhat other-worldly. *Duck Soup* takes place in that other world.

It starts with Groucho ascending to the throne of an entire country. It *starts* that way. More believable than that even is Groucho being the president of a college. What we seem to be asked for is the willing suspension of incredulity.

Worse, nobody flinches. No less surprising than Groucho's first words as President ("Take a card") is Margaret Dumont's determination at dignity ("I feel you are the most noble states-man in all Freedonia"). Nobody thinks twice (or even at all) when Groucho dictates a letter to his dentist in the middle of his inauguration. (He dictated a letter in *Animal Crackers*, too, so this is his second stab at being a dictator.) And when he slides down a fire pole to enter the ceremonial ballroom, we question not so much him as the architect who designed the building that way in the first place.

Groucho announces, "If any form of pleasure is exhibited, report to me and it will be prohibited," and the only difference between him and any other head of state is that coming from his mouth it sounds funny. Disrespect for crowned heads is what we're all set to see Groucho perform, but he executes the most ignoble sacrilege on the whole condition of sovereignty just by taking office, and determining our allegiance is a major tax on our ingenuity. It's no problem to his throng of admirers, however: He cheerfully proclaims he'll accept all the power due his office and none of the responsibility, and it gets a rise out of the people instead of an uprising. His conversation about Margaret Dumont's husband (who has died from a surfeit of Margaret Dumont) gets the same response out of her: Groucho is a baldfaced opportunist and makes no bones about it. He is the ideal ruler.

Groucho exits the palace and hops in the side car of Harpo's motorcycle. Harpo drives off without his side car. And now, since everyone has been so nice about swallowing *his* medicine, he decides to be just as gracious. He hops right out of the side car and declares, "It certainly feels good to be back again." And it certainly does. Wherever we are.

THE SHADOW

TRENTINO: Oh! Now, Chicolini, I want a full detailed report of your investigation.

CHICO: All right, I tell you. Monday we watch-a Firefly's house, but he no come out. He wasn't home. Tuesday we go to the ball game, but he fool us. He no show up. Wednesday he go to the ball game, and we fool him. *We* no show up. Thursday was a double-header. Nobody show up. Friday it rained all day. There was no ball game, so we stayed home and we listened to it over the radio.

TRENTINO: Then you didn't shadow Firefly?

CHICO: Oh, sure, we shadow Firefly. We shadow him all day.

TRENTINO: But what day was that?

CHICO: Shadowday! Hahaha! Atsa some joke, eh, Boss?

UNIVERSAL

All spies wear disguises. Even when reporting to their own superiors. All spies destroy messages. Even before anybody reads them. But how many spies light cigars with blowtorches? This is as great a mystery as any facing the world today.

Daredevil with cockiness, Harpo and Chico enter Trentino's office armed to the teeth with cigar butts, scissors, blowtorches, jars of paste, mousetraps and assorted bells—just as if they were on a real mission. (We presume they act this way on a real mission.) Their important conference with Trentino consists of singing lullabies, ringing alarm clocks, blasting phonograph records out of the sky, awarding each other cigars and making a lot of noise. After Harpo lights his cigar, he diplomatically lights Trentino's, and after he lights Trentino's, he cuts it in half. (A spy isn't much of a diplomat. When Harpo isn't severing ties, he's severing coattails and cigars.) They won't play ball with Trentino, but Harpo plays ball with a cigar, and Chico has a ball just playing on words. (This is his favorite sport. Each of his own limp gags gives him as much pleasure as if somebody had told *him* a joke. Everybody *he* tells a joke to has no fun at all. Apparently it isn't a spectator sport.) Harpo shows his frustration by tearing out some of Trentino's hair.

Trentino takes in all the horseplay as if it were a necessary formality, but they never get around to business because they are too light of heart and head to bother: Not only have they come back with no clues, but the one clue that was given to them they lost. When it turns out nothing's been accomplished, the real punchline is delivered by the straight man. "Gentlemen," he announces, "I'm going to give you one more chance." One more *chance?* What does he *want?* What are his prerequisites for despondency? Leprosy? The Black Plague? Fire, Famine, and Slaughter? Apparently games and disguises are all that's expected of a spy any more, just as death and taxes are all we want from our governments. This other world is beginning to look familiar.

PETTY PACES

MINISTER OF LABOR: The Department of Labor wishes to report that the workers of Freedonia are demanding shorter hours.

GROUCHO: Very well, we'll give them shorter hours. We'll start by cutting their lunch hour to twenty minutes. And now, gentlemen, we've got to start looking for a new Treasurer.

MINISTER OF LABOR: But you appointed one last week.

GROUCHO: That's the one I'm looking for.

SECRETARY OF WAR: Gentlemen! Gentlemen! Enough of this. How about taking up the tax?

GROUCHO: How about taking up the carpet?

SECRETARY OF WAR: I still insist we must take up the tax.

GROUCHO: He's right. You've got to take up the tacks before you can take up the carpet.

SECRETARY OF WAR: I give all my time and energy to my duties and what do I get?

GROUCHO: You get awfully tiresome after a while.

SECRETARY OF WAR: Sir, you try my patience!

GROUCHO: I don't mind if I do. You must come over and try mine some time.

SECRETARY OF WAR: That's the last straw! I resign! I wash my hands of the whole business!

GROUCHO: A good idea. You can wash your neck, too.

Back to Groucho. We get to see Rufus Firefly really holding a Cabinet meeting now and making light of governmental futility rites. And we find out that if there's one person in a conference who doesn't want to get anything done, anything doesn't get done. The pretense of politics has no attraction for Mr. Firefly: he doesn't want to do anything but make jokes about it all. (He is being played by a man who doesn't want to do anything but make jokes about it all.) His insistence on playing with all the customary political terminology just for the sake of turning it into a series of funny things is another pretense altogether.

Duck Soup may seem disconnected, but it really is. Outside Groucho's window there is a completely different movie going on. McCarey had almost nothing to do with Groucho's movie: it's all clever dialogue filmed from competent angles. Now Harpo and Chico do Laurel and Hardy's hat-switching routine with Edgar Kennedy, Leo McCarey has taken over entirely, and the dialogue is all on the level of "Wha . . . ?" "Ooop," and "Duh!" Harpo and Chico explain to Edgar Kennedy that they are spies (all false fronts are down this week), and if Kennedy were not obviously on loan from Hal Roach, and a refugee from another style of comedy, he might be to Harpo and Chico what Margaret Dumont is to Groucho or what Zeppo is to Groucho or Groucho to Chico or Chico to Harpo.

It is a tribute to Leo McCarey that when he puts together a mosaic of old impetuous Harpo and Chico gags and stitches it up with the old deliberate Laurel and Hardy style, he manages to impose his personality without spoiling the Marx Brothers' characterizations.

VERTIGO

GROUCHO: Now listen here. I've got a swell job for you, but first I'll have to ask you a couple of important questions. Now, what is it that has four pair of pants, lives in Philadelphia, and it never rains but it pours?

CHICO: Atsa good one. I give you three guesses.

GROUCHO: Now, let me see. Has four pair of pants, lives in Philadelphia . . . Is it male or female?

CHICO: No, I no think so.

GROUCHO: Is he dead?

CHICO: Who?

GROUCHO: I don't know. I give up.

CHICO: I give up too. Now I ask you another one. What is it got big black-a moustache, smokes a big black cigar, and is a big pain in the neck?

GROUCHO: Now, don't tell me. Has a big black moustache, smokes a big black cigar and is a big pain in the—

CHICO: Uh—

GROUCHO: Does he wear glasses?

CHICO: Atsa right. You guess it quick.

GROUCHO: Just for that, you don't get the job I was going to give you.

CHICO: What job?

GROUCHO: Secretary of War.

CHICO: All right, I take it.

GROUCHO: Sold!

---

*"I've got a swell job for you." There are vending machines who choose quarters with more care than Groucho fills government posts. Strictly speaking, *Monkey Business*

is still the only film where the brothers know each other from the outset, but that's only because it's never made clear from any of this dialogue whether Groucho and Chico have met each other before, whether they are meeting each other now, or whether they ever *will* meet each other. And if Groucho doesn't know the peanut vendor from under his window, what could ever be his reasons for picking him, with all the people in the world to choose from, to fill the Cabinet vacancy?

*". . . what is it that has four pair of pants . . ." I hope you've figured that out already, because now the questions have turned out to be a riddle.

*". . . lives in Philadelphia . . ." Now the riddle has an in-joke in it. Among ex-vaudevillians, the very mention of Philadelphia is still good for a laugh.

*". . . and it never rains but it pours?" The end of the riddle is a digression from the riddle.

*"I give you three guesses." Chico's task, you see, is not to *answer* the riddle. That would only spoil everything. His task is to top all those absurdities.

*"Now, let me see . . ." Groucho must fight nonsense with nonsense. It's the only way.

*". . . lives in Philadelphia . . ." The "Philadelphia" that is meant here is not the one in Pennsylvania but the small borough inside Freedonia (sometimes spelled "Phyladelphia"). This was the home of the Philadelphic Oracle, who uttered such enigmas as "A penny saved is a penny saved is a penny saved" and "I fear I've lost my powdered wig, and there'll be the devil toupee."

*"Who?" The "Who" referred to is, of course, Phineas T. Barnum, who was famous in Freedonian folklore for being born once every minute. He never reigned, but he ended his days in the Pourhouse.

*"I give up." Groucho can't be sure Chico is good enough for the job until he's asked him a riddle so tough that even he doesn't know the answer. Just the clues leave him stumped.

*"I give up, too." What does that mean?

*". . . a big pain in the neck." This was long believed to be a reference to Rufus Firefly's royal incestor, the treacherous Baron D'Omaine, whose story is told at every changing of the guard (Turn of the Sentry). It is now not believed at all.

°"Does he wear glasses?" Rufus Firefly was smothered in ticker tape and executive decisions in the Third Century after Nomenclature at the hands of an angry insurgent radical fascist separationist junta, who stormed the palace with cries of "Remember Philadelphia!"

°"Secretary of War." The Secretary of War was drowned in dashed hopes and broken promises seven years later at the hands of another insurgent faction, who stormed the palace with cries of "Forget about Philadelphia!"

°"Sold!" Chico gets the job. The conference is over and the business is settled. So *that's* how it's done.

If you really want to see sparks fly, wait till the rabble are off the street and the Marxes have just themselves to react to. (Have you ever seen sparks fly? No, but I've seen a Firefly.) First Groucho has a scene with Chico, then he has a scene with Harpo, then he has a scene with Zeppo. For Harpo, he is clearly reduced to a straight man; for Groucho, Zeppo is clearly reduced to a straight man; for Chico and Groucho, there is no straight man for miles. There are vending machines who choose quarters with more care than Groucho fills government posts. I said that already. Weren't you listening?

Chico's first act is to answer the phone and say, "He's not in," then turn to Groucho and tell him, "That was for you." To Groucho, this is the most sensible thing he's heard in the whole picture. Finally, after giving no one a straight answer to anything for the past twenty minutes, he is treated to the conversation of someone who won't give *him* one either. Now he's got somebody to communicate with. "I'm sorry I'm not in," he replies. "I wanted to have a long talk with you."

The phone rings again. Again Groucho isn't in. "I wonder whatever became of me," Groucho muses. "I should have been back a long time ago."

When Harpo comes in, he is asked to identify himself. This he does by rolling up his sleeve and displaying a picture of Harpo tattooed on his arm. That's very good identification. Who *else* would go around with a picture of himself tattooed on his arm? When Harpo writes with the quill pen, he does it to tickle his face with the feather. When Groucho writes with the quill pen, he does it to wave the feather in the air. When Harpo snips the feather in half, Groucho has to stop writing.

When Zeppo comes in he's got a great idea for undiplomatic relations, but Groucho must stop and make fourteen jokes on the matter before he can go out and do it, besides engaging Zeppo in a round-robin digression on a dirty joke that keeps on going until we've forgotten what the matter at hand was, and then they bring up the matter at hand again so that *it* sounds like a digression, too. It probably is.

Groucho hasn't been invited to Margaret Dumont's tea party, so he invites himself and he's been invited. Again he hops in Harpo's motorcycle and again he gets himself driven off without. "This is the fifth trip I've made today," he announces, "and I haven't been anywhere yet."

This makes everything much clearer. If he hasn't been anywhere today, then he hasn't been at the palace. Chico *said* he wasn't in when he answered the phone. The whole conversation never took place. They never *did* meet. Possibly what Chico was talking to was a projection of himself. That would explain why he was able to communicate so well. Actually, the dialogue only makes sense if we assume that Chico wasn't there either.

Which brings up a very interesting question. Can you find ten mistakes in the accompanying diagram? Can you find the accompanying diagram? What is the capital of the Chase National Bank? Give up?

HE WHO GETS SLAPPED

DUMONT: Your Excellency, the Ambassador's here on a friendly visit. He's had a change of heart.

GROUCHO: A lot of good that'll do him. He's still got the same face.

TRENTINO: I'm sorry we lost our tempers. I'm willing to forget if you are.

GROUCHO: Forget? You ask me to forget? A Firefly never forgets. Why, my ancestors would rise from their graves, and I'd only have to bury them again. Nothing doing. I'm going back and clean the crackers out of my bed. I'm expecting company.

DUMONT: Please wait.

GROUCHO: Let go of me, you bully!

DUMONT: Oh!

TRENTINO: I'm willing to do anything to prevent this war.

GROUCHO: It's too late. I've already paid a month's rent on the battlefield.

Viewed in its proper historical perspective, just about everything that's ever happened can be considered a grievous error.

Groucho wasn't *supposed* to start a war by insulting Trentino, but he would have thought it very uninventive of himself to go ahead with the scheme just the way it was planned. In scene after scene (two scenes) he strikes Trentino on the slightest provocation. (He is offered three provocations and he picks the slightest.) If Trentino were a nineteenth-century aristocrat, this personal grievance would lead to a man-to-man duel. But as it is he's a twentieth-century diplomat and it leads to war. He keeps trying to make amends and settle things peaceably, but every time he is hit he goes out screaming, "War!" Once Groucho gets the idea of striking Trentino into his head, there's no getting it back out. While Groucho goes ahead and treats this serious business as if it were a game, Trentino feels he must treat the game as if it were serious business. (Historical note: The trouble with Trentino is that he must treat *everything* as if it were serious business. He's not strictly a villain—the war isn't *his* idea—but he lives according to certain rules and he can't break them even when he wants to.)

The first time this happens is at Margaret Dumont's tea party, where Groucho arrives all set for a set-to and starts dunking invited guests' doughnuts into each other's coffee and eating them himself. Only the all-out attack on the captain in *Monkey*

Business is more brazen than this, but the actions are alike for conflicting reasons. (It is one thing to insult somebody, but quite another to do it when you're already in serious trouble and the man you insult could have you imprisoned for your very presence. It is one thing to steal doughnuts, but quite another to do it while a national anthem is being played to you and you are the President of a country who could have all the doughnuts you could ever possibly want if you just asked for them.) As an actor, Groucho has only one role to play; as a character, Groucho refuses all the roles and takes the doughnuts.

Later, Groucho lounges in bed eating soda crackers, a great mockery of the Idle Rich image. (And the bed was just made up, too. It wasn't a real bed; it was just made up.)

The second scene takes place at Margaret Dumont's house, where Groucho is almost to the point of nearing the verge of war, but Dumont wants him to be civil about it and make it a civil war. As with all arguments, this one consists of two parties: the wrong and the wronged. And, as with all arguments, each party is both.

Inserted between these battles of rival countries is a silent symbolic battle between rival concessions. Harpo submits Edgar Kennedy's hat to a slow burn, Kennedy turns over the peanut stand, and then Harpo plays grape-presser and goes wading in the lemonade. (Hysterical note: Things bode ill for heads of state when a peanut stand can't even coexist with a lemonade stand.)

THROUGH THE LOOKING GLASS DARKLY

(Note: This is a blank page. It is intended to represent "ghostly, unreal silence." Read on.)

The first routine performed is a revamped version of the door gag in McCarey's early Laurel and Hardy film *Early to Bed*. Harpo and Chico, trying to get into Margaret Dumont's house, lock a lackey out and then proceed to lock each other out until the lackey comes back and locks *them* out. The game, in this case, was either to see how many reversals they could pull on the lackey, each other, themselves, and the audience, or to add a touch of mystery to what could have been a very routine matter of breaking and entering. Laurel and Hardy can never quit doing this sort of thing, but for them it's because they're brainless. The Marxes do it because they're perverse. Laurel and Hardy once spent twenty minutes trying to break into a house in *Night Owls*. The act is something totally beyond their powers. With Harpo and Chico, it seems to be the other way around.

Once inside the house they seem to have some kind of compulsion, since absolute quiet is so clearly called for, to make the most *deafening* noises possible. When Harpo isn't dancing to music boxes, he's clanging bells or setting off the radio. (The safe turns out to be a radio, and a more spirited rendition of "Stars and Stripes Forever" you've never heard!) When he can't drown the radio, or hide its noise under a pillow, or coax it into clamming up, he smashes it to pieces and throws the pieces away and it's *still* sounding off. (It's amazing how energetic a radio can sound while it's being beaten to death.) Each, coincidentally, hits upon the outlandish idea of masquerading as Groucho and then dresses up that way unbeknownst to the other. When they converge in Margaret Dumont's room, we get the feeling that the scene is not everything it could be. Certainly three Marx Brothers all looking like Groucho and talking like themselves affords more opportunities than simply walking into a room and out again one after the other. In *Horsefeathers* they can walk in and out of a room and give us a great scene *without* being armed with such a pregnant situation.

But the mirror scene is everything it should be. It is more, in fact, than it seems it could ever in the world be *able* to be. We even feel a sense of outrage that it should be allowed to be all that, without anybody stopping it.

It is characteristic of the Marx Brothers that one of their best scenes should also be one of their least characteristic. 1) Our fondest memories of the Marx Brothers are loud, fast, chaotic ones. The mirror scene is fastidiously simple and takes place in a ghostly, unreal silence. It consists of two identical figures in white nightgowns alone in a room at night, gesticulating madly at each other. We don't even hear the padding of their stockinged feet on the rug. 2) What the Marx Brothers are good at doing is a lot of things that nobody else is good at doing. Their humor is generally original enough in tone to keep its relation to old familiar stock material shrouded in mystery. Yet here they rely on the old Mistaken Identity gag, a tradition in the history of buffoonery that is older than most of the hills in California. And the mirror business has made more film appearances than Tarzan: Chaplin's rendition in *The Floorwalker* in 1916 was followed by Max Linder's in *Seven Years' Bad Luck* in 1919, and only the Lord would know how many times it's been done on American vaudeville and English music hall stages (by everybody but the Marx Brothers, who never performed it outside of *Duck Soup*). 3) Any scene between Groucho and Harpo is something of a sore thumb. It's rare enough for Groucho and Harpo just to acknowledge each other's existence. What precluded the two greatest comedians in the team from playing to each other without being supervised by a straight man was either timidity, a deference to comedy tradition, or simply the fact that they had never done it before. McCarey was the first and last director to get away from this frame of mind, and 4) the scene has as much to do with Leo McCarey as it does with the Marx Brothers. It is entirely an improvised routine worked out in rehearsals and is probably the best example in the film of McCarey fashioning McCareyesque comedy inside of Marx Brothers logic and turning an old routine into a scene that nobody but the Marx Brothers could perform. Groucho and Harpo become mere slaves to Leo McCarey, who becomes a mere slave to the Marx Brothers.

Harpo smashes a mirror and when Groucho confronts him he tries to pretend that he's Groucho's mirror image. Now if it were *Chico* attempting such a transparent masquerade, Groucho would simply ask him, "Are you my mirror image?" and Chico would say, "Yes," and it would be settled. It is on just that level of credibility that we are presented with the most outlandish jigs, gyrations, and physical contortions and asked to believe that this is supposed to determine something. Very early in the scene the jigs are up: Groucho is quite obviously in a room with another person. Yet the shenanigans go right on; he is having far more fun with this game of determination than he could ever have by cornering the old spy. Groucho is wise enough to know that things are never what they seem, and since Harpo seems to be a real person, he assumes that he *couldn't* be. Harpo even gets a couple of chances to run away and hide, but he feels he must stick around and humor Groucho.

No less amazing than Harpo's resourcefulness in anticipating *every one* of the farfetched pantomimes that Groucho performs once in a row (sometimes Harpo is resourceful enough to perform them first) is the idea that this represents Groucho's search for Harpo's identity. When Groucho re-enters with a Panama hat concealed about his person, he manages, *while the two are walking around each other* (italics mine), to see that Harpo's got a top hat instead. Groucho smirks in triumph. Now he'll get him. The fact that they just walked around each other is immaterial. It might be one of those three-dimensional mirror images you're always hearing about. (The mirror image might be immaterial, too. Certainly the mirror is immaterial; even its pieces have disappeared.) He slaps the hat on his head and—harpo!—Bingo slaps his on, too, and it's the same hat. So Harpo smirks in triumph and grins and giggles, while Groucho concentrates on the problem of making his mirror reflection, who is dissolving into hysterics, give himself away. Groucho's concept of mirrors differs radically from ours. In Freedonia free speech is outlawed, but everyone is allowed to live in the physical dimension of his choice.

This threatens to go on till the end of the world. No matter *what* slip-ups Harpo makes, Groucho will still believe in him. The test now seems to have become: What could Harpo possibly do that would *not* give the impression he was a mirror image? Groucho's suspicion has turned into an unswerving faith. And

Harpo has forgotten about anything else but being a mirror reflection for the rest of his life. Groucho, fully cooperating, exists only to perform gyrations that Harpo can imitate, so he's been reduced to a reflection of Harpo's imitation of a reflection. Freedonia, Sylvania, the plans of war, international intrigue, the complex system of motivations that started all this, have vanished like the pieces of the mirror. There is nothing left but two blithe kindred spirits, reflecting each other for eternity.

The only way to make sense out of this scene is to remember Groucho's disturbing words, "I haven't been anywhere yet." If we accept the premise that he wasn't at the palace, then it's only natural to assume that he hasn't been here, either, and that what Harpo is really seeing is *his* mirror image, a homeless, neurotic waif whose whole world was shattered when Harpo broke the mirror.

THE TRIAL

GROUCHO: Chicolini, give me a number from one to ten.
CHICO: Eleven.
GROUCHO: Right.
CHICO: Now I ask you one. What is it has a trunk, but no key, weighs 2,000 pounds, and lives in the circus?
PROSECUTOR: That's irrelevant.
CHICO: A relephant! Hey, that's the answer! There's a whole lotter elephants in the circus.
MINISTER: That sort of testimony we can eliminate.
CHICO: Atsa fine. I'll take some.
MINISTER: You'll take *what?*
CHICO: Eliminate. A nice cool glass eliminate.

MINISTER OF FINANCE: Something must be done! War would mean a prohibitive increase in our taxes.
CHICO: Hey, I got an uncle lives in Taxes.
MINISTER OF FINANCE: No, I'm talking about taxes—money, dollars.

CHICO: Dollas! There's-a where my uncle lives. Dollas,
                         Taxes!
MINISTER OF FINANCE: Aww!

Look at the original version of this scene. The President of
Freedonia entered haggling with a taxi driver over a fare of sixty
cents. He told him he didn't *want* a taxicab; he was only *hitch-
hiking!* Groucho then bet Chico twenty to one he'd be found
guilty. He offered the judge half his bet, but Chico took it.

A pompous general stood up and declared, "I have gone
over the facts of this case very thoroughly and I feel . . ." but
was interrupted by Groucho fuming, "You feel! Why don't you
ask me how I feel? I could be sick in bed for all you care, and
you could be sick in bed for all I care." Then Groucho worried
about the budget and decided, "We should have no trouble keeping the wolf from the door," and Harpo went to the door and
found a wolf and shooed him away.

But it's all been eliminated (giving rise to the "eliminate"
pun) and in its place is the most heartless procession of excruci-
ating puns that even the Marx Brothers have ever been shameless
enough to palm off on us. As satire, this scene is less irreverent
than irrelevant (see "irrelevant" pun). As fantasy, it can't compare to what we have just seen. As comedy, it is contestable. As
puns, you can't beat it.

Puns? Whoever thought puns were funny? Puns aren't
funny. Just the nerve of saying them when they aren't asked for,
that's what's funny.

But I shouldn't be taking the scene to court. What this
sequence indicates is that solemnity and amusement don't mix;
they just cancel each other out. It has been said that the Marx
Brothers have destroyed politics in this movie just by making a
big joke of it all, but by the same token a serious discussion of
the jokes would destroy all the jokes. *Duck Soup* will always be
funny, of course, whether it's discussed seriously or not. And the
Marx Brothers, unfortunately, didn't destroy politics.

British sailors aren't *really* limeys. They just call them that.

THINGS BODE ILLIAD

Who *says* this scene doesn't make sense? Why, the war scene makes as much sense as any war ever fought. Let's analyze it.

One is struck by the way the parts fit in relation to the whole, and at the same time by the way the whole does *not* fit in relation to the parts. Take the porpoises who race to the rescue, for instance. For most of us, the horror of life is that it *is* porpoiseless. When we see Groucho calling for help and Harpo hanging out a "Help Wanted" sign, or Harpo doing his recruiting out on the battlefield ("Join the Army and see the Navy"), or Groucho wearing a different costume in every shot (symbolizing the transitory nature of all costumes), or even the ceiling beam that falls to the floor in the shape of a cross (also, miraculously, in the form of an "X," so that "X" marks the spot where the beam falls), it is because they are *there*. We certainly couldn't see them if they were *not* there. This is called "Visual Dynamics."

Or take the rich and complex "gas attack" pun. Zeppo brings the message that one of the generals is suffering a gas attack—a clever reference to the whole movie being a "gas," or "turn-on" (as in "turn on the gas"), as well as a sly comment on the proceedings in the form of the Danish word "*gas,*" for madness. Even the first line, "General Smith reports a gas attack," contains *two* double entendres—namely, that the fun ("gas") is an "attack" on the military, and secondly the suggestion that it is the "gas" that is being "attacked," as if this were a gasoline war. When Zeppo accepts Groucho's answer ("Tell him to take two spoonfuls of bicarbonate of soda in a glass of water"), his complicity in the madness (or "gas") is compounded (most gases are "compounds").

Surprise! There *is* no movie called *Duck Soup!*

After they've won the war by pummeling Trentino with oranges and grapefruit (turned out to be a private duel after all), Margaret Dumont sings that horrible national anthem again and they pummel *her* with oranges and grapefruit. "We didn't fight this war out of love for Freedonia, you know," the final image tells us. "We fought that war because we wanted to throw things." And before we have time to come to grips with *that* disclosure, everything stops.

1933 was just not the best of years to release your movie in, that's all. The big boom of sound had neutralized the big crash of the stock market, but that could last only so long. Sound was a novelty, and a six-year-old novelty is an antique, and the big boom had slowed down to an ominous rumble. And 1933 didn't help any by being the lowest financial ebb of the whole century. People simply didn't have any money to spend on movies, and they didn't care enough any more about the sensual thrill of hearing voices crackle over loudspeakers to spend their last dime on that.

The studios, with archetypal shrewdness, began firing everybody whose films didn't sell. Then they all found themselves with empty rosters and had to go back and hire them again. To top that off, these disruptions were aggravated at Paramount by a surrendering of the reins. Emmanuel Cohen, the new head of Paramount Pictures, didn't really like *Duck Soup.*

And to top all *that* off, neither did anybody else. The people who didn't have any money to spend on movies were absolutely in no mood to watch an uncompromising, exasperating comedy that refused to truckle to their tastes and concerned itself with dictatorships and wars. Audiences found it easier to take the attitude normally afforded to the unconventional: They pronounced it Wrong. *Duck Soup* was not being daring and novel by ignoring customary plot development; it was simply cheating.

Besides that, everybody had *seen* the Marx Brothers before. McCarey's genius for arranging their antics in an adept pattern is somewhat diluted by the fact that they're still the same old antics. Apparently the Marx Brothers, like corn chips, were something you could easily get too much of.

In the *Time* magazine cinema section their rise and fall is remarkable. They manage to progress from no mention at all for *Cocoanuts* to an incidental notice for *Animal Crackers* to the lead article for *Monkey Business* to a full-page spread and a cover photo for *Horsefeathers* back down to an incidental notice again for *Duck Soup*. *Time* said their latest offering was no different from the others; the New York *Times* said it was "rather disappointing"; and *Nation* was good enough to tell us, "Pretty near everyone seems to have agreed that in *Duck Soup* the Four Marx Brothers are not quite so amusing." According to *Nation*, Harpo comes off as "tiresome," Groucho is "badly provided for," and Chico and Zeppo have "less excuse than usual for their existence." As for the others, the intellectuals like *New Republic* and *New Statesman and Nation*, they fell condemningly silent.

No wonder the film has been disavowed by its makers. The question of an artist's integrity may really be worth talking about in any other field, but a comedian's only reward is the laughter of his audience. You can applaud yourself all you want to, but if nobody throws money you're in trouble. A movie that loses its investment and gets so few good notices is a bad movie, and no such arrogant cries as "It was over their heads!" or "It came at a bad time!" will suffice to assuage a performer's wounded ego. It probably *was* over their heads, and it probably *did* come at a bad time, but to say so in 1933 would only mean laying claim to the most desperate sort of rationalization.

McCarey has only said, "It really was not the ideal film for me," which, of course, is the truth. The Marxes themselves subscribed for years to the pat answer provided by studio heads and publicity men that the farther removed from the theater they came to be, the less sure of their material and therefore the less funny they became. They were perfectly convinced that *Cocoanuts* and *Animal Crackers* were the best films they had made. Years later Groucho voiced the intensest of disenchantments with all Marx Brothers movies that were not either *Night at the Opera* or *Day at the Races*. It is only recently, with re-releases of *Duck Soup* playing to packed houses, with the Museum of Modern Art declaring it one of the two Marx movies worthy of posterity, with Marx Brothers books calling it "the most highly regarded of their pictures" and "the Marxes at their most overwhelming," with Italian, French and German critics devoting reams of blather to it, with film festivals and film societies reviving it, that Groucho is able to do a characteristic about-face and declare that he always

did like the Paramount films better than those other ones. "In our early pictures," he says, "we were hilariously funny fellows, knocking over the social mores and customs of our times, but with each succeeding picture the receipts slipped just a bit. The reason we switched from being anarchistic in our humor to being semi-lovable was simply a matter of money." When asked recently which of the Paramounts he liked best, he responded simply, "*Duck Soup*. McCarey directed it."

It's characteristic of the Marx Brothers that when they do make a great film, they do it with all the consistency of a chameleon, all the determination of kittens in the courtyard, and all the bite of a goldfish. *Duck Soup* is simply an aberrant film about our aberrant nature. Its only really disquieting effect is achieved at the end, when it winds up in a war. For the first time, we have seen war right in the context where it seems to belong: at the climax of a Marx Brothers movie. *Monkey Business* had the logic of rebellion on its side, *Horsefeathers* had the logic of a daydream, and *Duck Soup* has no logic but the logic of familiarity. Its story line may be absurd, but don't tell me it isn't plausible, because it is too many true stories.

The Marx Brothers, who embodied everything that was human and real, are suddenly pixie muckrakers, dancing madly through a history that is nothing but a muck. "In individuals," said Nietzsche, "insanity is rare, but in groups, parties, nations, and epochs, it is the rule." In *Duck Soup,* it is both.

iv

do fury honor

The pedant and the priest have always been the most expert of logicians—and the most diligent disseminators of nonsense and worse. The liberation of the human mind has never been furthered by such learned dunderheads; it has been furthered by gay fellows who heaved dead cats into sanctuaries and then went roistering down the highways of the world, proving to all men that doubt, after all, was safe —that the god in the sanctuary was finite in his power, and hence a fraud. One horse-laugh is worth ten thousand syllogisms. It is not only more effective; it is also vastly more intelligent.

—H. L. Mencken, *Prejudices: Fourth Series*

COLLECTION OF HARPO MARX

A NIGHT AT THE OPERA 1935

Irving Thalberg was no more the common, everyday Hollywood producer than Herman J. Mankiewicz was—but for a different reason. Mankiewicz was the antithesis of the Hollywood producer. Thalberg was the ideal. To your typical, ordinary Hollywood producer, Mankiewicz was Beelzebub. Thalberg was the Savior. Hollywood producers prayed to their icons to deliver them from Mankiewicz, but they stayed up nights, they racked their brains, they beat their breasts, they kicked their wives, they pummeled their subordinates, they dashed their furniture and they rent their garments wishing a miracle would turn them from water into Thalberg. They would have hocked their jewels, forsaken their friends, bartered off their children, auctioned off their concubines, sold out their soul, even rented out their swimming pool to be Irving Thalberg. But they weren't Irving Thalberg. None of them was Irving Thalberg. Except Irving Thalberg.

Thalberg was one of the most practical, efficient men that bumbling, eccentric Southern California had ever seen. He was practical and efficient enough to realize that good movies were made neither practically nor efficiently. When injured temperaments came screaming to his office, Thalberg related to them as special individuals rather than cogs in machinery, because he knew that the cogs of the film-making machinery were special individuals. When whole fortunes had been squandered on the 1925 Ben-Hur just to get it half completed, and the entire studio wanted to cut corners on the rest, Thalberg knew that a profit could be turned only by squandering whole fortunes more. And he was right.

For reasons he preferred to keep contradictory, he never let his name get onto the credits of a film, thereby keeping alive the public fancy that if it was a really good movie there was no pro-

Harpo as Erich von Stroheim.

ducer at all. To Thalberg, a good picture was more important than anybody's ego, even his own.

As an assistant to Carl Laemmle, he had turned the infant and amorphous Universal Studios into a functioning operation by removing such nonessentials as clinging relatives and hard-headed artisans like Erich von Stroheim. As an assistant to Louis B. Mayer, he had helped create the conglomerate Metro-Goldwyn-Mayer and turn the man-eating lion into a symbol of quality, by insisting on careful story construction, smooth production polish, constant rewriting and reshooting, and the removal of people like Erich von Stroheim again. He fired Von Stroheim from *Merry-Go-Round* and cut *McTeague* into a Reader's Digest Condensed Version called *Greed* because giving an erratic genius his way was somewhat less to his liking than giving a Midwestern audience its joy and enchantment, and what was good for MGM Enterprises was good for the film industry.

Neither strictly a showman nor strictly a businessman, Thalberg saw with a shrewd eye in each direction, and the eye that watched the box office saw nice little families all in a row, and saw the maternal instinct deciding what the family's movie diet was going to consist of, and saw to it that any movie coming out of his studio was going to make substantial appeal to the Housewives of America.

Here and there, of course, arose the expected grumbles that MGM (or "Retake Valley") was more interested in perfection than in quality. And when the MGM screenwriting department got so interested in perfection that it turned itself into a gaggle of gag men for Buster Keaton and ganged up on his movies and gagged them all to death, Mr. Keaton was less than amused.

But most Thalberg underlings were stunned at his uncanny ability to tell them exactly what they were doing wrong and how they could do it right. They were impressed when he did things like import an expert from China's Central Military Academy to be technical director on *The Good Earth*, or when he hired a little man to run around and check the sound system of every theater that was going to run *Romeo and Juliet*. Thalberg could talk anybody who wasn't Erich von Stroheim or Robert Flaherty into anything, and one writer was so stimulated by Thalberg's presence that she swore she'd leave the film business if he died, and when he died she did.

The MGM Commissary, stocked with the finest food in Los Angeles so that all employees would eat at the same place, was decorated with a wall-size map of the world in which all roads led to Hollywood. Hollywood was the film-making capital of the world, and MGM was the capital of Hollywood, and Irving Thalberg was the Guiding Spirit of MGM. Thalberg and Mayer had gathered together more Stars than there were in the Heavens, and more Kings, Queens, Princes, and Princesses than there were on earth; they had built the finest mousetrap and the mice had beaten a path to their door; they had turned MGM into Hollywood's Palace of Prestige and Immortality, and for all good little show people on their way up it was the End of the Long Hard Road, it was the Happy Hunting Ground, it was the Great Sound Stage in the Sky.

But as show people the Marx Brothers were progressively on their way down. *Duck Soup* was not going over, and Paramount was finding reasons to avoid renewing their contract. By this time Zeppo was so fed up with having jokes made about him instead of for him ("He was constantly being embarrassed by the size of his part, which grew smaller with every preview," according to Arthur Sheekman) that he left his brothers and became an agent with Orsatti and Brene. Finally he was joined by Gummo, and the two of them set up shop for themselves, and the Marx brothers became agents and managers for the Marx Brothers.

The Marx Brothers (latter) made an attempt to return to the stage and went back to negotiating with Sam Harris again. They wanted a musical comedy built around them, to be written by Robert E. Sherwood and Moss Hart, with music by Irving Berlin. When even this failed to pan out, Groucho took off for Skowhegan, Maine, of all places, to enjoy the life of chicken farmers and other primitives, and to see some of the productions of the Lakewood Playhouse, and to be conned into taking the lead in one of them. His brief experience in Ben Hecht and Charlie MacArthur's *Twentieth Century* (later made into a film by Howard Hawks, with John Barrymore as the egocentric director) convinced him that plain old ordinary comic acting could beat the life of a comedian any day, and he considered following Zeppo out, and letting Chico and Harpo be the Marx Brothers.

But Chico was busy playing bridge. Since the struggle ahead was largely a political one (and the reason movie stars become politicians is that they have to be politicians before they can be movie stars), it was a day of smiling fortune that found Chico, the politician of the bunch, playing bridge with Irving Thalberg and deciding that anybody who was such a whiz at cards might be good at making movies too. When informed that Thalberg happened to be head of production at MGM, Chico's response was "Oh."

And Harpo was in Russia. All through the writing and shooting of *Duck Soup*, Alexander Woollcott was hounding him with insistent claims that the minute Roosevelt opened up diplomatic relations with the Soviet Union, the Russians should get a chance to glimpse genuine Marxist comedy. This gave Harpo the once-in-a-lifetime opportunity to ride through Germany and view the early signs of the Aryan persecution of the Jews and to brave Napoleonically the cold, forbidding Russian winter, brightened only by the cold, forbidding looks of Russian officials, ambassadors, and spies. Further cheer was in store for him when he got on stage (after being billed in Russian letters that seemed to be advertising not Harpo Marx but instead some foreigner named Exapno Mapcase) and discovered that Russian audiences refused to "understand" anything he did but play the harp. He treated them to the knife-dropping bit and to the prize lobby scene from *Cocoanuts*, where he drank ink and threw darts, and his audiences treated him to sounds of silence. They wanted to know what was the "purpose" of what he was doing. The impulsiveness of his actions made no sense to them. So he became equipped with two writers (whom he dubbed George S. Kaufmanski and Morrie Ryskindov) who conveniently supplied a "plot" to "explain" what he was doing and considerately left him ignorant of what it might be. For ten minutes he would stand genuinely stupefied while a doctor, a girl, and a jealous husband declaimed about something or other, and then they'd give him the signal and every nuance, twitch and facial catastrophe of this

ЛЕНИНГРАДСКИЙ ГОС. ЭСТРАДНЫЙ ТЕАТР

МЮЗИК-ХОЛЛ

Улица Ракова, 13   Телефон 37-57

с **18** по **24** ДЕКАБРЯ 1933 г.
Только 7 ДНЕЙ

ИЗВЕСТНЫЙ АМЕРИКАНСКИЙ КОМЕДИЙНЫЙ АРТИСТ КИНО и ЭСТРАДЫ

ХАРПО МАРКС

М. Д. КСЕНДЗОВСКИЙ
АРИИ ИЗ ОПЕРЕТТ

СЕРГЕЕВА и ТАСКИН
БАЛЕТ

НАРОВСКАЯ
ПЕНИЕ

КАЦУИТИ
ЯПОНСКИЕ АРТИСТЫ

ИСАЯМИ
АНТИПОД

3 ОСВАЛЬД 3
КОМБИН. АКР.

3 КАСТЕЛИО 3
ТАНЦЫ

2 РУФ 2
КЛОУНАДА

Нач. спектаклей ровно в 8 ч. в.

Касса открыта ЕЖЕДНЕВНО
в 1-9 час. вечера

Заявки на целевые спек-
такли принимаются в БЮРО-
помещение театра МЮЗИК-
ХОЛЛ тел. 3-86

Дети до 16 лет на спектакли
НЕ ДОПУСКАЮТСЯ

Вход в зрительный зал
после 2 звонка и во время
исполнения №№ь безусловно
воспрещается

"Exapno Mapcase" plays the Leningrad Music Hall.
COLLECTION OF HARPO MARX

vintage routine would burst forth *verbatim.* And back would come all the delirious laughter that was intended! All that was needed was that new twist, whatever the hell it was. Performing pantomime in a foreign language must certainly be an odd experience, but poor Harpo didn't even know who the character he was playing *was.* How alienated could you get?

Apparently Soviet totalitarianism had nothing on us, as this was just the dumb-show that Harpo had welcoming him on his return to his own country. Irving Thalberg was going to make the profoundly irrational characters of living legend and specialized appeal conform to the sensible, decent rationale of the big crowd-pleasing studio, and the world was going to be told that there is a readily discernible purpose behind everything we do whether it liked it or not.

What it boiled down to was a question of "class." The "class" struggle, you may remember, was one that had kept each Marx at war with Mother long past adolescence. There is good cause for the fact that the snotty and irreverent Marx Brothers pause to allow glowing, respectful prose to creep into their written reminiscences only twice: once to discuss their mother and then once again for the sake of Thalberg. That the class-ic argument had monopolized the sermons of both makes a pretty poor coincidence. Back as far as *Hi Skule,* the brothers had danced on the vague, fuzzy border between anarchic comedy and chaotic calamity, and, much as they resented their mother for being so class-conscious about everything, they came to be good at swallowing their medicine. They'd done without their mother for a long while, and now the time was overripe for Thalberg, in true maternal fashion, to take them under his wing, cluck his tongue at them for cutting class and set them straight.

Well, if Thalberg could talk some sense into the Marx Brothers' heads, he was even more of a genius than people thought he was. Reverence from the Marxes didn't come easy, and the three of them were just as ready to consider him a Hollywood producer and let him go choke on his prestige and reputation as to come away cheering his perspicacity the day they first held a conference with him in the dining room of a classy hotel called the Beverly Wilshire.

It was by now the fall of 1934. The Marx Brothers, facing a slump in prestige and a possible spell of unemployment, appeared more malleable than usual. Thalberg noted that Zeppo was missing. Yes, the other three nodded, he had decided to become an agent. Thalberg asked if the three of them would want to be paid as much as four had.

"Don't be silly," answered Groucho. "Without Zeppo we're worth twice as much."

Harmless sallies like that were exchanged throughout the meal, but nobody was in a mood for open warfare until *Horsefeathers* and *Duck Soup* were brought up. Usually, whenever anybody talked about *Horsefeathers* and *Duck Soup,* it was in terms of how funny they were. They were or were not funny. Thalberg said they *were* funny, but they weren't good movies. That did it.

"Oh, they weren't, eh?" snarled Groucho. "Well, I didn't think *Grand Hotel* was so great, either, what do you think of *that?*"

This offended Chico and Harpo more than it offended Thalberg. This was no way to talk to a good bridge player! Groucho seemed to be out to prove he was one of the Marx Brothers. But, as Groucho soon discovered, Thalberg most appreciated people who weren't afraid of him, as they seemed to comprise some kind of minority group.

Thalberg explained why he did *not* feel that the logical extension of their illogical dialogue was to string entire movies on an illogical premise. Women were put off by such an approach, for one thing, and that was no help. Groucho said women never did like cockeyed comedy and that was simply one of the facts of life. Thalberg said maybe so, but that they *could* be lulled into coming to the theater, and they could even be talked into liking the movie the comedians were in, so long as there were pretty hats and cute songs and other such enticements. And so could anyone else whose sensibilities were hurt by *Horsefeathers.* That was easy enough to say, but if you fixed up what people *didn't* like about Marx Brothers movies, wouldn't you destroy everything they *did* like about them? Thalberg didn't seem to think so. It was okay to be funny, he said, but be funny in legitimate movies with convincing stories and heart-warming romances and comedy scenes that were integral to everything else. Of course, adding romance to Marx Brothers comedy was nothing new. Their four-man harlequinade had been watered down with mush even earlier than *Animal Crackers* and *Cocoanuts*. But that wasn't entirely the point.

Thalberg had very definite theories about the construction of a film. One of his pet notions was that a film was like a football game: You were to know where you wanted to go and who your opponents were, and you were to know when you'd gained some ground and when you'd suffered a setback, and you were to be able to map out on a grid just how far away from your goal you were and how hard it was going to be to get there. And the best football game was the one that your home team was almost certain to lose because the opposition was driving it steadily up against the wrong end of the field—and then, just when things looked blackest, it miraculously recovered and, with seconds to spare, made that big 98-yard dash to their own goal and final victory. This, in the proper construction of football games, was the desired blueprint.

Another of the favorites was called, befitting the domesticated nature of the desired audience, the Clothesline Concept. According to this, sequence was to follow sequence sequentially, like squads in a platoon, each one making its contribution to the linear progression of the story and then departing the stage. It was the Well-Made Play, now become the Well-Made Screenplay, but with fades instead of curtains.

Thalberg succeeded in using his native persuasiveness to convince the Marx Brothers that he wasn't going to change their style of comedy; he was only going to change the mode of presentation. They could go on being a success without having to undergo an overhauling. This was the best news they'd heard in months. Thalberg and the Marx Brothers were going to get on fine.

But how were they going to fare with that man-eating lion? The hallowed portals of Paradise found themselves dimmed by demonic denizens.

Greta Garbo, for instance, was acknowledged as a goddess

Chico signs in at MGM.   COLLECTION OF HARPO MARX

not only by hordes of her fans but by cohorts at her studio. As
the biggest star in the MGM Heavens, and hence, by inference,
the biggest star in the known universe, she was treated to every
humanly possible deference, she was granted her every whim,
she was indulged in her every fancy. When she asked that her
performance before the camera be shielded from the camera
crew and the other rabble cluttering the set, her wish became
command. When the proper functioning of her moody temperament required that the very presence of Irving Thalberg absent

itself from one of her sets, the request was obeyed. Little preparation did she have, then, for the day she stood ascending in an MGM elevator, sulking languidly in slacks and one of the masculine broad-shouldered jackets later to become the height of feminine fashion, seeking isolation under a hat of enormous brim, ignoring a lowly crowd who glanced off and respected her stand apart, and was suddenly pounced upon by Groucho and Harpo, who peeped under the brim of her hat just to see who it was. Since they were standing behind her, what they were treated to was a million-dollar glimpse of the back of her neck. A million-dollar glimpse of the front of her face at length presented itself, however, and demanded repentance.

What could Groucho do? Decorum demanded that he offer at least the flattering solace, "Excuse me, I just thought you were a fellow I once knew in Pittsburgh."

In the interest of finery, MGM's most accomplished musicians were turned loose on the Marxes' musical numbers, and elegant harpists were known to pre-record for Harpo his more complicated passages. One prodigious maestro named Castel-Nuevo Tedesco, informed of his new assignment, went home in a grandiose stupor and concocted a fifty-seven-page harp sonata. Only when he showed up at the studio bearing this gift did anyone bother to inform him that the most famous harpist in the world had no idea how to read music, and he was going to have to find some other way to compose for him.

While dining out at the world-renowned MGM Commissary, the Marx Brothers had a nasty habit of sitting and eating with *the writers*. This just wasn't done. Writers had a rank on the Hollywood totem pole somewhere between the boom operator and the man in charge of the ashtrays. It was like fraternizing with lepers.

Once, on their way out of the commissary, they ran into old George Folsey, cinematographer of *Cocoanuts* and *Animal Crackers*. Folsey had proved himself too good for Paramount and had now become one of the crack cinematographers at MGM, where he pioneered the use of indirect lighting and eventually photographed *Meet Me in St. Louis, Forbidden Planet,* and many more of the studio's lush Technicolor productions. Harpo's face lit up when he saw George again. "Hi, Bob!" he said. "How ya doin'? Hey, lend me your belt, will ya?" Once more, Folsey lent him his belt, and once more he never saw it again as long as he lived.

Part of the indoctrination program at the new studio was a screening of *The Cameraman,* the classic comedy that Buster Keaton had made in spite of MGM in 1928. This had now gained official status as The MGM Comedy Training Film, but the lesson it was meant to teach was not the one it taught. When Keaton first came to work at MGM, Thalberg assigned the production of his films to Lawrence Weingarten, a man who had married into the noble family by wedding Thalberg's sister Sylvia. Thalberg knew that Keaton was accustomed to handling all the aspects of production by himself, and he instructed Weingarten to sign the bills and leave the man alone. Weingarten interpreted this to mean he should stand over Keaton every step of the way and tell him what to do, and run to Thalberg every time he refused to do it, crying that Keaton was uncooperative. Weingarten took to referring to *The Cameraman, Spite Marriage, Free and Easy,* and the steadily deteriorating films that followed as *"my* pictures," and the more he said it the more true it was. By 1934, Keaton had lost his integrity, his control, his popularity, and his mind, in that order (though MGM was fond of reversing it), and he was snowed in completely.

Herman Mankiewicz was outraged when he heard that the Marxes were going to string along with Thalberg. He maintained that audiences would never sit still for a plot and a romance in a Marx Brothers picture. (This is Herman J. Mankiewicz speaking, mass-media manipulator with his finger square on the pulse of middle America, all right. What he probably meant was that *he* would never sit still for a plot and a romance in a Marx Brothers picture.)

But the question soon turned out to be whether the Marx Brothers would sit still for Thalberg. The MGM production chief was notorious for filling his agenda full of crucial conferences with important and talented people and then getting so involved with every single matter that was brought to his attention that the important and talented people would have to wait for hours, sometimes for days, sometimes for *weeks,* before he had time for them. You could have kept a swell variety show running for two seasons with the talent that Thalberg left sitting around in his waiting room, and the expensive and impatient personalities might include Dorothy Parker, John Steinbeck (who once waited six months for an appointment), George Kaufman (who reported, "On a clear day you can see Thalberg"), and S. J. Perelman (who later wrote, "I seriously began to question whether Thalberg even existed, whether he might not be a solar myth or a deity concocted by the front office to garner prestige") all at once. Well, the finest and most prestigious writers in Hollywood may have been known to sit and burn in protest, but when the Marxes showed up for their first appointment sparked with excitement and bubbling with the energy to get their new production under way and it was announced that Thalberg was busy, they celebrated this news, rather than let their enthusiasm die, by lighting two cigars apiece and smoking them in the crack of his doorway. Eventually he emerged, smoked out of his sanctuary like a gopher. "Is there a fire?" he asked, anxious.

"No," they answered, "there's the Marx Brothers!"

This was a surprise. Though he recognized them clearly through the dolorous haze, it was still a surprise. Nobody had ever fumigated him out of his own office before. He had always been treated like the president of a bank or the archbishop of a diocese. This was not a good precedent.

The conference was punctuated with polite, solemn, gentle but firm admonitions to the effect that they might refrain, in future, from profaning the atmosphere in his office.

But he neglected to say something about jamming up his door with desks and filing cabinets, and when he was busy again the next time they roared, "Who does he think he is, Irving Thalberg?" and went about the business of rearranging his furniture. Shortly after sunset, the thin, frail executive struggled his way out the door, muttered something about insolence in the face of solemnity, and left.

It began to dawn on Thalberg that the more dignity he tried to pull off these arrangements with, the more indignities he got hurled back at him. It also began to dawn on Thalberg that this appealed to him enormously. He began casting about for the good, solid, stuffy backdrop that would make the most suitable contrast for their primeval perversity. James Kevin McGuinness, one of the good, solid, staff story men, came up with the idea of an opera house, and to him was assigned the dim prospect of writing for the Marx Brothers a story line.

McGuinness, who eventually worked his way up to head of the MGM Story Department, was at one time a sports writer and at another time a producer himself and writer on such screen-plays as *When Strangers Marry* and *Tarzan and His Mate*. It seems a shame to hold a man's background against him, but his story outline—which has more uncharacteristic Marx Brothers touches than a script by Salvador Dali and more idiot romances than a junior high school—might aptly have been termed "A Night at the Soap Opera." It is exactly what you'd *expect* a sports writer and an MGM story staff writer to write; it is Grover Jones work from its pearly, home-town-newspaper prose to its hokey, formula-film contrivance; it is an inauspicious beginning.

In it, Groucho is a wrestling entrepreneur who turns to opera contracts when he finds there's more money in it. Chico is a drudge, a prude, and a voice teacher. Harpo is the greatest tenor in all Italy. (No kidding. It just *happens* that in the course of the movie he never sings a note or says a word.) Pio Baroni is a wrestler who is in love with Lili, who is in love with Harpo, who is in love with Maria, who is in love with Ted. Who's Ted?

At one point, McGuinness informs us that "Pio returns from Rome and Lili gives him the air. He blames this on Groucho and assembles his behemoths march forth to vengeance. [That's right, Operator, assembles his behemoths march forth to vengeance.] There is nothing for it but to leave Italy at once." In America, a furor develops over whether Lili should be allowed to do the seduction scene from *Faust* on the stage, and, on the preposterous pretext that Lili is supposed to rest her vocal *speaking* cords, she must argue the matter in song—which progresses, naturally and inevitably, in true sports-writer-sense-of-humor fashion, into a singing argument between Lili, Groucho, and Chico. Why these two rebellious rapscallions should be offended by a seduction scene is a mystery. Almost as much of a mystery

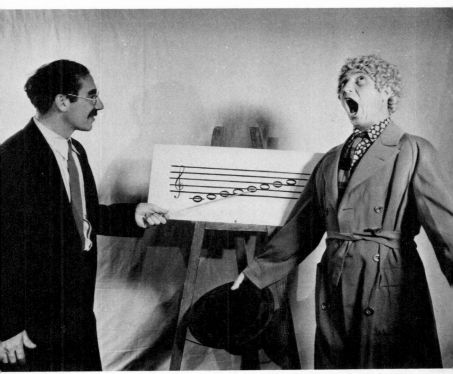

as why Lili shouldn't rest her vocal *singing* cords, if she's going to appear in an opera. But the best mystery is what the difference between a singing cord and a speaking cord might be. McGuinness wrote a mystery.

Thalberg rewarded McGuinness grandly for his mystery, and, clenching his teeth slightly, called his comedy stars in for another conference to talk it over. This meant involving them in his customary script-hopping program, in which conferences for three or four of his forthcoming films would transpire simultaneously and he would hop up and down the hall to keep the fires burning. With anyone else on the MGM staff, this was efficient procedure, but with the Marx Brothers it was like leaving pies on the windowsill. They started out rationally enough by looking at this heavily plotted and love-interested tale about two opera singers and deciding that it was a moderately entertaining intrigue that didn't seem to have much to do with the Marx Brothers. That's all right, said Thalberg, it's something to work from. Then he buzzed into the next room to see how *The Good Earth* was coming.

The Marxes began conferring among themselves unaided; they decided that they had already pulled the cigar gag and the filing-cabinet routine and that there was nothing to do now but strip to the toe and hold a picnic in the fireplace. Thalberg returned, four conferences later, to find potatoes being roasted by three naked men on his carpet. Now he was beginning to understand. He called the commissary and ordered some butter.

It was eventually agreed that Kalmar and Ruby, who were originally set to do only the music, would be the most natural collaborators at this juncture. Thalberg carefully instructed the two old-hand Marxists in his specific concepts of the proper construction of comedy, and they, duly awed, commenced work with McGuinness lasting ten weeks, from early October to mid-December, with a brief pause in November to turn in a progress report on the story changes they'd introduced.

In those ten weeks, the flatulent plotline was simmered down into an innocuous little burp, and some genuine gems of comedy were born. A place was reserved for Margaret Dumont, and Groucho became her business manager. Harpo and Chico were reduced to Baroni's lackeys, and all the romances were dropped but one. Plenty of long speeches were supplied for Groucho, and plenty of potential pantomimes were suggested for Harpo. Suspended all the way along Thalberg's Clothesline was the sweet Kalmar and Ruby whimsy of *Horsefeathers*.

The script opens with the Marx Brothers taking turns roaring in place of the MGM lion, the last being Harpo, who opens his mouth and honks. As before, the introductory locale is Italy. The first scene belongs to Groucho, who, as Otis B. Driftwood, busies himself by dashing back and forth from phone to phone making transatlantic calls to his offices in New York and London for the express purpose of telling them he's too busy to talk to them now.

"I am beside myself!" exclaims the director of the New York Opera Company, waiting for him to finish. "Move over, you're in bad company," Groucho tells him. He keeps introducing himself as Otis B. Driftwood, handing people his card and getting it handed right back to him. "You too?" he wonders after this has happened several times. "*Everybody* can't be Otis B. Driftwood."

Outside the opera house, he admonishes a cab driver who has gotten him there before the opera was over. "On accounta you, I nearly heard the opera," he scolds, and launches into an uncalled-for recitation. "Next time I go to the opera I'll take a turtle. At least, with a turtle, you've got something. When you get tired of it, you can make turtle soup. Of course, you can get turtle soup in cans. But you can't go to the opera in a can. On the other hand, you can't go to the can in an opera." Informed gratuitously by the cab driver that La Scala is the "mother of all opera houses," Groucho asks, "Who's the father?" and goes off on another rampage about the mischievous irresponsible beast who doesn't deserve to be protected by the bewildered cab driver's silence. "Picture all those little opera houses all over the world not knowing who their father is!" he proclaims.

Backstage at La Scala, the plot is introduced when Baroni, upset that he will be leaving his girl friend Rosa, sullenly refuses all the keen festivities Chico and Harpo have planned for him. "Whatsa matter you, boss?" Chico intones solemnly. "You no wanta Curly, you no wanta me, you no wanta contract, you no wanta food, you no wanta wine, you no wanta women. You just like a fly, who no wanta flypaper."

Margaret Dumont (Mrs. Fluffy Claypool) instructs Groucho to sign up Lassparri for the opera company at any cost; Groucho meets Chico backstage and signs up Baroni by mistake. When he reads the contract, he gets as far as "The party of the first part shall be known in this contract as the party of the first part," and Chico says, "That's good enough for me." "Do you realize New York is waiting to hear him sing?" asks Groucho. "Well," hedges Chico, "he can sing loud, but he no sing loud enough for that." Once Groucho has completed the deal he exclaims, "Did I ever pull a bloomer!" Then stops and stares into space contemplatively. "Let's see, did I ever?"

GROUCHO: That's the trouble with you women. All you think about is marriage. Why should you ask me to give up your career? You've got a goal. I've got a goal. Now all we need is a football team.

DUMONT: Otis, you do care a little.

GROUCHO: Fluffy, you'll never know how little. If only you could see me in the dark hours of the night, on my lonely couch. Tossing and tossing, rolling and rolling. Before I know it, it's four, five, six—and no matter how I try I can't roll a seven.

(*Dumont sings*)

GROUCHO: Come on! You're crazy if you stay here with this sort of thing going on.

DUMONT: That was me.

GROUCHO: That's all the more reason you should leave.

CHICO: Now, take a deep breath. Now, hold it and count-a ten.

GROUCHO: You couldn't make it a thousand, could you? (*Dumont sings*)

GROUCHO: I realize it's madness, but I'm staying. You should be singing over the radio.

DUMONT: Why?

GROUCHO: I haven't got a radio.

DUMONT: I adore singing.

CHICO: I like-a singing too. You know whatsa my favorite opera? The elephant opera.

DUMONT: The elephant opera. What's that?

CHICO: *La Tuska* . . .

DUMONT: It's hard to say which my favorite is. I love them all so much. But I just melt away when they play *Butterfly*.

GROUCHO: Play *Butterfly*.

On the ship to America, Groucho pays no attention to a kid shouting, "Paging Mr. Driftwood," until he finally interrupts him to complain: "See here, do you know you've been yelling that for the last half hour? What's the idea?" Guili-Guili, head of the New York Opera Company, discloses to Margaret Dumont that he has already signed up Lassparri, while Groucho was signing up some fraud named Baroni. They can get Baroni to break his contract by having him sing at the ship's concert. Once he's done this, however, Dumont-Claypool is so enthralled by his performance that she decides, as patron of the opera, that she'd rather have Baroni anyway, and it's Baroni who opens the opera season in New York (in an opera named *Louise*). It is a festive occasion, marred only by slight mishaps like Harpo's silent battle with the tailor, which costs him a sleeve (he doffs his cloak at the opera house and is met with Lassparri's inquiry as to the fate of the other sleeve. "He's-a lose it in the war," Chico tells him), and Groucho's perplexing speech to the members of the orchestra, none of whom have the faintest idea who he is:

> Boys, this is the beginning of a new season. Last year they said we were yellow; that we couldn't take it. But, that was last year. This is the beginning of a new season, which I said before. Mind you, I'm not blaming it all on you boys. We had a little tough luck. The trombone player lost his tonsils. Six months later we found them in the trombone. But that won't happen again, because we took away the trombone. The drummer got into a jam with a chorus girl. His wife sued for divorce and was awarded custody of the drum. But that won't happen again. We took the case to a higher court and got the drum back. The harp player's wife had a baby. But that won't happen again. We sent the piano player out of town. The breaks were all against us. But that was last year. This is the beginning of a new season. If I say that again, I'll scream. Boys, go out there and fight.

Once he is finished with this, he goes around announcing, "This is the beginning of a new season" to everybody.

Unfortunately, Baroni has picked just this night to lose his voice, and suddenly all three Marx Brothers are out of a job. They pound the pavements of Fifth Avenue and Wall Street looking for work but find nothing. ("I'm convinced now that the

country doesn't *want* a good bank president," sighs Groucho.)
Finally they all obtain employment in an Italian restaurant by
barging in and striking it.

Now they while away their hours toiling for a living and
nursing Baroni's throat back to health. Harpo, as a combination
cook and dishwasher, takes every order for pheasant or mon-
goose and whips up a plate of spaghetti. He earns time off by
hiding out in the freezer, wearing a fur coat and huddling around
the fire reading a newspaper. Groucho, as a combination waiter
and floor show, won't even answer a simple question like
"Where's Baroni?" without whipping a handkerchief over his eyes
and declaiming, "I see a boat! And at this boat I see Baroni."
"Why did he go to the boat for?" he is asked. "To get to the
other side," he answers. Even when an angry customer complains, "Where's my food?" out comes the old handkerchief
again. "I see a blue haze. You don't want a blue haze, do you?"

Finally, the federal agents come to take the immigrants
away, and, charged with desperation, the refugees hail a fire
truck ("In Case of Fire, Break Glass," says a sign on the wall.
Harpo smashes a window. It doesn't work) and ride like fury to
the opera house with Baroni (Groucho lighting a cigar in the
smokestack and saying it's the first car he's ever been in where
the lighter works). En route, they pass a real conflagration and
call out, "Keep it going till we get back."

Once at the opera house, they tie up Lassparri with a fire
hose and rush Rosa and Baroni on stage, where they do just swell,
and everybody is back in the chips and the good graces of
Margaret Dumont. Groucho closes the show with a grand scheme
("I'm going to get the government to put Baroni's picture on half
dollars. The government buys the pictures from us for a dollar
each. We sell the half dollars for a quarter and make seventy-five
cents on every half dollar") while Rosa and Baroni grab the
fadeout in song.

It was a very sketchy sort of script, and it quite obviously
would take another ten weeks to turn it into anything usable. It
would have to be ten weeks of somebody else's time, however, as

Kalmar and Ruby already had a prior commitment to a stretch at Warner's right about now, and they wormed out of the project. As it turned out, they didn't even do the music.

Thalberg, who had a reputation for everything but comedy, was at a loss to know where to go from here, but the answer that always came in handy when he ran into a scripting emergency was to put plenty more writers to work on the thing and see what they could come up with. When Groucho heard that there were two "unspoiled" neophytes named George Seaton and Robert Pirosh hanging around on contract with nothing much to do, he looked them up, told them he wanted a funnier story, and gave them Kalmar and Ruby's *A Night at the Opera* to show them what he wanted a funnier story than.

It was a cold, rainy winter's night when Seaton and Pirosh found their way to Groucho's home, their synopsis clutched in their trembling fingers. "Come into my parlor," intoned their wary host, and when they got as far as the parlor it occurred to them that they'd left Kalmar and Ruby's script in the car. "That's a good place for it," said Groucho. "Especially if it's an open car."

Dour as his mood seemed to be concerning the fate of the impending project, the story they brought to him that gloomy night cast upon his visage a ray of joy. An old Broadway legend and popular backstage tale served as the basis for a plot involving Groucho as a Broadway producer determined to stage the worst opera in the history of Western Civilization, just so that when the show closes after a phenomenally short run, the backers whom he has soaked for ten times what the show actually costs won't expect to be paid back, and he can escape to Venezuela with nine times what the show actually costs. Unfortunately, the opera becomes a hit by mistake (one of those hits by mistake that eternally plague show business), and now he *owes* ten times what the show actually *makes*.

That's great, said Groucho. It's just what we need. That's terrible, said Thalberg. It's just what we *don't* need.

Patiently, Thalberg sat down with Groucho and explained once more how to put a movie together. "I don't want a funny story," he insisted. "Let's stick with a good, simple story like the one we've got, and hang funny scenes on it. You can't build comedy on top of comedy. You might make a funny picture that way, but you won't bring in any customers."

(When Mel Brooks made *The Producers* in 1968, based on exactly that story, he seemed to disprove Thalberg on both counts.)

Sighing, Groucho faced the dilemma squarely between the eyes and yearned for the good old days of Kaufman and Ryskind, who, he recalled, were venerable masters at mingling nonsense with a story line and whom he considered the best writers they ever had. Thalberg was perfectly agreeable to signing them up and getting them involved in the struggle, but there were more dilemmas to be faced between the eyes. Kaufman's damning appraisal of the movie business went far beyond the faint disapproval of Mr. Perelman, and he had promised himself that he would mine salt in Nevada before degenerating into such hackery. Also, there was the problem of geographic location: Thalberg would naturally want them out in California under his watchful eye, and Kaufman, whose opinion of Southern California made Perelman's vision of terror and dread look like a savant's Valhalla, had made a promise to himself never to be more than twenty minutes from Times Square.

Thalberg's native persuasiveness, however, and the money Thalberg was willing to pay—which looked good to anybody in a depression year—turned his head slightly, as did Morrie Ryskind, who very much wanted to do the film and kept saying, "Look, a promise to yourself is pretty easy to break." But the deciding factor turned out to be George's wife, who said, "Oh, George, don't be silly. Go ahead."

Weeks passed. Kaufman and Ryskind never saw the Kalmar and Ruby script; they proceeded from November's outline. What they retained was about three gags and most of the proper names. They used the old story line, except for the Italian restaurant, but turned the old situations into whole new comedy routines. Their version of Otis B. Driftwood has no long speeches at all, and from the impulsive, self-contradictory, Wagstaffish character Kalmar and Ruby had drawn, Kaufman and Ryskind turned him into a very consistent fast-talking swindler who is all smart answers and snappy comebacks. Harpo—attesting to the hopelessness Kaufman always felt about writing material for him—became virtually gagless, and the three or four extended routines originally provided for him were replaced with not much of anything. Finally, in accordance with Thalberg's views on story construction, the point of joblessness was moved to a strategically more arresting spot just preceding the climax, so that they could make the old 98-yard dash to victory. The story was converted from that hackneyed bit about the down-and-out singer who rises again to fame, to that hackneyed bit about the unknown understudy who gets his big break.

Still there were problems. Nobody was particularly happy with this script, either. Kalmar and Ruby, in fact, took one look at it and asked that their names be taken off the credits.

Thalberg knew just the thing. Get another writer.

There was nothing Al Boasberg was better at doing than dreaming up dementia to doctor an ailing script. His monumental ingenuity at packing sentences with insanities was matched only by his monumental indifference to the logical progression of a plotline. At the very mention of his name, associates would either recoil as if attacked by a lunatic or roll around in hysterics and stay up half the night trading Boasberg gags. Boasberg was a friendly, 300-pound person, who wreaked his vengeance on people he didn't like by creating hilarious stories about them, or by turning his large neck widely red and getting good and angry. He liked to spend hours in a bathtub, yammering idiocies into a dictaphone.

Weeks more passed. Kaufman, being Kaufman, had found seven other projects to be busy with and returned to twenty minutes from Times Square, but Ryskind stuck around and, having little to do with Boasberg, sat alone in his hotel room bolstering the drooping sequences.

Finally he had something he thought would work, and he bounded to Thalberg with twelve pages fairly dripping with hilarity and offered it for his appraisal. Ryskind had known Thalberg to be solemn, serious-minded, but hardly humorless, from the age of eighteen, so he was hardly prepared for the solemn, serious-minded, remorselessly humorless scrutiny Thalberg applied to Ryskind's twelve helpless pages. After suffering mirthlessness for approximately three eternities, he was even less prepared for Thalberg's straight-faced verdict: "That's the funniest thing I've ever read."

Thalberg and his straight face suffered mirthfulness no more gracefully, typical of which was the day he checked progress with Boasberg.

"How are you doing, Al?" Thalberg asked him, and the inquisitiveness nettled him.

"I'll be done by tonight," Boasberg grumbled, "and you can come to my office and pick the stuff up."

When Thalberg and the Marxes popped over to see what had happened, they found an empty office. Writers, typists, receptionists, clerks, all had gone home; but deep in their hearts they knew that Uncle Al wouldn't disappoint them, and they began scouring the place industriously. Left alone with only logic to guide him, Thalberg might have searched for years; Groucho, having a better idea of what he was up against, figured things out more quickly. Boasberg, it turned out, had written an entire sequence, typed it up, shredded it like cabbage, and decorated the ceiling with it; and once they had found it, the three brothers proceeded directly to the business of patching it up again so they could read it. Thalberg only stood back against the wall and wondered if all comedies were done this way. He kept one arm poised for defense, in the event of bathtubs dropping from the ceiling or tennis balls leaping out of desk drawers.

The scene, when it was legible again, was something taking place in a stateroom in the middle of an ocean liner, at the point of the story where all the principals leave Italy and sail to America. When Boasberg's work was done, everything was done; the whole script was put together, and everyone met and had another look at it. It was better, they agreed, staring morosely at the accumulated screenplay, wondering how else they might tinker before taking the dread indelible step of committing the thing to film. And slowly, felicitously, grew the germ of the conception of the idea of The Tour.

Between the Marx Brothers and Irving Thalberg it was inevitable that The Tour should be conceived. The Marx Brothers knew that a joke wasn't a joke until fourteen different audiences had laughed at it, and no joke was a Marx Brothers joke until they'd figured out fifty different ways to fool around with it. It wasn't simply a matter of testing, or of sneak-previewing the movie and cutting out the lines that didn't sound funny, in the way that was suitable for ordinary comedians. Vivid memories of the caliber of disaster indicated by the first forty or so performances of *Cocoanuts* was enough to drive home the impression that live performances and infinite monkeying was the only way to ferment tepid material into something toastworthy.

Thalberg had toyed with the notion, too, in the dark days of early sound, by inviting audiences to the sound stage to witness pre-filming performances of *The Last of Mrs. Cheney* and *The Trial of Mary Dugan* (the latter of which is unwittingly referred to in *Animal Crackers*). So he was entirely sympathetic to the idea of extracting from the script the key comedy scenes, turning them into a vaudeville show and playing them in one city after another, giving the comedians ample time to ad-lib lines and horse around and play to each other like in the old days.

In the spring of 1935 the Marx Brothers embarked from Los Angeles to Salt Lake City, taking with them everyone who was to have a major part in the movie, including Allan Jones and Kitty Carlisle, as Baroni and Rosa, and including Margaret Dumont.

By this time Margaret Dumont was Law. She was a law that existed in Marx Brothers pictures for the sake of being broken. Miss Dumont (or "Old Ironsides," as Groucho fondly referred to her, in honor of her corsets) went through her whole life playing the part of the stately matron with her chin up in the air who looks like she has a plaster-of-Paris bust of God sitting at home on her dresser. Opinions differ as to whether she really *was* that part or whether her whole life was just a big put-on.

Groucho claims to this day that she almost never understood the jokes that were made about her. "This was also true of all my wives," he says. Some acquaintances insist she had next to no sense of humor at all. No wonder she "never got over her astonishment at the Marx Brothers," as Harpo's wife describes her. She thought they were the grandest people on earth and could never quite understand just why they were always pushing her off chairs or pulling her skirts up. Flattered as she came to be by all this attention, their entire behavior pattern was so wholly beyond anything she knew that there was nothing to do about it but ruffle her feathers and pout and then go on pretending that everything was in its place and all was right with the world so that she could be startled afresh by the next outrage. When they were on tours together, Harpo used to steal her wig, and she would be left to emerge from the train in the morning with a "Pullman" towel around her head. When they were on sound stages together, Groucho thought it would be fun to take her "lingerie" (large pairs of pantaloons) and drape it over the side of her trailer for all the world to see. Nowhere in her repertoire of reactions was there any way to deal with this, and it took everything she had just to fuss in exasperation and yell, "Julie!" (She could never bring herself to call anybody "Groucho.") "Julie, you can't *do* that!" Sometimes she got so mad she'd lock herself in her dressing room and refuse to come out for hours. In desperation, she once approached Harry Ruby and exclaimed, "Harry, I don't know what to do. I love the boys, and they're very considerate to me, they're always putting me in their pictures and thinking of me all the time, but they just do the *darndest things!* It's rather embarrassing!"

But when they asked her to work with them again, there was never any argument. What else could she do? Nobody could accept her as a *serious* version of a stately woman. Every time she appeared, audiences anticipated the cue for Groucho's entrance. She lived alone, with one maid, just waiting for the next time she would be asked to appear with the Marx Brothers.

Groucho is fond of relating how she went up and asked him what he meant by his line in *Duck Soup,* "Remember that we're fighting for this woman's honor, which is probably more than *she* ever did." Less frequently does he tell how, on the train for the *Night at the Opera* tour, "we went into her compartment, locked the door, took off our clothes, and *showed* her what that line meant."

"Scenes from *A Night at the Opera*" was too bizarre to be called quaint but too old-fashioned to be called novel. Vaudeville was on its way out, but as there were no other acts on the bill, this wasn't really vaudeville, and it wasn't really a play either, since it told half of its story live and half of it by proxy with slides and expository monologues. The disconnected whimsy of, say, *Horsefeathers* would actually have lent itself more readily to such treatment, but now of a sudden the Marx Brothers were telling a story, and the scenes looked their best when understood in relation to a concurrent plot. It isn't a play, folks, it's a movie that isn't shot yet, but it's not the *whole* movie, so here's something else you should know. The shows were five times a day, six days a week, and for eight weeks. For the inveterate performers of Broadway success, this was somewhat of an unwelcome trip back Home, the five-a-day being an old vaudeville synonym for the Galley—a rigor to which they hadn't exposed themselves for nearly fifteen years. First show, after a month of rehearsals, was Monday at noon in Salt Lake City, and this scared little screenplay saw its first light of day and shriveled like a prune. Salt Lake City in the middle of the Depression was no fit home for hysterics, but to *Night at the Opera,* Salt Lake City was, so far, the world, and its titters and smirks only indicated that there was work to be done. It was another inauspicious beginning.

Morrie Ryskind and Al Boasberg had followed along, still having little to do with each other, and held conferences with the clowns between each of the fifty-minute shows that were spaced at handy intervals such as 12:30, 3:00, 5:00, 7:30, and 9:30, to give them time to decide what had worked and what hadn't and to retire into a corner for a minute and quick come up with something that would. These were perhaps the most dynamic of script conferences, and, given the cold-water-in-the-face impetus of a daily audience, the comedy minds of the company found themselves startled into wittiness like dancing tenderfeet. No major rewriting could be done at this point, but an abundance of cuts were made, and emphasis was shifted around, and funny lines were being originated on the hour. Once again they discovered to their dismay that some of their favorite lines were not getting the laughs from audiences that they had gotten from writers, but, conversely, it turned out that some of the presumably weaker lines proceeded to fare just fine. One exchange ("I'm Henderson, plainclothesman." "You look more like an *old* clothes man to me") was formerly considered a likely candidate for omission by everyone who was asked and some who weren't, but the minute Groucho said it on stage, it became one of the few laughs they could count on.

It had been agreed that if the tour didn't go well, there would be no movie, but by the light of the silvery eighth week such trepidations appeared to be groundless. Things finally seemed to be going well. When Thalberg saw the show in San Francisco, it was to the sound of raucous laughter, though he succeeded in giving the cast the jitters by refusing to crack a smile again.

All that was left to do now were some minor bits of rewriting, consisting in the main of motivations to clear up and sub-scenes to be strengthened. Thalberg trusted his old reliable policy of distributing the problems to a variety of writers, and after the naïve little cubs Pirosh and Seaton had hammered away at the various tasks for two whole days in one corner of the lot, it startled them to pause in the midst of brainstorming to hear two strange voices drifting in from the next office verbally masticating the selfsame matters. Contriving at noontime on the third day to have their lunch break coincide with their neighbors', they crept out of their office to espy none other than Bert Kalmar and Harry Ruby creeping out of theirs. It was even more of a surprise to discover that they'd been given precisely the same assignments. But it was no surprise to Kalmar and Ruby, who said, "Oh, we know. We've been listening to you through the wall for two days."

––––––

Would this erstwhile masterwork ever come to pass? It wasn't until the middle of June that Sam Wood took his post and, at long last, *A Night at the Opera* started to become a movie.

Sam Wood was the oldest and most conventional of all the Marx directors, but also the one with the greatest amount of previous success. Wood had a career of over a decade behind him, the bulk of it in Hollywood house-fillers like *Bluebeard's Eighth Wife, The Dancin' Fool, So This Is College,* and *They Learned about Women;* and in those years he had managed to

Sam Wood's attempts at becoming one of the Marx Brothers were doomed from birth.   ACADEMY OF MOTION PICTURE ARTS AND SCIENCES

direct practically every star of the silent era that you've never heard from since: William Haines, Wallace Reid, Wanda Hawley, and Ethel Clayton among them.

Reportedly chosen on the basis of Thalberg's notion that he hadn't had a successful film in so long that he'd have no compunction against conforming to policy, Wood's decidedly dramatic tendency was continually finding itself at odds with the Marxes' own peculiar ideas of how a film was made. He didn't quite cotton to this business of making up new lines of dialogue just before the scene was shot, any more than they could accommodate his idea of preceding every take with the exhortation, "All right, gang, let's get in there and sell 'em a load of clams!" And when the Marxes arranged to have Wood's customary morning milk brought to him in a baby bottle, he was just confused. Not having been along on the tour, the director was not quick to adjust to the notion that the tempo of some of the scenes had been worked out to the bat of an eyelash, and whenever he had the bright idea of speeding up this exchange to get some life into it, or slowing it down to make it flow more evenly, the writers would run up to him with their stopwatches and point out that this pause was supposed to be five seconds, not three, because the audience was laughing that long. But what finally got everybody's goat was his little old directorial habit of sitting back in his chair and ordering that every scene be shot twenty times. *Every* scene. Working from the principle that everyone wasn't tired enough already, Wood adopted a technique that left them totally sapped. It takes a moderate amount of energy to go through *anything* twenty times in a row, but when it's exuberant Marx Brothers mania, and when each time you're giving your all, knowing that this particular shot could just be the one, and sent to theaters all over the country as sole representative of all the work you've been going through, it begins to tax the very limits of your stamina. By the end of Take Four, there was nothing left that could be called funny.

Groucho got annoyed again. So did Harpo and Chico. Once or twice had been enough for a scene even when they *hadn't* tested it two hundred and forty times in front of an audience. They understood all this stuff about being perfectionists, and developing a feeling for the scene, and obeying the call of a demanding art, but they *didn't* understand why they should do every scene twenty times. "This jerk we have for a director doesn't know what he wants," grumbled Groucho, "so he shoots everything twenty times and hopes there's something good in it." Harpo spent one whole day hanging on a harness that held him under his arms and between his legs so he could swing on ship rope and peer into portholes. Twenty takes of all those shots, and he was bleeding at the crotch and underarms, but he had to go right on being cute and impish. Harpo also submitted to day after day of swinging from rope to rope and from rope to railing, without benefit of a harness, a stunt man, or a process shot, for the final scene in the catwalks of the opera house—which he later admitted was a stupid thing for a forty-seven-year-old man to be doing, especially one who was never much of an acrobat to start with.

Punctuating the recurrent demands for perfection, Wood imposed a fifty-dollar fine on anybody who showed up late. This imposition was fine with Groucho, whose sleepless nights were sweetly suited for fine points of early-morning punctuality, but Harpo and Chico felt imposed upon and responded by sneaking over to Groucho's house one night and jamming a wedge of wood into the workings of his garage door. The first brother to have the fine imposed on him, then, was Groucho, which punctured his appreciation for it appreciably. As it went on to be imposed on the others, however, and the standard answer went on to become "I'm at you double or nothing," followed by wagers hedged against wagers and bets being batted around, it punctured Wood's appreciation too, and he decided to call the whole thing off.

———

Finally it was all done. Conferences, screenplays, rewrites, revamps, tours, takes, retakes, and headaches, and finally they had a film to show for it. Everybody who had anything to do with *Night at the Opera* and everybody who was anybody at MGM attended the historic sneak preview at Long Beach, where a full-fledged throng of an audience sat through this long-hard-fought-and-won classic comedy and never opened their mouths except to yawn. *Another* inauspicious beginning.

And then everybody was in the lobby wondering what they had done wrong and what they could do to make it right. Groucho—who could have told you at any single point in their career that doom was just beyond the next rise of the curtain—wore the blackest face. He had been right all along. The more enthusiastic grew their hijinx on the screen, the sillier and more old-fashioned looked the whole idea of the Marx Brothers.

Now he'd have plenty of time to try his hand at being a writer. Now he'd have no choice.

As writers and vice-presidents joined the depressing throng, the beaming face of Louis B. Mayer failed to brighten things. Mayer and Thalberg had made it official policy not to agree on anything, and when Mayer insisted that the days of the Marx Brothers were numbered and that hiring them was folly, Thalberg had refused to listen. Mayer gave himself several points for being right and went home.

One remaining face refused to admit defeat. "I know what it is!" said Chico. They all turned to him. If he could get them through *Cinderella Girl* he could get them through this. "The mayor of Long Beach died today," he said, "and everybody was so sad they couldn't laugh."

He was right about the mayor, and the connection had as much basis in rationality as any idea born of enthusiasm, but it had precious little effect on the man who was mentally preparing new careers for himself. "Bah!" said Groucho.

But his brother wasn't through. "I know what it is," he said again. "There was no bingo tonight. Everybody came expecting bingo, and they were so disappointed they couldn't laugh."

A lot of money and several careers were hanging on these decisions, but even so it was hard to swallow the bingo bit. "Humbug!" said Groucho.

Further suggestions from Chico only served to heighten the dismay, and finally Thalberg, as perplexed as anybody, suggested that there was no explanation, and if they went elsewhere to have their sneak preview they would get the response they had worked for. This didn't sound plausible, but it did sound easy, and, animated by Chico's incomprehensible high hopes, they agreed to suspend disbelief until the following evening.

Oddly enough, Thalberg was right. Not so odd, of course, since Thalberg had been right before, but it was disconcerting to have their embarrassing shenanigans turn into red ripe juicy comedy as soon as they were displayed at another theater somewhere else where the people weren't sad about anything, and have no explanation for it.

Eventually the explanations materialized. Not only is Long

Beach as fully an unfertile soil for ecstatic audience response as Salt Lake City, but the audience that was assembled that night for reasons other than to see an unannounced comedy was not necessarily the most prone to prostration. But by then *A Night at the Opera* was one of the comedy hits of the year, and the explanations grew increasingly uninteresting.

Perfectionism hadn't ceased even yet, all indications of smash success to the contrary. Here and there a line in an untested scene would turn out to be a dud, and it was gracefully, skillfully cut out of the negative. One perfectly successful bit of dialogue was removed from the final scene simply in the interest of tempo: Groucho, seeing the police stomp on stage in the middle of the performance, calling out, "Either there are cops in *Il Trovatore*, or the jig is up." (For some reason, they left in the shot of the cops in *Il Trovatore* walking in front of the scenery, so you're *waiting* for a punchline, but it never turns up.) It was then up to the individual censor boards in every single one of the states to cut the sexual innuendo of Margaret Dumont asking, "Are you sure you have everything, Otis?" and Groucho replying, "I've never had any complaints yet."

A Night at the Opera is a view of the Marx Brothers decked out in refinery like a Christmas shopping window, going through some very funny motions against a stops-out backdrop of posh set design, realistically reacting extras, careful choreography, and first-class camerawork. (The Paramount cameras never seemed to care what was going on.) This keeps them from being the figures of fantasy that Mankiewicz allowed them to be: Harpo can never step outside the bounds of reality any more, for one example; he may use an ax for a job as simple as slicing salami, but now it must be an ax lying handily on a nearby barrel, not concealed mysteriously on his person. As if this restriction were not enough to ground him entirely, he is left in this picture so devoid of material that, but for a gag here and a funny face there, he has abdicated domination fully to Groucho. Being back in the real world again (or MGM's idea of the real world) has a tendency to suggest that a relationship among the three of them does indeed exist, so that when Groucho and Chico strike up a spontaneous conversation over Lassparri's unconscious being, requiring none of the formal amenities that Claypool and Gottlieb demand, much more is meant than could ever be indicated by Groucho's and Chico's spontaneous conversation in *Duck Soup,* where nothing is meant by anything. Though the Marxes occupy considerably less than 100 percent of the screen time, the moments that are theirs are loud and strong and almost enough to make up for the moments that are not.

The music, by Nacio Herb Brown and Arthur Freed, who are better remembered for *Singin' in the Rain* and music in movies that people go to see music in, reaches shades of excellence that make most of the former interludes look pretty pale by comparison, but that hardly seems an ambitious enterprise. Allan Jones is working so hard to be charming that his synchronization is off. Harpo and Chico are expertly handled, however, and Harpo's rendition of the show's hit song "Alone" is probably his most beautiful solo.

The only apparent difference between the carefully developed story of *Night at the Opera* and the awkward frames of *Horsefeathers* or *Monkey Business* is that the one in *Night at the Opera* has more time spent on it. Kalmar and Ruby were able to accomplish in six bad lines what it takes Thalberg six bad scenes to do. The trouble with Sam Wood is that he thinks the dramatic scenes are just as interesting as the comedy scenes. He's wrong. Thalberg's rationale was that nobody remembered *Duck Soup* when they were through laughing at it, and if you gave them a good solid story and a romance, they'd have something to come away with. This is rather an odd way of looking at it, considering the great number of people who can recite whole pages of *Duck Soup* dialogue verbatim, and the great number of people who have seen *Night at the Opera* a hundred times and still can't remember whether Polly Bergen or Kitty Carlisle is in it.

This film changes mood so many times that it's hard to keep in mind that it was Thalberg's insistence on a unified entertainment package that got it made in the first place. It can hardly be said to be one movie at all, in fact, but a lot of little ones instead.

Five of them are Marx Brothers movies, though, and they're awfully good.

MRS. CLAYPOOL, MR. GOTTLIEB, MR. GOTTLIEB, MRS. CLAYPOOL

DUMONT: Mr. Driftwood: three months ago you promised to put me into society. In all that time, you've done nothing but draw a very handsome salary.

GROUCHO: You think that's nothing, huh? How many men do you suppose are drawing a handsome salary nowadays? Why, you can count them on the fingers of one hand . . . my good woman!

DUMONT: I'm not your good woman!

GROUCHO: Don't say that, Mrs. Claypool. I don't care what your past has been. To me you'll always be my good woman. Because I love you. There. I didn't mean to tell you, but you . . . you dragged it out of me. I love you.

DUMONT: It's rather difficult to believe that when I find you dining with another woman.

GROUCHO: That woman? Do you know why I sat with her?

DUMONT: No.

GROUCHO: Because she reminded me of you.

DUMONT: Really?

GROUCHO: Of course. That's why I'm sitting here with you. Because you remind me of you. Your eyes, your throat, your lips! Everything about you reminds me of you. Except you. How do you account for that?

Our first glimpse of Groucho goes unheeded, as the back of something we take to be an extra's head. His true identity isn't revealed until a boy is asked to page him; Groucho leaps out of his seat to call him down for it. ("Do I go around yelling *your* name?") From here he turns on Margaret Dumont, who would like to protest being stood up, and berates her for sitting there all evening with her back to him. ("When I invite a woman to dinner,

I expect her to look at my face. That's the price she has to pay.") This goes on until she is turned off about the idea of eating with him at all, then he goes ahead and joins her at her table—but not before getting good and outraged at the bill he has incurred and handing it to his blond floozy to pay. Margaret Dumont seems to be putting up with Groucho for the time being only because she has put up with him for so long already. She bears a strange, unsettled non-reaction to his spectacular effronteries, and sometimes she just looks away, as if she could pretend they weren't happening.

After Groucho tires of insulting only one large and dignified person, he tosses off a bit of exposition and invites a second one in. So, once he is through behaving indecently toward Margaret Dumont, he can flare up at Herman Gottlieb for behaving decently toward her. ("Making love to Mrs. Claypool is *my* racket.") The more annoying he is to everybody concerned, the more annoyed he gets at *them*. Cheerfully aware of the fact that he depends upon not one but both of these horrendous figures for his livelihood, he continues to have every sort of fun at their expense.

George S. Kaufman and the well-made playwright permeate the proceedings, drenching them with skillful construction and rich dialogue simultaneously. The scene does us a favor by clearing the air of the tiresome matters of exposition and still keeping up a high level of low comedy. Otis B. Driftwood, it turns out, has a fine mind for determining the meet and seemly course of action, then turning around and doing something else. All of *us*, knowing full well where duty lies, lend our sympathies to the man who doesn't do his. He ends up emerging victorious, while Gottlieb and Claypool retire in disgrace.

THE CONTRACT ROUTINE

GROUCHO: "The party of the first part shall be known in this contract as the party of the first part."

CHICO: Well, it sounds a little better this time.

GROUCHO:	Well, it grows on you. Would you like to hear it once more?
CHICO:	Just the first part.
GROUCHO:	What do you mean, the . . . the party of the first part?
CHICO:	No, the first part of the party of the first part.
GROUCHO:	All right, it says the, uh, "The first part of the party of the first part shall be known in this contract as the first part of the party of the first part shall be known in this contract . . ." Look, why should we quarrel about a thing like this, we'll take it right out, eh?
CHICO:	Yeah, ha, it's-a too long, anyhow! Now, what do we got left?
GROUCHO:	Well, I got about a foot and a half. Now it says, uh, "The party of the second part shall be known in this contract as the party of the second part."
CHICO:	Well, I don't know about that . . .
GROUCHO:	*Now* what's the matter?
CHICO:	I no like-a the second party, either.
GROUCHO:	Well, you shoulda come to the first party, we didn't get home till around four in the morning. I was blind for three days!

The contract routine is one of the few great scenes in the history of film in which two people do nothing but stand and talk. The longer they stand and talk, the more hopeless becomes the idea of standing and talking, and the more hopeless becomes the idea of standing and talking, the longer they stand and talk. The scene consists of a pointless pyramid of perplexities, in which a lot of time and effort are involved in getting nothing accomplished. Five or six comic personalities have converged upon the confusion and rendered it fathomless, and countless rounds of experiments and experience have calculated laughs like compound interest. The scene proceeds merrily along a carefully established thread, and every time it departs from the thread it gets merrier and merrier.

Groucho and Chico descend like falcons on the money their little agreement is supposed to produce for them, and they have it all devoured before they even get started. Then they descend like falcons on the agreement that is supposed to produce the money, and that gets devoured before long. All formality in this agreement is abolished, including the formality of reading the agreement. "I haven't said anything worth hearing," says Groucho. "Well, that's why I didn't hear anything," answers Chico. "Well, that's why I didn't say anything" is the only sensible reply. The party of the first part is defined, then the first part is done away with and the party is attended till all hours of the night. Disagreements become the only thing they can agree on. Baboons are invoked.

Groucho and Chico grow increasingly aware of the contract's inadequacies, until, finally, clause by clause, they reduce it to shreds and tatters like the logic that produced it and wipe it off the face of the earth. Chico insists on coming up with aesthetic critiques of the prosaic verbiage. ("Hey, look, why can't-a the first part of the second party be the second part of the first party? Then you *got* something.") It's this idea that you can treat a formal agreement with any kind of individualized response that finally kills the whole deal. If there's one thing you're not supposed to concern yourself about in the reading of a contract, it's whether or not you enjoy the sound of the words. There wouldn't be any contracts left if people went around worrying about that. When all the clauses but one have been evaluated out of existence, only the signature remains to be squabbled about. Chico can't write. This is immaterial; there is no ink in the pen. Then, with a "Sic Semper Tyrannus" of a pun ("That's the sanity clause." "You can't fool me, mister, there ain't no Sanity Clause!"), they laugh off the solitary remaining shred of paper as a myth. Their work is done.

Their victory has somewhat of a hollow ring to it when you consider that they had set out to *use* the contract to effect a business relationship, not to pass judgment on it and condemn it to death. Their rejection of the intellectual bog of exactitude has taken them up the rosier road of impasse, and now the rest of the movie will have to be spent accomplishing what should have been accomplished by the contract. But in all likelihood we'd rather see the rest of the movie than see them conclude their agreement properly. Their blessed inefficiency is the best part of the deal. If it is true that the most hideous crimes are committed in the name of obedience, it is equally true that the most monotonous are committed in the name of efficiency.

THE VERY FAMOUS STATEROOM SCENE

GROUCHO: Two fried eggs, two poached eggs, two scrambled eggs, and two medium-boiled eggs.

CHICO: And two hardboiled eggs.

GROUCHO: And two hardboiled eggs.

HARPO: Honk!

GROUCHO: Make that three hardboiled eggs . . . and, uh, some roast beef: rare, medium, well-done, and overdone.

CHICO: And two hardboiled eggs.

GROUCHO: And two hardboiled eggs.

HARPO: Honk!

GROUCHO: Make that three hardboiled eggs . . . and, uh, eight pieces of French pastry.

CHICO: And two hardboiled eggs.

GROUCHO: And two hardboiled eggs.

HARPO: Honk!

GROUCHO: Make that three hardboiled eggs.

HARPO: Honk!

GROUCHO: And one duck egg. Uh, have you got any stewed prunes?

STEWARD: Yes, sir.

GROUCHO: Well, give 'em some black coffee, that'll sober 'em up!

CHICO: And two hardboiled eggs.

GROUCHO: And two hardboiled eggs.

It starts out very simply. One man in a hallway. Groucho finds his trunk being moved to his room and decides to be moved on top of it. There's one altercation with another porter (where he swindles him out of a dollar. Groucho is making some kind of a fortune bamboozling Madam Dumont out of a handsome salary, but he still considers it worth the time it takes to stand

and deliver a sales pitch and swindle some poor steward out of one dollar. What he could be doing with all the money he makes we'll never know, as he seems to spend most of his time in the act of not spending money.), then a long glide down the hallway like a rajah, tossing insults to the rabble. (And a love note from Baroni to Kitty Carlisle. This is supposed to make Groucho a sympathetic character. Does Thalberg really think that we're going to sit and watch Groucho swindle porters, insult waiters, and tear up contracts, and then not lose our hearts to him until he delivers a love note to Kitty Carlisle?!? Haw haw!) He finishes off with Margaret Dumont, striding into her room and singing, in the hopes of embarrassing her in front of her bed; this accomplished, he takes advantage of her succeeding ill humor by inviting her to his stateroom for a seduction scene. (Margaret Dumont loves Groucho because he is remorselessly unromantic and opposes everything she stands for. Groucho loves Margaret Dumont because she is remorselessly unappealing and has a lot of money. Love is a funny thing.) Then, to finish up his tour, he arrives at his own micron compartment, aghast that it is scarcely larger than his *Monkey Business* barrel. He is further aghast to find Harpo, Chico and Baroni inside his trunk, and aghast on top of that to hear that they won't leave till they've been fed.

"Don't make any noise, you're stowaways," Groucho keeps saying. Chico keeps telling him, "We no say nothing," and then feels free to shout, "Two hardboiled eggs!" no less than four times from behind the door. The fact that he has done this makes even less impression on him than the fact that he promised not do it, so when Groucho tries to get mad at him about it, all that comes back is a jovial, "Oh, sure, that's all right." The power in Chico's simple-mindedness is that anything it doesn't believe just vanishes from the earth. It never happened. No second thoughts. Just vanishes from the earth.

Two maids come to make up the beds. The engineer crawls to the back of the room to turn off the heat. He is followed, in a persistent succession, by a manicurist, the engineer's assistant, a homeless wanderer looking for her Aunt Minnie, and a determined cleaning woman intent on mopping the place up whether it is physically possible or not, and *these* are followed by a staff of waiters bearing dinner—everyone not only occupying the same spatial and temporal milieu ("Tell Aunt Minnie to send up a bigger room," hollers Groucho in the midst of the throng), but continuing to perform their various functions and getting in each other's way—all in a room that was crowded as soon as Chico and Harpo stepped out of the trunk. ("I've got plenty of room," hollers Chico. Just vanishes from the earth.)

The sense of the ridiculous is amplified in a geometrically ascending ratio each time the intruders asking Groucho for permission to enter the room increase arithmetically. He *encourages* them in. "Sure!" he is saying. "Already we can't breathe! Come on in!"—the apparent rationale being that if you can't have a large, comfortable room all to yourself, you might get a perverse pleasure out of stretching your discomfort to its fullest measure. This would have the effect of ridding your life of all those pesky annoyances you're always running into and turning them into full-blooded vexations. The people who enter the room, of course, don't question the rationale for their actions. By this point in the movie, the infectious Marx Brothers logic has spread like a contagion and is spinning the heads of everyone in the vicinity.

When a single scene gains a stature as great as this one has, the story of how it came to be grows cluttered with clashing gospels. Morrie Ryskind says simply that Al Boasberg wrote it and that extensive performances helped to improve it. Harpo's wife Susan claims that the written version wasn't much at all, and it took a host of ad libs and impromptu clowning to turn it into something even remotely passable. As Allan Jones remembers it, only the size of the stateroom changed. People didn't laugh when they saw everybody crowding into a stateroom, but they laughed when they crowded into a *small* stateroom. Another story is that Groucho in the middle of the tour suggested having waiters come into the room with trays of food, to top off all the jokes about what a tiny room it was. Salt Lake City was so amused by the presence of waiters in a stateroom that the writers quickly populated it with engineers and manicurists to see if that would get a rise out of them, too.

How all this congestion could be performed on the stage at

all, much less five times a day, is something we might spend the rest of our days trying to grasp, but, according to Harpo's account, it was not only being done, it was, worse, falling completely flat, and talented men were chafing their elbows to embarrass themselves in front of an audience. But one day one little ad lib made all the difference. The problem, you see, was to get the crowd laughing *before* the pandemonium began and sweep them along with a momentum greater than they were. And what was needed for that was one of those ridiculous gags that strikes you viscerally, even while insulting your intelligence—the verbal counterpart of being tickled. Hence the two hardboiled eggs, and the idiotic repetition of the honk, and the phlegmatic three hardboiled eggs, so that we are tittering senselessly before the parade of intruders even begins.

But make room for one more. The most farfetched story was prepared by publicity agent Teet Carle. According to this one, the original version was nothing more than a weak excuse to get some laughs by having Groucho stand in the hallway in his shorts. Now, this would never have gained any stature as a classic scene, especially since clothing styles were to change and treat us to the comedy of seeing *everybody* in his shorts at one time or another. In this condition the scene was getting no response, and the writers had begun to suggest that it go, and it was already reaching for its hat and coat and starting for the door—when all of a sudden Groucho got it into his head one day to start tossing stagehands, prop men, electricians, and script girls into the stateroom, and, what do you know, folks, the audience burst into hysterics and rampant applause.

And Margaret Dumont opens the door and they all fall flat on their face.

ADVENTURES WITH HENDERSON

HENDERSON: Who you talking to?

GROUCHO: I was talking to myself, and there's nothing you
            can do about it, I've had three of the best doctors
            in the East.

HENDERSON:	Well, I certainly heard somebody say something.
GROUCHO:	Oh, it's sheer folly on your part.
HENDERSON:	What's this?
GROUCHO:	Why, that's a fire escape. And, uh, that's a table, and this is a room, and there's the door leading out, and I wish you'd use it, I . . . I vant to be alone!
HENDERSON:	You'll be alone when I throw you in jail.
GROUCHO:	Isn't there a song by that name? . . .
HENDERSON:	What became of that fourth bed?
GROUCHO:	What are you referring to, Colonel?
HENDERSON:	The last time I was in this room there were four beds here!
GROUCHO:	Please! I'm not interested in your private life, Henderson.
HENDERSON:	Oh-h-h. Say! What's that bed doing here?
GROUCHO:	I don't see it doing anything. . . .
HENDERSON:	Hey, you!
GROUCHO:	Coming!
HENDERSON:	Am I crazy, or are there only two beds here?
GROUCHO:	Now, which question do you want me to answer first, Henderson?

Although the stateroom sequence is the most canonized of Marx Brothers scenes, and the one most often damned with the stifling stigma "classic," it is the scene that follows it that is most likely to walk off with the laughter and applause. It is just as skillfully structured, its chaos has a much more energetic exuberance, and, besides that, it's the old in-and-out-of-doors scene all over again.

In a *modus operandi* diametrically opposed to Keaton's, who was known for accomplishing the impossible in deft, easy moves, the Marxes in this scene demonstrate their eternal insistence upon employing the most elaborate machinations conceivable to achieve what the rest of us would regard as pretty simple ends. When presented with the problem of sneaking off the ship, the three stowaways settle upon terms the most blatantly bogus available. When they might slip off disguised as passengers, or dress up in uniforms and call themselves the captain, they don beards and strange inverted accents and hope to be mistaken for the three great aviators and have to bluff their way through speeches and whole parades.

In what must be the low point of comedy for the entire movie, Chico explains that when they flew across the ocean they kept running out of gas halfway over and having to turn around and go back, and that they finally flew across the ocean by taking a steamship. The assembled audience accepts this news with a shrug, but the instant Harpo's beard comes off from an overdose of ice water, the mob realizes it's been duped and leaps to its feet in a fury. The lameness of the jokes is rivaled only by the lameness of the pretext.

("Did you hear what he said? He said you boys are imposters and you absolutely don't belong here at all." "Did he say that about us?" "I've never been so insulted!" "He said he didn't mean it and he wants to know if you'll stay here." Some of the dialogue in this scene is spoken in a strange Far Eastern dialect that can be interpreted only by running the projector backwards.)

Next morning they further complicate the situation in Groucho's hotel room, where two cots have been set up to accommodate the three stowaways and one to accommodate an alarm clock. Harpo, after demolishing the clock with mallets aforethought, ravishes the defenseless breakfast table and constructs a meal out of pancakes, neckties, cigars, boyish glee, and powdered sugar. Groucho, whose beam reflects unadulterated adoration of everything his brother does, is given a lot of lines about how annoyed he is.

Then enters Henderson, in the role of Propriety and the Law, and all but Groucho dash onto the fire escape. Baroni, the man the whole story is supposed to be about, simply edges along the building and gets away, but Harpo and Chico stick around to attend industriously to the business of staying out of Henderson's sight. The detective inspects the bedroom, and they all dash into the living room again to grab a bite. Henderson goes out on the fire escape, so they scoot into the bedroom, this time taking one of the beds with them on their trip back into the living room again. Henderson can't figure out where the bed came from, so

Harpo and Chico bring another bed from the bedroom into the living room through the bedroom doorway, while he's chasing them from the living room into the bedroom by way of the fire escape. By the time he gets to where the first bed came from, the second bed is gone too, and the next time he goes into the bedroom, the bedroom door turns into another bed. The camera glances, swishes, and jumps from room to room as Chico and Harpo rearrange furniture in a furtive fury and Groucho charges in at Henderson's beck and call to give him pointless answers to his frantic questions.

Chico, who seemed an invincible moron when Groucho wanted to pore over contracts, is suddenly found to be possessed of a superhuman mental and physical dexterity, as he deftly performs the incredibly complicated act of maneuvering small beds from one room to another while keeping out of the sight of a determined detective. This is simply the simple face of a simple man who can't do anything right unless it becomes vital, significant, necessary, and ultimately desirable for him to do it, at which point he proceeds to accomplish miracles. We've all seen that before. (Parents still wonder why their children can't learn arithmetic.)

And Groucho, calling encouragement to the invisible gremlins and discouragement to the official inquisitor, is the *last* person anybody should turn to for counsel at a time like this, as Henderson discovers on his last trip into the room with all the beds. What beds? The living room now has all the beds, and the room with all the beds is bedless. All it contains now is two bizarre, cloaked figures and one Italian masquerading as a chair. Henderson says he must be in the wrong room. He certainly must be. The Marx Brothers, whatever their differences, have established their allegiance.

A NIGHT AT THE OPERA

"This is the opening of a new opera season—a season made possible by the generous checks of Mrs. Claypool. I am sure the familiar strains of Verdi's music will come back to you tonight.

And Mrs. Claypool's checks will probably come back in the morning." Thus begins the proof of Thalberg's pudding: the infectious attack on the opera house on opening night. Thalberg contended that, while it was amusing enough to confront Marxes with officers of ships and heads of state, who are all pretty much dignified people, the penultimate climax of all their efforts would feature a gathering of the clan deep in the insides of a body of dignitarians so obsessed that they had lost all sense of perspective. They seem to have found the perfect target: Anyone who has ever sat through an altercation on the refinements of the finer contraltos knows what pretension is. We don't even have to see a single gag; the very idea of primal enthusiasm coming into conflict with conscious culture is comedy enough. The word "opera" itself is just asking for it—it's Italian for "work" and comes from an old Latin word that meant "efforts." What *more* could you want? "At every one of these concerts," says Bernard Shaw, "you will find rows of weary people who are there, not because they really like classical music, but because they think they ought to like it." People, in other words, who see where duty lies.

Through various matters of pomp and circumstance, our heroes have found themselves thrust out in the cold, moping on a park bench in despair, when news arrives that Rosa, too, has been fired. Strategy then is planned for an all-out assault on *Il Trovatore*'s premiere, all of which we are supposed to enjoy immensely because it succeeds in getting Rosa and Baroni signed by the opera company. Well, we have not come through Allan Jones's intrusions into the comedy with a pulsating wish to see him get ahead, and the contrivance we are presented with to excuse all the nonsense is even less appealing. The idea, see, is that if they *steal* Lassparri while *Il Trovatore* is on, the opera company will *have* to put Baroni in. Sure. Not only is that a ridiculous rationalization for throwing Gookies at the audience, or starting a duel with the orchestra conductor, or calling out Saturday-matinee remarks like "How'd you like to feel the way she looks?" from the plush boxes, but it presupposes that we need a rationalization at all. These actions may make the opera look pretty silly, but they make their plot look even sillier. And what's more, once Harpo has entirely destroyed any semblance of a

straight opera, and swung back and forth in the catwalks and clambered all over the backdrops, and plopped down the battleship *Potemkin* in the middle of Lassparri's recitation, once the whole enterprise has become a lost cause, you would not expect anybody to have any inhibitions left about heading straight for the stage and nabbing him. But some altruistic sense of duty restrains them, and they stand off in the wings making signals, laboring under a grand delusion that the show must go on, even when it's become a travesty of itself. Let's face it, it just doesn't make sense. Whether anybody likes it or not, the Marx Brothers have returned to good old *Horsefeathers* surrealism. What the *plot* is telling us is that opera is all right, just so long as Allan Jones and Polly Bergen (or Kitty Carlisle) sing it. What the *scene* tells us is something entirely else.

If you listen to an audience watching *Night at the Opera* you'll hear great bursts of delight that speak of a release far surpassing simple laughter. It is probably based on the feeling that sitting through an interminable performance of grand opera would probably fill *us* with no desire greater than to leap from one box to another screaming like Tarzan or to dash across the stage ripping the skirts off half the chorus. It is all symptomatic of a common disease that spreads like the plague through Sunday schools, filibusters, piano recitals, and political-science lectures, building to an intensity that is scarcely expunged by coughing, shifting your feet, or even sneaking over to the side exit. In most cases, it simply remains bottled. The best cure, in cases like that, is this final scene from the Marxes' favorite movie.

When you juxtapose great music and great comedy, the music shouldn't *necessarily* come out second best. There's something not particularly right about an affair if we get such a big kick out of seeing it go all wrong. Were the Marx Brothers to barge in personally and disrupt a performance of Stravinsky's *Rite of Spring*, let's say, or Mussorgsky's *Night on Bald Mountain*, or Ligeti's *Atmospheres*, or a Rolling Stones concert, or a screening of *Duck Soup*, or a public reading of this book, I should only be annoyed, no matter how funny they were.

There are, after all, limits.

Otis Ferguson, *The New Republic,* December 11, 1935:

In terms of rhyme, reason, good taste, and formal plot structure, *A Night at the Opera* is a sieve, a leaky ship, and caulked to the guards with hokum. It has three of the Marx Brothers and absolutely no pride. It seems thrown together, made up just as they went along out of everybody else's own head—it steals sequences from René Clair, it drives off with whole wagonloads of the Keystone lot without so much as putting the fence back up; it has more familiar faces in the way of gags and situations than a college reunion. In short, *A Night at the Opera* is a night with the Marx Brothers, who have a zest for clowning and a need to be cockeyed that are either genius or just about enough to fit them all out with numbers and a straitjacket, and who troop through this impossible hour and a half of picture with such speed and clatter as to pin up a record for one of the most hilarious collections of bad jokes I've laughed myself nearly sick over.

You realize even while wiping your eyes well into the second handkerchief that it is nothing so much as a hodge-podge of skylarking and soon over. Their picture is done the minute it fades on the screen. But the boys themselves are still with us, and I estimate an average period of ten days to three weeks, as the picture gets around, before the American public will be able to open its garbage can in the morning and not duck, involuntarily, anticipating that a Marx Brother will pop out and clout it over the head with a sackful of tomatoes.

They tear into it by guess and by god; their assurance, appetite, and vitality are supreme; they are both great and awful.

A Night at the Opera was greeted with waves of applause and roars of laughter deafening to the ear and to the other organs as well. Critics, knowing in their hearts they had missed them the season before, now recalled their old movies with a misty-eyed fondness and referred to them as the venerable past masters of comedy, rather than those young whippersnappers who throw things. The movie was hailed as a beautiful desecration of civilization's most claustrophobic art form, a great satire on opera movies, and one of the funniest comedies ever made. It was considered to be the greatest Marx Brothers picture of all time by almost everybody, including the Marx Brothers and all the writers and directors of their other films, including men who had written *Duck Soup* and never bothered to look at *Duck Soup* again, even on television, including critics, historians, comedians, and film-series chairmen ever since, including everybody but Pauline Kael, who kept saying, "It isn't."

Nobody knows what Mankiewicz thought. Nobody asked him.

A Night at the Opera defines the Marx Brothers once and for all as the most positive negativists in the cinema: they master one art form to demolish another, they belittle dignity so that indignities reign, and they smash the limits of good taste and proper conduct just so you won't forget their infinite, boundless personalities. The glory of this movie is that for every ounce of cynicism there's a pound of joy.

But recently its stature has begun to weaken. After all, is it still possible to enjoy a movie after it's been called "a classic comedy" for so long? In one sense, *Night at the Opera* is Marxist anarchy in its most perfect form. In another sense, how the hell do you get anarchy into a form? To Marx Brothers purists, the whole idea of this film has grown to be palpable anathema. This guy Irving Thalberg had profaned their nothing-sacredness! Perhaps the Marx Brothers weren't *meant* to travel first class. To anybody who thinks the matter over, the whole idea of a Marx Brothers purist is palpable anathema; you start getting pure about the Marx Brothers, and it's all over. For some reason, even the most iconoclastic of artists seem not to be immune from this kind of sanctification. "The deadliest blow the enemy of the human soul can strike," said James Agee, "is to do fury honor." But there are deadlier blows the enemy of the human soul can strike than to make *A Night at the Opera.*

Sam Wood, urging the Marx Brothers on.   MGM, PHOTO BY TED ALLAN

A DAY AT THE RACES 1937

It was somewhere, at some point in the production of *Night at the Opera,* that it entered Irving Thalberg's head what an overwhelming undertaking a sequel was going to be.

The natural first choice for a script writer was Kaufman

again, but Venerable George, out west to supervise *Opera* production, decided he had tons of pressing engagements in New York. He pointed out that MGM already had on salary a "Flywheel, Shyster, and Flywheel" man, who came at a far lower weekly rate than Pulitzer Prize winners did. So George Oppenheimer (a man whose name seemed more appropriate to a concert pianist than a gag writer—a man, in fact, who had an impressive background at Williams and at Harvard and on Broadway as a musical and comedy writer, and a great future as New York drama critic and theater correspondent for the London press; a man, in other words, who had been somewhere and was going somewhere but was right now only a screenwriter) was put to work conceiving of a new story involving the Marx Brothers in a sanitarium situation, with the stipulation that it include some stabs at the medical profession. For this assignment Oppenheimer recalls being teamed with an unspecified staff writer left over from silent films (screenwriters from the silent films are faceless animals—even the people who knew them don't remember their names), but this man's hangup was facts and statistics and amusing incidents rendered dull by the telling, and the two of them very quickly got nowhere.

After two stories were prepared in this manner of speaking, Groucho and Thalberg took time out from their other duties to shake their heads in dismay and bemoan the fate of the second *Night at the Opera*. Recalling what a big help Pirosh and Seaton had been last time, Groucho, at his own prompting, sought them out again. He found them at Republic Pictures, of all places, grinding out a sausage, and he popped in and made his offer.

Here was a real dilemma! Forced to choose between laboring for the low man on a triple bill and accepting a request from a boyhood idol comedian to work for Hollywood's biggest and most powerful producer. [Their decision in favor of Thalberg was the first big step in a couple of substantial careers. Pirosh, a former advertising man from Baltimore, was to write, produce, and direct Westerns and war movies, win an Oscar, and then switch over to television and write and produce some more. Seaton, a former radio and stock-company actor from South

Bend, Indiana (he was radio's first Lone Ranger and invented the "Hi-yo, Silver!" call because he was incapable of whistling for his horse), became a prominent writer-director, won three Oscars, advanced as far as president of the Motion Picture Academy, and made films like *Miracle on 34th Street, Country Girl, The Bridges at Toko-Ri, 36 Hours,* and the film that all Middle America took to its heart, *Airport*. Actually, neither one ever did comedy very often, and the two of them never worked together again until they wrote the recent *What's So Bad About Feeling Good?*] Honored as they were, the two cubs had to admit to being somewhat intimidated by this business of doing a follow-up to a Kaufman–Ryskind act. Not to help matters any, they got an advance screening of *Night at the Opera* when it was finished, and that, no matter how exhilarating it proved to others, only served to depress them. The harder they laughed, the more discouraged they became.

Don't forget, they had the Clothesline Concept and the Football Game to worry about. Marxian madness was to be sewed together with a prejudice for continuity, as had been done only once before in the History of Man. Also at work on these problems, besides Oppenheimer, were Will Johnstone, Carey Wilson, and whomever else Thalberg could round up for one more hour or one more day.

By the time *A Night at the Opera* was released and the receipts started pouring in and 1935 was over, a fifteen-page treatment was the fruit of the combined labors of Pirosh, Seaton, Oppenheimer, and Johnstone: a screwball story reverting back to the maniacal deviations of *Horsefeathers* and *Duck Soup.*

In it Groucho is Syrus P. Turntable, a questionable doctor at work in a den of out-and-out thieves called the Quackenbush Medical Building. Allan Jones is a friend whose life he once saved by not treating his throat. Jones is in love with Millicent Rittenhouse, daughter of Margaret Dumont and victim of a heavy barrage of doctors and pills. She is worth so much in medical bills, in fact, that she fosters a deadly rivalry between doctors Turntable and Waltzer (of the Vienna Waltzers), who (after Turntable sings a "song about what a great doctor he is") proceed to present their respective cures for the horrors of modern civilization. To satirize the contemporary influx of German and Austrian pretenders to the throne of Freud, the writers placed the first scene in a ballroom full of bearded quacks with their white coats and stethoscopes on, all dancing to "The Blue Danube" with each other. The frayed nerves attendant on mechanized life are so graphically depicted by Waltzer that a woman in the audience faints. "Is there a doctor in the house?" Groucho cries out. One little man in the back of the room stands up—only to be met with "What are you doing here? Throw that man out!"

The roomful of medics is anxious for the discovery of a new, all-purpose cure. Nonsense, says Turntable. What we need is a new disease. He resolves to boost business by concocting one. Harpo and Chico enter as process servers and get through to Groucho by telling him that Harpo is sick, which is the cue for a comedy examination scene. The Groucho–Chico encounter takes place immediately afterward at a train station; when they catch up to him on his way to Maine, he pulls out a timetable and proves with the aid of symbol arithmetic that Chico and Harpo have already gotten to Maine, while he's only reached New York. (This was Groucho's idea for a routine to match the labyrinth logic of the contract sequence.) After a riotous train ride, the three of them meet again in Maine to converge on Mrs. Rittenhouse in a furious examination where blood counts are marked up like football scores and the rivalry between doctors practically demolishes the patient. Waltzer whisks everybody off to his tranquil Colonial Village, from which they are finally rescued, in a recreational war finale, by the Marx Brothers and Allan Jones, with the help of a band of wild Indians. Millicent is cured by romance and exuberance, Groucho marries Mrs. Rittenhouse, and Harpo and Chico give him a bill for $2.50.

THE END

Now there arose the age-old problem of executive approval. This consisted in the main of everyone sitting outside Thalberg's office waiting for him to get around to being late for their appointment. If he kept you waiting long enough, you began to wish he'd keep you waiting even longer, because he'd treat you to dinner if it got to be late enough. He was always in a good mood when you finally got through to him, anyway, and usually made you forget that you'd been cursing his mother's grave for two days in a waiting room. "You felt in his presence that you were talking to Mr. Hollywood," attests Seaton. "But he never made you feel uncomfortable about it." (This was the reverse of events undergone when Groucho Marx was your firing squad. Writers up before his critical eye usually found him punctual, efficient, and with nothing good to say. In the end, it was probably a more pleasurable experience to have a script unconditionally refused by Thalberg than to have Groucho decide to accept it.)

Unfortunately, this was the pleasurable experience the four of them had in store. Affable as Thalberg proved to be, appreciative as he was of everything, and good as dinner tasted, the story was all wrong and would have to be done over. The grand total number of things he approved, in fact, amounted to four:

1. The Colonial Village
2. Millicent Rittenhouse being a hypochondriac
3. Margaret Dumont's examination scene
4. The name "Quackenbush"

The first scene, he pointed out, was "too sophisticated and satiric." (A strange complaint, that, considering that barbs at the medical profession were all he had asked for in the first place.) They all smiled, munched on their celery, and agreed (they *had* to agree) and harbored a hope that it could be salvaged regardless. But Thalberg remained precise, exacting, and a man of irreversible decisions. Happy New Year, boys, he said, and keep at it.

The next treatment bore the title *Peace and Quiet* and the names of Pirosh, Seaton, and Oppenheimer, without Johnstone, and was two weeks in the making. Quackenbush becomes Groucho's name, and his first appearance is in the midst of a medical emergency—when an ambulance pulls up in front of a rest hotel in Maine, he shows up asleep on the stretcher. Chico is a law student who supports himself by playing piano in the hotel ballroom; he also supports law books instead of sheet music on his piano so he can study while he's working. Harpo is a tree surgeon who sits in trees and stares at girls' rooms through binoculars. He and Chico first see Groucho one day when they saw themselves out of a tree and land on top of him. He tells them he'll sue, which prompts Chico to announce he's a lawyer, which prompts the two of them to map out a trial: Chico will be Groucho's prosecuting attorney and also his own defense; Chico will charge Groucho a fee for being his lawyer that will far exceed the amount of the damages; Groucho will forget the whole thing; Chico will now sue Groucho for breach of promise; but Chico will offer to act as Groucho's defense attorney for a very reasonable fee.

Chico wants to find a doctor who will admit to Mrs. Rittenhouse that Millicent isn't sick. He would like to enlist Groucho, but Groucho is only a vet; then he decides that's all right because Millicent is sick as a dog. So Groucho storms up to Margaret Dumont's room (at two in the morning, this is) and bangs on the door till she comes and answers it. Then when she does, he says, "What are you doing up at this hour? Don't you know you should be in bed!" She says there was this knock at the door. He says don't change the subject.

Dr. Waltzer escorts the enraged Dumont out of the hotel the next morning, and Groucho has the bellhops route her luggage outside the door so that it comes back in again. "Look at all the patients moving in!" he tells her. "Why, this place is a mecca for broken-down women." Dumont is impressed and decides she *won't* move out, but then begins to realize it's *her* baggage he's talking about. "Well," answers Groucho, "you're a broken-down woman, aren't you?"

She and her daughter head for the train station, but Waltzer, in a separate car, is delayed by an accident with the Marx Brothers. Groucho tumbles out of the car, effusive with apologies, claims total responsibility and offers him a drink. Dazed, Waltzer keeps accepting drinks and apologies every time Groucho offers them. Then a highway patrolman shows up and asks what happened. "Arrest this man," says Groucho. "He's a drunken driver."

Now everything gets serious. The directions for this stage of the *Peace and Quiet* narrative read: "We now go to Millicent and Allan on horseback and play a love scene, with a possibility for a romantic duet. We see Millicent's fondness for horses, particularly for the horse she is riding, a magnificent animal, who, for the lack of a better name, we will call Zeppo."

The examination of Mrs. Rittenhouse follows, with some added embellishments in the form of Harpo the tree surgeon propping a ladder up against her bed and spraying her with lime. When he makes ready to saw off a limb, Groucho the vet says he'll just have to shoot her. Chico the law student says what she's got looks like habeas corpus. The football atmosphere is built up to a furious pitch, and the three of them tear down the bedposts.

Then the Colonial Village bit again, with a squadron of policemen substituted for the Indians, and Harpo running around dressed as Sanity Clause. Allan Jones proves that Millicent isn't sick at all, Groucho marries Mrs. Rittenhouse *again,* and everybody waves into the camera lens for a smasheroo crescendo. Plenty funny, no?

Thalberg said plenty funny, no.

Three weeks later, Mrs. Rittenhouse had become Mrs. Standish, Millicent had become Judy, Quackenbush had been changed to Quackenbrush, and Dr. Waltzer was Dr. Leach, of the Bedside Manor Sanitarium. The examination of Margaret Dumont is out, but the hypochondriac plot is still in; the Colonial Village is out, but the drunken-driving gag is in; and sprung out like a sapling from the fertile soil of the drunken-driving gag is a new routine where the three Marx Brothers and a guy named Muggs finagle each other around a race track (we're getting there!) to get $500 of bail money done away with. In the hopes of keeping Dr. Leach incarcerated, the Marxes talk Muggs into throwing it all away on a sure loser. (Racing is supposed to be Muggs's weakness. It never had any attraction for the writers, however, as anything but a situation. "I came to the conclusion as a child that one horse was capable of running faster than another, and that's been the extent of my interest ever since," claims Seaton.) Chico consults all the tips he can accumulate and finds ten of them for the next race—one for each horse. "Should make racing history," he remarks. "Ten horses in a dead heat." They substitute for No. 10 a plowhorse with Harpo aboard and bet all his money on that. (Chico coaches Harpo, "At the first quarter you start holdin' him back. At the second quarter you start holdin' him back still more. The third quarter I think maybe you better tie him to a post.") Unfortunately, the race has been *rigged* in favor of No. 10, leaving the other nine jockeys to figure out how to stay behind a horse that isn't going anywhere.

Groucho has a dozen highlights in the course of events, including a chance to weasel into the Standish mansion ("I happen to know she *is* in," he says, before the butler gets a chance to say anything); a big surprise for Mrs. Standish which he's so excited about he wants her to guess at, and which, when she refuses, he guesses at himself ("Now, don't *tell* me," he giggles, while she stands around and fumes); and a long, smug interrogation of the rotting inmates of his sanitarium ("I never saw a sicker looking crew! Well . . . that's what we're here for. And how are you, Skippy, you're looking worse!" "I feel terrible." "Well, never you mind. Remember . . . here today and gone tomorrow!"). Most priceless of all is the Groucho–Chico routine (the third such created), where Chico sets up a Lost and Found Department at the railroad station and Harpo helps him get started by stocking it full of Margaret Dumont's luggage. Groucho comes up looking for his little black doctor's bag, and the two engage in a satire on bureaucracy that comes out sounding like Orson Welles's version of *The Trial:*

GROUCHO: You haven't seen anything of a black bag around here, have you?

CHICO: How do you know we haven't?

GROUCHO: Oh . . . call it a hunch.

CHICO: You mean it was a hunch bag. . . . What does he look like?

GROUCHO: Well, it's black and it's about this size and it's got my initials C.Q. on it and . . . that's it right there!

CHICO: No, we no find it.

GROUCHO: What do you think I ought to do?

CHICO: Well, you better aska the Information Department.

GROUCHO: Where's that?

CHICO: I no can tell you. I got a deal with the Information Department. I no tell anything and they no find anything.

And prefacing the whole mad affair is Margaret Dumont's ridiculous Civic Anti-Noise Campaign, a million-dollar setup designed to give her daughter bucolic silence in the midst of New York City—people with a house burning down are requested to go to the window and whisper "Fire!" out into the street, and the fire engines tear across town tinkling like a kitten's collar. The Marxes profane the whole thing at the end of the picture by getting hold of those same fire engines and clattering noisily all the way down to the pier to save Judy from being sent to Vienna. En route, they pass a genuine conflagration, and Groucho calls, "Keep it going till we get back!" (This is the second time that gag has popped up in a script. Thalberg must have had them read old *Night at the Opera* drafts. Maybe some day somebody will come along who will take that gag and put it in a movie.)

In the days before all this had started, Kaufman suggested he act as adviser to whatever writers were found. Thalberg, with *Peace and Quiet* looming up in front of him, shipped Pirosh and Seaton (Oppenheimer was taken off this project to try making loose ends meet on a spy picture called *Rendezvous*) to New York, through the Panama Canal, by boat, with George Kaufman and Moss Hart, so they could get a past master's views. Kaufman, who was on his way to see how his latest project, *Of Mice and Men* ("The best-laid plans . . ." according to Burns), was doing on Broadway and talking over his next project with Moss Hart, found time here and there to lend an ear to this Marx Brothers project with Pirosh and Seaton. He considered it a dandy diversion, made some comments and suggestions, warned them that Chico's questions were going to have to be as funny as Groucho's answers or Chico would get mad, and sent them smiling into New York to view *Of Mice and Men* (". . . gang aft agley," said the noble Scot) at a matinee performance. The thing had gotten so out of hand while Kaufman's back was turned that he sent a telegram to his Lennie, Broderick Crawford, at the end of Act One, which read, "I am out front. Wish you were here."

Pirosh and Seaton went back to California, made their revisions, incorporated Kaufman's ideas, amalgamated the variations, and displayed their handiwork to Thalberg once more.

He said he liked the bit about the race track. Move the whole thing to Saratoga and start over.

And that went on till the summer of '36: Groucho neurotic and fussy, Thalberg charming and fussier, Harpo and Chico amused and disinterested, Pirosh and Seaton in and out of everybody's office. "Thalberg wasn't particular about the time element," recalls Pirosh. "It could take three days, or three weeks, or a month, but he got what he wanted." All in all, it was going to take two years.

By the time the writing and rewriting was over, and situations had been concocted and thrown out and brought back in again, and gags shuffled in and out and around, the story had been sifted and refined into a conventional situation-comedy plot—a horse doctor finds himself the head of a sanitarium and hopes no one will reveal his background; a friendly jockey from the nearby race track comes to the rescue on a winning horse; if everyone can keep his head above water and hold off his creditors long enough, all will be roses; Hallelujah, brother, Dance, Fool, Dance!

Night at the Opera was so much of a hit that it had left them with a legacy of rules to follow: start with a Groucho scene, set up a relationship between Chico and Allan Jones, touch off a Groucho–Chico confrontation, throw in a crazy scene with all three Marx brothers, take time out for a musical interlude, do the in-and-out-of-a-bedroom routine, have them thrown out of somewhere, get them depressed about it, then send them back for a rousing, hysterical, grand-slam finale.

The drunken-driving gag has been discarded, but the old comedy examination of Harpo is back in. Dumont's examination has made a return from the dead, but the football flavor is drop-kicked out. Judy Standish *owns* the sanitarium by this time, but Margaret Dumont has given up being her mother and turned into an inmate. The Quackenbush Medical Building and the Bedside Manor have become simply Standish Sanitarium. The masquerading Dr. Waltzer becomes Dr. Steinburg, a legitimate doctor from Vienna. Harpo is reduced from a gremlin to a mischievous kid who doesn't like spinach. Groucho becomes a charlatan doctor who can't make jokes about anybody else's incompetence and is afraid to make jokes about his own and has very little left to make jokes about but sex and money. (He has no less than four variations on the line "That's the prettiest girl I've *ever* seen!" Like "A prettier number I've *never* seen!" and "You're the prettiest owner of a sanitarium I've *ever* seen!" Like that.)

It was Script No. 18, entitled *A Day at the Races,* that was approved by the front office. By that time the writers had probably given up thinking it was ever going to happen and resigned themselves to writing unused Marx Brothers stories all the rest of their lives. But writing the script was only half the battle. There was still the *de rigueur* of another tour to go through, and Al Boasberg was put on the crew again to help dress up the show for its public appearance.

There were two weeks of rehearsals at the Biltmore Theater in Los Angeles, at the end of which Thalberg was invited to drop on over and lend his stamp of approval to the proceedings. Thalberg sat in a big, empty theater, watched "Scenes from *A Day at the Races,*" and didn't approve. There wasn't a whole lot he could do about it, of course, as train tickets had all been bought and theaters booked, and the show would have to go on, one way or the other, but it just didn't seem funny. Maybe he should have turned down that last script, too. He said, "Good luck," and hoped invention would flourish in the Midwest.

The show opened in Minneapolis and in Duluth and in July and, from its first night, had its audiences in stitches. Even when the fun dragged on for over an hour, the house was in a constant uproar, warm receptions being afforded not only to the comedy but to the harp and piano performances and to the songs that Harry Stockwell and Lorraine Bridges were singing. Thirty thousand reaction cards were passed out to the corn farmers and insurance brokers, asking them what parts they liked, what parts they could do without, and what they thought of the whole shebang. Esther Muir, a kind of quick-frozen Thelma Todd and a veteran of Wheeler and Woolsey escapades, was being tested along with the dialogue to see if she had it in her to be straight man for all three Marx Brothers through the whole production. (Groucho commented that casting one of these parts practically required a physical examination. I can imagine it did. By the time she made it to the end of the tour, she had convinced everybody she had what it took.)

George Seaton, attesting to the hopelessness of giving any Marx Brothers line a prior evaluation, recalls writing some utterly hopeless stuff while on the road and finding it very successful. In one scene, a seductress bids Groucho hold her close . . . then closer! . . . Closer! Groucho's line is "If I hold you any closer, I'll be behind you." "Now, that's just *silly*" is its creator's own opinion, but when you put it in the middle of a Marx Brothers scene it seems funny at the time.

Both Pirosh and Seaton were amazed when the tour started out and Groucho refused to "punch" anything. There were no wiggles of the eyebrows, no wicked leers, and precious little emphasis given to anything. They thought he'd lost all heart and a year's work was doomed to disgrace, but backstage his reticence had a more experienced air about it. By now, it transpired, he had a well-developed theory of the proper approach to a pre-filming tour. "I know I can get a laugh on almost any line with my eyebrows and my eyes," he said, and so he was testing each one clinically and scientifically, without embellishments.

This went on for five weeks, with the writers concentrating on a different scene every week, tinkering with the wording and delivery. They found that something that didn't suit people when phrased as a question might always come across better if it was turned into a statement. (Al Boasberg's famous line upon Groucho taking Harpo's pulse, "Either he's dead or my watch has stopped," wouldn't get a laugh if it went "Is he dead or has my watch stopped?" because people would sit and wait for the funny answer to come.) Groucho's retort to Siegfried Rumann's beard, "Aren't you a fugitive from a mattress?" didn't make the grade either way, and they dropped it. His excuse for Harpo and Chico's existence, "They must have come out of a test tube," didn't quite go over, but its replacement, "You just rub a lamp and they appear," did fine. A reference to a doused wrist watch, "I'd rather have it rusty than disappear," became "I'd rather have it rusty than gone," and then "I'd rather have it rusty than missing." A line that went "That's the most obnoxious proposal I've ever had" was not getting the laughs it seemed to deserve, and so it became a "revolting" proposal, a "disgusting" proposal, an "offensive" proposal, a "repulsive" proposal. Still not funny enough. It became "disagreeable" and "distasteful," and it bombed altogether. When it was a "nauseating" proposal, it was hilarious. One blank spot in the show, just previous to the bedroom scene, was filled only with Harpo making faces at Chico to the effect that Groucho was going to get in trouble with some seductress, and a comedy scene seemed called for. Harpo's pantomime was sheer exposition, but it always got a laugh, even when it was expanded, and more gags were stuck in it, and guesses on Chico's part as to what he might mean by his signals were put in and taken out and written and rewritten like wildfire, until it was finally extended, elaborated, stretched out, and amplified into a whole routine, and turned into one of the great Harpo— Chico scenes of ever.

By the time they left Chicago, the laugh gauge was approaching maximum, and "Scenes from *A Day at the Races*" looked like another hit. By the time they opened in Cleveland, there were no laughs at all, and it looked like the end of the road. Panic struck the entire company. What were these Cleveland people, hayseeds? Were the Marx Brothers really washed up? Would they have to write the show all over *again*? Somebody had the temerity to speak up and ask if the Cleveland house had suitable acoustics. Research disclosed that it didn't even have a loudspeaker system. Nobody had heard anything. Minnie always said there'd be days like that.

And there was trouble from the legal department. After all the fuss about the name Quackenbush, and after everyone had decided it was the most preposterous name imaginable for any doctor in the world to have, thirty-seven Dr. Quackenbushes, within the continental United States alone, were reported well and doing fine and just itching to sue the very minute they were portrayed on the screen by Groucho Marx as horse doctors. Now, right in the middle of the tour, a new most preposterous name imaginable was going to have to be found, something a little less popular. "I've already got Quackenbush painted on my shingle," Groucho complained. "Let them change *their* names if they don't like it." But they settled on an innocuous "Hackenbush" regardless, so Groucho fell in love with that instead. Now he signs it to letters, answers to it at parties, and identifies himself with it over the telephone, satisfying, presumably, his lifelong urge to be a doctor.

Thalberg saw the show in its last week in San Francisco. It was down to fifty minutes. Invention had flourished. Things looked fine.

But they didn't stop there, no sir. For three weeks they went back to work on the script again and fashioned a new, improved movie around the comedy scenes. One part of the legacy of rules (the part where they get depressed after being thrown out of somewhere, as in the park-bench scene in *Night at the Opera*), wasn't close enough to the pattern yet, and Pirosh and Seaton were told to "keep coming up with park-bench scenes" till they had the right one.

Redoubtable Kaufman was flown out from New York to assist Pirosh, Seaton and Boasberg in punching things up. Kaufman, who had money flowing in from more directions than he could count, abruptly remembered one day that he hadn't picked up his MGM pay checks in quite a spell, and, much to the shock, dismay, and chagrin of his fellows, popped over to the cashier's window, rounded up all twenty of his $4,000 checks, pocketed them, and went back to work.

The comedy scenes weren't left alone either. The Marx Brothers hired a team of vaudevillians (Harry Lash, Bobbie Dooley, and "Skins" Miller) to act out their routines for them so that *they* could sit and look at them for two weeks and test their *own* reactions.

Actually allowing the cameras to go ahead and roll would have seemed too impetuous an act at any stage of this procedure, but the Marxes wanted to film their routines as shortly after the tour as possible to keep them from growing stale. Deliberations proliferated; the brothers were ready to forgive Sam Twenty-Takes-a-Shot-Sell-'Em-a-Load-of-Clams Wood all his eccentric-ities and get him back in charge again, but he was tied up in a project with Edna May Oliver, which Thalberg had to postpone to grant the Marxes' wish. Shooting on the comedy scenes was scheduled to begin September 12, even though the rest of the film was still in the process of being written; but it was moved up to August 27 to avoid staleness, and then moved back again to September 4. It finally did begin on Thursday, September 3, and after two days of hard work the comedians repaired to Del Monte for the weekend to exhale.

The next week things went well. Al Boasberg sat by with a book of notes, wherein was recorded which word and which inflection was most suitable to which line, and everyone went and consulted it from time to time. Cast and crew knew they had a good thing going, and events progressed with all due confi-dence and satisfaction, until Sam Wood came onto the set one day with tears all down his face and said, "The little brown fellow just died."

The doctors had told him he wouldn't live past thirty-five. Now he had lived to see thirty-seven. But, what with a flimsy constitution, a twelve-hour workday and the kind of pressures he submitted himself to, well, it was just inevitable that when Irving Thalberg caught a severe head cold on Labor Day, it would multiply into lethal complications and kill him. It was a big blow not only to the *Day at the Races* company, not only to the whole Irving Thalberg production unit, not only to the entire MGM studio, but to everybody who had ever had anything to do with making a movie. Hollywood was full of people who either re-spected him professionally or felt very close to him personally, or both. Even if you knew Irving Thalberg only as a name, you were so full of awe and reverence for him that it hardly seemed possible a being of such power and glory should ever come to the end of his days. The film colony became a chorus of mourners, affected and sincere, as associates, rivals, friends, and enemies spread their eulogies across the nation's papers. All activity at

MGM was halted for twenty-four hours, as of midnight of the day he died. All activity at every studio in Hollywood was halted at ten o'clock on the morning of his funeral, while heads were bowed in prayer for five minutes.

For the Marx Brothers, it meant the End of the Line was at hand. Their personal grief was intensified by their sense of professional doom. Irving Thalberg was the last of the prodigious talents to lend his genius to the making of great Marx Brothers films. From here on in, there were to be no more Thalbergs, no more Kaufmans, no more Mankiewiczes, no more Boasbergs, no more McCareys, no more Kalmars, Rubys, Ryskinds, or Sheekmans; the Marxes were grist for the run of the mill.

After Thalberg's death, shakeups at the studio included script renovations, shooting hiatuses, nervous breakdowns, and rampant resignations. Production was halted on *A Day at the Races,* and all matters pertaining to the film were turned over to Thalberg's brother-in-law, Lawrence Weingarten.

Pirosh and Seaton sat down burdened with a host of revision assignments and resumed the seemingly infinite task of writing the script for *A Day at the Races.* Among their other problems, they were asked to come up with a love scene in a boat between Allan Jones and Maureen O'Sullivan (who had since replaced Harry Stockwell and Lorraine Bridges) that would accomplish their reconciliation after an unfortunate series of tiffs. The death of Thalberg didn't mean a dearth of perfectionism, and Pirosh's friends Ellis and Logan, who began writing a musical feature for Fox about the time Pirosh and Seaton started their love scene, were reasonably startled to meet Pirosh again weeks later when their film was just about ready to go before the cameras and find Pirosh and Seaton still sweating it out on that boat.

It wasn't until the eighth of December that the screenplay was wrapped up and ready to go again, but just because production was being resumed, did you think that was going to mean the end of the rewrites? Nonsense. Love scenes continued to expand and contract, and musical numbers came and went with the whims. By March of 1937 they were rewriting dialogue for scenes that had already been shot. One of the least serious omissions was "I've Got a Message from the Man in the Moon," a song which is never sung in the course of the picture, though it pops up in the overture played during the credits and Groucho does a "reprise" of it during the finale; one of the *most* serious omissions was "Dr. Hackenbush," a very funny song by Kalmar and Ruby that Groucho was to perform (it was not the last contribution they were not to make) and which Groucho always *has* performed, whenever he gets the chance (it's his "song about what a great doctor he is"), everywhere but in *Day at the Races*.

Even the comedy scenes—the clinically tested, laboratory-proven, doctors'-recommended comedy scenes—were taken out and monkeyed with. Now gone by the wayside are: Groucho's latest insult to Chico, "I don't know what I'd do without you, but I'd like to try sometime"; his lethargic remark when his alarm clock is smashed, "Well, it's broken. Now I won't have to get up tomorrow"; the spirited cry, "Don't touch that phone! It hasn't been sterilized," when a telephone rings and interrupts a commotion over sterilization and is instantly dumped into the sink to drown; a whole to-do at the Water Carnival, prompted by Harpo and Chico clambering into the boat with Groucho and Margaret Dumont and being outrageous in their buffoonery, while Groucho lectures Margaret Dumont for having the presumption to object, "Have you forgotten Jefferson's immortal words? I have. Say, I've even forgotten the music. We've come a long way since the Pilgrims landed on the rocks. We've come through muck and mire, rain and sleet, fire and theft, shot and shell, and we won't come back!"; and a whole seltzer-water scene, apparently removed on the basis of somebody's prejudice against seltzer water, replaced with Harpo and Chico masquerading as detectives. Groucho orders a bottle of Scotch sent up to his room, and Harpo and Chico dash in dressed as bellboys and instantly start spraying the place with seltzer water. Harpo, holding the obstreperous bottle, tries to keep the spray within reasonable bounds, while Groucho and Chico climb under tables and behind couches arguing about the matter, and finally everyone heads for the door and goes out, claiming, "This is no place for a man who hasn't been in the Navy," except for Groucho, who heads for the door after Harpo and Chico have gone out and slams it shut.

Characteristic of the rewrites is Chico's line, "Look at that.

Harpo, Hi-Hat, Harpo's double, and "half the population of Culver City, California," between shots at Santa Anita.

"The dirtiest, messiest set I've ever seen."

Judy likes him. Thatsa swell!" which becomes "She loves him. Everything's going to be *all right now.*" You get the idea.

But scripting suddenly becomes a minor consideration when you've got a ten-ton superspectacular gargantuan to get on film. There was the grand festivity of the Water Carnival sequence to do, with sheets of water spraying in the air, so that all the grand festive extras got soaking wet. There was the climactic race-track sequence to do (at Santa Anita, after all the real racers had gone home), where the Marx Brothers kept dropping in at surrounding stables and sizing up likely steeds. Chico began making bets with an extra and placed his money on the horse which the script specifically stated was going to lose. When asked why, all he could say was "The odds were fifteen to one."

There were the musical scenes to do, and Harpo went around humming "Boom, Boom, Boooom!" all day, because he couldn't remember the name of the piece, but that was what he wanted to play when it came time to play the harp. "He's been playing it for a year and he doesn't know what it's called yet," Chico would scold. "It's Rachmaninoff, you!" Harpo would remember it was Rachmaninoff and then go and forget it again, but he didn't forget about humming "Boom, Boom, Boooom!" until MGM informed him that the rights to that particular tune would run in the neighborhood of $1,000 and he could just go around humming something else for a change.

Then there was the wallpaper scene. "As I remember it, people in the cast were getting buckets of wallpaper paste dumped over their heads for at least three weeks," says Robert Pirosh. "The dirtiest, messiest set I've ever seen. When a director insists on twenty takes of a scene in which a bucket of paste is splashed in your face, it makes you wish you were in any other line of work but that. Sam Wood enjoyed every minute of it. I don't think it was as much a case of his being a perfectionist as of his liking to see people get smeared with paste."

Shortly before the film was released, at a time when nerves were on edge, there came the days of the Incredible Credit

Harangue. It all started early in May when the first notice of the writing credits were issued to the production world. It read:

ORIGINAL STORY and SCREENPLAY
by
Al Boasberg, Robert Pirosh, and George Seaton

and was accompanied by the parenthetical comment that George Oppenheimer, unbilled in the title, would get additional mention in the *Academy Bulletin.* (Oppenheimer was put back on the staff again after the tour was over to put on more of those finishing touches. He had played an integral part in the creation of many of the rejected stories, but now that most of the work was done he returned to the roost to assume his accustomed role of Also Ran. He was *always* being put at the tail end of somebody else's screenplay credit. One woman met him in person and remarked, "I thought your name was *And* George Oppenheimer.") The billing was suitable to all except, strangely enough, Al Boasberg. It didn't satisfy him to be first. He wanted something better.

Boasberg sent a wire to Donald Gledhill of the Motion Picture Academy that said, "THIS PICTURE IS A MUSICAL PICTURE OF AN UNUSUAL CATEGORY AND REQUIRES SPECIAL CREDIT." His suggestion was:

ORIGINAL STORY and SCREENPLAY
by
Robert Pirosh and George Seaton
COMEDY SCENES and CONSTRUCTION by Al Boasberg

(George Oppenheimer will get
additional credit in the *Academy Bulletin*)

He acknowledged that this would have to be agreed to by everyone else involved, but added that if real arbitration were undertaken, with the Marx Brothers and everyone participating, he wanted the radio rights. Ho ho ho ho.

When consulted about the matter, the studio made the

natural objection that his version, in effect, gave no credit to anyone else. With a picture whose key attraction was a series of comedy scenes, the men who weren't given credit for the comedy scenes wouldn't seem to have been much help. On top of that, it simply wasn't true. The studio did, however, like the *order* he presented. Four days later, they came out with the new version of the credits, which read:

ORIGINAL STORY and SCREENPLAY
by
Robert Pirosh, George Seaton, and Al Boasberg

(George Oppenheimer will get
additional credit in the *Academy Bulletin*)

Bystanders three blocks away from Boasberg when he found this out have reported that he was furious. His eyes bulged, his neck grew red, his face went purple, his bellow shattered glass. His reaction was a big surprise to everybody since they all had assumed (somehow) that he wouldn't mind. Writers are such touchy people.

Now everyone got involved. The problem was taken to Larry Weingarten, it was taken to George Seaton, it was taken to Groucho Marx. They all agreed that the listing was more or less suitable and accurate as it stood. They did not agree on how to handle the apoplectic Boasberg. First he said that if he couldn't have credit the way he wanted it, then he didn't want any at all. Then he said he'd be willing to arbitrate, but only if Sam Wood were the mediator. The producers decided that if he wanted Wood so badly, there must be something funny going on, and refused. Then they printed a new credit:

STORY and SCREENPLAY by Robert Pirosh and George Seaton

Somebody jokingly pointed out to Boasberg that every time he complained about his credit he went down a peg. Boasberg's reply was an impolite remark, bordering on the sacrilegious.

Pirosh and Seaton were just innocent little neophytes caught up in the ego nightmare of an ogre. Now when he gave the radio routine, it was in deadly, sinister earnest. "I'm going to go on *national radio*," he declared, "and tell the world the *truth* about the credits to *A Day at the Races!*" The truth was that the studio was fed up with fussing with him and dropped him from the argument, at which point, the third, final, and definitive notice came out:

ORIGINAL SCREENPLAY
by
Robert Pirosh, George Seaton, and George Oppenheimer

(Al Boasberg will get
additional credit in the *Academy Bulletin*)

The Academy shortly received a letter from Boasberg's lawyers. Mr. Boasberg, they wished it known, did not want any credit, in any way, anywhere, in any connection with *Day at the Races*, whatsoever.

This last wish they complied with.

The six key comedy routines of *Day at the Races* share the nearly two hours' running time with an endless succession of lavish production numbers and terse business conferences. Each routine is preceded by as much preparation and explanation as any play by Bernard Shaw, yet the whole of their contributions to the story cannot equal one. The story could actually get along with only the first ten minutes of the movie and the last fifteen, but that doesn't stop them from slowing up and plotting it all over again after every fadeout. Subplots spring up, falter, and die as fast as dandelions. There seems to be a considerably earnest attempt to get Harpo entered as a patient in the sanitarium, but after one try the effort is abandoned. Esther Muir makes a grand exit on the line "I'll get even with you, you dirty, lowdown, cheap, double-crossing snake!" but we never see her again. At one point Groucho turns to Chico and says, "I thought I told you guys to stay down in that room with those pigeons." What pigeons? (A pigeon enters five minutes later, apparently having just come from "down in that room.") Chico has a line "That's Whitmore, and I think he's in with Morgan," although there is no clue to how he happened on this revelation. Groucho is a horse doctor, but nobody bothers to relate this to the fact that half the movie is about horse racing or that the story is resolved by a horse. On top of that, there is such a plethora of debts being run—Groucho is out of money, Allan Jones can't pay the feed bill, Judy is going to lose the sanitarium—that each one seems to be trying very hard to be *the* debt around which the plot revolves but just doesn't have it in it.

The comedy scenes are given overabundant rationalization, but no such care is afforded to the music, and now that it has nothing to do with either the comedy or the plot, it looks particularly useless. As if the sight of the Marx Brothers waving their fingers in the air and making with the heighdy-ho were not appalling enough, a big thing is made of "All God's Chillun Got Swing," a silly song which seems to make mock of the attempt of *Duck Soup*'s "All God's Chillun Got Guns" to make mock of the original. And whatever it is that Harpo's playing on the harp, it certainly wants to be "Alone."

Turns out the "Races" of the title means more than we thought it did. Situation comedy, hoked-up romance, uninspired music, sex and money weren't enough for them; the producers were out to get *every single one* of Hollywood's hangups in this film, even if it meant going miles out of their way to bring in a host of stereotype Negroes to recognize Harpo as Gabriel and make with some more heighdy-ho. (The assumption of the role of Gabriel lends a somewhat impious, obscene aura of respectability to Harpo's supernatural qualities. In *At the Circus* he becomes Swengali, but that's sort of a comedown if you've ever been Gabriel.)

This is the movie where Dr. Hackenbush Groucho announces, in lieu of a medical alma mater, "Dodge Brothers, late '29." The Chrysler Corporation was so inexplicably pleased by this reference to a shady past (the Dodge Brothers, having sold their Dodge to Chrysler for some millions of dollars, celebrated with a drunken orgy that killed both of them) that they presented Groucho, Harpo and Chico each with their own spanking

MGM

The splendiferous Water Carnival scene.

clean bright shiny Dodge. Apparently insults from Groucho had come to be worth even money in the marketplace.

When *Day at the Races* came out, it was advertised as "MGM's Monster Musical." One envisions King Kong doing the Charleston.

A BITTER PILL

WHITMORE: Just a minute, Mrs. Upjohn. That looks like a horse pill to me.

GROUCHO: Oh, you've taken them before.

WHITMORE: Are you sure, Doctor, you haven't made a mistake?

GROUCHO: You have nothing to worry about. The last patient I gave one of those to won the Kentucky Derby.

WHITMORE: May I examine this, please? Do you actually give those to your patients? Isn't it awfully large for a pill?

GROUCHO: Well, it was too small for a basketball and I didn't know what to do with it. Say, you're awfully large for a pill yourself.

WHITMORE: Dr. Wilmerding, just what is your opinion?

DOCTOR: It must take an awful lot of water to swallow that.

GROUCHO: Nonsense, you can swallow that with five gallons.

WHITMORE: Isn't that a lot of water for a patient to swallow?

GROUCHO: Not if the patient has a bridge. You see, the water flows under the bridge and the patient walks over the bridge and meets the pill on the other side.

By the time *Day at the Races* has started, fifteen minutes of it is already over—which is to say that in the script finally accepted, Groucho's prick of a bombastic bubble is given the ax, to make way for a lot of conventional exposition, with Chico Marx making concessions to sentimentality like "Miss Judy, you can stop paying me, but you can't fire me!" This sort of thing is all right in its place, but it's about as appropriate to a Marx Brothers comedy as a nose on a rhino. If you look at the whole MGM battery, you'll find opening shots of singing Italians in *Night at the Opera,* an expository Dukesbury Manor sequence in *At the Circus,* a meeting of the Railroad Board in *Go West*—and you'll find all of them either excised or relegated to a slot less noxious. The same mistake was made and then rectified time after time: Opening one of these films without a comedy routine was like starting a race without an opening gun.

And when it finally does get started, what a feeble start it is! The reason, possibly, is not so much the material, which is fine, as the approach, which is just plain wrong. In charges Groucho, with a majestic dolly punctuating his predatory crouch—and then he proceeds to cower and whimper and belie that whole head start. He evades the questions directed to him about his medical background, for one thing. He tries to make up for it by boasting of his hardships during the flu epidemic, but when challenged about them he shrivels. "I caught the flu," he says, and stops dead.

This ante-climactic opening proceeds from a basic misunderstanding of what Groucho is all about. Professor Wagstaff is a fraud, too, but you don't see him going around making excuses about it.

THE CODEBOOK ROUTINE

CHICO: Hey, hey, boss, boss. Come here. You want-a something hot?

GROUCHO: Not now, I just had lunch. Anyhow, I don't like hot ice cream.

CHICO: Hey! Come here! I no sell ice cream, that's-a fake to fool the police. I sell-a tips on the horses, I gotta something today can't lose, one dollar.

GROUCHO: No, some other time. I'm sorry. I'm betting on Sun-Up. Some other time. Two dollars on Sun-Up.

CHICO: Hey, come here. Sun-Up is the worst horse on the track!

GROUCHO: I notice he wins all the time.

CHICO: Aw, just because he comes in first!

GROUCHO: Well, I don't want 'em any better than first! Two dollars on Sun-Up.

CHICO: Hey, boss! Come here. Come here. Suppose you bet on Sun-Up. What-a you gonna get for your money? Two to one! One dollar, and you remember me all your life.

GROUCHO: That's the most nauseating proposition I *ever* had!

CHICO: Come on, come on. You look like a sport. Come on, boss. . . . don't be a crunger for one buck.

GROUCHO: All right. . . . What's this?

CHICO: That's the horse.

GROUCHO: How'd he get in here?

CHICO: Getta you ice cream! Tootsie-Frootsie ice cream!

GROUCHO: "ZVBXRPL." I had that same horse when I had my eyes examined.

Now things start happening. We finally get a chance to meet Harpo, and this proves to be just as discouraging an experience as meeting Groucho and Chico. Chico's introduction, after all, was only an impediment, and Groucho's attack was only a defense, and now, red wig or not, Harpo dressed up in a jockey's suit and cap looks just like any other jockey. And that clever idea of making him a lackey for the opposition and arousing sympathy for him by having him beaten savagely at periodic intervals, so ingenious when somebody thought it up for *Night at the Opera,* is now well on its way toward becoming one of MGM's more beloved clichés. Even at that, he does marvelous things, left alone with naught but a blade of hay, when the sheriff demands to be paid for the feed bill, and it is at just the point of Harpo's insolence that *Day at the Races* gets into full swing and we can forget that the three of them have ever been introduced at all. Up to now, the writers have been slaves to the idea that we can't enjoy the comedy scenes until we are interested in the characters. The truth, of course, is just the reverse: We simply aren't interested in these characters until they've given us something to laugh at.

Harpo makes a strategic withdrawal at the behest of the sheriff, and Chico's eyes alight on Groucho as a suitable subject for his Chicanery. A clever enough choice, we must admit, after watching the man be made a fool of by a handful of doctors. This ought to be duck soup for an illiterate Italian.

Woeful Groucho has found it his lot to venture a bet on a horse named Sun-Up. No good, says Chico, I've got a hot tip. Groucho blows a dollar on the hot tip, but finds it unintelligible. Just at the point where he regrets losing the dollar, he is sold a Codebook to understand the tip, then a Master Codebook to understand the Codebook. He's sunk. Now he needs a Breeder's Guide to find out what the Master Code is about, then an entire series of nameless volumes to elucidate the Breeder's Guide. If he stops at any point, the money he's already spent becomes Instant Loss. If he keeps going, the reckless squandering takes on the flavor of an investment, and that ought to mean *something.*

It reminds us of days at the carnivals and arcades, where we know that every nickel spent is a nickel lost, yet illogic tells us that losing more nickels will step things up and make the first ones worthwhile. By the time we've spent everything, we have no recourse but to convince ourselves we've had a ball.

Now it seems the entire approach of the Groucho–Chico encounter has been changed: Normally it was Groucho who had something to gain from Chico, even though he normally lost it, and lost Chico, and lost his train of thought, and never found his way back home again. Normally, there was no such pattern to their conversation; it was a series of divergent strands that led around each other like spaghetti. The Marx Brothers always could get along without a pattern or without a comedy routine. Two guys stand in a hotel lobby, three guys go to a speak-easy, four guys fight in a war—these are not comedy routines. But the Codebook Routine is a comedy routine. Aside from the sparkle and glitter of the splendiferous settings, it is this approach which most sets apart *Day at the Races* and *Night at the Opera* from the films that precede them. It is only a shame that nobody here seems to have mastered the knack of balancing gags one on top of another so that they all spill out like jelly beans out of a jar. One laugh following another with relentless assurance is a method with considerable merit, but with the Marx Brothers we usually expect to be titillated in our precipitous rush down the roller coaster by some unexpected hills and surprise swerves at the bottom. The Codebook Routine flows smoothly but never tumultuously.

So what makes this scene great is not the noodle-soup logic that is no longer at its base, but the invincible straight line of its progress and the Greek-tragic inevitability of Chico burdening Groucho with books that elucidate nothing but each other and, only after an effort, tell him to bet on Rosie. Chico, meanwhile, uses his earnings to bet on Sun-Up. Groucho doesn't even get a chance to throw away *more* money, as by the time he gets to the window the race is over and Sun-Up has won. This, remember, is the horse Groucho was about to bet on in the first place. Now he's left with nothing but books. He dumps them into the wagon and takes up the "Tootsie-Frootsie Ice Cream" chant. He hasn't simply been exploited. He's inherited a racket.

The well-educated writers of *Day at the Races* (Pirosh is an alumnus of the Sorbonne!) could tell you all about that satire on

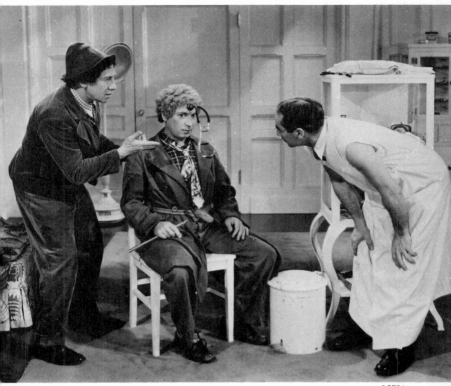

MGM

education that the writers of *Horsefeathers* were trying to get at. Groucho has nothing to do but shout "Tootsie-Frootsie" for the same reason that the most "promising" college students have nothing to do but turn around and become professors.

THE SINGING DOCTOR

GROUCHO: Take it easy, now, huh? Say, am I stewed, or did a grapefruit just fly past?

CHICO: I no see anything.

GROUCHO: If that's his Adam's apple, he's got yellow fever.

CHICO: He's got ingrown balloons.

GROUCHO: He has, eh? Well, we'll soon find out. Hold it till I get a rock, will you?

CHICO: Look, look! He's got a blister on his tongue!

GROUCHO: Is that what it is?

CHICO: Yeh, I think he's a Ubangi.

GROUCHO: Well, I'll get a hammer and Ubangi that right off. I had a case like that once in Düsseldorf many years ago, and . . . Say, it's grown considerably, hasn't it? What's that hairy fungus all over him?

CHICO: Some fungus, eh, Doc?

GROUCHO: Not a great deal, no. I don't know.

CHICO: Hey, you're making a mistake, that's his head!

GROUCHO: If that's his head, he's making a mistake, not me.

Groucho turns innocently enough to the receptionist and says, "Have the florist send some roses to Mrs. Upjohn and write, 'Emily, I love you' on the back of the bill"—which manages to get things going again after they've simmered down considerably. Groucho discovers that a plot is afoot to look into his background, and he leaps into his office to get Business Manager Whitmore on the phone so he can treat him to his Florida Medical Board impersonation. Uncharacteristically, he is given another comedy routine to perform—that is, a story line. Characteristically, the comedy routine is completely uncalled for, as he mercilessly defeats the purpose the screenplay carefully prepares for him. His original intent was presumably to allay all suspicions by assuring Mr. Whitmore that everything was well with Hackenbush's record. But he elaborates endlessly on the masquerade and ends by doing nothing more than make Whitmore angry. He fabricates a hurricane, he pretends he can't hear, he pretends he's forgotten what the call was about, then he turns into Dr. Hackenbush again and calls Whitmore to the dictograph in the middle of every sentence. Rarely has Groucho heckled anyone so methodically. This scene is very well done and almost makes the grade, but it could really use a handful of nonsensical lines that were lost in the rewrite. As it stands now, there is not one good Groucho line that would be funny out of context; the business is all Southern imitations and straight-faced reprimands. The lines that they did leave in would be funnier if the lines that they didn't leave in were left in. It's the conglomeration of absurdities that provides a lot of the kicks, after all, and whether every single one of them is a gem is a little beside the point. Not all the lines in Groucho's battle with Alky Briggs are funny, either. What's that got to do with it? We'd still rather see them all there than be left with just the best three.

This bit is linked with its inverse: a noncomedy routine embellished with formless balderdash. The situation is this: Groucho is the doctor who will examine Harpo the patient. Chico will kibitz. That is all. Happens thousands of times every day. But it is excuse enough, in its homey fashion, to monkey about with the stethoscopes and swallow thermometers and insult each other, all three stumbling through the tools and devices of the medical trade with concentrated unconcern. Groucho assumes command of the situation and Chico lends him his support by tossing offhandedly some credentials to Harpo ("Good doctor . . . been a doctor for years . . . Singing doctor."). Neither Chico nor Harpo has the wispiest faith in the man in white robes until they have undeniable proof that he is a fraud ("A horse doctor!"), and then, of a sudden, he has their unshakable confidence, and the minute his leg is shot full of Novocain (with a needle the size of a jackhammer), so he walks with one leg wrapped behind the other, they make their exit as blind, trusting followers, walking exactly the same way.

There's no denying that it is a happy scene, but one hopelessly full of grotesque dialogue: There is much talk of desiccation, fungus, decay, poison, yellow fever, and other such uncharacteristic allusions. Had there perhaps been something more suggestive of the bizarre, the Gothic, the old-fashionable in the setting and decor, something comically sinister might have come across. All we get, though, is that antiseptic, spic-and-spanitary atmosphere that dominates the film. We are only reminded of our last trip to the hospital and all the grim details still associated with it. We are only left with a slight nausea which the comedy does its best to triumph over. It's a close fight, but the comedy wins.

BUFFALO BILL GOES ICE SKATING

CHICO: Hey, Doc! Doc! I'm telling you a secret! She's out to get you!

GIRL: Why, I've never been so insulted in all my life!

GROUCHO: Well-l, it's early yet.

GIRL: Well, I'm leaving! I'm certainly not going to stay here with these . . .

GROUCHO: You're not leaving, they're leaving!

GIRL: Oh! My cape!

GROUCHO: You fellas are busting up a beautiful romance. What's the matter with you?

CHICO: Doc, Get her out! She's gonna make trouble!

GROUCHO: You've got her all wrong. This is my aunt; she's come to talk over some family matters.

CHICO: I wish I had an aunt look like that!

GROUCHO: Well, take it up with your uncle.

Now that the Water Carnival sequence is over (and in *Day at the Races* the musical confection comes less as a breather and more of a damper than it did in *Night at the Opera*—not so much a restful eye in a comedy hurricane as a patch of sawdust in a bobsled race) we get back to the business of creating legends. Once again, the ever-increasing mythos of the Marx Brothers is delved into for inspiration, and an old bit is linked with a new idea. The new idea is Harpo's pantomime to Chico, sparked from the notion that one of the day's more popular pastimes, a current living-room rage called charades, provided a snugly fitting vehicle for a mute comedian. Fortuitously discovering a plot to frame Groucho, Harpo runs off to get the news across to Chico (he knows he'd never get anywhere with Groucho). The sheer idea of a pantomimed sentence is not in its essence a matter of hilarity (as two witless revivals in *Night in*

Casablanca and *Love Happy* went on to prove), but when cleverly handled it becomes a prime opportunity to display Chico's skill at misinterpreting the obvious while at the same time evaporating impossible enigmas—a *series* of opportunities, end on end.

Harpo starts out with a broad outline of a large moustache to indicate who the message is about. Chico gets it—Buffalo Bill. Harpo tries again, with an unmistakable imitation of the Groucho crouch. Buffalo Bill goes ice skating? It's clear now that surface simplicities are no good at all. This is a job for a conundrum. Harpo turns around and leaps furiously into an attack on the shrubbery. Oh! says Chico. Hacken-a-bush.

Chico understands Harpo the way we understand our impulses, which is to say randomly and inexplicably, but not necessarily at all.

Before this, Harpo had always been a character who *didn't* speak, not one who *couldn't*. His refusal to utter words had always, perversely, been one of his major strengths. This scene is the first step in its gradual transformation into a weakness. It's a great scene, of course, but like the intercom scene unambitiously cut short, and the real fun in this picture, even when inspiration fails, is provided by the whole Unholy Three at once. This new situation (Groucho being framed) is only new clothes on an old friend: the dash-back-and-forth-in-a-bedroom routine that stretches clear back in a broken line to *I'll Say She Is*. (Though the room they dash back and forth in has come a long way from the patchwork flats of the Napoleon boudoir. From the looks of this palatial layout, they could save the whole sanitarium just by selling the chandelier.) The attempt to mask the chaos in clear and unquestionable motivation is not only somewhat crippling; it is openly unsuccessful. Chico bursts upon Groucho with frank distress and in all seriousness warns him, "She's gonna frame you!" In no seriousness whatever, Groucho replies, "I wouldn't mind framing *her*," a comeback which is neither good plotting nor good comedy. As if that were not quite soggy enough, he goes and tops it with "A prettier picture I've never seen!" (Won't he *ever* stop saying that?) So much for reasons.

The kick in all this is limited strictly to the nonsense:

Groucho playing up to Miss Marlowe, but so inept and downright rude about it that he couldn't possibly be in earnest ("Tomahto soup?" he inquires, then produces a can and asks if she has a can opener with her); Chico dreaming up insane and unconvincing pretexts for barging into the room again and again, apparently less interested in getting rid of the girl than in proving himself a nuisance to everybody (A German Jew doing an imitation of an Italian doing an imitation of an Irishman is about as far removed from narrative necessity as you can get); Harpo gleefully delighting in each costume for its own sake, and content, if he can't remove the girl, to heap wallpaper, cosmetic powder, and other indecencies upon her all night. (When Groucho throws the steak in Chico's pocket and sics the bloodhounds on it, they drag Harpo around the couch, under the table, and out into the hall, and nothing could he enjoy more heartily.)

But it starts with an excuse for existence and it ends the same way: Margaret Dumont marches in, doesn't see anything but wallpaper, and marches back out again. It kills the old uncalled-for air of the entrance and exit games they used to play with Thelma Todd. But it's fun while it lasts.

EXAMINATION

MARX BROTHERS: "Down by the old mill stream, Where I first met you . . ."

STEINBURG: May I say I've seen quicker examinations.

GROUCHO: Maybe, but you'll never see a slipperier one!

STEINBERG: Gentlemen, are you ready to proceed?

GROUCHO: We'll proceed immediately.

WHITMORE: Doctor . . . and what do you expect to do next?

CHICO: The next thing I think we should do is . . . Wash our hands!

GROUCHO: Yeah, wash our hands!

MARX BROTHERS: "Down by the old mill stream, Where I first met you . . ."

GROUCHO: Sterilization! Sterilization!

ASSORTED VOICES: Doctor! Doctor! I don't know. Get away from me! No, we're not mad, just terribly hurt, that's all.

GROUCHO: Hey, just a moment, just a moment, just put that gown on, not the nurse, huh?

NURSE: Aah!

GROUCHO: Why is it a dame like *that* never gets sick?

DUMONT: But I am sick, Doctor, will you please pay some attention to me?

GROUCHO: You'll have to step in line, Mrs. Upjohn, there's three orders ahead of you. Just think of that poor girl catching her death of cold! Say, nurse! Sterilization!

CHICO: Hey, Doc, get away from there.

STEINBURG: This is absolutely insane!

GROUCHO: Yes, that's what they said about Pasteur!
    (Sound track degenerates into a lot of shouting)

We waited through the intermission, we waded through the exposition, we sat through tame and amusing comedy scenes, we counted curtains during the Water Carnival, we stood in line to get tickets, we forsook an evening of domestic comfort and connubial bliss, we may even have waited out the week to see this movie—the climactic scene had better be worth it.

This is where they finally get around to making fun of doctors. The way they do this is to present us with an unquestionable victory of sham doctors over qualified ones—a task which any ordinary comedian would undoubtedly find too momentous even to think about bringing off, much less making it look like a real victory. But it is a perfect assignment for the Marx Brothers, who have more to do with what keeps people alive than medical science even knows about. Just ask one of these Knights in White Linen what's deep inside of a man. He'll tell you a pancreas, a liver, and a lot of intestines. Smart guy!

And this is where Groucho at long last tells the world that he hasn't forgotten what he has always known: that the cleanest way for a fraud to behave is as a straight-off, out-in-the-open fraud. Captain Spaulding sneers at a recapitulation of his own exploits, Groucho the stowaway complains to the captain of living conditions in the hold, Professor Wagstaff informs his pupils that whatever it is they want to do he's not going to let them, Rufus Firefly declares to his subjects that the government will be full of corruption from here on in, Otis Driftwood is sure to let his benefactors know that they are throwing their money away on him, and now Dr. Hackenbush confronts all the dignitaries with his ignorance, accuses *them* of incompetence, and dares them to make something of it. Typically, they are stupefied (directness *does* have a habit of baffling people), leaving him free to emphasize the importance of sterilization and declare himself an expert in the art of washing his hands. Harpo and Chico are introduced to Dr. Steinburg as two more Dr. Steinburgs, providing an excuse to run around the room and introduce skeletons, diagrams, tables, and lamps as just so many Steinburgs. Ignorant of even so fundamental a technique as how to take a pulse, they denigrate its significance ("I don't do any pulse work!"), then they rush over and sterilize; they chase each other to dry their hands on their white gowns, they chase Steinburg to dry their hands on his, they give the patient a shave, a shoeshine, and a roller-coaster ride in her chair, they tear uniforms off nurses, they shove bed pans under the doctors, they sell newspapers, and, through it all, they sing a nostalgic song. Finally they put a capper on their unbridled energy by riding through the operating room on an unbridled horse. In the rain. Everyone is taken abath.

All of which does nothing to save the sanitarium, but as we were never very concerned about the sanitarium, we can't consider it much of a loss. What is far more important is the pure catharsis, the cleansing of the joints, the pruning of doubt, hesitancy, and fear from the Tree of Life, the actions of men with something besides a pancreas inside. What is important is that a great outburst of insistent madness come as a climax to the evasion and the spastic momentum of the rest of the film. *Day at the Races,* alone of all Marx movies, creates within its own borders the mild amusements and petty disappointments we daily encounter, and then, to bring it all to a head, must purge it all in an explosion of the demonic self terrifying enough to leave the specialists to stand alone and wonder what they forgot to specialize in.

What a pity, then, that it doesn't quite do that. By this time in the Marxes' career, they are expected to do what is not expected of them; they are supposed to do whatever it is they are not supposed to do. By this time they have gotten their madness down to a science, and it isn't really madness any more. The Marx Brothers are so intent on sterilizing, they've set themselves on the path to sterility.

A DAY AT THE RACES

Now there is a nice scene where Allan Jones's horse is stolen from the sheriff and smuggled into the race track, where valiant efforts by all concerned help it to gallop courageously to final victory.

It's strange to see a long sequence appended to a movie that has already come to an end. There are reasons, of course, for jamming up the operations of a race course. The sanitarium has to be saved *sometime,* for one thing; a sequel really ought to be provided for the opera-house monkeyshines, for another. But nonetheless, we are no longer in the mood for excess nonsense, and the final scene can only look like a loose flap.

In the cloistered atmosphere of the opera house, the slightest irreverence exploded into blasphemy. But in the wide-open spaces of the race track, so many things are going on at one time that a million desecrations add up to nothing. Horse racing is such a simple and unaffectedly exciting way to spend an afternoon, anyway, that no matter how funny the Marx Brothers are in the middle of it, they don't satisfy any primal urges by gumming things up and they are simply not doing us any good by being there. But it is a nice scene.

A Day at the Races was received with open arms by the critics and the moviegoing public as just what they had in mind. If *Night at the Opera* made three million dollars, its sequel made four million, which ranks it, on the basis of initial release, the most instantly popular of all their films. (But then, 1937 was such a good year for the film business, it was hard to bring out a movie and *not* clean up on it.)

Mark Van Doren, in *The Nation*, found its appeals for sympathy and its tireless perfectionism particularly suited to his tastes; it was as if a fan of Chaplin and Langdon, apparently liking the Marx Brothers but feeling he shouldn't because of their apparent disorder and seeming lack of discipline—everything, in short, that makes them distinctive—could now deign to consider them great for all the wrong reasons. "The film is as funny as any of its predecessors, and in addition it is more charming, more loveable. It places the comedians clearly among the few fine comedians of our day." As if charming and lovable were prerequisite qualities to greatness.

One of the more perceptive reviews was turned in by Frank Nugent of the New York *Times:* "The brothers busied themselves for two years getting material together for this picture and carefully plotting a curve of audience response. They were so deliberate about this research that many of the whimsies they had in mind became public property—gag-stealing, they called it. Somebody must have stolen the gags, because they aren't in the picture."

Though *Races* won crowds of new fans for the Marxes, it turned away disgusted old admirers and dyed-in-the-wool anarchists. Insignificantly enough, the film was banned in the Republic of Latvia on the grounds that it was "worthless."

A Day at the Races suffers from a bad case of wishing it was *A Night at the Opera*. The more money *Opera* made, the more obligated Thalberg seems to have felt to sail after the Golden Fleece on the good ship *Ergo* and turn the pattern of his success into a formula. The restless sense of discovery so evident before, culminating in a grand air of triumph, is replaced here by the complacent self-satisfaction that so discourages us when we encounter it in the world: There is a low-lying level of energy suggesting that this is all there is to life and that it is vanity to hope for more. *Day at the Races* is a lot of fun, but it's all polish and no spit.

It makes us see what a perfect combination of the old and

the new that *Night at the Opera* was. In the first film the flavor of the abstract and the supernatural and the iconoclastic still re-mains. In the second, that has all been distilled away, and the flavor is the flavor of Micrin. Even those who had their hearts in this project through most of the two years of its preparation remain today among the hordes of wholehearted adulators of the other—an indication that running a good thing into the ground is no way to erect a monument.

A Day at the Races, which looks to most like a pleasing shadow of *A Night at the Opera,* actually resembles most of all a comedy in mourning, not only for the little brown fellow, but for a stillborn child called *Peace and Quiet.*

MGM

V

intermission

ROOM SERVICE 1938

There is a common assumption that the Marx Brothers appeared in *Room Service* on Broadway. This is not true. *Room Service* was written by John Murray and Allen Boretz and produced and directed for the stage by George Abbott in 1937, with Sam Levene, Philip Loeb, and Teddy Hart in the leads.

There is also a common assumption that *Room Service* is a Marx Brothers movie. This is not true either. It is an easy mistake to make, however, and can be corrected simply by providing a clear definition of the term "Marx Brothers Movie." Let us consult Webster:

> **Marx Brothers Movie** *n:* a motion picture intended, conceived, written, and committed to film directly by and/or for the Marx Brothers with the express and stated purpose of creating an experience dominated by their personality and intended for those receptive to that personality, with, to, and for all detriments and attributes pertaining thereto syn Marx Brothers Film; Marx Brothers Picture; Marx Brothers Flick (*slang*); *archaic:* Marx Brother*f* Movie

If we take the phrase "intended, conceived . . . directly . . . for the Marx Brothers" in its literal sense, the conclusion is inescapable that any film made from a play written to be acted out by normal people and then bought up by RKO with the bright idea of putting the Marx Brothers in it, is not a Marx Brothers movie. If we look closely at the phrase "dominated by their personality," it is clear that it has no relation to the finished film of *Room Service*. If we think hard about the phrase "detriments and attributes pertaining thereto," we can only assume that Webster was trying to be cute.

Part of the problem of the film comes from the mistaken

notion—a veritable byword among people who don't understand show business—that "good" is a measurable quantity; that if you take a "good" script and put it in the hands of "good" comedians, you will get a "good" result. Good airplanes may be made that way, but good films are not.

RKO, a studio dedicated more to the importance of the individual product than to the perpetuation of a series, was willing to pay $225,000 for the rights to the play. It was also willing to transport almost the whole supporting cast of the original production to Hollywood to play the same roles in the film. Neither of these moves was within the bounds of tradition, and RKO applauded itself mightily for being so unconventional about the whole affair.

It was Morrie Ryskind's job to turn Murray and Boretz's play into a Marx Brothers screenplay. "Don't think that's easy, trying to get them into a show that wasn't written for them," he warns. The transferral was mostly a matter of adding superfluous gags to already existing dialogue, so that Gordon Miller's perfectly acceptable expository line, "You can't shake backers out of your sleeve," is turned into a chance for Groucho to shake his sleeve hopefully and mutter, "Anyhow, I can't." Harry Binion's appraisal, "The rehearsal was terrific. The play looks better all the time," is voiced by Chico's Harry Binelli as "Oh, the rehearsal's a-wonderful. Yes, sirree, boss, it's a-wonderful. I still think it's a terrible play, but it makes a-wonderful rehearsal." Then it was up to Harpo to add his own embellishments, as when he takes his cue from the playwright's pathetic plea, "I've burned my bridges behind me," and looks under the man's jacket at the seat of his pants and disagrees.

The Marx Brothers were signed, through their agent, Zeppo Marx, for $250,000. It was the first and last deal he was ever to make for them. He got no thanks at all from them for the tidy arrangement, except for the snide remark from Groucho that it should have been $350,000.

Rehearsals were held all through June of 1938, though the script wasn't finished till the eighteenth. Then filming went on all through July, though the script was being changed till the twenty-fifth. The Marx Brothers approached their new "legitimate" roles with professional acumen, and shooting went efficiently and well (in the phenomenally short time of five weeks) under the semi-skilled hand of director William Seiter, who had done perfectly well by Laurel and Hardy in *Sons of the Desert,* one of their best features. Philip Loeb, the original for Harry Binion, was supposed to act only as technical adviser, but at the last minute he was rushed into the role of Timothy Hogarth, the bill collector from the We Never Sleep Collection Agency, where he did a great job. Leonid Kinskey (the "agitator" from *Duck Soup*) was set to play Sasha Smirnoff, the waiter, but at the same last minute was called back for retakes on another film, and Alexander Asro, one last original from the George Abbott production, was flown in from Manhattan. (He's good, too. Most of the others from the original cast are pretty awful.)

Room Service is the story of a shoestring producer's frantic attempts to get a backer for his shoestring production before he and his whole cast are kicked out of his brother-in-law's hotel for not paying the huge bill they've accumulated. There is a painstakingly worked-out series of situations, recriminations, and plot reversals. People disappear into the closet at intervals and come out wearing fifteen hats. A turkey gets loose, and the gang chases it all over. The one great scene in the picture is probably the eating scene. The best moments are provided by the Marx Brothers being funny in spite of their structural material, or the material being funny in spite of its nonstructural comedians. This tug of war gets tiresome after a while. Gordon Miller, who sincerely cares about the fate of his production and the people involved in it, is being played by Groucho Marx, who sincerely cares about nothing at all.

Reviewers called *Room Service* "typical" and "entertaining for Marx Brothers fans." *Room Service* is not typical, and the reviewers were apparently not Marx Brothers fans.

vi

joy becomes laughter

The simplest solution became the adaption of the products themselves so they could be reproduced by modern machinery. If it means that wholesome cake-like bread has to become soggy cellulose mush, with all food value lost, then it is a small price to pay because look how much faster and cheaper the machines can reproduce the new inferior product! Naturally it was difficult for them to even consider that it might be better to produce something of worth in an inefficient way than to produce worthless things efficiently. Efficiency was everything.

Beauty became Utility; Joy became Laughter; Creation became Labor; Art became Productive; and Man became Machine. It is this disaster that some would define as Progress.

—James Drought, *Drugoth*

COLLECTION OF HARPO MARX

AT THE CIRCUS 1939

Once the Dell Publishing Company got their hands on a great character like Bugs Bunny, they turned him into a suburban homeowner, and the chief concerns of his life became parking his car and getting his driveway shoveled. In the same way, the deathless, mythical clowns of *Horsefeathers* and *Night at the Opera* are hereby pummeled and subdued into a pack of sniveling, chiseling, weaseling nitwits who get in the way and mess things up a lot. What comes between the punchlines of *At the Circus, Go West* and *The Big Store,* even the best punchlines, are pretty plain old ordinary 1940s movies.

But the Age of Heroic Comedy was over all around. Chaplin was trying to overthrow the government with farce and violins, in his Hitler satire *The Great Dictator,* a black comedy whose audiences preferred their comedies sunny. Lloyd made *Professor Beware,* looked at *Professor Beware,* and quit. The Laurel and Hardy product of 1939, *Blockheads,* was hardly even worth the effort, and after they left Hal Roach and fell into line at the larger studios, the effort was greater and the worth was even less. Buster Keaton was a $100-a-week gag man at MGM. Harry Langdon was one of the gag men for *Blockheads.*

Only W. C. Fields, whose fortunes had declined to the point where he was working for Universal Studios, had at his disposal a small enough unit and a great enough degree of cooperation to turn out something like *The Bank Dick* at the age of sixty-five. After that, the well was spent. Twenty-five years of brilliant gags, incisive characterization, and dynamic, subversive comedy had come to an end. There was nothing left but disintegration, demoralization, heartbreak, and Abbott and Costello.

When Irving Thalberg died, the Marxes' enthusiasm for movie-making died with him. With the last of the Hollywood producers who could figure out what to do with them out of the way, an awfully good reason was going to have to be trumped up before they would ever set foot on a sound stage again. Groucho had several fortunes salted away and stayed home with his family whenever he got the chance. Harpo had recently married Susan Fleming, adopted his first child, and settled down to the domestic life he had never missed. Chico had spent every cent he ever earned and had to have an income or he couldn't eat. That was the reason.

Mervyn LeRoy was no Erich von Stroheim, but then, he was no Irving Thalberg either. LeRoy, who, by many standards, was quite a good director (*Waterloo Bridge, Little Caesar, I Am a Fugitive from a Chain Gang*), took it upon himself to see what kind of producer he could be for the Marx Brothers—who made their return to MGM and signed a three-picture contract providing them with $250,000 a picture and, just to keep them in place, a $50,000 bonus when the film got made for under a million.

Mervyn LeRoy really had no idea what to do about broad, farcical comedies, but, like everyone else who doesn't make them, he thought of them as one big lark that would be lots of fun to go and try. Plans had been circulating in the studio ever since *Day at the Races* to place the Marxes either at a World's Fair or at a circus. LeRoy decided that the Marx Brothers belonged in a circus. And he was right. The Marx Brothers *do* belong in a circus. Which is why they shouldn't be put there. They do *not* belong in a college, or in an opera house, or in a sanitarium, or on a placid ocean liner. Which is exactly why their best movies put them in those places. Strike One.

The handiest junior writer around was a twenty-four-year-old radio gag man that LeRoy had under personal contract. Irving Brecher had never yet written a screenplay, but he had written a lot of gags for radio comedians and, as his career progressed, came to be called the "undisputed king of all Gag Men, living or dead," and to be singled out in later years by Groucho and S. J. Perelman as one of the fastest men on the draw for one-line impromptus, right up there with Oscar Levant and George S. Kaufman. Brecher's style is characterized by a caustic, acid wit softened by a soapy sentimentality, evident in *Meet Me in St. Louis, Sail a Crooked Ship,* and the TV series "Life of Riley" and "The People's Choice." His promising New York Semitic background was enhanced by his amazing resemblance to Groucho (he had done imitations of him from the age of twelve, and today even smokes cigars the same way), but was offset by the fact that he was a producer's choice rather than the Marxes'. His other drawback was that he was, perhaps incurably, one person. Marx Brothers writers, like parents, tend to come in pairs. Without two men to build on each other's ideas, there was always the danger that one gag wouldn't lead to another—it would just lead to itself and then turn around and go back. Brecher's only collaborator was Harpo, who visited him in his office when the spirit moved him and invented visual gags with him. There was no tour, there was no second draft, there was no Al Boasberg. Strike Two.

Another New Yorker was hired to handle the directing. (The difference between New York people and Hollywood people is of more than geographical import. Eddie Buzzell was a Hollywood person born in New York.) Buzzell, a breezy little song-and-dance man (Five feet three. Just about the size of Mervyn LeRoy, by the way. Brecher, by contrast, is very tall), was an old buddy of the Marxes from Broadway, where he starred in musical comedies with titles like *Sweetheart Time* and *The Gingham Girl.* (He had a cute habit of referring to the Marx Brothers as "the O-boys.") His theatrical career had proceeded out of a childhood as one of the Gus Edwards originals, along with Eddie Cantor and George Jessel, and had progressed to being writer, director, and star of two-reel quickies for Columbia. He remained a good friend of the Marxes so long as he was anything but a movie director. By the time he got to this post, he was as firmly entrenched in his own particular style of comedy as they were in theirs.

They didn't mesh. There wasn't one scene, there wasn't one gag that didn't get argued over, sometimes bitterly. Buzzell would tell them how to play the scene, they would tell him how they were *going* to play the scene, Buzzell would tell them they didn't know what they were talking about. Right from the first day there was friction. Buzzell told Groucho, "Now, let's really act this scene," and Groucho piped up, "The Marx Brothers will do anything but act. If you want dramatics, use our stand-ins."

The directorial approach of *At the Circus* hits a good, fast-moving, high-spirited pitch, but one that seems strangely unlike the specific approach already established by the Marx Brothers. (Groucho is so chipper in his first scene that his voice rises several octaves.) Nor is it especially suited to Brecher's cutthroat sardonics. It's not enough that a comedian be given a chance to be funny; he really must have an entire production, from story line down to camera angle, geared to his own personal style. There are several possible ways to pull off any single gag. If you do it any one of these ways, and do it well, and follow it through properly, it will work. If you try to do it both of any two, it will fall flat on its face and die. Strike Three, and the Age of Heroic Comedy was over for the Marx Brothers.

The Marxes were out but they weren't yet down. Buster Keaton was both. It was the ghost of a dead Buster Keaton who was called over to be one of the gag men on *At the Circus*. Try to imagine Harpo performing this gag Keaton came up with:

Harpo walks past a camel with two baskets of straw on its back. He can't see the keeper on the other side, but the keeper is holding the camel's halter and looking around for a match to light his pipe with. Harpo sees some straw fall out of the basket and he puts it back. He finds some extra straw on the ground and he puts that in the basket too. At just that moment the keeper bends down to strike his match, and the camel sinks to its knees. Harpo, in horror, quickly brushes the offending straw out of the basket, the keeper straightens up to light his pipe, and the camel rises again. Harpo walks away, convinced.

It's certainly too mechanical and laboriously contrived to be a good Marx Brothers gag. It would be better if there *were* no explanation, and the camel simply went through the floor. "Do you think that's *funny?*" Groucho asked Keaton with disgust. Harpo and Chico just looked at him.

Now—imagine the whole routine with *Buster Keaton* performing it. And you see the problem.

The brothers were heartsick when the studio decided that the movie would be made without the benefit of a road tour. Now that they knew how to make a Marx Brothers movie a sure thing, they couldn't do it.

By 1939 Groucho was nearing fifty, and Harpo and Chico had passed it. They didn't need any extra stumbling blocks. "Why should I let myself get upset over a movie?" Groucho would go home and ask his family. "A movie that in three months will probably wind up on a double bill at the Oriental Theater, with bingo and free dishes? It's not worth it. I'd rather retire than be constantly aggravated." Then he'd go down to the studio the next day and be constantly aggravated. Harpo was less interested in fighting a lost cause. He determined to do his best, but when he saw doom threaten he responded with a shrug of the shoulders and turned his attention elsewhere. Nevertheless, Harpo and Groucho made certain that Chico invested half of his money before he spent the rest of it. There was no sense going through *this* again.

Then there was the old romantic duet business. This they didn't fight about; it had been one of Thalberg's insistences, so they went along with what they were told was right rather than what they felt was right, little realizing that what had every outward appearance of being a suitable adjustment to reality would be greeted with abject dismay by the sharp eye of posterity. Goes to show what happens when you lay yourself on the line for values belonging to people who aren't you.

The casting side of the talent of Mervyn LeRoy, who made a star of Edward G. Robinson, was cast aside the day he signed up Kenny Baker. It's even more surprising to find out that Kenny Baker was a radio star, since his Mickey Mouse whimper is without a doubt his worst feature. The "straight" part of the story is about how he saves a struggling circus from bankruptcy, and yet from the look of the idiot grin on his face one would tend to be hesitant about giving him a nickel and trusting him to put it in the gum machine. After one shot we've lost interest in him and couldn't care whether he saves his old circus or not. And the songs he and Florence Rice are asked to sing are no help. "Two Blind Loves" and "Step Up and Take a Bow" weren't even considered good in the Thirties, as all the songs that bored us in *A Day at the Races* were.

MGM wanted to give their circus a "streamlined" look. They filled the sets with chromium plating and put neon signs on the animals' cages. They made the tent completely round and constructed it out of imitation silk. (I guess they thought we were going to notice all that. There were imitation silkworms in the audience, and even *they* didn't catch it.) Shooting went on round the clock much of the time, the second unit taking over at night and working till three in the morning doing circus background shots that Buzzell wasn't needed for. They found a super-duper acrobatic act belonging to Janet May, who walked upside down suspended hundreds of feet in the air. They bought the act for the movie and got Janet May to double for Eve Arden in the far shots. But do you think they could get a gorilla? No.

It seems there's this gorilla, Gibraltar, who figures importantly in the story, especially the climax, where he comes out of his cage and terrorizes everybody. But it seems in Hollywood there was *no* gorilla, none that didn't have his calendar filled for the next two years. MGM had to hire a man to play a gorilla. They hired the man, and then they found out he didn't have a gorilla suit. (They watched him do a gorilla imitation without a gorilla suit. They weren't convinced.) They hired a gorilla suit for the man to wear. The man had an agent who examined the gorilla suit. Even the gorilla suit had an agent, and he examined the man. The problem, as Groucho recalls, was that "Mother Nature, with her customary slipshod design, had neglected to equip the gorilla with a window." After two hours of shooting under bright lamps on one of the warmer days of a Los Angeles summer, the man fainted, right in the middle of his gorilla imitation. The gorilla imitator's agent said the man had been inside hundreds of gorilla suits before, and he'd *never* fainted. The gorilla suit's agent said that hundreds of gorilla imitators had been inside his suit before, and they'd *always* fainted. Buzzell said, "Lunch!"

Hot arguments ensued on a hot day over a hot lunch. The gorilla man refused to do his gorilla imitation unless he got a chance to breathe, too. The gorilla-suit man said he would have to take his choice; he couldn't do both. ("Let's make up our minds what we're here for," he said, "to imitate gorillas or to breathe.") The gorilla man, when nobody was looking, crept back onto the set and perforated the old gorilla pelt with an ice pick. The afternoon then passed without incident. When there was no incident by 4:00 P.M., the gorilla-suit man started getting annoyed. "Hey!" he said. "My experience has been that the man inside that skin always faints inside of two hours."

Well, he took one look at his air-conditioned gorilla and stomped off the premises with it, swearing revenge. Production was held up for days while gorilla skins were being looked for, with or without ventilation. All of those were booked up too. The gorilla man, of his own accord, went all the way to San Diego and found an old orangutan skin and bought it. And not till he showed up at the studio with it did he realize that an orangutan is so much smaller than a gorilla that the suit wouldn't even fit him. He had bought himself right out of a job. "We were obliged," says Groucho, "to engage a smaller monkey man who specialized in impersonating orangutans in and around San Diego."

Brecher, recalling his work with Buzzell, felt that "they were very difficult pictures to make, and the Marx Brothers not easy to handle." It was during the second week of production that Buzzell was standing on the set waiting for the O-boys to materialize, when a small messenger boy with a beard rode up on a bicycle and handed him a telegram. He tore it open and read a message that went "HAVE DECIDED TO TAKE SHORT VACATION IN HONOLULU. HOPE TO BE BACK IN A MONTH. GROUCHO, HARPO AND CHICO." The small messenger boy, it turned out, was Chico with a beard.

When the Marxes met Florence Rice, they introduced them-

WANTED

Harpo.

Love Italian

To Berni

by Thomas Gainsborough.
1727 – 1788.

50 CENTS REWARD

August 18th **FOR** *1939.*

JAY-WALKING

it. My house of Harpo Marx.

An *At the Circus* prop, autographed by Harpo.
COLLECTION OF HARPO MARX

Chico, Harpo and Groucho talk business with Gummo.
COLLECTION OF HARPO MARX

selves by locking her in the gorilla cage and leaving her there for an hour. Apparently the fact that they had struck out wasn't going to stop them from getting to first base on balls.

Doctors were called to the set only once, and that was when Harpo, who wanted feathers to spew from his mouth in the scene in the strongman's bedroom, suddenly swallowed them all when Chico hit him on the back.

But shooting went what was called smoothly for a Marx Brothers picture, and the schedule was fairly well stuck to. "I believe it will be better than I thought," Groucho wrote to Arthur Sheekman during production, but then admitted that "this isn't saying a hell of a lot." Brecher wasn't paid to be on the set and have anything to do with the shooting, but he was still on salary at the studio and they were kind enough to call for him to make revisions as occasions arose. One scene in particular, in a midget's cabin, was given a heady going-over before it was photographed. It was decided, for example, to have the infuriated midget threaten to sue the three of them and for Groucho to answer, "Well, if you need a good lawyer, I'm your man." (We might remember what a great routine this once was in *Peace and Quiet*.) The scene was even more thoroughly worked over during the cutting of the film, even to the point of trimming off the exits and fading in mid-scene, for the sake of a stronger ending.

Where Chico was called upon to ask Groucho if he was dressed and Groucho replied, "After a fashion—of 1800," the line was changed to read, "After a fashion, and a pretty old fashion, and I wish I *had* an old-fashioned." Harpo, too, was able to elaborate on the inherent comedy in a way that wasn't obvious from the script. When Groucho is ascertaining that the midget is just a little fellow, Harpo pantomimes that he gets smaller all the time, and thereupon tramples him to death.

Finally, the picture was finished, and Buzzell announced he was leaving for Europe to take a rest. Immediately the Marxes threw him a party: they took him to dinner at the Trocadero, to soup at card tables on a sidewalk, to snacks at a café, to dessert at ringside in the American Legion Stadium, and finally to coffee and cakes served solemnly at a mortuary. After that, he *deserved* a rest.

At the Circus marks a return to the spirit, at least, of *Day at the Races*. Unfortunately, it also marks a return to some of the same jokes. (Groucho even gets to say, "You're the prettiest millstone I've *ever* had around my neck.") And you would think that the last thing they would *want* to copy from *Day at the Races* would be that silly and patronizing Negro business, but there it is, all over Harpo's harp solo, and it seems even worse taste this time than it did before. (If Harpo looks a little awkward in this scene, it's because he had bursitis in his right arm and couldn't raise or lower it without contortions. He had had the misfortune to fall off his ostrich.)

But nothing could be more degrading than the *Lassie* morality that creeps inexorably everywhere. When Kenny Baker is knocked out and wakes up to find $10,000 stolen from him, everybody—even Groucho and Chico!—tells him, "You've got to get some sleep. Never mind the money. You can worry about that in the morning."

Or picture the moment where Groucho phones Kenny Baker and lets him know that he has solved all of Kenny's problems at once. His circus is salvaged, his career is secured, and his girl can marry him. And what does Kenny do? He hangs up the phone, stares straight out the window, and whimpers, "Oh, *boy!*"

Oh, boy!

THE BADGE ROUTINE: There's definitely something to be said for a comedy scene based on a double standard. It is a very common, human thing to have such strong faith in both of two contradictory ideas that you never examine them closely enough to see that they'll never get along with each other. Chico *must* remember that he's the one who hired the lawyer in the first place, but he also knows he's not supposed to let anyone on the circus train without a badge. So Chico the good buddy welcomes Groucho to the departing train, and Chico the circus employee won't let him on. Chico the sympathetic friend looks out for Groucho's welfare and Chico the uptight official keeps kicking him out into the rain. Finally, goodhearted Chico lends Groucho his own badge, but he can't get past officious Chico, who discovers that it's last year's badge and kicks him off the train again.

But Buzzell seems to have missed the point. He emphasizes all the wrong things: Groucho sloshing around uncomfortably in a puddle, Chico misunderstanding Groucho's wisecracks. The way Brecher wrote the scene, it was punctuated by Chico intoning at various intervals, "Bless you, good luck, good health, and I think you caught a cold"—each time complicating the disease until he got to pneumonia—and finally calling out from the embarking train, "Bless you, good luck, good health, and goodbye!" A scene that depends so much on its situation urgently needs such punctuation, as the stateroom scene needed its "hardboiled eggs." But that's been cut out, and the situation has gone to the dogs. There's nothing left to laugh at but the individual lines. And some of those are dogs too.

And here's the topper: Groucho never gets on the train. Originally the scene called for Harpo to ride by in the observation car and whisk him on board with a fishing pole. This was considered either too way out or too expensive. So the last shot shows us Groucho sulking in the gutter and the next scene shows us Groucho on the train. But he never *gets* on. He just *is* on. In *Duck Soup* we might have called this surrealism. But in *At the Circus* it's just bad continuity.

MIDGET:	Let's shake on it.
GROUCHO:	Oh, uh, let's smoke on it, uh? Oh, heck, I, uh, I seem to be all out of cigars. Uh, you don't happen to have a spare cheroot on you, do you?
CHICO:	Hey, I find one more! Are you lucky! I thought this cigar was in my other suit.
GROUCHO:	I wish *you* were in your other suit, and your other suit was being pressed. No, mangled.
CHICO:	Hah, I just remember, this *is* my other suit. Hey, you know these cigars are imported? They're hard to get.
GROUCHO:	*I* haven't had any trouble getting 'em! Not with that plantation under your vest.
CHICO:	Hey, boss! You're not getting any evidence!
GROUCHO:	No, but I'm getting tobacco heart.

HAVE YOU GOT A CIGAR?: Now we're catching on. This movie really *isn't* structured as a series of comedy scenes. For one thing, the Marxes are always making incidental gags every time they come on the screen. For another thing, the routines they put together are so dissipated that they never generate any hysteria. In 1931 Groucho held a gangster at bay with simple verbal acuity. In 1939 a strongman says, "How you like I should break you in two?" and all he can think of is "Could I file separate income taxes?" He's lucky to get out of the room alive.

It takes all three of them together, talking and gesticulating at once and each other, to do anything that merits a full-scale giggle. The best that can be said for the scene in the midget's house, for instance, is that it is fast. Groucho asks the midget for a cigar, Chico gives him one of his, Harpo lights it, and Groucho hides it in the lamp and asks the midget for another cigar, in a rapid succession of lines and actions that maneuver all over and around one another almost too quickly for anyone to notice that it isn't really funny. This is the opposite of the first scene. This is all punctuation and nothing else. Chico keeps offering his god-dam cigars until you want to reach into the screen, yank him by the hair, and yell, "Stop that!"

There is, unfortunately, no finish a scene like that can have, so Harpo contracts allergies out of the clear blue sky and starts sneezing so that the furniture flies around. Right here, of course, things start promising to grow as chaotic and crowded in that tiny little room as they got in that tiny little stateroom. Right here is where the scene starts to get really interesting. And right here is where the fade arrives.

THE FLIES AND ME: Brecher claims to have had a lot of lines stolen from him. You begin to wonder, when you hear Groucho say, "I have an agreement with the house flies: The flies don't practice law and I don't walk on the ceiling." The varieties we've heard on that one are endless. Either Brecher invented one of cheap comedy's most ingratiating clichés or he's stooped to a form of humor more befitting a PTA pageant.

We are much more impressed when the girl slips $10,000 down the front of her costume and Groucho muses, "There must be some way I can get that money back without getting in trouble with the Hays Office." Groucho has claimed that at the preview of this film the biggest laugh he ever heard in a movie theater was triggered by that line. Its glow has dimmed slightly over the ages, but at the time it was the very mention of censorship by a character on the screen that was enough to bring down the house. (It would never have even found its way into the movie if Brecher and Groucho hadn't been called back for retakes on this sequence. As it was, the substitute director, Sylvan Simon, didn't "like" the line and couldn't be talked into shooting it until they had written and shot an alternate.)

Groucho's duel of wits with Eve Arden results in yet another defeat for him. Eve Arden, of all people! The nastiness that trickles through every pore of this interchange—the sneers, the insults, the affected reactions—would be enough to rancidize funnier dialogue than this.

GROUCHO: Oh, Hildegarde!

DUMONT: My name is Susannah.

GROUCHO: Let's not quibble. It's enough that you've killed something fine and beautiful. Oh, Susannah! Oh, Susannah! Oh, won't you fly with me? For I need ten thousand dollars 'cause the sheriff's after me!

DUMONT: Get out of this room, or I'll scream for the servants.

GROUCHO: Let the servants know! Let the whole world know! About *us!*

DUMONT: You must leave my room. We must have regard for certain conventions.

GROUCHO: One guy isn't enough, she's gotta have a convention. Oh, Susannah! Susannah! At last we're alone! Couldn't the two of us be . . . oh, how should I say it, uh, a man, and a woman? There, I said it! Oh, Susannah! If you only knew how much I need you! Not because you have millions, I don't need millions, I'll tell you how much I need. Have you got a pencil? I left my typewriter in my other pants.

OH, SUSANNAH!: Margaret Dumont has never been such a relief. After the second revival of "Two Blind Loves," Miss Dumont's grandiose babble sure sounds better than Our Miss Brooks'. And Groucho is right back where he belongs: where he doesn't belong. When he lopes around through Mrs. Dukesbury's mansion ("I've been in bigger hotels than this"), everything he does seems right—even when it isn't.

This whole bit is pretty open to criticism for being uncharacteristic, but it's not open to criticism for not being funny. When Groucho offers his greeting to the butler, "Well, Succotash, what's eatin' ya?"; or when he gives him a dime and says, "Go get yourself a clean shirt," and then announces to Margaret Dumont with the greatest of satisfaction, "He's going to get himself a clean shirt!"; or when he decides halfway through the scene that he's a Frenchman and starts jabbering in a French accent that wouldn't convince a cow—we don't really feel that this is the familiar Groucho Marx going through his paces, but that seems like an uninteresting thing to worry about right now.

Rock-a-Bye Baby: All that is strictly called for here is for Harpo and Chico to break into the strongman's compartment and look for the money while he is sleeping. Not a particularly hilarious idea, and not just a little reminiscent of a lot of other times that they broke into places and tried to be quiet and weren't. But Harpo's elaborations are priceless. This scene comes off so beautifully because it *is* so much like old times, not in spite of the fact that it isn't.

When there are feathers floating all over the room, how does Harpo respond? He turns the fan on, so they will whirl around the room like snow. Then he ice skates on the floor. Then he picks up a spittoon and clangs a bell and plays Santa Claus. When Chico steps on his hand, Harpo goes and drowns the hand in iodine, and then paints the wall with it. When the strongman wakes up, he hears a disembodied voice from his mattress singing a lullaby and a strange honking sound whenever he rolls over. He runs out of the room screaming for the porter.

They *could* have kept quiet; they just didn't bother. What havoc they caused, they caused out of prankishness, not out of some misguided situation. In their touch-and-go relations with the picture's pedestrian plot, they have suddenly become its tormentors rather than its victims.

SAMSON AND THE PILLARS OF SOCIETY: The great thing about this is watching Groucho return to his old role as the shocker of encrusted nobility, as well as Margaret Dumont resuming the role of The Great Shocked One. There are better lines for upsetting somebody than "Good evening, frie-ends!" but it's pretty hard to top the image of Groucho counting the heads of the Newport 400 as they enter the room ("396, 397, 398, 399, 400. . . . Everybody showed up. Looks like no second helpings") or the fun we have watching all 400 rise until Groucho says, "I'll have another cup of coffee," and then watching all 400 sit down again.

And a more skillful blending of impudence and situation comedy it is hard to imagine than the moment where Jardinet, the imported musician, finally does show up. Jardinet, who is the only one in the room besides Groucho to know anything of the fact that a circus is just that moment being set up on the front lawn, marches indignantly into the room and announces his outrage to the entire assemblage. "And when I get here, what do I find?" he fusses in exasperation. "Animals!" Animals? everybody murmurs to each other, What could that mean? "Animals!" he repeats, for the benefit of all. Groucho leaps to his feet indignantly. "Animals, eh?" he screams, grabbing the flustered Jardinet and rushing him to the door. "Any friends of Mrs. Dukesbury's are friends of mine! I'll take care of him!"

But then the climax. We are asked to believe that when that puny orangutan trundles onto the scene, everybody is really going to be scared. Everybody, that is, but the orchestra, which immediately strikes up a spontaneous rendition of "Hold That Tiger" (which I guess we're supposed to read as "Hold That Orangutan") and keeps it up for the whole of the scene. Margaret Dumont is shot out of a cannon, like rice. Nobody seems to have taken the time to work out the special effects until they work. Minor provocations are supposed to send people flying in the air, but the speed isn't exactly right, so they all just float around mysteriously, to the tune of slide whistles. Groucho restricts himself to the most piddling one-liners available, like

COLLECTION OF HARPO MARX

"Calling Tarzan" and "Is there an insurance man in the house?" And, needless to say, old Kenny Baker gets his money back.

It is when we cut away from something like this to a great shot of poor old Jardinet, floating on his bandstand in the middle of the ocean, delivering a concert to the dolphins, that we are most fully aware of what a checkerboard experience this film has been.

What is annoying about *At the Circus* is that so many things *are* done well. If *nothing* had come out right, it wouldn't be such a frustrating film. Sometimes the level of humor is fairly creditable. Sometimes it sinks to the level one would expect to hear exchanged between foremen on a construction crew. Even when the jokes are funny, they are not paced, and they never get to snowball. They just clutter.

The attempt to appeal to Marx Brothers fans and to the average public at one time is just too much of a strain; the result is something that doesn't greatly appeal to either.

Groucho's only comment was that he "didn't much care for it." He never bothered to see the rushes during production, and he wouldn't even go out of his way to see the film until it played at his neighborhood theater. (He claimed that he wouldn't have even bothered to see it there, if the theater up the street had gone ahead with its plans to raffle off a Buick.)

Variety reacted well enough to the movie. They said it was staged fine, it was very funny, and the story didn't get in the way of the comedy. Very few others agreed with them. "A matter more of perspiration than inspiration," said the New York *Times*. *Life* suggested the Marx Brothers find another formula. *Time* said that, for their fans, it was their best film since *Night at the Opera*. Note the phrase "for their fans." It's the sort of phrase a reviewer uses when he doesn't actually like a movie and he hopes somebody else will. "Only for their fans," said *The New Yorker*, for instance, "who must see them in everything."

Paul Zimmerman, in *The Marx Brothers at the Movies*, postulates that "in the career of almost any other comedy team, this would be considered a classic." If you are that much of a

Marx Brothers fan, you can almost believe that statement. But if you were enough of a Marx Brothers fan, you would wish it *was* in the career of some other comedy team.

GO WEST 1940

"Looks like the boys at the studio are lining up another turkey for us," wrote Groucho in 1939. For the second picture of their three-picture contract, the Marxes and all their production headaches were handed over to Louis B. Mayer's nephew, Jack Cummings, who later made a lot of musicals. His decisions for *Go West* reflect not so much a patriarchal wisdom as a nostalgic envy for the good old days when the Marxes were surefire money winners. First off, he decided to do a comedy Western, an idea that was big cheese at the box office ever since Laurel and Hardy made *Way Out West*. Then, once he'd hopped on the covered bandwagon, he contacted those old pros Bert Kalmar and Harry Ruby, who hadn't been listened to on a Marx Brothers project since *Duck Soup*. Kalmar and Ruby wrote a script about a rodeo and called it *Go West*. And in a chaotic series of front-office decisions, front-office indecisions and general neurotic fancies, production dates were set and then canceled, and the Kalmar–Ruby script was turned down and replaced by a whole new screenplay by Irving Brecher and Dore Schary, with new situations, new gags, new routines. Only the name was not changed to protect the publicity. Then that one was turned down, too. This wasn't going to be easy, was it?

The only thing left to do was to let Brecher work by himself again. It was the only thing left to do, because nobody else wanted any part of it. "I think most of the writers were smarter than I was, in one respect," says Brecher. "They ducked it. Too

rough." It was rough going for Brecher, too, but he had a name to establish and he kept fighting.

So a third script called *Go West* was finished. This one was reluctantly agreed to—but the Marxes wanted one condition met, and that was where Cummings' nostalgic wisdom came through again: He agreed to let them take the show on tour! It wasn't a big tour, now, just three weeks this time, but it was really a tour, an honest-to-goodness tour. Think of it!

Then, scant hours before it was all scheduled to start, Brecher got a phone call from Groucho. He was informed that he was desperately needed, not as a writer but as a stand-in. Publicity photos of the Marx Brothers were being taken that morning for the tour, and one of the Marx Brothers was too sick to get out of bed. So, reliving *his* good old days, Brecher got to do his Groucho imitation in front of a camera. And even the closest observers never noticed that the photos displayed the incredible sight of a Harpo and a Chico well into their fifties sharing the stage with a twenty-five-year-old Groucho.

"Scenes from *Go West*" played to 103 audiences, five a day, in Chicago, Toledo, and Detroit. Jack Cummings, in his nostalgia, enlisted Nat Perrin to join Brecher in mid-tour and accompany him through the grueling grill of the last-minute-change sessions that went on every night and every day. The tour was a good way for the Marxes to realize what a talented man Mervyn LeRoy had rounded up for them. When they got back to Los Angeles, they requested that he stay on the payroll and keep the company company during production. Cummings, to the credit of his nostalgia, agreed to that one too.

Shooting was slated to begin the first of July 1940, a month after the end of the tour, "By which time, I'm sure," said Groucho, "we will have forgotten all the dialogue so carefully rehearsed on the road." Brecher used the time to work the script over.

One weekend in June, which Groucho spent at Arrowhead "getting confused in a sailboat" and Chico and Gummo spent in Catalina, threatened to prove disastrous when Chico came back stricken with streptococcus and had to be taken to Cedars of Lebanon Hospital. As it turned out, it proved nothing; production was held up again, but for different reasons.

Everybody in the front offices started worrying about the story. Everything that hadn't been tested on the road was revised and rewritten to suit the old neurotic fancies. One executive producer got all upset over the budget estimates and decided that $200,000 worth of gags could be cut out of the big scene at the end. Brecher tried to convince him that cutting out the best part of the movie wasn't going to solve any financial problems, but a writer has little voice, and it took the concerted energies of Brecher, Groucho, and Harpo to talk him back into leaving it in.

As the deliberations wore on, the dye in Groucho's hair

faded and had to be touched up every once in a while to match his moustache. Then once a week they would redesign his costume and he had to go to the Wardrobe Department and be fitted all over again. In various letters written over the summer, Groucho expresses his dismay: "*Go West* is constantly being postponed. I read the script and I don't blame them. . . . My theatrical career has dwindled to being fitted once a week for a pair of early American pants and having my hair dyed every three weeks. This is a fine comedown for a man who used to be the Toast of Broadway. . . ."

By August the poor script was a hacked-up chaos, a plethora of pink sheets, white sheets, new pages, old pages, disjointed page numbers and out-of-sequence sequences. Finally MGM took a deep breath and let them get started. The neurotic fancies didn't take them so far as to dispense with Eddie Buzzell, and so the team whose talents had meshed like square pegs and round holes on *At the Circus* were back together once more.

Buzzell was the last of a small band of intrepid men who succeeded in getting all the way through a picture with the Marx Brothers as often as twice. He, Sam Wood, and Norman McLeod formed a trio whose track record could be worn with pride if not affection. Quitters like Leo McCarey and Victor Heerman could only shake their heads with a kind of modified respect. By now Buzzell realized that the only way to get through it all was to stop appreciating their lovable, behind-the-scenes humor. When he suggested to Groucho that he needed more make-up on his nose and Groucho answered, "Don't quibble. What I need is a new nose," the only reaction he could think of was to not laugh. As a comedian with a past, Buzzell knew that to an attention-hungry performer laughter was license. As a director with a future, he knew that if things started turning into a gag session, there wouldn't be any movie made. "Look at Harpo, not at the camera," he would say to Chico, and Chico would say, "Personally, I'd rather look at the camera." No response. Now he became a real challenge. Finally, when he told Harpo in one scene that he wasn't stalking slowly enough, and Harpo answered brightly, "But I'm not a stalking actor, I'm a silent actor," and he *still* wouldn't curl the corners of his mouth, people started to think he had problems.

Unfortunately, the rushes gave the same impression. He had calmed his comedians down, all right, and he had gotten the scenes shot, and he had kept all three of them in viewfinder range. That was about all you could say for it. Groucho and Irving Brecher got together and had little hope for the "less than larger than life" results of all their efforts. Not too terribly surprisingly, the Marxes started turning to Brecher when they needed advice on their delivery. That was no help to the neurotic fancies involved, either, and Buzzell picked a rather arbitrary moment to stomp off the set, but Groucho had gone to Brecher and asked him how a line ought to be read just once too often. The young writer had not exactly intended to be another one of *Go West's* problems, and after he was lectured on the protocol he was transgressing, and after apologies were exchanged all around, they quit this nonsense and got back to making the movie.

As usual, some awfully good lines were made up at the last minute, and just as many good ones were tossed out. We never get to hear Groucho say, "Well, if she gets insulted just because I insulted her . . . !" Nor are we treated to the following interchange: "Wait till your wife hears about this!" "I have no wife." "Well, she's a lucky woman."

What we *do* get includes one ad-libbed line that floats in from off camera: "One mint julep, coming up." "What! Before I drink it?" And another impromptu pops up during the climax: When Groucho is stuffing a gag in the mouth of one of the railroad engineers, he turns and explains to us, "This is the best gag in the picture." But that sounds a little like desperation.

Strangely, the plot for *Go West* is just like the one for Laurel and Hardy's *Way Out West*. A man's worthless deed, suddenly turned valuable, must be restored to his daughter (or granddaughter), but first it has to be retrieved from the wicked saloon owner who has wrangled possession of it through illegal means and the bungling of the heroes. Thing is, it's *right* for Laurel and Hardy to be bullied and cowed as the timid Easterners in an alien environment. It isn't an affront to their characterizations.

For the Marx Brothers, rehashing all this warmed-over stew is simply a mistake.

But *Go West,* for all its faults, certainly has its moments. Befitting its title, the movie is most like the Grand Canyon: Its peaks are genuinely awe-inspiring, but at times it sinks to depths that are unbelievable.

GROUCHO: Now, let's see, that's twenty plus one, that's, uh, twenty-one.

CHICO: We meet you halfway. We give you one.

GROUCHO: You must have come the short way.

CHICO: Come on, Rusty, give him a dollar.

GROUCHO: Well, that's fine—adios, gentlemen.

CHICO: Uh, nine dollars change, please.

GROUCHO: Change?

CHICO: Yeah, atsa ten spot.

GROUCHO: Oh, so it is. Say, it looks a lot like the other one, doesn't it?

CHICO: It should.

GROUCHO: Say, uh, did you see something flying across here?

CHICO: Might've been a pigeon.

GROUCHO: No, it wasn't a pigeon. It was green.

CHICO: Must've been a frog.

GROUCHO: It had numbers on it.

CHICO: Those were the license plates.

THE FLYING DOLLARS: No movie that starts with this scene can be *all* bad. In less than sixty seconds after the titles have faded away, all three Marx Brothers are on the screen and pulling stunts on each other. The bang that this movie starts with is either the kickoff to a cross-country marathon or the sound of somebody shooting his wad.

Groucho enters the train station with an army of porters bearing luggage. "Have any of you fellows got change for ten cents?" he asks them. No, they reply. "Well," he says, after the hint of a deliberation, "*keep* the baggage." Then, imitating a banjo, he goes to the ticket window and gets outraged at the price of "one ticket to the West." "It's highway robbery!" he screams. "No wonder you're behind bars!"

No sooner does he find out he is ten dollars short than Harpo and Chico enter with ten dollars. And no sooner does he plug ahead with his con games than we find out he's up against a couple of pros. *We* find out. *Groucho* doesn't find out until half-way through the scene. By then he has bartered off all his earthly possessions for one dollar apiece, and each transaction has, through underhanded sleight of hand, cost him ten dollars. It is a tribute to the whole idea of the Marx Brothers that when they perform a routine that is basically nothing more than good Abbott and Costello material, they raise it by sheer force of personality out of the Abbott and Costello bog. Harpo is pantomiming everything Chico says, Groucho is insulting Harpo, Chico is babbling nonsense, Groucho is dickering with Chico, and Harpo is robbing Groucho blind—everything on top of everything else. There is so much going on that the situation of the scene becomes about as important as the plot of the movie.

Hastily, Groucho deposits the remainder of his wad in his hat. Deftly, Harpo makes off with his hat. Groucho has shot his wad. Uh-oh.

———

Six Isn't a Crowd: Chico and Harpo should get their money back; their ticket to the West has gotten them only as far as an MGM rear-projection screen.

Why two characters should go unconvincing on us in such a hurry is a question whose answer lies not in the wide-open spaces of the West but in the narrow, confined minds of the film-makers. When Chico whines, "We don't wanna no trouble," his resemblance to that brash cornet player who barged into the party in *Animal Crackers* and glibly announced his rates for not rehearsing is very hard to make out. It is impossible to believe they are the same person. And Harpo is as far removed from the whirling dervish of *Horsefeathers* as he could get without singing tenor. Time was, he could produce candles from his pockets, masquerade as a camera, cut coattails behind people's backs, and bamboozle anybody who tried to interfere with him, and all without an ounce of effort. Here he can't even twirl a gun on his finger without dropping it. He is reduced in the main to doing silent impersonations of whoever is talking and nodding his head yes and shaking it no.

When they go into a saloon, they are instantaneously laughed out of it, and we don't even crack a smile. The only person who actually makes a joke, in fact, is the bad guy, who calls an I-O-U an I-O-Me. That doesn't sound like much, but if context alone were any criterion, *Punch* would have snapped him up in a minute.

Then they find themselves on a crowded stagecoach with Groucho. (And it's never made clear how Groucho gets out West, just as it was never made clear how he got on that train. Ubiquitous fellow, that Groucho.) This marks a halfhearted attempt at being the stateroom scene, but it's just six people being slightly uncomfortable in a stagecoach. The saloon scene was uncomfortable enough.

BRANDY: Funny gags do not a good scene make. This has neither a fanciful, free-fall air nor a solid sense of structure. A comedy scene must know what it is getting at every minute, even when what it is getting at is that it isn't getting at anything.

Harpo gets the deed back by plowing through the cash in the cash register and hurling it all over the room. He provides the accompaniment to one of Chico's best piano solos, by leaping up and down at one end of the bench. Groucho comes in and greets one of the chorus girls with "Lulubelle! I didn't recognize you standing up!" The classic parody of the Big Draw, between Harpo and Rex Baxter, is good for a Big Laugh at the close and for a semi-triumph for the Marx Brothers. (Although originally it was intended as yet another of Brecher's crushing blows for them, when Harpo's whisk boom didn't go off.)

We can see now that *Go West* features less of that annoying mutual interruption between comedy scenes and plot scenes. Now the plot moves right in and sits down on the comedy. And Groucho's attitude toward the plot hasn't been made clear, even to Groucho. He's too concerned about the money he is being

MGM

swindled out of, then he comes out of it and shrugs, "Well, that's one way of reducing your overhead," then he goes back to being too concerned again. How can you reverse yourself before you make up your mind which way you're going?

GROUCHO: White man red man's friend! White man want to make *friends* with red brother!

CHICO: And sister too.

INDIAN: Beray! Beray! Kulah! Kulah! Cocko! Cocko! Rodah! Nietzsche! Pardo!

GROUCHO: Are you insinuating that the white man is *not* the Indian's friend? Huh! Who swindled you outta Manhattan Island for $24?

CHICO: White man.

GROUCHO: Who turned you into wood and stood you in front of a cigar store?

CHICO: White man.

GROUCHO: Who put your head on a nickel, and then took the nickel away?

CHICO: Slot machine.

RESERVATIONS: Rarely have the Marxes let us down in consistency and determination so consistently and determinedly as they do here. For every funny line there are two clinkers, and the scene thuds along with the comic pacing of a drippy faucet. Groucho and Chico end up so drunk that eventually they have to be ushered out of the room like children. This is the Marx Brothers? Rarely has comedy been so unheroic. The day wouldn't be saved at all, in fact, if the hero wasn't to show up and straighten things. He even gets to deliver the laugh line on the exit, which he does while pushing Harpo out of the way. This is at least a step up from letting the bad guy do it. (Apparently the film-makers haven't decided whether they were making a spoof on Westerns or a real Western. Maybe they were making a spoof on comedies.)

What's this about anachronisms? Chico mentions a telephone at one point, and Groucho says, "Telephone! This is 1870! Don Ameche hasn't invented the telephone yet!" This is one of the best lines in the film. But when they stop for the night at an Indian camp and Groucho complains, "I don't know why we don't sleep at a regular motel," it is simple time displacement we are supposed to laugh at. It would be like laughing at all those "Twilight Zone" episodes where a man found himself in 1870 and couldn't figure out how he got there.

What's this about double-takes? Groucho keeps doing double-takes. Comedians like Larry Semon and Billy Bevan do double-takes. And the Ritz Brothers. And Soupy Sales.

The really funny bit in this section is prompted by the grand takeoff, "Drop that cannon!" Villains and heroes alternately enter the room and tell the last person who entered to put his hands up. Finally, a line is formed that stretches all the way across the room, and every other set of hands goes up or down when the next guy comes in and says, "No, put *your* hands up." Somebody ought to have the Marx Brothers do something funny like that.

———

THE END OF THE LINE: By now, the only way this movie could possibly redeem itself is to close the show with one of the greatest scenes the Marxes ever did. Oddly enough, it does exactly that.

You would think, if somebody told you about a manic-destructive comedy team who made a lot of high-paying movies, that somewhere along the line they would do an insane, stops-out, whoopee chase scene on a fire engine or something. But no. Time after time their climaxes have been the most anemic disappointments of the films.

There's nothing anemic about this. All three of them have taken over a train, and they have to keep it going even when it's run out of fuel. So they chop the train to pieces and feed it to itself. Without slowing it down. This has been done before and since, and sometimes seems a lot like *The General*, but, just as in *Duck Soup*, they have given a familiar bit such a maniacal twist that even the people who performed it wouldn't recognize it. It bears less relation to anybody else's comedy scene than it does to the train intrigues of the Thirties, like Hitchcock's *Number Seventeen*, where somebody always finds it expedient at some point in the action to leap out the window and sidle along the edge of the car. *Here* whenever somebody tries a trick like that he gets clobbered by a signal or hung on a mail hook. Harpo gets swung clear into the baggage car and the baggage man gets swung clear out of it. Harpo, Chico, and Groucho take axes and start demolishing the passenger cars, and paying passengers have to stand back in horror and watch doors and windows and walls being carted away.

All of which is pretty artificially hoked up with stunt men and process work and speeded up cameras. As a matter of fact,

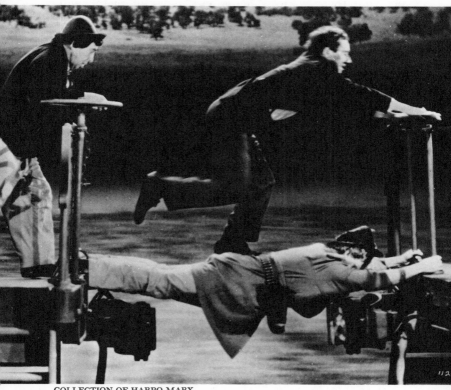

COLLECTION OF HARPO MARX

the scene brings up every possible technical problem that film-making has to offer, and each one is handled so smoothly and well that at last you are more impressed and stupefied than you are annoyed. It's all furiously and idiotically convincing, even when they pour popcorn in the furnace and yell, "Pop goes the Diesel!" and then get drowned in the stuff. Buzzell's giddy energetic style seems just what is called for in this emergency, and Brecher's remarkably diverse visual gags, all of them worked out on paper and never even given a chance to be tested on the road, come across very effectively.

In the end, it is the bare skeleton of the ruins of a derelict train that goes steaming off into the sunset, loaded with baffled people. Finally, for the fadeout, the ceremonious Driving of the Golden Stake. Harpo unceremoniously on the backswing drives in one of the railroad officials instead, and the three Marx Brothers shake hands all around, as if they'd *meant* to do that.

Now it was decision-making time at the old corral again, and the bad decisions were leading the stampede. Chico set up a nightclub band called "Chico Marx and His Ravellis" and took off for New York as soon as shooting was done. Groucho and Irving Brecher set to work laying out a radio series called "The Life of Riley." Unfortunately, no sponsor wanted "The Life of Riley," but the minute Brecher replaced Groucho with William Bendix it went over with a bang. Groucho was offered the chance to emcee a quiz show called "You Bet Your Life," but he said he hated quiz shows and didn't want to do it. When "Life of Riley" switched over to television, the network people vetoed William Bendix on the grounds that he wouldn't make the grade as a television personality and replaced him with Jackie Gleason. After twenty-six weeks, the show was canceled, because Jackie Gleason "has no future in show business."

Even the most enthusiastic of *Go West* reviews had to admit that the show was stolen by the last scene. More sober journals like the New York *Times* and *The New Yorker* reported gruffly that the chase was the only scene worth watching and had done with it. But the picture struck the right chord with house organs like *Variety* and the *Hollywood Reporter,* where it apparently fulfilled all the contemporary qualifications for a merry evening. They would say that it was "in some places hilariously funny" and then work around that, apparently having all gone home recovering from the effects of that great climax. They also said it was "better than their last two." That wasn't hard to say. Later Bosley Crowther was to include the final sequence of *Go West,* along with such classics as the eating of the shoe from *The Gold Rush,* in his list of the ten greatest sequences ever filmed.

But the best assessment was supplied by William Cullen Bryant, without even seeing the movie:

> And suns grow meek,
> And the meek suns grow brief,
> And the year smiles as it
> Draws near its death.

THE BIG STORE 1941

At the Circus looks like situation comedy. *Go West* operates on an Abbott and Costello level. *The Big Store* is as good as anything the Three Stooges ever did. *At the Circus* is disappointing; *Go West* is uneven; *The Big Store* is a mess.

Just because it takes place in a store, they apparently felt it had to be called *The Big Store*. It's not like it was *really* a big store. It's not like it was Macy's or anything. There's no line of dialogue about what a big store it is. It's just a store. But you can't make a movie about a store and call it *The Store*. You have to call it *The Big Store*.

Hollywood seems to have something out for the word "big." It makes something that isn't impressive sound impressive. If it's big it's better. Glance just briefly into the history of the movies and you'll find *The Big Beat, The Big Bounce, The Big News, The Big Punch, The Big Chance, The Big Combo, The Big Cube, The Big Hangover, The Big Heat, The Big Noise, The Big Time, The Big Sleep, The Big Cat, The Big Clock, The Big Knife, The Big Cage, The Big Sombrero, The Big Farmer's Ford, The Big Happy Bed, The Big Oil Change, The Big Day, The Big Night, Big Leaguer, Big Little Leaguer, Big Sister, Big Brother, Big Boy, Big Bully, Big Business, Big Business Girl, Big Brown Eyes,*

COLLECTION OF HARPO MARX

Big Hand for the Little Lady, Big Happiness, Big House, Big House, U.S.A., Big Gusher, Big Boodle, Big Risk, Big Bonanza, Big Money, Big Freeze, Big Trees, Big Timber, Big Apple, Big Trail, Big Pond, Big Wave, Big Land, Big Country, Big Sky, Big Street, Big City, Big City Blues, Big Town, Big Town Ideas, Big Town After Dark, Big Town Scandal, Big Town Czar, Big Town Girl, Big Town Roundup, Big Market on the Corner, Big Bluff, Big Bounce, Big Break, Big Question, Big Medicine, Big Picture, Big Fix, Big Frame, Big Jump, Big Lift, Big Steal, Big Diamond

Robbery, Big Gamble, Big Killing, Big Gundown, Big Shake-
down, Big Blast, Big Stampede, Big Race, Big Chase, Big Adven-
ture, Big Caper, Big Fight, Big Game, Big Game Fishing, Big
Game Hunt, Big Parade, Big Parade of Comedy, Big Show, Big
TNT Show, Big Carnival, Big Circus, Big Broadcast, Big Broad-
cast of 1936, Big Broadcast of 1937, Big Broadcast of 1938, Big
Boss, Big Fella, Big Brain, Big Shot, Big Show-Off, Big Tip-Off,
Big Operator, Big Executive, Big Wheel, Big Mouth, Big Little
Person, Big Bad Wolf, Big Bad Bobcat, Big Green Caterpillar,
Big Pal, Big Guy, Big John, Big Red, Big Dan, Big Jack, Big
Hearted Herbert, Big Hearted Jim, Big Jim Garrity, Big Jim
McLean, and, of course, The Big Store.

If Chaplin had made The Pawnshop in 1941, they would
have made him call it The Big Pawnshop.

The most important man in the big story of The Big Store is
probably Georgie Stoll, who was the musical director. He must
have had his hands full. There are more songs, solos, duets,
accompaniments, arrangements, renditions, reprises, themes,
points, counterpoints, concerts, recordings, rehearsals, and incidental background ditties than it seems one man could possibly
have kept track of. What comedy there is in this movie is
peripheral; this time the production numbers have taken over.
That way, Tony Martin becomes just as important as any one of
the Marx Brothers, and he's easier to write for. But Tony Martin,
with his greasy pomade hair and his granite chin, is just about
tops on the Nausea Rating (see Fig. 1).

Louis K. Sidney, the producer, had worked his way up from
an usher to the head of Loew's Theaters, and eventually became
vice-president of the studio. Before the frenzied finagling of Go
West was finished, and before the studio had the nerve to release
it, Sidney took over the job of getting the Marxes' last picture
done (and Groucho had announced that this was to be their last
picture). Brecher was the first to be asked to take care of the
screenplay, but he'd had it. Now he was in a position to refuse.
Finally, Sidney turned to a three-man team of song writers and ex-
newspaper reporters put together by an agent named Nat Gold-
stone.

(Figure 1) NAUSEA RATING

1. Tony Martin (*The Big Store*)
2. Kenny Baker (*At the Circus*)
3. Oscar Shaw (*The Cocoanuts*)
4. Hal Thompson (*Animal Crackers*)
5. Charles Drake (*A Night in Casablanca*)
6. John Carroll (*Go West*)
7. Allan Jones (*A Night at the Opera, A Day at the Races*)
8. Frank Albertson (*Room Service*)
9. Zeppo Marx (you remember)

It takes more than good looks and straight teeth to pass the test of time with the Marx Brothers.

The story idea for this one was Nat Perrin's. When the writers—Sid Kuller, Ray Golden, and Hal Fimberg—had worked it up into a workable story line, the producers came in and had them change it; when they changed it, the Marxes went and told them how to revise it some more; after they worked out a 150-page treatment from their workable story line, the producers had more suggestions; then when they were through compromising with them, the Marxes came back and fussed over it again. "The shortest thing," says Sid Kuller, "was writing the screenplay." During the ten months of drafting, the title was changed from *Bargain Basement* to *Step This Way*. Finally the Publicity Department decided that the label no moviegoer could resist was— you guessed it—*The Big Store*.

None of the acerbity that marked the previous two experiences was encountered here. The only friction that did develop was between Ray Golden and L. K. Sidney, and that simply resulted in having Golden dropped from the company. Otherwise, things were peachy keen on all fronts, even when Sidney gave a pep talk halfway through the preparatory stage and announced, "Your last two pictures have lost money. *I* have never had a loser. *We* are not going to lose money. And we're going to have a good picture. And to make a good picture I want all of you to promise me your undying cooperation." Although neither of his brothers responded to that with anything but grunts or mild gesticulations of approval, Chico spoke right up without hesitating: "L.K., you're a great man, you're a great showman, I love you! I'm going to be with you all the way, I'm going to help on the story, I'm going to help on the gags, I'm going to go all the way with you, all the way."

The writers launched into the reading of the second draft of the story line. By the time they got to page 15, Chico was sound asleep and snoring.

Big Store's director was Chuck Reisner, a stocky ex-vaude-villian whose training in comedy had taken him all the way from Keystone and Vitagraph to Universal, where he starred in two-reel comedies, to every other comedy studio in town, including Chaplin's. Reisner was associate director for *A Dog's Life, The Kid, The Pilgrim,* and *The Gold Rush.* After that, his mighty directorial turnout included little that would be of interest today, except for Keaton's. *Steamboat Bill, Jr.,* which is only of interest because Keaton managed to direct his own films no matter who was in the chair. Reisner's was also an amiable nature, and he took part in the general affection that prevailed.

Shooting went on for sixteen weeks; exorbitant as that seems today, it was anything but unusual for a comedy in that extravagant day. The chase scene alone was labored on for four. The comedians insisted on having at least one writer follow through on the shooting, and they chose Kuller, the youngest of the three, and the only one with tenacity enough to keep on hacking away at comedy all his life. (Kuller, who had once ghosted for Al Boasberg, has been chiefly a writer of nightclub and television material ever since. Golden, who had worked with Kuller on Ritz Brothers scripts, went into producing; Fimberg, who was once a stand-up comic, became a broker during the war and didn't come back to movies until doing the *Flint* pictures with Ben Starr.) All three Marxes started inviting Sid Kuller to various soirees at their homes or on the town, and then, aiding and abetting the close-

Groucho and Margaret Dumont in their farewell appearance.

MGM

ness that was already abounding, his father died in the middle of production, and he began turning to Reisner for emotional support. They, too, would spend meals and evenings together.

In fact, the only time this big happy family ever went so far as to clench teeth at each other was after shooting was done and the film was first sneak-previewed in Pomona. There had been a disagreement over a punchline late in the film, in the midst of Groucho's love-making to Margaret Dumont, when her reservation, "I'm afraid some little blonde will come along, and you'll forget all about me," was supposed to prompt his retort, "Nonsense! I'll write you twice a week!" L. K. Sidney, for no particular reason, hated the line and ordered it out of the film before the preview. Reisner, retaining his amiability, loved it: he and Groucho went and had it put back in. And it was right there when it played in Pomona, and it got the biggest laugh of the evening. But that didn't stop Sidney from being riled all to hell. At the end of the film he stormed out into the lobby and confronted Kuller (naturally he would pick the person *least* responsible) and demanded that he tell him how that line got back into the picture. Kuller, who didn't know, and didn't know whether he should say he didn't know, didn't say. There were tense stutterings and glance exchanges between Kuller and the comedians until Louis Mayer and the unit manager Al Lichtman happened into the family quarrel and wanted to know what was up. Harpo leaned over and explained softly, "There's a line in question."

"Which one?" asked Mayer.

"The one where he says, 'I'll write you twice a week.' "

"Greatest line in the picture," said Mayer.

"I fell out of my seat," said Lichtman.

Now Sidney was *really* angry—if only because nobody agreed with him. "All right," he said, "all right. I just want to know how the *hell* did it get in the picture after I'd ordered it out!"

Nobody had an answer for that. Until Chico, with a mote of reverence, said, "Well, let's just say the god of comedy put it in."

Lovable imp though he may be, it can rarely be said of the god of comedy that he smiles on *Big Store* other than this once. Yes, the bitter taste of *At the Circus* and *Go West* is gone. But it takes more than love to make a great comedy. *Big Store* is a much more likable picture than the other two, but it is also a far less funny one.

Its script seems determined to be a Grover Jones effort, as indicated by the "Night at the Soap Opera" prose describing the last scene: "Tommy's right fist shoots out, hitting Grover on the chin, and dropping him like a felled ox." It is up to Groucho to turn a dull exchange ("You have no objections if I ask him a few questions?" "Go ahead, ask her anything you want." "No, it's you I'm asking") into a pretty funny bit ("Well, I just heard you ask her if you could ask me a few questions. After all, I'm not blind!").

Visitors to the set had already discovered that the Marxes seemed to have their minds on other things. For Chico, this was nothing unusual, but when Groucho spends more of his time poring over *The Devil's Dictionary* than he does tinkering with his dialogue, and when Harpo is itching to get the music rehearsals over with so he can go out and play golf, something is amiss. In an interview Groucho gave voice to some of the sentiments that may explain what it was.

"We're tired of making the same old story—even if it is a howling success. . . . I was talking with Harpo about it this morning. Eleven pictures in twelve years is about all anyone can stand of us, including ourselves."

"*You* take the moustache," Groucho told Brooks Atkinson in another interview. "It would be an improvement."

And nothing was more infuriating to him than being called back for retakes the day his son Arthur was playing a big tennis match. It was obviously more important to him to watch his son play a game than to stand around and utter lines that didn't amuse him. The movie had been previewed twice by this time, and the monkeying around that followed the first preview had caused it to be a total flop at the second. MGM hadn't the faintest notion how to handle comedies or comedians, but they caught on that sneak previews had something to do with it. Invariably, their appraisal of audience response was centered around the story line. "They imagine the audience hasn't laughed because the plot wasn't understood," remarked Groucho. "The fact of the matter is, the audience hasn't laughed because they didn't understand the jokes!" Groucho noted with some pride that the new jokes he was given were "six times as unfunny" as the rejected ones.

It hardly seems to matter. The dialogue in question (some

asides in reference to clothes being demonstrated by models) comes in the middle of Groucho's song "Sing While You Sell," which, on its own merits, is one of the most obnoxious, shameful spectacles we've ever had to watch him parade through, full of silly couplets like "You can't sell no pan/Without Chopin."

But nothing in the film beats Tony Martin's horrifying "Tenement Symphony," a pretentious bit of pseudo-cultural hokum whose music is everything the Marxes exploded in *Night at the Opera* and whose couplets are as silly as "Sing While You Sell" 's. The song is introduced in the film by a sweet woman who explains that Tony Martin would never have had his splendid musical education and this grand piece of music could never have been written if it hadn't been for the contributions of that fine old philanthropist, the late Hiram Phelps. Two bars, and you wish the old guy had taken it with him. At the song's conclusion, the film audience naturally breaks into appreciative applause, where you would by rights expect them to rise as one and give throaty indignant cries of "We want Zeppo back!"

Some of the music is pretty nice. Harpo and Chico do a piano duet that is rather a treat and, like the Marx quartet in *Duck Soup*, the only one of its kind on record. Chico gets to the keyboard *twice* in the film, which is rather startling in a picture that can't afford him that many laugh lines. Harpo does the same with his harp, besides tossing in some bits on violins and bass viols in a three-way-mirror dream scene that is at least worth watching for its technical wizardry.

But it is all bogged down in one of the most distressingly morbid story lines since the days of de Sade. The villain goes skulking around his department store making plans to kill a bunch of people so that no one will ever find out the books have been tampered with. He never mentions how he plans to hide the fact that he's killed a bunch of people. He discusses with a blond harlot his plans to marry Margaret Dumont and offhandedly remarks that he'll probably kill her, too. Jesus!

And the villain isn't the only one with a morbid sensibility. The writers seem determined to kill every good gag they make. Groucho, for instance, finishes his morning paper and says to

Harpo, "Take this newspaper out and sell it"—but then he says, "Never mind." When he gets angry at a reporter he instructs Chico, "Take out a subscription to the *News* and cancel it!"—and then he adds, "Sign the cancellation 'Disgusted Reader,'" and another good line bites the dust.

And no *Big Store* diatribe would be complete without a Tired Old Gag Catalogue:

TIRED OLD GAG A: The one where you rattle off a whole list of things and one word keeps popping up as every other item on the list. (Music and sex and music and money and music . . .) This is used twice in the movie—once referring to sex and once referring to money.

TIRED OLD GAG B: The one where the lights go out and when they come back on everybody is in a funny position. This is used twice, too; these guys don't stop at using an old gag, they go and use it twice.

TIRED OLD GAG C: You won't believe this unless you actually see it on the screen, but they even have a version of what is often referred to as The Classic Tired Old Gag: "That's no lady, that's my wife." When Harpo is identified as Groucho's driver, Chico announces, "Atsa no driver, atsa my brother." So you see, they've managed to drain all the humor out of even that.

The Big Store is a failure in a way that even *Room Service* never was. The only trouble with *Room Service*, after all, was that it wasn't a Marx Brothers comedy. That's excusable. *Gone with the Wind* wasn't a Marx Brothers comedy either. Didn't hurt it a bit.

———

GANGBUSTERS: For openers, we actually get one of those precious, rare scenes between Groucho and Harpo that grace the screen about once every five movies. This one, sadly, has few of the attributes of vintage wine, except that it looks like it was dug up out of somebody's cellar. Even at that, it must have been a bargain basement. Two Marx Brothers for the price of three.

When Margaret Dumont comes to Groucho's detective office, he and Harpo pull every stunt in the script to convince her they are running a big-time operation. The beds flip into the wall and become enormous files reading "Liabilities"and "Assets," mechanical hands break in with telegrams, and Harpo makes such a racket transcribing the proceedings that the proceedings stop proceeding. The only objections I have to this scene are that Harpo's name is "Wacky" (and Groucho's is Wolf J. Flywheel. The names given to the characters seem to be some kind of barometer of the level of wit to be expected from the film. Wait till we get to *Night in Casablanca!*), cutesy music accompanies the action (to tell us how funny it is), Groucho, for some reason, is talking like a supper-club agent (what detective ever said, "I'm just dripping with offers"?), half of these gags were done before by Snub Pollard (some of them are stolen from *At the Circus,* of all places), Margaret Dumont has a line, "Your best friends are the police," which belongs in a grade-school propaganda film in civics. Outside of that, it's the best scene in the film.

GROVER: Do you object if I ask him a few questions?

DUMONT: Oh, not at all.

GROUCHO: Go right ahead, ask her anything you want!

GROVER: No, it's you that I'm asking the questions.

GROUCHO: Well, I just heard you ask her if you could ask me a few questions.

GROVER: Just a minute—

GROUCHO: After all, I'm not blind!

GROVER: We will assume that I am a customer. I am returning a baby carriage.

GROUCHO: Are you married?

GROVER: Why, of course not!

GROUCHO: Then what are you doing with a baby carriage? This man is a cad! A yellow cad!

GROVER: The v   thing is utterly ridiculous! Now I'll ask you a   uestion: it's Bargain Day, the store is crowded, a woman faints. What do you do?

GROUCHO: How old is she?

GROVER: What difference does it make?

GROUCHO: You hear that? A woman's life is in danger and he asks, "What difference does it make?"

A MADHOUSE: Here Groucho meets Mr. Grover, the head of the department store. Then Chico comes in and Groucho meets him. Then Harpo meets Mr. Grover and Chico meets Harpo. That's really all that happens. There aren't many gags, but there are certainly a lot of reactions. People are too busy saying things like "That's his little joke" to get many jokes said. At one point, Grover exclaims, "Why, this place is becoming a madhouse!"—which seems to be the script writer's way of saying, "Oh! If this place were only becoming a madhouse!" The only action that has the guts to go and happen is Harpo running away from a cop and smashing a lot of vases into a lot of pieces. It has less than nothing to do with the logic or the sense or the direction of the scene, it's completely out of Harpo's character, and it comes too abruptly and nonsensically to be funny, but it is *action*.

CHICO: Don't letta your wife call the police. Remember the grapes!
GROUCHO: Remember the grapes.
CHICO: The grapes!
            (*General commotion*)
GROUCHO: Now, wait a minute—Quiet. Now, let's get this straight. You say you came in here with twelve grapes and now you've only got six grapes.
ITALIAN: No grapes—six-a kids!
GROUCHO: Well, you just said you had twelve kids. She says you've got eighteen; how many kids have you got? How many grapes have your kids got?
ITALIAN: I don't wanna no grapes!
CHICO: You gotta no grapes, I getta you some grapes.
GROUCHO: Go down and get him a buncha grapes.
ITALIAN: My kids!
GROUCHO: You shoulda gone to the department. This is the furniture department.

THE BEDS OF BEDLAM: By 1941 the Marxes are so out of energy they can hardly keep awake. This scene takes place in the bed department, so the Marx Brothers can show off a lot of funny beds. (Instant Humor. Just push a button and funny beds pop out of the wall.) An Italian family with twelve children comes in looking for beds. Warmhearted Chico discovers that the father is an old friend from Naples, so they can talk about the good times they had pressing grapes. Then Harpo comes in and it turns out he's an old friend of the family too, so they each have a jolly old reunion with the grape-presser just like the jolly old reunion they had with each other in the preceding scene. (The script writers have gained an incredible insight into what a funny thing it is for people to meet old friends. Wish they'd tell *us* what's so funny about it.) Six of the Italian grape-presser's kids disappear, and they are replaced, in succession, by six Chinese children, six Swedish children, and six American Indian children, while they all argue about grapes. Finally everybody goes dashing all over and around the beds, and the Marx Brothers go back to sleep.

The premise of this scene asks us to believe that it is funny to look for six Italian children and come up with six Chinese children, and that bands of six to twelve children of some minority ethnic group are constantly going shopping in the bed departments of department stores, to the exclusion of anyone else. I, for one, don't believe it. What *I* believe is that when you have the Marx Brothers on your set, you shouldn't need to bring in wild Indians and Chinamen to run around.

OVER, GROVER: It's hard to tell whether the rest of these scenes are supposed to be funny or not, so let's get on to the climax. (In one interchange there is a discussion over the developing of a negative. "You can do it two ways," says Groucho. "You can use the potassium or the silver nitrate." "Use the nitrate," says Chico. "It's cheaper." It took me three viewings to realize that was supposed to be a joke. Night rate, get it?)

Only naturally, when the Marxes do a great scene in one movie, there is an eager-beaver attempt at a sequel in the next one. Sometimes the sequel gets to be just as good as the scene it is copying. But sometimes it ends up like the chase scene in *Big Store*.

Not that this is never funny. But there isn't any momentum. An action scene with a lot of running and skating and sliding and flying has to have a solid, steady rhythm to keep it going. The *Go West* climax had the constant motion of the train to sustain it; the action never *could* stop. This scene grinds to a halt and starts over so many times, it is just as apt to inspire nausea as hilarity. And they haven't taken the time to work out the special effects again, so the mysterious floating from *At the Circus* reappears. The scene is *so* tricked up and animated, in fact, that it looks more like one of George Pal's Puppetoons than a Marx Brothers scene. The Marx Brothers don't even seem to be present. There are three guys who look just like them running around hollering straight lines, like "Help, Flywheel!" and "Come on, Wacky!" They even have to bring in a funny janitor for comic relief.

———

The critics' kindness to *Big Store* borders on clemency. Only *Newsweek* was biting enough to say, "The boys might have left their friends something more substantial to remember them by." The rest of them seemed to act on the assumption that so pitiable an object ought not to be picked on. "A pleasure," said *The New Yorker*, "though this is just one of their more offhand efforts." What the New York *Times* said was that *The Big Store*, "as the last remnant on the counter, is a bargain." Samuel Taylor Coleridge once said, "A weary time, a weary time." Coleridge never saw *The Big Store*, or he would have said it twice.

There are funnier things in this world than *The Big Store*, you know. They include:

1) Voting for Willkie.

2) Singing "Hello, Dolly!" to the tune of "Stardust."

3) A crutch.

4) Running around and around the room, all the time shouting "Barbara Frietchie!"

5) Wearing knickers.

Three bored Marx Brothers waiting for the shooting to start.

A NIGHT IN CASABLANCA 1946

There are some things rational people should never even *try* to do, and one of them is make Marx Brothers movies.

There is always the compulsion to keep on doing something even after it has ceased to be the novel and exciting thing to do. There is always the temptation, once you have made a hit, to repeat the old patterns and see if they go on working. No one was more aware than Groucho that there were other things for an active mind to be engaged in than being one of the Marx Brothers. "I am a serious man with a comic sense," he himself declared, "but I don't see why, if you hit one note and are successful, you must stick to that all your life. I've had enough of those scenes climbing out of the window or hiding in the closet. There are other facets to be explored."

And yet there comes a time in the life of even the most active mind when the ego needs a pure and simple boost. For four years since the completion of *Big Store*, he had been mining the prospect of radio. When nothing panned out, however, he was forced to satisfy himself with guest appearances and tours of Army bases, where laughs come easy. He didn't need the money (he *never* needed the money), but his lifelong career had left him with an insatiable urge to hear applause. The temptation must have grown very strong.

To cinch matters, Chico *did* need the money. "You're wasting the best years of our lives," he complained, and Groucho weakened.

David Loew, one of the many producers bent on convincing the Marx Brothers that their names were still worth gold, was the lucky man to make his bid when they were in a mood to listen. He and the three brothers pooled their resources and formed Loma Vista Films, a name that was to stand as a beacon in the entertainment world for almost an entire year.

Joseph Fields, a *Ziegfeld Follies* veteran (and one of the sons of Weber and Fields' Lew Fields) who had a strange habit of rewriting bad plays and producing them himself, was hired by Loma Vista to do one from scratch. Fields drew up a parody of the Humphrey Bogart film *Casablanca* (which was already three years old) and filled it with characters named Humphrey Bogus and Lowan Behold. Then a slight case of dissatisfaction set in, and a whole Greek chorus of new writers was engaged before the tour was begun. (As three of the backers were Marx Brothers, there was to be *no arguing* the tour idea.) The new writers included Howard Harris and Sydney Zelinka, who came out of God Knows Where for the production and returned there afterward, and Roland Kibbee, who had written radio gags for Fred Allen, Fanny Brice and Groucho Himself and who was to fashion the final screenplay. In the eventual version, the parody names are dropped, and Groucho is given the even more repulsive title Ronald J. Kornblow. When it finally was taken on tour, it was only a four-week tour, and even at that consisted mostly of Army camps.

Archie Mayo, the director of *Night in Casablanca,* actually has some good films to his credit (*Three Men on a Horse, The Black Legion*), even though *Night in Casablanca* isn't one of them. His handling of comedy is discouragingly ponderous, and he accentuates it by dollying around in all the wrong places. Actually, the only interesting name that comes up on this whole roster is Frank Tashlin's.

Frank Tashlin's name (Frank Tashlin) once came up in connection with nothing but cartoons. At the Warner Brothers cartoon studio, he was ribbed continually for one of his strange habits, which was going to Chaplin and Laurel and Hardy comedies with a little black book in his hand and writing down every gag that appealed to him. (His other strange habit was going around peeking in doorways and running away, which got him fired while an errand boy for Dave Fleischer.) Tex Avery, one of his colleagues at Warners, later remarked, "He sure got the laugh on us!"

By 1948 his name (Frank Tashlin) was appearing on Red Skelton and Bob Hope comedies (like *The Paleface,* which Norman McLeod directed), and by 1952 he was directing some himself (like *Son of Paleface*). Finally, pictures like *The Girl Can't Help It, Will Success Spoil Rock Hunter?* and Jerry Lewis' *Rock-a-Bye Baby, Geisha Boy* and *Cinderfella,* all written and directed by Tashlin himself, made him one of the most conspicuous names in comedy during one of comedy's biggest dry spells. When World War II opened, Tashlin had left the cartoon business, figuring the screenwriter shortage was severe enough to leave room in the field for him. He had overestimated the shortage. His job devising sight gags for Harpo in *Night in Casablanca* was the first film job he ever cleared for himself. He earned it in competition with three old-time gag men one morning at the Hollywood Woman's Club rehearsal hall when the stage version of the movie was being prepared. He then followed the production through the tour, through the rehearsals and on into shooting. His contributions to *Night in Casablanca* include its most celebrated gags (the famous opening gag, where Harpo is asked, "What do you think you're doing? Holding that building up?" and it turns out he is; Harpo raising a pair of glasses to his eyes and then blowing bubbles through it).

Tashlin was too much of a novice at the publicity game to comprehend the importance of fighting for a credit and was therefore given none. (He wasn't even given additional credit in the *Academy Bulletin.*) This is a real pity, since he has such an interesting name.

But then, Casablanca is an interesting name too, and it was getting to be harder to come by all the time. Warner Brothers, who made the original film, announced their plans to take the parody in little of the joking spirit in which it was intended. When the Warners Goliath wrote to David Loew and made a lot of threatening noises, Groucho took it upon himself to cast the first stone—thereby touching off the famous correspondence that earned for *Night in Casablanca* its most endearing reputation. "Apparently there's more than one way of conquering a city and holding it as your own," he wrote back, incensed. "Do you maintain that yours is an original name?" he asked Jack Warner. "Well, it's not. It was used long before you were born. As for you, Harry, you probably sign your checks, sure in the belief that you are the first Harry of all time and that all other Harrys are imposters. I can think of two Harrys that preceded you." He then signed off, adding warmly that "Some of my best friends are Warner Brothers."

Warners couldn't take that as a joke either. They presumed Groucho was trying to be reasonable and wrote back a very nice reply asking him to explain himself. Groucho answered by explaining the movie instead. "There are many scenes of splendor and fierce antagonism," he waxed rhapsodically, "and Color, an Abyssinian messenger boy, runs Riot. Riot, in case you have never been there, is a small nightclub on the edge of town. When I first meet Chico, he is working in a saloon selling sponges to barflies who are unable to carry their liquor. Harpo is an Arabian caddie who lives in a small Grecian urn on the outskirts of the city. All this has been okayed by the Hays Office, Good Housekeeping, and the survivors of the Haymarket Riots." Warners assumed that the reason this made no sense to them was that they didn't understand it. (Their only experience with comedians had been nice tame fellows like Joe E. Brown.) With the tirelessness of Job, they asked for a few more descriptive details. Groucho answered that there had been some changes in the script and wrote out a whole new story line: "In the new version I play Bordello, the sweetheart of Humphrey Bogart. Harpo and Chico are itinerant rug peddlers who are weary of laying rugs and enter a monastery just for a lark. This is a good joke on them, as there hasn't been a lark in the place for fifteen years. In the fifth reel, Gladstone makes a speech that sets the House of Commons in an uproar, and the King promptly asks for his resignation."

Warner Brothers, finally catching on to the fact that an infinity of complaining would only result in an infinity of funny answers, gave up dealing with the renegade Loma Vista and went straight to the Hays Office, demanding that they restrain the production. They *couldn't* have gotten the same answer from the Hays Office. But they got the same result, and the matter was dropped.

Later, Groucho wrote to Warners and complained that *Night and Day* was a title stolen from *Night at the Opera* and *Day at the Races*. That was dropped, too.

On the set for *Night in Casablanca:* Harpo's children get to meet their uncles in make-up and seem rather terrified at the prospect.

COLLECTION OF HARPO MARX

Shooting began at General Service Studio late in September 1945. Somebody in charge of make-up decided that Harpo would look better without a wig. So they went and dyed his real hair and curled it up and filled it out with fluff. His hair doesn't hang all over his head any more; it just sits there piled up on top of his scalp. The effect is to make him look more like an old man and less like a gremlin, if that's your idea of better. The producer was hoping to compound this desecration by having Harpo shout "Murder!" at one point in the film. He even offered him $55,000 for the single line of dialogue, presuming that posters proclaiming "Harpo Speaks!" would be worth much more. (Never in all of film has there been a Golden Egg that somebody didn't want to capitalize on by killing the goose. There wasn't one Buster Keaton picture where some wise guy didn't come up with the clever idea of having him smile at the end. To some people, characterization is nothing more than a gimmick.) When asked whether he wanted to do it, Harpo thought it over. And then shook his head.

And once again it was impossible to get all three Marx Brothers on the set at once. Sometimes it was hard enough to get one of them. They would sit in their trailers and argue politics. Harpo said the sound of Groucho's bones creaking was drowning out the dialogue. When an interviewer wrangled herself onto the set of *A Night in Casablanca*, she was greeted by one of the writers, who told her that the movie was "a darned good yarn that stands up by itself without the special, high-powered comedy scenes." That gives us a darned good idea what we're in for.

When Groucho foretold doom, he did it on purpose: "This picture," he mourned balefully, "is quite likely to be the opening gun in a new world-wide disaster." The most that can be said for *Night in Casablanca* is that it is better than *The Big Store*. That's not very much.

Night in Casablanca concerns some Nazi spies (the Nazis, though recently defeated, were still going strong as the most convenient villains in the history of storytelling and were just embarking on a long and eventful career that will probably extend well into the next century) who are trying to find valuable art treasures hidden in a hotel in Casablanca. In order to avoid the treasure's being discovered by the manager of the hotel, they murder him. This means that they have to keep on murdering hotel managers as fast as they can be hired. Groucho is hired as the fourth manager of the hotel.

As you can see, the situation is just brimming with comic possibilities. No sooner have the titles dissolved away than a man drops dead, getting us right in the mood for some hilarious Marx Brothers comedy. Once again, the plot is as full of holes as a leaky sponge and sometimes makes no sense at all but is taken so gravely somberly seriously that it becomes dead wood rotting away half the picture. The production has been done on such a low budget that when Chico sits down at the piano he plays "The Beer Barrel Polka," while Harpo's harp solo is "The Hungarian Rhapsody"; the only song that is sung is that old Kalmar and Ruby staple, "Who's Sorry Now?" No comment.

And then, once we are not in the mood for Marx Brothers comedy, we have to admit that the comedy the Marx Brothers give us is hardly worth not being in the mood for—hardly even worth sitting through to get to the uninteresting plot scenes. Groucho, Harpo, and Chico do pretty good imitations of Groucho, Harpo, and Chico, but the gags they recite are all stolen from other films. (How long are we to be handed that limp old line where Harpo pantomimes a female form and Chico thinks he means a snake?) Once again, *Day at the Races,* that gold mine of success, is dug into and shafted interminably, and all the little nuggets of inspiration carefully chiseled out, while the tawdry rocks remaining are hammered into cliché and contrivance. It is as if the audience of *Horsefeathers,* still not understanding half the jokes, is trying to write them. Whoever came up with the line where Groucho, seeing Charles Drake and Lois Collier and telling them about being chased up a date tree by a murderous taxi driver, cracks, "Till I saw you two, I thought every date in town was broken," just doesn't have any idea what he's doing. There are gags that are funny, all right (most of them Tashlin's sight gags), but, like the gags in *Monkey Business* that are not funny, they are the exceptions.

The first key comedy scene, which we might call "Taking Over," doesn't appear until pretty deep in the film. Groucho steps into the shoes of the manager of the hotel in a labored remake of the first scene in *Day at the Races,* strained as applesauce. The second, "Duels," gives us Harpo in a sword fight with some Nazi, followed by Groucho in a banter volley with some woman. Harpo's scene has some good gags rendered impotent by cumbersome dolly shots and a morbid running commentary by Sig Rumann. (Hey, some writers' attempts at being serious just end up being depressing.) Groucho's has good gags ("You wouldn't say no to a lady." "I don't know why not, they always say no to me") rendered impotent by bad gags. The scene is faintly amusing but not hilarious until it is capped by Harpo's confrontation with the same woman. Not a sound is uttered for an entire minute, as Harpo mocks all her affectations and then mocks his own mockery, and for an entire minute it is a wonderful film. "Buffalo Bill Skates Again" is the charade scene that dares to steal not only its comedy premise but even its narrative situation from *Day at the Races*. It does end on some good sight gags, though, as Harpo and Chico pretend to be guinea pigs for Groucho's food. There is even one whole great scene in *Night in Casablanca,* and it is three minutes long. While Groucho is clerking at the hotel desk, a well-starched gentleman dignified enough to be minor royalty deigns to ask for a room. Groucho instantly assumes that his wife, a woman about as appetizing as a plate of yesterday's prunes, is a pickup and demands to see their marriage license. Both sides trade incredulous stares, until the old fellow charges out of the lobby proclaiming, "My attorneys will be here in the morning!" and Groucho shouts back, "Yeah? Well, they won't get a room either unless they've got a marriage license!" "Hey Boss!" has an interesting idea behind it, with Chico foiling Groucho's attempts at seduction in the interest of playing his "bodyguard" and finally ending up with the girl in his own lap, but it would have to be a whole lot funnier than it is to be as good a scene as it could be. The funniest line in it is Groucho's (apparently ad-libbed) aside, "Let's call the whole thing off." The climax could most appropriately be called "Nadir." The business of running around unseen in the Nazi's hotel room is performed so slowly that it reminds us less of Henderson's scene in *Night at the Opera* than of those Abbott and Costello routines where there is a gorilla in the room and nobody seems to notice. The airplane scene, like the airplane, never gets off the ground. The fight scene is stupid and pointless. One of the last lines, uttered when the plane crashes into the jailhouse, is "Home Again!" and it marks a welcome touch of nostalgia.

GROUCHO: Have you got any baggage?
SMYTHE: Of course. It's on its way over from the airfield.

GROUCHO: In all the years I've been in the hotel business, that's the phoniest excuse I've ever heard. I suppose your name is Smith!

SMYTHE: No, it's Smythe—spelled with a "y."

GROUCHO: Oh, that's the English version. Mr. and Mrs. Smythe and no baggage! Let me see your marriage license.

SMYTHE: What!? How dare you, sir?

GROUCHO: How do you like that, puts a "y" in Smith and expects me to let him into the hotel with a strange dame!

SMYTHE: Str-strange dame!!

GROUCHO: She is to me, I've never seen her before.

SMYTHE: Sir, you may not be aware of it, but I am President of the Moroccan Laundry Company.

GROUCHO: You are, well, take this shirt and have it back Friday! Mr. Smythe, or Smith, this is a family hotel and I suggest you take your business elsewhere.

SMYTHE: Sir—this lady is my wife. You should be ashamed!

GROUCHO: If this lady is your wife, *you* should be ashamed.

People certainly were glad to see the Marx Brothers back again. There were mobs of fans crowding every theater in every big city the picture played—even in Los Angeles, where it opened in four theaters at once. Harpo's charade, his duel with the Nazi and the running-around-the-room sequence all got big laughs from audiences. *Hollywood Reporter* went so far as to call it "hilarious entertainment" that "should chalk up a riotous hit." The Los Angeles *Times* thought the film was "great razzle-dazzle entertainment—probably the best they've had since the days at Paramount." They even managed to make the claim that the plagiaristic charade scene "outdoes any other the brothers ever offered." (!!)

The state of American comedy must have been on the verge of collapse to allow its heart to be gladdened by this sorry old film. As James Agee pointed out in his review, "It certainly looks as if nobody in Hollywood any longer knew or cared how really to strip the last drops out of even a verbal joke, not to mention a piece of comic pantomime." The New York *Times*, possessed, apparently, of a longer memory than the average newspaper, commented that "the world should be noticeably happier this morning, considering that the Marx Brothers are back on the screen. But the sad truth is that this battered old world is not much merrier than it was, say, on Friday." *The New Yorker* reaffirmed that "there are times when you hardly know whether you are watching a Grade B melodrama or a comedy."

But Cecilia Ager in *PM* said it best—not only for *Night in Casablanca* but for the Marxes' whole career. "The Marx Brothers," she pointed out, "have never been in a picture as wonderful as they are." Amen.

LOVE HAPPY 1949

Atoll K, A Countess from Hong Kong, Two Marines and a General—these are formidable names, names powerful enough to conjure up horror, depression and nausea in the heart of any comedy fan. Add to these the name of *Love Happy,* that unique film in which the beloved grotesqueries so consistently funny in *Monkey Business* and *Night at the Opera* simply wander about wondering what to do. The pain of seeing the Marx Brothers in their dotage has, so far, been offset by the joy of seeing them at all. But there has to be a limit. *Love Happy* is the limit.

You may notice that not one autobiography, not one biography, not one interview, not one straw vote, not one independent poll, not one Marx Brother ever admits to having anything to do with this picture. Apparently they've repressed the whole experience and sincerely remember *Night in Casablanca* as their last film. Actually, the fact that they made a film in 1949 is quite impressive. It is impressive that a show-business career that began in the days of Weber and Fields and *Cyrano de Bergerac* should extend into the postwar years of Martin and Lewis and *Death of a Salesman.* It is impressive that a fifty-nine-year-old Groucho, a sixty-one-year-old Harpo and a sixty-two-year-old

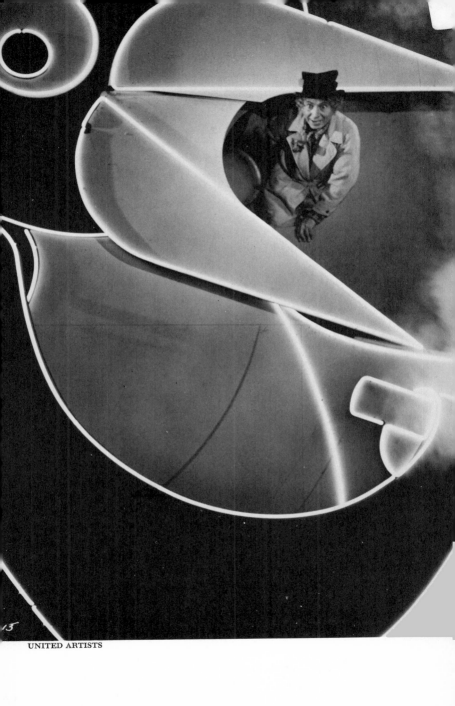

13

Chico should still be at it. Yet age has necessarily impaired, if not their wit, then their ability to make witty films. Inevitably, the fact that they made a film in 1949 is far more impressive than the film ever gets to be. God never meant for sixty-two-year-old Marx Brothers to make movies.

Love Happy was produced by Lester Cowan, producer of *G.I. Joe,* who had to round up his stars from all over the world: Chico from Australia, Groucho from New York and Harpo from a cross-country tour. (They were *still* refusing offers from producers, now on the grounds that the long, hard hours wore them out and that the money came in too slowly. "On tour," they said, "we get that pay check every week.") Lester Cowan is the man of whom the really well acquainted have often said, "He will do anything to make a buck." Executive producer was Mary Pickford, who had been backing multied and various productions since her retirement from the screen in *Secrets*. Miss Pickford, like the Marx Brothers, withdrew from film activity after *Love Happy*. When asked about the film recently, her only reply was "Love *what?*"

The original script of the film, written by Ben Hecht and Frank Tashlin and called "Diamonds in the Pavement," was lost in translation. The movie was planned as a sweet, unpretentious story revolving around Harpo alone, and it's clear even in the truncated version provided by radio gag man Mac Benoff that there had been no intention to create a Marx Brothers movie, and that any vague and uncertain resemblance to one is wholly coincidental.

Chico is stuck in at random, and Groucho seems to have made his obligatory appearance for the sole purpose of being nice. His place as narrator and last-minute problem-solver hardly gives him a chance to show whether or not he still has it in him. He had some pretty feeble jokes in *Night in Casablanca,* but here he can hardly even be said to have jokes. All he has are straight lines like "Let's go up on the roof." The picture is nearly over before two whole Marx Brothers get together on the screen at one time.

David Miller, the director, a man capable of such heights as *Lonely Are the Brave* and such depths as *Hail Hero,* is the man

David Miller, director; Harpo Marx, star; Ben Hecht, writer.
COLLECTION OF HARPO MARX

of whom Andrew Sarris, perhaps the most encyclopedic of all film critics, once said, "Who is David Miller?" Miller, whose easygoing temperament was a good match for Harpo's, could find very few targets in the world worthy of full-boiling wrath, but one of the few, undoubtedly, was Lester Cowan. As long as Harpo lived, he and Miller would get together, talk about old times, have a few laughs, then mention Lester Cowan and get genuinely, vehemently, mad. Once during the production of *Love Happy* Harpo came home visibly shaken, and told his wife, "Do you know what I just did today? I stood over Lester Cowan, trembling with rage, and I said, 'I hate you! I hate you! I think you are the vilest man in the whole world! I *spit* on you!' And I spit on him!"

"What did he do?" asked Susan.

"Oh, nothing special."

There is yet another charade scene in *Love Happy*, and it is one of the most tragic things since *Camille*. The same goes for Chico's foray at the piano, which is all the worse for the desperate laugh line he tosses out to his accompanist on the violin: "Hey, are we playing the same tune?" As soon as we hear this, we presume that it's a lead-in to some punchline that might go "The same tune as what?" or "I'm playing the same tune, but you're not." And yet it is followed by nothing, and we are apparently being asked to rouse up a grin on the strength of just the cue. One gets the feeling through the whole of the film that some prodigious talents are being capitalized on by some sharp opportunists.

Toward the close of production, Cowan ran out of money and United Artists withdrew from its agreement to release the film. In a last-ditch attempt to keep the picture alive, Cowan went around to major corporations and sold them advertising space, which, at the time, was a practice approximately as common as the Irish measles. This is why the climax is a chase across rooftops full of neon signs advertising Bulova watches and Kool cigarettes. Some of the sight gags here, offensive though the method may be, and slow and pointless as the sequence has turned out, provide the most genuine laughs in the whole movie. There is one great shot where Harpo mounts a neon image of the Flying Red Horse, the first in a series of four that blink on and off to give the impression that the Red Horse is really Flying. Conveniently, as one blinks off and the next blinks on, Harpo appears on that one, too. This goes on until he is magically transported, with each blink of the lights, to the top of the sign and out of the reach of the thugs. It almost makes up for the rest of the film. Old comedians never die; they just float away on Mobilgas signs.

Love Happy is the film of which Bosley Crowther once said, "Does anybody have any idea whatever became of the Marx Brothers?" It is the film about which *Variety* said, "Even production numbers fail to come off because of their poverty-stricken appearance. Marion Hutton sings one song in exact style of her

COLLECTION OF HARPO MARX

sister Betty. Ilona Massey's talents are wasted. Paul Valentine gets no opportunity to show any ability. David Miller's direction just isn't strong enough." The picture had a great deal of trouble on its release, but not for the reasons that would make sense. One exhibitor's magazine, *Harrison's Reports,* tried to get theater owners to claim they should be paid for running the film by the advertisers featured in the last scene. Cowan tried to get out of that by saying the advertisers were already paying an awful lot to advertise the movie.

Then in England the film encountered resistance when somebody found out about Ben Hecht's uncredited contribution. It seems there was a ban on all films Ben Hecht had anything to do with, being staged by the Cinematograph Exhibitors Association of Britain. Mr. Hecht had been imprudent enough to criticize the British Empire's intrusions into Palestine, and even to comment that there was "a little holiday in my heart" every time a British soldier was killed. For the past year, Hecht had been deemed, with characteristic understatement, "anti-British."

Then Groucho turned against them too. In November of 1950 he sued Lester Cowan and Mary Pickford for $35,000 salary he had never gotten.

What somebody *might* have attacked *Love Happy* for is being a bad movie. But that wasn't much of a sin in 1950. *Love Happy*'s most salient redeeming feature is that it features Marilyn Monroe in a micro-role. It was the third film she appeared in, though it was later rereleased as "the picture that discovered Marilyn Monroe." That's probably the nicest way to remember it.

vii

three strange angels

What is the knocking?
What is the knocking at the door in the night?
It is somebody wants to do us harm.

No, no, it is the three strange angels.
Admit them, admit them.

—D. H. Lawrence,
"Song of a Man Who Has Come Through"

Regrettably, the story doesn't end with *Love. Happy.* The Marx Brothers went down for the last time in 1957 in a horror of a comedy, called *The Story of Mankind,* produced by Irwin Allen (who has since turned to doing very funny horror shows, like "Land of the Giants"). Irwin Allen actually hired all three Marx Brothers and then didn't have the sense to put them in the same scene together.

The last, final, ultimate, this-is-it appearance of Groucho, Harpo, and Chico on one screen simultaneously came in 1959 on a "G-E Theater" episode called "The Incredible Jewel Robbery." It was a totally wordless Harpo and Chico story for twenty-five minutes, then Groucho made a surprise entrance at the end and said, "We aren't talking till we see our lawyer." Harpo gave Groucho his leg, Groucho gave Chico his leg, and the "You Bet Your Life" duck came out of the sky with an "End" title. And it was all over.

After that, there were hundreds of plans to bring them back again. Billy Wilder planned a United Nations current-events comedy with them, Sol Siegel had a *Minnie's Boys* film in the work and only got as far as the finished script (a typical Hollywood-Life-Story melodrama with some very funny lines, bearing little relation to the recent play, except in its bearing little relation to the actual story), Norman Prescott wanted to use a new process called Tri-Cinemation to do a cartoon series based on their characters, and a TV series called "Deputy Seraph" actually got its pilot completed.

But the Marx Brothers as a phenomenon had died with *A Day at the Races.* Groucho was now the evil-eyed sharpster with the predatory lope and the wiggling eyebrows, ever on the lookout for a pretty girl or a lot of money. Harpo was the funny little man who made leering expressions and played the harp and couldn't talk. Chico was the swell fellow who had a little bit of an accent, but deep down inside was the soul of generosity. The Marx Brothers were explained. The Marx Brothers were dead.

A lot of progress has been made since *A Day at the Races,*

and rational people have killed a lot more than Marx Brothers. They went on buying and selling, bartering and trading, signing contracts, sailing steamships and putting on bad comedies. They have gone on replacing sets of old oppressive rules and regulations with sets of new oppressive rules and regulations, sending alternating flags up and down their flagpoles and re-evaluating their currency in terms of other re-evaluated currency until *nobody* knows the value of the dollar any more. This has all been very boring. And it has inspired us to nothing but to ask ourselves whether the death of the Marx Brothers has really meant that the Marx Brothers are dead or simply that Julius, Adolph, and Leonard don't make movies any more.

Long live the Marx Brothers. Admit them, admit them.

notes

and answers to riddles

I: OF THEIR HOLOCAUST

HEAVEN KNOWS WHAT

Shaw quote: Los Angeles *Times*, September 17, 1967.

Kerr quote: *The Groucho Letters*.

Agee quote: *The Nation*, May 25, 1946.

New York *Times*, June 21, 1949, quoting *The Times* of London, unsigned article.

Sheekman quote from a person interview.

For intellectual "railing on" against the movies, see the essays in *Film: An Anthology*, Daniel Talbot, ed.

BIRTHMARX:

CHICO

The business of the Marxes' actual birth dates is certain to be a matter of controversy. Studio biographies, which have supplied the commonly accepted dates, are famous for falsifying. The dates I give are backed up by several reliable sources, including stated ages at the time of death, newspaper and magazine articles written in their younger days, and the testimony of Harpo's wife and eldest son.

Impressions of Chico are derived from Harpo Marx and Rowland Barber, *Harpo Speaks,* and Groucho Marx, *Groucho and Me,* plus personal interviews with Sid Kuller, Irving Brecher and Willy Clar, a personal friend of Chico's since 1914. For specific references, see below:

Kaufman's quote about financial idiocy is from a review of Kyle Crichton's book *The Marx Brothers* in the New York *Times*, June 18, 1950.

The movie with the empty suitcase is *The Cocoanuts.*

Chico's quote about the Cohens and the Levys and the story about the Mexican are from Hal Humphrey, "Chico Marx, the Dubious Smuggler, Is Back Again," Los Angeles *Mirror*, March 7, 1959.

Chico's methods of entertaining in Hollywood are derived from the testimony of Sid Kuller.

Friars Club story from Joe Schoenfeld's column "Time and Place," *Daily Variety*, September 15, 1954.

Groucho's philosophic "That's His Life" is quoted from Los Angeles *Times*, June 11, 1961, and Los Angeles *Herald-Examiner*, June 11, 1961.

Irving Brecher's story is from a personal interview, but he claims to be supported in this impression by George S. Kaufman.

Morrie Ryskind tells his story in a personal interview.

Time magazine, August 15, 1932, is responsible for the "irrelevant vehemence" statement.

George Oppenheimer, *View from the Sixties*, relates Chico's relations with writers.

Rabbi line: Los Angeles *Times*, October 14, 1961.

HARPO

Impressions of Harpo from Harpo Marx and Rowland Barber, *Harpo Speaks;* Ben Hecht, *A Child of the Century;* and personal interviews with Mrs. Harpo Marx, Sid Kuller, George Folsey, Irving Brecher, and Margaret Dumont's stand-in, who was present for the filming of all their MGM films (and who prefers to remain nameless). Harpo's first adopted son, Bill Marx, has read this section and also added impressions.

George S. Kaufman quotes Harpo about winding his watch in his review of *The Marx Brothers, op. cit.*

The film with the peanuts is *Duck Soup.*

Joseph Schenck case, Los Angeles *Times*, March 11, 1941.

Alexander Woollcott quote from "Portrait of a Man with Red Hair," *The New Yorker*, December 1, 1928, and the Amalfi story from his article in *Cosmopolitan*, January 1934.

George Burns is quoted in Los Angeles *Herald-Examiner*, September 29, 1964.

"Another friend" is Mrs. Herman Mankiewicz, who knew the Marxes in New York and Hollywood and gave this account in a personal interview.

Polyp story, Oscar Levant, *The Memoirs of an Amnesiac.*

The one direct quote from Ben Hecht is from *Life*, May 19, 1961.

The quotes at the finale:

Harry Ruby and D. A. Doran are quoted from personal interviews with the author.

Guedel: Los Angeles *Herald-Examiner*, September 29, 1964.

Goldwyn quote: New York *Times*, September 29, 1964.

Red Skelton: *Newsweek*, October 12, 1964.

Groucho and Harpo, both quoted from Los Angeles *Herald-Examiner*, September 29, 1964.

GROUCHO

Impressions of Groucho from a variety of sources, salient among them being Arthur Marx, *Life with Groucho;* Groucho Marx, *Groucho and Me;* and personal interviews with Arthur Sheekman and Sid Kuller.

Concerning the battle of the instincts, see Robert Ardrey, *African Genesis.*

The five quotations in order of appearance are from:

Lewis Carroll, *Alice in Wonderland.*

Robert Benchley, "The Menace of Buttered Toast."

Oscar Wilde, *The Importance of Being Earnest.*

Dialogue from *Horsefeathers.*

Dialogue from *Animal Crackers.*

The necktie story is from Charles Isaacs, "Comedians Can Be Funny," *Daily Variety,* November 2, 1953.

World War II gag from Leo Rosten, "The Lunar World of Groucho Marx," *Harper's,* June 1958.

Eddie Cantor on children, "Look Who's a Father," Los Angeles *Times, This Week* magazine, June 19, 1949, though Groucho's son, Arthur, provides more firsthand evidence in *Life with Groucho.*

Groucho's opinions of movie-making are a combination of *Groucho and Me* and *Life with Groucho* observations and the impressions of Margaret Dumont's stand-in.

Comment on the networks from Los Angeles *Times,* January 5, 1967.

"Naturally I was touched": Groucho Marx, "What This Country Needs," Los Angeles *Times, This Week* magazine, June 16, 1940.

"Nostalgia": New York *Times,* April 13, 1967.

"Approaching forty" from "Groucho . . . The Man from Marx," Leo Rosten, *Look,* March 30, 1950.

Skates gag from Rosten, "Lunar World," *op. cit.*

Hair-trigger mind remark from "Groucho Marx: A Sharp Knife in a Stale Cake," *Newsweek,* May 15, 1950. As far as the "I like my cigar" remark is concerned, Groucho recently (*Esquire,* July 6, 1972) insisted he never said such a thing. The remark is so famous it would seem to be some kind of a sin *not* to include it, like the Warner Brothers letters for *Night in Casablanca,* and it is just possible that Groucho is wrong (he also insists that there *was* no Marx Brothers script by Salvador Dali; those who have read the script disagree with him). At any rate, in the interests of accuracy, it's worth a footnote.

"Fall out of a patient": *Time* cover story, December 31, 1951.

Comment on commercials from Pete Martin, *Pete Martin Calls On* . . .

Free speech from Groucho Marx and Leslie Lieber, "Groucho's Who's Who of Ha-Ha's," Los Angeles *Times, This Week* magazine, March 11, 1962.

Clergyman crack, Los Angeles *Times,* May 21, 1961.

Gershwin line from Sid Kuller.

Closing remark from Hal Humphrey's column in Los Angeles *Mirror-News,* March 17, 1958, and Groucho Marx, *Groucho and Me.*

GUMMO AND ZEPPO

Impressions of Zeppo and Gummo culled from Kyle Crichton, *The Marx Brothers,* and personal interviews with Harry Ruby, Arthur Sheekman and Mrs. Harpo Marx. That Zeppo stood in for Groucho for several weeks is related in Arthur Marx, *Life with Groucho.* Gummo's wisecracks from *Newsweek,* June 22, 1953, and Earl Wilson's column in Los Angeles *Daily News,* April 22, 1950.

II: ANTIQUITY

Major sources for this stage in their careers include Kyle Crichton, *The Marx Brothers;* Marx and Barber, *Harpo Speaks;* Groucho Marx, *Groucho and Me;* and Arthur Marx, *Life with Groucho.* As the opening paragraph states, the accounts are wildly contradictory, and straightening them all out was a herculean task. In addition, the chronology is almost consistently off and had to be straightened out through the researches of Abel Green and Joe Laurie, Jr., in *Show Biz from Vaude to Video,* which consists in the main of facts and dates derived from old copies of *Variety.* Also, Bill Marx was of some help in confirming the fact that the Marx Brothers were vaudeville comedy stars by 1911, even before Chico joined them.

THE NIGHTINGALES ET AL.

The dates I have given for the ragamuffin series of variously titled playlets that precede *I'll Say She Is* depart radically from the timetables suggested by Harpo in *Harpo Speaks* and Arthur Marx in *Life with Groucho,* but this serves only to point out how unreliable these off-the-cuff accounts turn out to be in particulars. The exact years (when not preceded by a "c.") are the result of the diligent searching of British researcher Geoffrey Brown through old copies of *Variety, Billboard, New York Clipper, Show World, New York Dramatic Mirror,* and several other trade magazines of the period. These were of little or no value in ascertaining the exact nature of the act, but did help to clarify some dates. Brown's research also disclosed that *Home Again* was written *and staged* by Uncle Al Shean, making him the first of a long line of father figures to foster the career of the Marx Brothers, including George S. Kaufman, Herman Mankiewicz, and Irving Thalberg.

Two articles by Groucho Marx, "Up from Pantages," New York *Times,* June 10, 1928, and "Bad Days Are Good Memories," *Saturday Evening Post,* August 29, 1931, were of help in constructing the account of the Nightingales.

The Nacogdoches story is a familiar one, told in almost all of the above sources.

The memories of Willy Clar and Harry Ruby, two surviving members of Marx Brothers audiences, were called into play here, in reconstructing the early vaudeville act, through personal interviews.

Stan Laurel, W. C. Fields: See John McCabe, *Mr. Laurel and Mr. Hardy,* and Robert Lewis Taylor, *W. C. Fields: His Follies and Fortunes,* for conflicting approaches to show business.

The dialogue quoted is derived from several of the above sources, chiefly *The Marx Brothers* and *Harpo Speaks.*

S. J. Perelman, "A Weekend with Groucho Marx," *Holiday,* April 1952, is reconciled with the other accounts of *Home Again.*

THE CINDERELLA GIRL

Chico Marx, "Time Marches on for the Marxes," New York *Times,* September 18, 1938, describes *Cinderella Girl,* though he confuses it with *Mr. Green's Reception.*

HUMOR RISK

Marx, "Bad Days Are Good Memories," *op. cit.,* is the key source here. Crichton is probably wrong when he says a print still survives. Or probably kidding.

I'LL SAY SHE IS

Impressions of the Twenties derived from F. L. Allen, *Only Yesterday,* and other similar accounts. The list of comedians is from

William Cahn, *The Laugh Makers;* Corey Ford, *The Time of Laughter;* Charles Chaplin, *Autobiography;* and Kevin Brownlow, *The Parade's Gone By* . . .

Description of a typical revue, plus assurance that that's what *I'll Say She Is* was, is from Morrie Ryskind in personal interview.

Impressions of Will Johnstone from D. A. Doran, in personal interview.

Description of *I'll Say She Is* from Harpo Marx, "My Brother Groucho," *Coronet,* February 1951, and a review of *Cocoanuts* in New York *Times,* December 13, 1925, as well as the above accounts.

Story of the dramatic show is from Morrie Ryskind. Success of *I'll Say She Is* based chiefly on Crichton, plus John Corbin's review in New York *Times,* May 20, 1924, and New York *Times,* June 1, 1924.

TOO MANY KISSES

Studebaker story from *Life with Groucho.*

Chico story from New York *Times,* December 1, 1924.

The story of *Too Many Kisses* is derived from articles in the New York *Times* on the following dates: March 3, 1925; March 8, 1925; March 15, 1925; May 19, 1929.

Since this section was written in 1970, *Too Many Kisses has* been found, and, true to the prediction, lost all claims to greatness in the process. In all fairness to the film, Harpo *is* allowed to do more than one bit; it was Harpo's memory in a 1929 interview that curtailed his part more seriously than Paramount's editors. He appears at one point strumming a ladder like a guitar; at another he pours wine into his mouth from a flask held at arm's length. These are cute enough, but at every one of his appearances he is treated like a moron who is, unprotestingly, shoved, kicked, and punched around. His part is extremely small, and, considering the Marx Brothers' great popularity with vaudeville and theater audiences nationwide, surprisingly little attempt is made in the publicity or the titles of the film to blow any trumpets for him.

THE COCOANUTS (SHOW)

Accounts of the Broadway years come chiefly from Crichton, *The Marx Brothers,* and Marx, *Life with Groucho,* with additional information from Marx and Barber, *Harpo Speaks,* and personal interviews with Morrie Ryskind and Harry Ruby.

Impressions of Sam Harris and George Kaufman are from Moss Hart, *Act One,* and Morrie Ryskind.

The "one witness" who caught the show in Philadelphia is Alma Gluck's daughter, Marcia Davenport, in *Too Strong for Fantasy.* Reactions to *Cocoanuts* in New York *Times* article of December 9, 1925; December 13, 1925; April 18, 1926; June 11, 1926.

Similar stories of stars getting fed up with their shows proliferate elsewhere, but the Orson Welles business is the testimony of Richard Wilson, a colleague, and the Al Jolson story is from Ryskind.

ANIMAL CRACKERS (SHOW)

Gilbert Seldes is quoted from *New Republic,* November 14, 1928.

Story of "Who Sorry Now?" from Harry Ruby. See Bob Thomas, *King Cohn,* for Ruby's days with Cohn.

Ryskind affirms that the Marxes were hard to deal with here, and Ruby reinforces Crichton's description of the stock-market squabbles.

The baseball story, the "Three Musketeers" story and the story of Dumont's slip are from Harry Ruby. Rhinelander is from Crichton. The "Edison" story is from Groucho Marx's address to the Motion Picture Academy, September 29, 1969. The story about the harp and piano, as well as the new line for Groucho, is from Morrie Ryskind.

The Great Bathrobe Intrigue: I might as well go into a detailed examination of how I assembled this story so that I may be spared the bother of explaining the others and so that scholars may ascertain just how far they can trust me. I have combined the account given by Morrie Ryskind in "Marx Brothers vs. Kennedy Brothers," Los Angeles *Times,* July 6, 1962, with the story as it was told to me by Harry Ruby. When the accounts differed, it was only in minor details, and I simply accepted what I considered the most likely. The conversations between Ruby and Groucho are set down just as Harry Ruby related them, and, though it is not likely that he has got the words right precisely as they were spoken in 1929, it is probable that conversations very much like this did take place. The only sheer fabrication on my part is the line "That's not a funny thing," which I considered a natural extension of the situation and not unlike many funny remarks that must have been said around this time and not recorded. The really unbelievable part of the story—Ruby's popping up out of the trunk—is *not* a fabrication, as will be found to be the case in every instance, and is backed up by both Ruby and Ryskind. Further research disclosed that January 27, 1929, was a *Sunday.* However, as there was no performance on Sunday, Ruby must have had good reasons for expecting the gift on Saturday, which I considered rather uninteresting and unworthy of the text.

THE COCOANUTS (FILM)

The making of The Cocoanuts is a combination of evidence given by George Folsey, the cinematographer, in personal interview; Robert Florey, the director, in Hollywood d'Hier et d'Aujourd'hui; and Morrie Ryskind, who devised the screen version of the play, in personal interview. Other sources for specific details:

Zeppo and Zukor story recounted by Walter Wanger in The Real Tinsel by Bernard Rosenberg and Harry Silverstein (Macmillan, 1970).

Robert Florey stuff from Jack Spears, "Robert Florey," Films in Review, XI, pp. 218–19; story of Hollywood Extra from Lewis Jacobs, Rise of the American Film. Harpo remembers Florey breaking up at everything, but Folsey is adamant that if anybody broke up, it was Santley. This is one of those cases in which Harpo's admittedly faulty memory has to be discredited.

Soaking the paper is out of Life with Groucho. Arthur describes this occurring on the set of Animal Crackers, but this is very obviously an error. There are no actual blueprints in the blueprint scene in Animal Crackers.

I'm not about to enter into any of those who-did-what-first arguments, as they all seem incapable of ever being settled, and I'm certainly not out to blow any horns for Robert Florey, but Florey claims that Busby Berkeley's style and Rouben Mamoulian's "innovations" originated here, and as I can find no arguments to refute him, it might be worth the time it would take for historians to consider the evidence in Cocoanuts.

The encounter between Groucho and Walter Wanger is an obviously hoked-up account of an actual confrontation. In Groucho and Me, Groucho says simply that the producers gave him trouble on these accounts, and it was not until a short test scene was screened at a nearby theater that the matter was settled. I find the test scene somewhat farfetched, though it is possible.

Impressions derived from several viewings of The Cocoanuts. Screenplay by Morrie Ryskind, from the play by George S. Kaufman. Directed by Robert Florey and Joseph Santley. Released by Paramount Pictures, August 3, 1929. Dialogue transcribed from a recording of the film.

Some have asked me to clarify the rationale for chopping the Marx Brothers' movies up into submovies and giving them quirky and odd titles. Though I don't expect my rechristenings to last beyond my own pages, and though I recognize that some of the divisions and regroupings may seem somewhat haphazard and random (though none of them is), I felt some attempt was necessary to discuss each Marx Brothers *scene* as a separate entity, varying as they do in quality from one to another within an individual film, and being, as I felt, the particular unit of expression that was improved and perfected and usually expected to stand on its own merits, at the time of performance. There is no single Marx Brothers *movie* that can be singled out and hailed as a masterpiece, though there are several Marx Brothers *scenes* that make neat and indisputable statements of their own.

There are many indications that the film was a success, including *Hollywood d'Hier et d'Aujourd'hui* and the testimony of Teet Carle, who provided the unbelievable information about the multiple bookings, as part of the American Film Institute's Oral History of the Motion Picture in America Program in 1968–69.

REVIEWS

From Mordaunt Hall, New York *Times*, May 25, 1929; Harry Evans, *Life,* June 21, 1929; A. M. Sherwood, Jr., *Outlook,* June 12, 1929; Groucho Marx, "Bad Days Are Good Memories," *op. cit.*

Jesse Lasky provides the story of the destruction request in *I Blow My Own Horn.* This was backed up by Walter Wanger in *The Real Tinsel, op. cit.* Morrie Ryskind tells of the party. *I* tried showing the film to an audience in 1967. Good heavens.

ANIMAL CRACKERS (FILM)

First is an amalgamation of no less than three different accounts of the nude Harpo story: that in *Life with Groucho,* that in *Hollywood d'Hier et d'Aujourd'hui* and the version Bill Marx told me in an interview, as Harpo had told it to him.

Stories of the Crash from *Life with Groucho* and *Harpo Speaks.*

The making of *Animal Crackers* falls roughly into three sections: the writing of the script, from interview with Ryskind; Heerman's effect on the shooting, from interview with Folsey (and Harpo recalls being locked into a cell for *Cocoanuts.* Again, Folsey seemed very definite, and his is the kind of memory against which Harpo's pales.

There can be no doubt that the cell incident occurred); and Lillian Roth's viewpoint, from her autobiography, *I'll Cry Tomorrow*, written with Mike Connolly and Gerold Frank.

Impressions of the motion picture are those that follow repeated viewings. *Animal Crackers:* Screenplay by Morrie Ryskind, from the play by George S. Kaufman and Morrie Ryskind. Music by Bert Kalmar and Harry Ruby. (Kalmar and Ruby had nothing to do with writing the actual play, despite the claim of the film's title.) Directed by Victor Heerman. Released by Paramount Pictures, September 6, 1930.

Story of Ryskind's sister told by Morrie Ryskind in interview.

Here, once and for all, is that mysterious bit of dialogue about the house next door that Arthur Knight, *et al.*, have circulated about the world in scrambled versions:

CHICO: Now to find the painting, all we gotta do is-a go to everybody in the house and ask them if they took it.

GROUCHO: You know I could rent you out as a decoy for duck hunters? You say you're going to go to everybody in the house and ask them if they took the painting? Suppose nobody in the house took the painting!

CHICO: Go to the house next door.

GROUCHO: That's great. Suppose there isn't any house next door.

CHICO: Well, then of course we gotta build one!

GROUCHO: Well, now you're talkin'! What kind of a house do you think we oughta put up, huh?

CHICO: Well, I tell ya, Cap. You see, my idea of a house is something nice and-a small and comfortable . . .

REVIEWS

See Harry Evans, *Life,* June 21, 1929; Alexander Bakshy, *Nation,* October 1, 1930; Mark Forrest, *Saturday Review* (London), December 6, 1930; Celia Sampson, *Spectator* (London), December 20, 1930; Sime, *Variety,* September 3, 1930; Mordaunt Hall, New York *Times,* August 29, 1930; (Unsigned) *Time,* September 8, 1930.

The "recent critics" referred to at the end are Allen Eyles, *The Marx Brothers: Their World of Comedy,* and Paul Zimmerman, *The Marx Brothers at the Movies.*

Concerning the final point, see Bela Balazs, *Theory of the Film.*

III: NOTHING BUT AMOK

MONKEY BUSINESS

The story of the making of *Monkey Business* is based chiefly on four main sources: S. J. Perelman's article "The Winsome Foursome," *Show,* November 1961, which describes how he and Johnstone got involved in the project, how Perelman reacted to Los Angeles when he got there and what were the reactions to their first script; interviews with Arthur Sheekman and Nat Perrin, who each described how they came to be involved and what their impressions were of every step of the journey; Arthur Marx's book *Life with Groucho,* which was employed chiefly as a supplier of details concerning the trip to London and the fateful re-entry mission through the customs rigamarole. Specific details were also provided by other sources, as specified below:

As far as brushing off their first three films is concerned, see Crichton, *Marx Brothers,* and Marx, *Groucho and Me. Harpo Speaks* accomplishes roughly the same effect; so does Arthur Marx in *Life with Groucho,* since the Hollywood observations he inserts at this point in his chronology have less to do with these films than with *At the Circus* and *A Night at the Opera.*

To be truthful, I know nothing of the *order* of the gag men, only that each one was signed up. Nor am I as aware of Groucho's mental processes as I pretend to be. When Groucho read this chapter, however, he seemed to have no serious objections. The Sheekman quote on his obscurity is from *The Groucho Letters.*

Impressions of Hollywood gathered from five years of living in the area, in addition to endless reading on the subject, including Kenneth Anger, *Hollywood Babylon;* Lewis Jacobs, *Rise of the American Film;* Bob Thomas, *King Cohn;* Rudi Blesh, *Keaton;* and some notes on Orson Welles by Pauline Kael in *Kiss Kiss Bang Bang.*

Description of Mankiewicz is a collection of impressions from George Oppenheimer, *View from the Sixties;* Ben Hecht, *A Child of the Century;* Bob Thomas, *King Cohn;* and the personal reminiscences of Arthur Sheekman, Nat Perrin, Mrs. Harpo Marx and Mrs. Herman Mankiewicz. See also Pauline Kael, "Raising Kane," *The New Yorker,* February 20, February 27, 1971. The fact that he produced these films (though he gets no screen credit), which is very important to an understanding of this stage in the Marxes' career, is attested to by the above interviewees, plus Harry Ruby and George Seaton, and S. J.

Perelman in "The Winsome Foursome." The only written proof I have found is his credit as "Executive Producer" on the script of *Horsefeathers*. The "one writer" describing the noise is Nat Perrin.

Furniture story from Groucho Marx, *Memoirs of a Mangy Lover*. Perelman is wrong when he ascribes the penny-pitching incident to this engagement. That occurred on their first trip to London.

Groucho's statements to the press about visas recorded in New York *Times*, February 15, 1931. The "Proof of Purchases" bit is true according to Arthur Marx, *Life with Groucho*, but I made up the "eyes" gag myself. I couldn't resist it.

"Limitless fictions abound": These are from Kyle Crichton, *The Marx Brothers;* Sara Hamilton, "The Nuttiest Quartette in the World," *Photoplay*, July 1932; and RKO publicity releases. Harry Ruby, Arthur Sheekman and Nat Perrin have conspired in debunking them.

The Marxes' reactions to Hollywood are related in Arthur Marx, *Life with Groucho*, and Marx and Barber, *Harpo Speaks*.

The story of the first reading of the first script is primarily Perelman, but Sheekman and Perrin have added their viewpoints.

Mankiewicz definitely made the crack about dispensing with plots, Sheekman tells me.

"A lot of the Marx Brothers' recent trip to Europe seems to have found its way into the screenplay": Maurice Chevalier story from Florey, *Hollywood d'Hier et d'Aujourd'hui*. Ladies' fashion wear man from New York *Times*, February 15, 1931, *op. cit.* Marx, *Life with Groucho*, is also called into play. I really have no evidence for any relation between the real events and those in the film, except for their rather definite similarity.

The Norman McLeod story is derived from the impressions of Harry Ruby, Arthur Sheekman and Nat Perrin, as well as a glowing account in Corey Ford, *The Time of Laughter*, and some research into his record. As far as *It's a Gift* is concerned, see William Everson, *The Art of W. C. Fields*. For that matter, see *It's a Gift*.

"They began to exercise not restraint but caution." Arthur Sheekman affirms that there was some concern involved—more than was evidenced during *Animal Crackers* or *Duck Soup*, or any of the other shows where success seemed imminent.

Johnstone's comic strip on movie-making appears in the same issue of *Life* as the *Monkey Business* review. The "one reviewer" who makes the snide remark about Zeppo is *The New Yorker's*.

Impressions are from repeated viewings of the motion picture *Monkey Business*. Screenplay by S. J. Perelman, Arthur Sheekman,

Will Johnstone, and (uncredited) Nat Perrin, J. Carver Pusey and Solly Violinski. Directed by Norman Z. McLeod. Released by Paramount Pictures, September 19, 1931.

The Groucho statement about thinking you're an individual happens to be one of the few things said by Groucho to this writer in person. The other things were caustic remarks and one gag from *At the Circus*. Harpo's statement about inhibitions is from Jim Marshall, "The Marx Menace," *Collier's*, March 16, 1946.

REVIEWS

Harry Evans, *Life*, October 30, 1931.

Dorothy van Doren, *Nation*, October 28, 1931.

(Unsigned), *New Statesman and Nation* (London), October 3, 1931.

Mark Forrest, *Saturday Review* (London), October 3, 1931.

Creighton Peet, *Outlook*, September 23, 1931.

Mordaunt Hall, New York *Times*, October 8, 1931.

(J. C. M.), *The New Yorker*, October 17, 1931.

(Unsigned), *Time*, September 19, 1931.

HORSEFEATHERS

The surrealism argument derives chiefly from Roger Shattuck's introduction to Maurice Nadeau, *The History of Surrealism*, and from Martin Esslin, *The Theater of the Absurd*. Concerning man's innate fascination for extra-reality, see R. D. Laing, *The Politics of Experience*; Rollo May, *Love and Will*; J. B. Priestley, *Man and Time*; Carl G. Jung, *Man and His Symbols*.

Groucho quote from an article by Hedda Hopper, Los Angeles *Times*, March 31, 1946.

Soupalt translated and quoted by *Living Age*, December 1932.

Antonin Artaud quoted from *The Theater and Its Double*.

The Dali story is a combination of accounts given by Susan Marx in personal interview and by Salvador Dali in Dick Blackburn, "In Cadaques the Name of the Game is Dali," *On View*, December 1968. The sketches were printed with a commentary by Marie Seton, "Salvador Dali & 3 Marxes," *Theater Arts*, October 1939.

Norman Krasna's ideas on comedy writing related to the author by Bill Marx in an interview. Harry Ruby's ideas related by Harry Ruby. The succession of testimonials is from personal interviews, except for the following:

Teet Carle, from an Oral History prepared for the American Film Institute.

George Oppenheimer, from *View from the Sixties*.

Leo McCarey, in an interview by Serge Davey and Jean-Louis Noames, "*Leo et les aleas*," *Cahiers du Cinéma*, February 1965. These views were reaffirmed on his deathbed in an Oral History prepared by Peter Bogdanovich for the American Film Institute.

Eddie Buzzell, in "Mocked and Marred by the Marxes," New York *Times*, December 15, 1941.

S. J. Perelman, in "The Winsome Foursome," *op. cit.*, and in an interview with John Hall, *Manchester Guardian*, November 30, 1970.

Mary Jane Higby's account comes from her book, *Tune in Tomorrow*.

The Marx Brothers interview is from Philip K. Scheuer, "Three Marx Brothers Interviewed," Los Angeles *Times*, June 13, 1937.

For more evidence on the subject of the Marxes' intractability, the reader is referred to Howard Dietz's attempt to gather all four for a rehearsal, recounted in "A Night at the Marx Brothers," *Weekly Variety*, January 7, 1970.

Harry Ruby supplied the skeleton for the story of *Horsefeathers* in two interviews.

The "soft racket" bit is based on Arthur Marx, *Life with Groucho*.

S. J. Perelman's nonsense quoted from *The Most of S. J. Perelman*.

Two Vince Barnett stories from interviews with Harry Ruby and Arthur Sheekman. Sheekman seemed rather definite that Ruby's version never took place, though Ruby allows that both may have occurred.

The idea that McLeod had it rougher here than on *Horsefeathers* is a somewhat tenuous one. Sheekman describes him as calm and unruffled on *Monkey Business*, while Harry Ruby describes him as absolutely lost on *Horsefeathers*. Also, more control is evident on the first film than on the other.

Sheekman attests that Will Johnstone became Harpo's gag man, and the two worked independently of the rest of the company.

The foot race and the committee of gag men, testimony of Sheekman and Ruby. Chico's accident from New York *Times*, April 10, 1932.

Notes on script changes based on the (apparently one and only) script, *Horsefeathers*, dated March 7, 1932, signed by Harry Ruby, Bert Kalmar and S. J. Perelman.

Notes on disappointing line performance from interview with Harry Ruby.

Lewis Jacobs' citation of Ray June from *Rise of the American Film*.

Description and dialogue based on *Horsefeathers*, written by Bert Kalmar, Harry Ruby, S. J. Perelman, Will Johnstone and (uncredited) Arthur Sheekman. Directed by Norman Z. McLeod. Released by Paramount Pictures, August 19, 1932.

My description of "Harpo's adventures alone with Connie" derives chiefly from Allen Eyles in *The Marx Brothers: Their World of Comedy*. I have never seen the sequence. (From Eyles' description, it seems to be derived directly from some of the bedroom shenanigans in the Napoleon scene of *I'll Say She Is*.) It is Eyles who blames the MCA-TV prints for the omission, and other English correspondents tell me they have seen the scene sometimes included and sometimes omitted; however, even 35mm theatrical prints are without this scene, at least in America, and so it is possible that the footage was removed years before MCA ever acquired the film, perhaps on its initial release. Skullduggery after the fact, however, is always possible.

Will Cuppy is quoted from *The Decline and Fall of Practically Everybody*.

REVIEWS

Forsyth Hardy, *Cinema Quarterly*, Winter 1932.

(Unsigned), *Living Age*, December 1932.

Alexander Bakshy, *Nation*, August 31, 1932.

Cy Caldwell, *New Outlook*, October 1932.

Francis Birrell, *New Statesman and Nation* (London), October 1, 1932.

(Unsigned), *Stage*, September 1932.

Sime, *Variety*, August 16, 1932.

DUCK SOUP

Stories are chiefly from *Life with Groucho, Harpo Speaks* and *The Groucho Letters*, except for the following:

Brown Derby story from Harpo Marx, "My Brother Groucho," *Coronet*, February 1951.

Louella Parsons story from Arthur Sheekman, who said that afterward they wondered just why they had treated her this way.

Name-plate and exit-conference stories from Teet Carle's publicity release on the Marxes, "From Gags to Riches." I had discounted their credibility and had even included them under the "fiction" heading in the *Monkey Business* chapter, but Mr. Carle insisted, as part of the American Film Institute's Oral History Program, *op. cit.*, that they were undeniably and irrefutably true.

Impressions of McCarey and parallel with McLeod made on the basis of the films of each, but Harry Ruby and Arthur Sheekman supplied information, as did Bob Thomas, *King Cohn*, and McCarey himself in *"Leo et les aleas," Cahiers du Cinéma*, February 1965, *op. cit.*

Calling *Duck Soup* a political satire: See Ernesto G. Laura, *"Il contributo dei Marx Brothers alla nascita del film comico sonoro," Bianco e Nero*, November–December 1964; and André Martin, *"Les Marx Brothers ont-ils une ame?" Cahiers du Cinéma*, February, March, May, June 1955. If that's your idea of a good time.

Opinions on the political-satire question have all been made personally to the author, except for McCarey's, which is from Peter Bogdanovich's Oral History, *op. cit.* Groucho's Vietnam statement from Israel Shenker, "Is Groucho Serious? You Bet Your Life!", New York *Times*, April 8, 1969.

"Ruin, disruption and collapse"; *Harpo Speaks, Groucho and Me, View from the Sixties, Life with Groucho* and interview with Sheekman.

Kean Thompson and Grover Jones: narrative supplied chiefly by Harry Ruby, with research into Thompson's and Jones's records done on my own.

Marx Brothers, Inc.: New York *Times*, March 18, 1932; March 10, 1933; April 4, 1933; May 20, 1933.

Rewrite with Sheekman and Perrin: Reminiscences of Sheekman and Perrin. Arthur Marx places the radio show between *Duck Soup* and *A Night at the Opera*, but Sheekman and Perrin both remember it as before *Duck Soup*. Nobody remembers Ed Kaufman being on this film, but Kaufman signed a release that is appended to the script. Impressions of Kaufman from Sheekman.

Spaghetti joke and gag about Zeppo from Teet Carle, "Laughing Stock: Common or Preferred," *Stage*, March 1937.

Conflict with McCarey: testimony from *Life with Groucho*, the script of *Duck Soup*, Arthur Sheekman, Susan Marx.

"A fit of *auteur*": Evidence for the alteration is the revised version of the script, *Duck Soup*, dated July 11, 1933, with releases signed by Nat Perrin, Arthur Sheekman and Ed Kaufman.

Harry Ruby tells the story of finding his script radically departed from.

Rehearsal-till-six story told by Leo McCarey in his Oral History by Peter Bogdanovich, *op. cit.*

Chico's remark about quitting time from RKO publicity release, 1938.

Harpo's "character" story is told by George Seaton. Rushes and big-tits anecdotes: Harry Ruby. Groucho's recipe is quoted by Harpo in *Saturday Evening Post,* August 5, 1951. Mayor of Fredonia story from *Time,* November 20, 1933.

Impressions of *Duck Soup:* Screenplay by Bert Kalmar, Harry Ruby, Arthur Sheekman, Nat Perrin and (uncredited) Grover Jones, Kean Thompson and Ed Kaufman. Directed by Leo McCarey. Released by Paramount Pictures, November 17, 1933.

Movie Trends, 1933: See Lewis Jacobs, *Rise of the American Film.*

Loss of Paramount contract: See *Life with Groucho;* Crichton, *The Marx Brothers.*

REVIEWS

Time, September 8, 1930; September 19, 1931; August 15, 1932; November 20, 1933.

William Troy, *Nation,* December 13, 1933.

(Unsigned), *Newsweek,* December 2, 1933.

Mordaunt Hall, New York *Times,* November 23, 1933.

Later reflections: McCarey, *"Leo et les aleas."*

Marx, *Life with Groucho.*

The book quoted is Allen Eyles, *The Marx Brothers: Their World of Comedy.*

Groucho's later comments from Los Angeles *Mirror,* February 15, 1961, and *Weekly Variety,* June 10, 1964.

Final quote: Friedrich Nietzsche, *Beyond Good and Evil.*

IV: **DO FURY HONOR**

A NIGHT AT THE OPERA

Impressions of Thalberg from Bob Thomas, *Thalberg;* Kevin Brownlow, *The Parade's Gone By . . . ;* Rudi Blesh, *Keaton;* clippings from issues of *Variety* during this period, and the memories of Robert Pirosh, George Seaton and Morrie Ryskind.

Groucho in Maine, Harpo in Russia and Chico at the bridge table: New York *Times,* November 19, 1932; November 22, 1932; January 10, 1934; March 30, 1934. See also *Life with Groucho* and *Harpo Speaks.* Harpo places the trip to Russia between *Horsefeathers* and *Duck Soup,* but, again, this is a minor lapse of memory easily straightened out by examining the record.

Conference with Thalberg: See *Life with Groucho, Harpo Speaks, Groucho and Me* and *The Marx Brothers.* The Football Game and the Clothesline Concept are related by George Seaton.

The Garbo story is in John Bainbridge, *Garbo,* and also in *Groucho and Me.*

Experiences at MGM: interviews with Sid Kuller, Bill Marx, George Folsey.

Keaton and Weingarten: Rudi Blesh, *Keaton.*

Mankiewicz's outrage: interview with Susan Marx.

Trouble seeing Thalberg: interview with Seaton and remarks quoted in Bob Thomas, *Thalberg.*

Smoking cigars, moving furniture, roasting potatoes: These stories have been told so often it seems superfluous to document them at all, but I cite *Groucho and Me, Life with Groucho, The Marx Brothers,* and *View from the Sixties,* just to be thorough. See also Thomas, *Thalberg.*

Script references: "Outline—Marx Brothers Story," by James Kevin McGuinness, October 9, 1934.

A Night at the Opera, by Bert Kalmar, Harry Ruby, and James Kevin McGuinness, December 17, 1934. Actually, there are two dates stamped on this script, the first one being November 9. This couldn't be explained by the present MGM Story Department. However, Harry Ruby claims that they spent ten weeks on the script, and as December 17 is almost exactly ten weeks from October 9, it would seem to be the most likely date.

Pirosh and Seaton episode: interviews with Harry Ruby, who admitted that the script was not yet ready to be filmed, and Robert Pirosh and George Seaton, who recalled the story outline they devised.

Kaufman and Ryskind involvement: interview with Morrie Ryskind. The metamorphosis I describe is actually derived only from a comparison of Kalmar's and Ruby's script with the finished film. However, Morrie Ryskind, like Pirosh and Seaton, insists that there is very little *basic* difference between the script before the tour and the script after the tour.

Description of Al Boasberg from *Life with Groucho* and interviews with Sid Kuller and Susan Marx, both of whom seemed to feel that Boasberg saved these two films single-handedly. When I asked Ryskind about him, he simply replied that I probably knew more about Boasberg than he did; they apparently didn't work together.

Shredding the script from Arthur Marx, *Life with Groucho*.

The Little Tour and How It Grew: Bosley Crowther, *The Lion's Share*, and Arthur Marx, *Life with Groucho*.

Margaret Dumont described by George Folsey, Harry Ruby, Susan Marx and Dumont's stand-in. The punchline is from Groucho Marx's address to the Motion Picture Academy, September 29, 1969.

Descriptions of the tour from George Seaton, Robert Pirosh, Morrie Ryskind, and *Life with Groucho*. Ryskind claims that the show's first nights were not as bad as *Life with Groucho* claims they were, but they still were not all that was expected. "Plainsclothesman" exchange verified in New York *Times*, July 26, 1936.

Duplicated rewrite story told by George Seaton.

The Viking Press has published the script to this and *Day at the Races* as part of their MGM Library of Film Scripts. Though Stanley Kauffmann in *The New Republic* applauds the series for giving the writers their due credit, the books make no attempt to mention the names of those terribly important but heretofore uncredited writers for these two films—including Bert Kalmar, Harry Ruby, Al Boasberg, or George S. Kaufman. To top that off, they have made a great show in each case of printing the script separately from the actual film dialogue, in order to demonstrate the degree of divergence, and then gone ahead and printed the *post-tour* film script, and then further clouded the issue by referring to this *final* version of much-rewritten script as "The Original Script."

Presuming that what Viking has published in the MGM series is the Kaufman and Ryskind script as it stood *after* the tour and *before* the Kalmar-Ruby-Seaton-Pirosh revisions (and Viking gives us no particulars, but this is what the evidence would indicate), it would seem that what was most heavily worked over at the point immediately following the tour was the climactic opera house shenanigans. From the point of Groucho's "speech" to the house to the end of the film, the script has very little in common with the film (it involves an elaborate fire situation that is distantly related to the Kalmar-Ruby original). It is unlikely that this particular scene could have been staged as part of the tour (it would have required a complicated *Helzapoppin*-like staging that no one connected with the project has any memory of), but definite evidence for or against this opinion seems lacking. However, all the comedy scenes in the Viking edition (in the section labeled "Original Script") are in quite polished and final form, all but the night at the opera.

Pauline Kael (in "Raising Kane," *op. cit.*) claims that Herman Mankiewicz was fired from his executive post on *Duck Soup* but later hired by MGM to supervise the Marxes on *A Night at the Opera,* and, after similar shenanigans ensued, fired again and replaced by George S. Kaufman. When I questioned her about this, she claimed to have gotten the information from Groucho Marx indirectly through Harry Ruby, but she has recently informed me (in a letter dated January 13, 1973) that Groucho verified this in person after having read "Raising Kane." There can now be no doubt about the truth of the matter, but just what a "Supervisor" post might have entailed, in a production on which director Wood and producer Thalberg had so much authority, is an investigation I must take up one of these days.

Tales of Sam Wood, as told by George Seaton, Morrie Ryskind, Dumont's stand-in, Mrs. Harpo Marx, and *Life with Groucho,* plus the milk-bottle anecdote from New York *Times,* November 19, 1939. Seaton claims the "twenty takes" was not a mechanical thing; sometimes it was somewhat more, sometimes less, but twenty was not unusual. That the conflict in film concepts resulted in universal exasperation is attested to by one source, who says, "They drove Sam Wood crazy," and Mrs. Harpo Marx, who says, "Sam Wood drove them crazy." The fifty-dollar fine is told in *Life with Groucho,* but a reliable source dated it at this period, as a measure by Wood to enforce discipline.

Harpo and his harness: Susan Marx has told me that it is the scene on the ship rope for which a harness was used, and not the scene on the catwalks. When I look at the movie, it seems quite obvious that there was a harness used for the catwalk scene, and there doesn't seem to be one in use on the ship rope. Mrs. Marx's memory has been known to slip in particulars. That's about all I can say.

Memories of the sneak preview by George Seaton in personal interview and Harpo Marx in *Harpo Speaks.* Ryskind doesn't remember anything like this, but Seaton was very definite and supplied the Groucho–Chico dialogue. Harpo's version seems somewhat farfetched;

they would *have* to have had time to arrange another screening. The version in Bob Thomas, *Thalberg,* is too tame; the important part of the story is that there *was* no change made in the film between the first preview and the second preview.

The accounts of the final cuts are from, respectively, Oppenheimer, *View from the Sixties,* and Groucho's address to the Motion Picture Academy, *op. cit.*

Impressions: My experience of *Night at the Opera* has been of countless viewings, good and bad. I've seen this film loved and hated so many times, it's impossible to know what to think of it any more. Screenplay by George S. Kaufman and Morrie Ryskind, and (uncredited) Al Boasberg, Bert Kalmar, Harry Ruby, George Seaton, Robert Pirosh. Story by James Kevin McGuinness. Directed by Sam Wood. Released by Metro-Goldwyn-Mayer, November 15, 1935.

The Very Famous Stateroom Scene: testimony from the following sources: Morrie Ryskind and Susan Marx in personal interviews; Allan Jones quoted in Zimmerman, *The Marx Brothers at the Movies;* New York *Times,* July 26, 1936; Harpo Marx and Rowland Barber, *Harpo Speaks;* Teet Carle, "Laughing Stock: Common or Preferred," *op. cit.*

Otis Ferguson is quoted from "The Marxian Epileptic," *The New Republic,* December 11, 1935.

Reviews consulted include those in *Newsweek, Time,* and *The New Yorker,* besides the New York *Times,* October 20, 1935; *The New Republic, op. cit.;* and *Literary Digest,* November 16, 1935.

Harry Ruby, Arthur Sheekman, and Nat Perrin all claim they haven't seen *Duck Soup* since the night of the premiere. They remain among the adulators of *Night at the Opera,* as does Robert Florey in *Hollywood d'Hier et d'Aujourd'hui.* Pauline Kael's remark is from old program notes reprinted in *Kiss Kiss Bang Bang.*

James Agee is quoted from *Let Us Now Praise Famous Men.*

A DAY AT THE RACES

The story of getting a script approved is an amalgamation of accounts given by Seaton and Pirosh in personal interviews, George Oppenheimer in *View from the Sixties,* an examination into the records of all three men and a close inspection of some of the scripts and treatments written during this period: "Marx Brothers Story," treatment by George Oppenheimer, George Seaton, Robert Pirosh, and Will Johnstone, December 27, 1935.

"Marx Brothers Story," treatment by George Oppenheimer, George Seaton, Robert Pirosh, and Will Johnstone, December 31, 1935.

"Peace and Quiet," treatment by George Oppenheimer, Robert Pirosh, and George Seaton, January 15, 1936.

"Peace and Quiet," story with some dialogue, by George Oppenheimer, Robert Pirosh, and George Seaton, February 7, 1936.

Both Pirosh and Seaton claim that neither Oppenheimer nor Johnstone worked with them at this time. The facts, however, speak differently, as does Oppenheimer in *View from the Sixties*. It is likely that all of Johnstone's work preceded theirs and that Pirosh and Seaton scripts simply incorporated the Johnstone material. However, Pirosh and Seaton have denied that, too. A couple of Judases, these guys.

Story of the Tour from Pirosh and Seaton, plus *Life with Groucho*, plus "Laughing Stock: Common or Preferred," plus articles in New York *Times*, July 19, 1936; July 26, 1936; September 13, 1936.

Post-tour deliberations: tales from Pirosh and Seaton, as well as accounts in Los Angeles *Times*, August 30, 1936; short notices in contemporary issues of *Variety* trace the indecision over the starting date.

Death of Thalberg from Bob Thomas, *Thalberg;* Arthur Marx, *Life with Groucho;* and the New York *Times*, September 15, 1936; September 16, 1936; October 4, 1936. Again, the common notion that the film was three weeks into production at the time of his death is not borne out by the facts; the actual time is more like a week and a half.

Revision assignments: Pirosh and Seaton testimony again, mingled with an examination of the final script *A Day at the Races*, approved by Larry Weingarten, December 8, 1935.

Production stories from participants in the shooting and *Life with Groucho*.

Rachmaninoff story from Los Angeles *Times*, January 3, 1937. "Buckets of paste" paragraph from a letter from Robert Pirosh to the author, October 24, 1969.

The incredible credit harangue is told in a neat little bundle of memos, all carefully dated, arranged chronologically, stapled together, and resting to this day in the *Day at the Races* folder at the Academy of Motion Picture Arts and Sciences in Hollywood. Pirosh and Seaton added their viewpoints.

Examination of *A Day at the Races:* Screenplay by George Seaton, Robert Pirosh, George Oppenheimer, and (uncredited) Al Boasberg,

George S. Kaufman, Will Johnstone. Directed by Sam Wood. Released by Metro-Goldwyn-Mayer, June 11, 1937.

Chrysler story from *Life with Groucho.*

". . . Books that elucidate nothing but each other." Footnotes work the same way. What, exactly, is an *ibid?* Where do you find *op. cit.?* Nobody *reads* footnotes until they learn how to *write* footnotes. What are *you* reading footnotes for? You waiting for a bus?

Countless reviews have been consulted, including those in *Time, Newsweek, The New Yorker, Christian Science Monitor,* New York *Sun,* New York *World-Telegram.* Those of most interest are Mark van Doren, *The Nation,* July 10, 1937, and Frank Nugent, the New York *Times,* June 18, 1937, as well as two unsigned articles in *Literary Digest,* June 26, 1937, and *Commonweal,* July 2, 1937.

See Jacobs, *Rise of the American Film,* for conditions of the industry in 1937.

"Banned in Latvia." See John Hawley, *World Wide Influences of the Cinema.*

v: INTERMISSION

ROOM SERVICE

Story of *Room Service* from an examination of the RKO file on the film, courtesy of Vernon Harbin. Screenplay by Morrie Ryskind, dated June 18, 1938; personal interview with Morrie Ryskind; New York *Times,* July 24, 1938; Los Angeles *Times,* April 13, 1937. Also, a copy of the original play provided contrasts.

vi: JOY BECOMES LAUGHTER

AT THE CIRCUS

Introductory material derived from *Life with Groucho, Harpo Speaks,* and interviews with Irving Brecher and Sid Kuller.

The making of the film is derived from accounts given by Irving Brecher, Mrs. Harpo Marx, and Margaret Dumont's stand-in in personal interviews; by Groucho Marx in *Groucho and Me* and· *The Groucho Letters;* by Arthur Marx in *Life with Groucho;* by Buster Keaton in *My Wonderful World of Slapstick;* by the shooting script of *At the Circus,* by Irving Brecher, 1939; by Kenneth Tynan in "Funny World of Groucho and Perelman," Los Angeles *Times,* June 28, 1964, originally printed in the London *Observer* under the title "Groucho, Perelman, and Tynan talk about Funny Men"; by Eddie Buzzell in "Mocked and Marred by the Marxes," New York *Times,* December 15, 1940; and by the following New York *Times* articles: August 22, 1937; July 16, 1939; November 19, 1939. That there was friction between Buzzell and the Marxes was indicated most especially by Mrs. Harpo Marx and Dumont's stand-in.

As far as *why* the last three MGM films are so discouraging and unfunny (rather than *in what way,* as I chronicle so lovingly) Arthur Marx has offered perhaps the best reason available in *Son of Groucho* (David McKay Company, Inc., 1972). It is that Louis B. Mayer, who contested many of Thalberg's decisions, hated the Marx Brothers both personally and aesthetically, and refused to make for them the extraordinary concessions Thalberg was always coming up with. Though there are several things Arthur Marx's explanation *doesn't* cover (such as why the Kalmar and Ruby script would be turned down), and though he differs from the accounts I consulted on some particulars (*At the Circus* was *not* taken on tour, according to Irving Brecher— *At the Circus* was not called *A Day at the Circus,* according to the titles of the film), his story of Mayer's arguments with the Marxes seems to me to be very important to an understanding of this period.

A few thoughts on *At the Circus:* Screenplay by Irving Brecher. Directed by Edward Buzzell. Released by Metro-Goldwyn-Mayer, October 20, 1939.

Bursitis: Harpo's wife said he had bursitis on *Day at the Races.* It doesn't *look* like he had bursitis on *Day at the Races.* Besides, there is no ostrich in that movie at all.

Reviews: *Variety,* October 12, 1939; New York *Times,* November 17, 1939; plus contemporary issues of *Life, Time, Newsweek, The New Yorker.* Groucho's reaction from *The Groucho Letters.*

GO WEST

Main sources here are an interview with Irving Brecher; "Mocked and Marred," by Eddie Buzzell, *op. cit.;* shooting script to *Go West* by Irving Brecher, 1940; some remarks by Groucho in *The Groucho Letters;* Los Angeles *Times,* October 6, 1940; New York *Times,* June 12, 1940.

I have it on the best of secondhand authority that Norman Krasna has read the Kalmar-Ruby script for *Go West* and thinks it is one of the funniest things he ever read. A subject for further research if there ever was one.

Some ideas about *Go West:* Screenplay by Irving Brecher and (uncredited) Nat Perrin. Directed by Edward Buzzell. Released by Metro-Goldwyn-Mayer, December 6, 1940.

Chico and his band: Los Angeles *Times,* October 5, 1940, and New York *Times,* November 27, 1940. "Life of Riley" story told by Irving Brecher. Reviews summarized are from Daily and Weekly *Variety, Film Daily, Hollywood Reporter,* New York *Times,* London *Times,* and other periodicals, contained in a book of clippings compiled by MGM.

William Cullen Bryant quote from "October: A Sonnet."

THE BIG STORE

The big story of *The Big Store* culled from an interview with Sid Kuller; an article by Thornton Delahanty entitled "Groucho Plans to Write After Quitting Films," in New York *Herald Tribune,* April 20, 1941; an examination of the script *Step This Way,* by Sid Kuller, Ray Golden, and Hal Fimberg, February 17, 1941. *Variety* clippings of March 4, 1941, indicate the change of title to *Bargain Basement.* The Brooks Atkinson interview is from the New York *Times,* September 26, 1941. Some Groucho comments from *The Groucho Letters.* The list of titles from copyright listings of 1919 to 1969.

Louis K. Sidney is apparently the fellow Groucho refers to in *Groucho and Me* with several pages of uncomplimentary remarks describing how he terrorized the three timid, talented writers from the East by pounding on his desk and shouting "It stinks!" Among other things. As I have no positive proof of this, I would not like to repeat those uncomplimentary things on these pages.

Impressions of and dialogue from *The Big Store:* Screenplay by Sid Kuller, Hal Fimberg, and Ray Golden. Story by Nat Perrin. Directed by Charles Reisner. Released by Metro-Goldwyn-Mayer, June 20, 1941.

Reviews: New York *Times,* June 27, 1941, plus *Time, Newsweek, The New Yorker, Variety, Hollywood Reporter.*

Samuel Taylor Coleridge's snappy comeback is from "The Rime of the Ancient Mariner."

A NIGHT IN CASABLANCA

The chronicle of *Night in Casablanca* comes from Cecilia Ager, "News: Girl Chases Marx Brothers," *PM,* January 27, 1946; "How to Be a Spy," *Life,* April 1, 1946; New York *Times,* July 1, 1945; a letter from Frank Tashlin to the author, November 3, 1971; as well as a few details from *Life with Groucho* and *The Groucho Letters.*

The Groucho–Warners correspondence has been reprinted so often that I believe it would be difficult to find a Marx Brothers book that did *not* contain it. You will find the whole thing in *Groucho and Me, Life with Groucho,* and *The Groucho Letters.*

The paragraph on Frank Tashlin is based on material from Joseph Adamson, "Tell Me the Story You Told Me on Tuesday: An Oral History of Tex Avery"; Joseph Adamson, "Where Can I Get a Good Corned Beef Sandwich?: An Oral History of Dave Fleischer"; Joseph Adamson, "He Was a Chicken, but They Treated Him Like a Farmer: An Oral History of Friz Freleng," all prepared for the Oral History of the Motion Picture in America Program, under the direction of Dr. Howard Suber, sponsored by the American Film Institute and the National Endowment for the Humanities. See also Joe Adamson, "You Couldn't Get Chaplin in a Milk Bottle," *Take One,* Vol. 1, No. 9, December 19, 1970.

Detailed examination of *A Night in Casablanca:* Screenplay by Joseph Fields, Roland Kibbee, and (uncredited) Howard Harris, Sydney Zelinka, and Frank Tashlin. (Contrary to popular belief and some well-meaning film historians, Frank Tashlin received no credit for his work on this film.) Directed by Archie Mayo. Released by United Artists, May 10, 1946.

Reviews: *Variety; Hollywood Reporter; The Nation; PM; The New Yorker,* August 10, 1946; Los Angeles *Times,* July 31, 1946; the New York *Times,* August 12, 1946.

LOVE HAPPY

Screenplay by Frank Tashlin and Mac Benoff and (uncredited) Ben Hecht. Story by Harpo Marx. Directed by David Miller. Released by United Artists, March 3, 1950.

This story comes from *Daily People's World,* San Francisco, October 26, 1949; Los Angeles *Times,* March 12, 1950; the New York *Times,* November 2, 1950; personal interview with Susan and Bill Marx; Los Angeles *Daily News,* March 9, 1950; *Variety,* September

21, 1949; the New York *Times,* April 8 and April 23, 1950; letter from Frank Tashlin, *op. cit.*

Andrew Sarris is quoted from *The American Cinema.*

vii: THREE STRANGE ANGELS

Los Angeles Times, September 13, 1961, and the MGM script for *Minnie's Boys,* as well as a copy of the play, are among the sources for this section.

"Long live the Marx Brothers." See Joe Adamson, *Groucho, Harpo, Chico and Sometimes Zeppo,* Simon and Schuster, 1973.

bibliography

CENTRAL SOURCES

RECORD OF INTERVIEWS:

Subject	Date
Irving Brecher	May 1967
Willy Clar	March 21, 1970
D. A. Doran	December 22, 1968
George Folsey	April 8, 1969
Sid Kuller	April 10, 1969
Mrs. Herman Mankiewicz	April 11, 1969
Mrs. Harpo Marx, Bill Marx	March 22, 1970
Nat Perrin	May 2, 1968
Robert Pirosh	January 1968
Harry Ruby	May 1967
	May 17, 1968
Morrie Ryskind	November 28, 1969
George Seaton	March 1967
	January 1968
	October 23, 1969
Arthur Sheekman	September 1968
	October 29, 1969

SCRIPTS AND TREATMENTS:

Horsefeathers, script by Harry Ruby, Bert Kalmar and S. J. Perelman, March 7, 1932.

Duck Soup, script by Bert Kalmar, Harry Ruby, Arthur Sheekman, Nat Perrin, Ed Kaufman, July 11, 1933.

"Outline—Marx Brothers Story," treatment by James Kevin McGuinness, October 9, 1934.

A Night at the Opera, script by Bert Kalmar, Harry Ruby, James Kevin McGuinness, December 17, 1934.

A Day at the Races:
"Marx Brothers Story," treatment by George Oppenheimer, George Seaton, Robert Pirosh and Will Johnstone, December 27, 1935.
"Marx Brothers Story," treatment by George Oppenheimer,

George Seaton, Robert Pirosh and Will Johnstone, December 31, 1935.

"Peace and Quiet," treatment by George Oppenheimer, Robert Pirosh and George Seaton, January 15, 1936.

"Peace and Quiet," story, with some dialogue, by George Oppenheimer, Robert Pirosh and George Seaton, February 7, 1936.

A Day at the Races, script by Robert Pirosh, George Seaton, Al Boasberg, George Oppenheimer, December 8, 1936.

Room Service, script by Morrie Ryskind, June 18, 1938.

At the Circus, script by Irving Brecher, 1939.

Go West, script by Irving Brecher, 1940.

Step This Way, script by Sid Kuller, Ray Golden and Hal Fimberg, February 17, 1941.

ARTICLES: A PARTIAL LIST

Ager, Cecilia, "News: Girl Chases Marx Brothers," *PM,* January 27, 1946.

Buzzell, Edward, "Mocked and Marred by the Marxes," New York *Times,* December 15, 1940.

Carle, Teet, "Laughing Stock: Common or Preferred," *Stage,* March 1937.

Delahanty, Thornton, "Groucho Plans to Write after Quitting Films," New York *Herald Tribune,* April 20, 1941.

Hamilton, Sara, "The Nuttiest Quartette in the World," *Photoplay,* July 1932.

McCarey, Leo, *"Leo et les aleas,"* interviewed by Serge Davey and Jean-Louis Noames, *Cahiers du Cinéma,* February 1965.

Marshall, Jim, "The Marx Menace," *Collier's,* March 16, 1946.

Marx, Groucho, "Bad Days Are Good Memories," *Saturday Evening Post,* August 29, 1931.

Marx, Harpo, "My Brother Groucho," *Coronet,* February 1951.

Perelman, S. J., "The Winsome Foursome: How to go batty with the Marx Brothers when writing a film called *Monkey Business,*" *Show,* November 1961.

Ryskind, Morrie, "Marx Bros. vs. the Kennedy Bros.," Los Angeles *Times,* August 6, 1962.

Scheuer, Philip K., "Three Marx Brothers Interviewed," Los Angeles *Times,* June 13, 1937.

Seton, Marie, "Salvador Dali + 3 Marxes," *Theater Arts Monthly,* October 1939.

Tynan, Kenneth, "Funny World of Groucho and Perelman," Los Angeles *Times*, June 28, 1964.

(Unsigned), "Marxmen Shoot to Kill," New York *Times*, November 19, 1939.

BOOKS:

Bogdanovich, Peter, *Leo McCarey Interview*, November 25, 1968– May 6, 1969. Unpublished. Furnished by the American Film Institute.

Marx, Arthur, *Life with Groucho*, New York: Simon and Schuster, 1954.

Marx, Groucho, *Groucho and Me*, New York: Bernard Geis Associates, 1959.

Marx, Harpo, with Rowland Barber, *Harpo Speaks*, New York: Bernard Geis Associates, 1961.

PERIPHERY

BOOKS THAT WERE OF SOME HELP:

Allen, Steve, *The Funny Men*, New York: Simon and Schuster, 1956.

Bainbridge, John, *Garbo*, Garden City, New York: Doubleday and Co., 1955.

Brownlow, Kevin, *The Parade's Gone By . . .*, New York: Alfred A. Knopf, Inc., 1968.

Crichton, Kyle, *The Marx Brothers*, Garden City, New York: Doubleday and Co., 1950.

Crowther, Bosley, *The Lion's Share*, New York: E. P. Dutton and Co., 1957.

Davenport, Marcia, *Too Strong for Fantasy*, New York: Charles Scribner's Sons, 1967.

Esslin, Martin, *The Theater of the Absurd*, Garden City, New York: Doubleday and Co., 1961.

Florey, Robert, *Hollywood d'Hier et d'Aujourd'hui*, Paris: Editions Prisma, 1948.

Ford, Corey, *The Time of Laughter*, Boston: Little, Brown and Co., 1967.

Hawley, John Eugene, *World Wide Influences of the Cinema*, Los Angeles: University of Southern California Press, 1940.

Hecht, Ben, *A Child of the Century,* New York: Simon and Schuster, 1954.

Higby, Mary Jane, *Tune in Tomorrow,* New York: Ace Publishing Company, 1966.

Jacobs, Lewis, *The Rise of the American Film: A Critical History,* New York: Harcourt, Brace and Co., 1939.

Keaton, Buster, with Charles Samuels, *My Wonderful World of Slapstick,* Garden City, New York: Doubleday and Co., 1960.

Levant, Oscar, *The Memoirs of an Amnesiac,* New York: G. P. Putnam's Sons, 1965.

Martin, Pete, *Pete Martin Calls On . . . ,* New York: Simon and Schuster, 1962.

Marx, Groucho, *Memoirs of a Mangy Lover,* New York: Bernard Geis Associates, 1965.

Nadeau, Maurice, *The History of Surrealism,* New York: The Macmillan Company, 1965.

Oppenheimer, George, *The View from the Sixties,* New York: David McKay Co., Inc., 1966.

Roth, Lillian, with Mike Connolly and Gerold Frank, *I'll Cry Tomorrow,* New York: Frederick Fell, Inc., 1954.

Sheekman, Arthur (ed.), *The Groucho Letters,* New York: Simon and Schuster, 1967.

Thomas, Bob, *King Cohn: The Life and Times of Harry Cohn,* New York: G. P. Putnam's Sons, 1967.

Thomas, Bob, *Thalberg,* Garden City, New York: Doubleday and Co., 1969.

"STUDIES" OF THE MARX BROTHERS: The question of whether or not such a thing is appropriate in this case is mitigated by the fact that these would probably not be valid even if it were.

Artaud, Antonin, *Theater and Its Double,* New York: Grove Press, Inc., 1958; tr. by Mary Caroline Richards.

Durgnat, Raymond, *The Crazy Mirror,* London: Faber, 1969 ("Four Against Alienation").

Durgnat, Raymond, *The Marx Brothers,* Wien, Germany: Osterreichisches Filmmuseum, 1966.

Eyles, Allen, *The Marx Brothers: Their World of Comedy,* London: A. Zwemmer, Ltd.; New Jersey: A. S. Barnes and Co., Inc., 1966.

Laura, Ernesto G., *"Il contributo dei Marx Brothers alla nascita del film comico sonoro," Bianco e Nero,* November–December 1964.

Martin, André, *"Les Marx Brothers ont-ils une ame?" Cahiers du Cinéma*, February, March, May and June 1955.

Rowland, Richard, "American Classic," *The Penguin Film Review*, No. 7, 1948. Originally appeared in *Hollywood Quarterly*.

Sarris, Andrew, *The American Cinema: Directors and Directions*, New York: E. P. Dutton and Co., Inc., 1968. ("The Marx Brothers")

Thomson, David, *Movie Man*, New York: Stein and Day, 1969.

Zimmerman, Paul D., and Goldblatt, Burt, *The Marx Brothers at the Movies*, New York: G. P. Putnam's Sons, 1968.

index